Multiculturalism in the Criminal Justice System

Robert McNamara

The Citadel

Ronald Burns

Texas Christian University

Mc Graw Hill **Higher Education**

Boston   Burr Ridge, IL   Dubuque, IA   New York   San Francisco   St. Louis
Bangkok   Bogotá   Caracas   Kuala Lumpur   Lisbon   London   Madrid   Mexico City
Milan   Montreal   New Delhi   Santiago   Seoul   Singapore   Sydney   Taipei   Toronto

The McGraw·Hill Companies

Graw
Hill
Higher Education

Published by McGraw-Hill, an imprint of The McGraw-Hill Companies, Inc., 1221 Avenue of the Americas, New York, NY 10020. Copyright © 2009. All rights reserved. No part of this publication may be reproduced or distributed in any form or by any means, or stored in a database or retrieval system, without the prior written consent of The McGraw-Hill Companies, Inc., including, but not limited to, in any network or other electronic storage or transmission, or broadcast for distance learning.

This book is printed on acid-free paper.

2 3 4 5 6 7 8 9 0 DOC/DOC 0 9

ISBN: 978-0-07-337994-4
MHID: 0-07-337994-8

Editor in Chief: *Michael Ryan*
Publisher: *Frank Mortimer*
Sponsoring Editor: *Katie Stevens*
Marketing Manager: *Leslie Oberhuber*
Developmental Editor: *Teresa Treacy*
Production Editor: *David Blatty*
Manuscript Editor: *Margaret Moore*
Cover Designer: *Stacey Anthony*
Photo Research: *Sonia Brown*
Production Supervisor: *Louis Swaim*
Composition: *10/12 Times by Aptara®, Inc.*
Printing: *45# New Era Matte Plus, R. R. Donnelley*

Credits: The credits section for this book begins on page 333 and is considered an extension of the copyright page.

Library of Congress Cataloging-in-Publication Data

McNamara, Robert Hartmann.
   Multiculturalism in the criminal justice system / Robert McNamara, Ronald Burns. —1st ed.
      p. cm.
   Includes index.
   ISBN-13: 978-0-07-337994-4 (alk. paper)
   ISBN-10: 0-07-337994-8 (alk. paper)
   1. Criminal justice, Administration of—United States. 2. Multiculturalism—United States. 3. Discrimination in criminal justice administration—United States. I. Burns, Ronald G., 1968- II. Title.
   HV9950 .M43 2009
   364.973089—dc22   2008025390

The Internet addresses listed in the text were accurate at the time of publication. The inclusion of a Web site does not indicate an endorsement by the authors or McGraw-Hill, and McGraw-Hill does not guarantee the accuracy of the information presented at these sites.

www.mhhe.com

Contents

To Carey, who sees no color.

To Lisa, Ryan, and Lily. A special thanks to "Gram" (aka Shirley Crites) for the childcare.

Preface

There can be little doubt that race and ethnicity are defining features of American life. Despite the fact that many people attempt to downplay its significance, attributing past negative experiences to a lack of enlightenment or sensitivity to multiculturalism, race and ethnicity, along with gender and age, are important factors in understanding social life in the United States. Perhaps nowhere else does the impact of negative attitudes, values, and beliefs about these variables become apparent when punishment in the form of arrest, conviction, and/or incarceration is involved. Because of the implications it has for those involved, the criminal justice process becomes an important symbol for the larger society in terms of its stance on the treatment of minority groups. Further, because this system also contains minorities as employees working within the system, a host of issues are generated and a series of potential problems can be identified.

This textbook is an attempt to explore the many issues relating to the treatment of minorities in the justice system as well as to call attention to issues stemming from minorities working within it. Not only do we hope to describe the realities of different minority groups when they are arrested or sentenced, we also want to explore what life is like, for example, for African American police officers who work in low-income neighborhoods comprised primarily of other African Americans. Is it more difficult for them to relate to citizens, or does the common heritage make cooperation more likely? As we embrace the inevitable changes brought about by social progress and technology, social issues, such as prejudice and discrimination, are also likely to change. It is our hope that those changes are progressive ones, meaning that we gain a much greater understanding and appreciation for issues relating to cultural diversity.

Acknowledgments

A project of this magnitude cannot be accomplished without a substantial amount of assistance. While authors often get all the credit, success usually comes from those behind the scenes making things happen for them. This is true in our cases, where we had many people picking up the slack while we were distracted and encouraging us to work harder. From a professional standpoint, we cannot express enough gratitude to Katie Stevens and Frank Mortimer, our editors at McGraw-Hill, for their support, encouragement, and belief both in the project and in us. Katie, in particular, deserves a great debt of thanks. She made us better thinkers, writers, and, with her emphasis on the students' needs, better teachers as well. One would indeed be hard-pressed to find a more dedicated and talented person with whom to work. We also owe our families a debt of gratitude for their patience and understanding while we were completing this project. Families of academics often bear a considerable cost that is often overlooked, and it is something we wish to acknowledge and to express our thanks for the gift of being able to pursue our passions.

An Introduction to Multiculturalism

Introduction

Chapter Objectives

After reading this chapter, you should be able to

❖ Define the issues surrounding race and ethnicity in the United States.

❖ Define concepts such as race, ethnicity, minority groups, multiculturalism, prejudice, and discrimination as they are used in the social science literature.

❖ Contrast the debate of whether multiculturalism is a valuable idea in American society.

❖ Understand how race and ethnicity play a role in the criminal justice system.

On October 7, 1998, Matthew Shepard, age 21, a student at the University of Wyoming, met Russell Henderson and Aaron McKinney in a bar in Laramie, Wyoming. Henderson and McKinney posed as gay men and offered Shepard a ride home in their car. Subsequently, Shepard was robbed, severely beaten, and tied to a fence in a remote area, where he was left to die. About 18 hours later, a bicyclist discovered Shepard, barely alive. Shepard suffered a fractured skull and had severe brain damage. He died five days later.

In response to the growing fear about illegal immigration, and the concern that immigrants are stealing jobs from American workers, the Minuteman Defense Corps Project (MDCP) was created for citizens to actively take part in addressing the problem. The name of the group comes from the minutemen who fought in the American Revolution. Critics of MDCP, including former Mexican President Vicente Fox, President George W. Bush, and the Anti-Defamation League, argue that the program has been infiltrated by White supremacist groups, such as the Neo-Nazi party and the Ku Klux Klan. An added problem is that some MDCP members have carried weapons while on patrol, lending to the perception that they appear to be a vigilante group rather than a supplement to the U.S. Border Patrol.

In September 2005, William Bennett, who served as President Reagan's chairman of the National Endowment for the Humanities from 1981 to 1985, as U.S. secretary of education from 1985 to 1988, and as "drug czar" during George H. W. Bush's administration, told a caller on his radio show, "If you wanted to reduce crime, you could—if that were your sole purpose—you could abort every black baby in this country and your crime rate would go down." Clearly, Bennett's comments gave the appearance that racism continues to permeate Americans' understanding of crime, specifically as it relates to African Americans. In a larger sense, Bennett's comments seem to suggest that the historical experiences of African Americans continue to affect Whites' perceptions of the issues and problems relating to crime.

On November 26, 2006, hours before he was to be married, Sean Bell, a 23-year-old African American, was leaving his bachelor party at a strip club in Queens, New York, that was under police surveillance, when he was shot and killed. At the time, Mr. Bell was accompanied by two of his friends, both of whom were wounded, one critically. According to police and witness accounts, Mr. Bell and his friends walked out of the club and got into their car. Mr. Bell then drove the car half a block, turned a corner, and struck a black unmarked police minivan bearing several plainclothes officers. Mr. Bell's car then backed up onto a sidewalk, hit a storefront's rolled-down protective gate, and nearly struck an undercover officer before racing forward and slamming into the police van again. In response, five police officers fired over 50 rounds at the car, hitting it at least 21 times. The bullets ripped into other cars and slammed through an apartment window nearby. Mr. Bell was shot in the neck, shoulder, and right arm and was taken to Jamaica Hospital Medical Center, where he was pronounced dead. The two wounded men, Joseph Guzman, 21, and Trent Benefield, 23, were taken to a nearby hospital and released. Officers involved in the shooting were subsequently indicted and are awaiting trial.

Incidents such as these suggest that the United States has a long history of tension between different groups, particularly as they relate to race, ethnicity, sexual orientation, and religion. While many people refer to America as a **melting pot,** or a society that blends a variety of backgrounds and cultures into a cohesive whole, this is actually a misnomer. Though there is a great deal of diversity in the United States, there is also considerable intergroup conflict. According to the U.S. Census Bureau, there are approximately 300 million people living in the United States, many of whom come from a host of different backgrounds.[1] This diversity is one of the defining features of American culture and, at the same time, presents one of the more difficult and enduring problems.

On one hand, living in a society where everyone is the same has advantages. For instance, in small **homogeneous societies,** people tend to know each other more intimately, they tend to see the world the same way, making disagreements less common, and the sense of conformity and treatment of others is more equitable. People in homogeneous societies tend to be figuratively and literally on "the same page" with regard to social life. They also feel more connected to the larger society. As the song from the comedy *Cheers* suggests, there is comfort in going to places "where everyone knows your name."

The downside to living in such a society, however, is that change happens slowly, if at all. Additionally, people can be too intimately involved in each other's day-to-day lives, making privacy difficult. Ask anyone who lives in a small town: one of the things they like the most, and, at the same time, the least, about living there is that they are known by most people. In general, social control is easier to achieve in small towns because there is general agreement about what is right or wrong, good or bad, legal or illegal. It is what sociologist Émile Durkheim called the "**collective conscience.**"[2] In other words, the morality of a homogeneous society is stronger because there is greater consensus on the meaning and importance of social life.

In contrast, in **heterogeneous societies,** people come from a wide range of backgrounds and experiences. They may come from other countries, and participate in cultures with different attitudes, values, norms, and belief systems, and there tends to be a lower degree of consensus on how individuals should meet their social responsibilities. In other words, people living in diverse societies tend to have different ideas about how the world works as well as their place in it. In Durkheim's terms, the collective conscience tends to be weaker since there is a lack of consensus as well as a generally lower degree of connectedness to the larger group.[3]

This also means that people in diverse societies tend to think of social relationships in a different way than those in homogeneous societies. Instead of building trust and intimacy, people tend to interact based on what those around them can offer in meeting their individual needs. It is this distinction that surrounds much of the efforts of community policing. How does the government or the police department generate a sense of community in places where little collective conscience exists? How can police officers bring people in a neighborhood together to solve problems in the spirit of cooperation?

Living in a diverse society also means that some groups are going to acquire more economic, social, and political power than others. In fact, that is often how groups distinguish themselves: by their ownership or control of scarce resources. How does living in a diverse society create problems for groups that do not have much power? How are they treated? What are the consequences for being placed in a less powerful status? Much of this discussion relates to criminal justice in that differences in crime statistics, sentencing practices, the use of police discretion, and the overall treatment of minority group members are all symptoms of larger issues. While this textbook does not attempt to solve the problems of the unequal treatment of some groups, it does explore how some groups are treated when they come to the attention of the criminal justice system. This book also examines what it is like to be a member of a minority group and to work within the system itself.

Prior to any discussion of how some groups are treated with regard to crime and criminal justice, a number of terms must be defined. In research methodology, this is called **operationalization.** In simple terms, it refers to the way concepts are defined. For example, when people talk about minority groups, they might have different ideas about what that really means. Some might think in terms of numerical size (e.g., the smallest number of redheads in a group of people), or they might use political influence (e.g., they do not have a lot of political power, so they are not able to change policy or laws regulating certain behaviors). In the next few sections, we will spend some time defining our terms so that when we use them in the rest of the text, you will know how we are using them.

✖ Race

Race has a variety of meanings, which can make its discussion confusing and difficult. In fact, probably the only thing about race that is clear is that people are confused about the proper use of the term. If you looked at the definition of race in biology textbooks, you would likely find that race has a precise meaning,

Al Sharpton was discovered to be a distant relative of Senator Strom Thurmond.

something like, "A biological race is a genetically isolated group characterized by a high degree of inbreeding that leads to distinctive gene frequencies. This distinctiveness is made most apparent by the presence of inherited physical characteristics that differentiate members of a group from others."[4] What does that mean? It means that, essentially, you can see the differences between people from different races.

However, it is very difficult to consider race in a strictly biological sense. Given that people have migrated over a wide range of geographic areas for hundreds of years, pure genetic types have not existed for some time, if ever. Think about it for a minute: Are there mutually exclusive races? Can you really tell where one race begins and another race ends? If so, on what basis? It is not as though a person can take a blood test to determine his or her race; these tests do not work with any real accuracy. Given interbreeding of races over the sweep of history— for example, many African Americans are light skinned and a large number of Whites have African American ancestry—is it even possible to tell where to draw the line between races?

As an illustration, in 2007 it was discovered that the Reverend Al Sharpton, a Black community activist who has spent his career exposing racism and mistreatment of African Americans, is related to former U.S. Senator Strom Thurmond, a conservative Republican from South Carolina who spent a good part of his career maintaining the White-dominated status quo in the South.[5] This ironic familial tie serves as an example of the difficulty in drawing the line between races.

Though race is not a useful biological category, it is clear there are certain groups with similar traits. What is important is that race becomes significant, not because it matters in a biological sense, but because society has constructed it in such a way to symbolize certain attitudes, values, and beliefs about members who possess those physical traits. Race matters, in other words, because society has made it matter. This is sometimes referred to as the **social construction of race.** Every culture must determine which physical features are used to define membership in certain races (Americans typically use skin color) and also determine which attitudes and values are associated with a particular race. Simply put, people attach significance to the concept of race and consider it a real and important way to categorize people. As long as people believe that differences in certain physical traits are meaningful, they will act on those beliefs, which influence how they see and interact with others. Unfortunately, in doing so, people often rely on stereotypes to determine the behavior patterns of certain groups.

Another problem with using the term "race" is that it often suggests a type of homogeneity among the different races. To many Americans, "Blacks" are African Americans, or those whose ancestry dates back to American slavery. However, there are a host of differences among Jamaicans, Haitians, and even immigrants from various parts of Africa, who have little in common with African Americans. Similarly, another example might be to use the term "Whites" as if all are part of the same cultural group. There are significant differences between Polish Americans and Jewish Americans as well as between Irish Americans and Italian Americans, yet we often do not see those differences when using those labels.[6]

☆ Ethnicity

For the sake of simplicity, let's define an ethnic group as a collection of individuals and organizations identified by national origin, cultural distinctiveness, racial characteristics, or religious affiliation. This gets a bit tricky since most textbooks define ethnicity as being a distinction based on cultural heritage and racial groups based on physical features. However, because of the problems and disagreement on its scientific validity, many social scientists have avoided using the term "race" and instead use "ethnic group" to describe those groups commonly defined as racial. In the United States, African Americans, Chinese Americans, and Native Americans all have the elements of ethnic groups—unique culture and in some cases even physical territory—but at the same time, most members of these groups are physically differently from Americans of European origin. Calling these groups "ethnic" seems reasonable because there are always consistent and significant cultural traits that set them apart from other groups.[7]

☆ Minority Groups

This seems simple enough, right? The group with the fewest members. But minority status is not necessarily the result of being outnumbered by the majority group. In the social sciences, a **minority group** is defined as a subordinate group whose members have significantly less control or power over their own lives than the members of the dominant group. While numerical size may be important and related, the issue is really one of power.[8]

In one sense, the idea of minority groups seems fair to people. After all, this is a democracy and the majority rules. The subordination of a minority, however, is more than its inability to rule over society. Members of a minority group experience fewer opportunities for education, wealth, and success that go beyond any personal shortcomings they may have. In other words, a minority group does not share in proportion to its numbers in what a given society defines as valuable.[9]

Moreover, a group's being numerically superior does not guarantee power, control over its destiny, or majority status. For example, think of the Republic of South Africa during apartheid, a system of government that segregated native Blacks from access to social, economic, and political institutions and ended in the mid-1990s. During the apartheid era, the majority of people in South Africa were Black, but under the apartheid system of government, Blacks did not have any significant control over their lives. In terms of making sense of understanding minority groups, the following are important characteristics to consider.

Part of the definition of a minority group involves access to social, economic, and political power. While Blacks in South Africa are numerically superior to Whites, under apartheid they had virtually no political power.

Distinguishing Physical or Cultural Traits

Each society has its own arbitrary standard for determining which characteristics are most important in determining if a person belongs to a minority group. Examples might include skin color (as in the case of African Americans in the U.S.) or fluency in a certain language (as in the case of Hispanics/Latinos).

Unequal Treatment by Those in Power

As mentioned earlier, minorities experience unequal treatment and have less power over their lives than members of a dominant group. Social inequality may be created or maintained in a variety of ways including prejudice, discrimination, and/or segregation. In extreme cases, the dominant group attempts to eliminate minorities completely, sometimes referred to as *extermination*.

Involuntary Membership

Membership in a minority group is not voluntary. A person does not choose to be African American nor would he or she likely make such a choice if it meant being treated unfairly. Often this involuntary membership is not changeable either. This is particularly true in American society, where skin color and other physical features often identify a minority.

Solidarity of Members

Perhaps due to the mistreatment or denial of equality, minority members are very conscious of their status. They also tend to be more sympathetic to other similarly stigmatized groups. This can explain some of the relationships that minority groups form with each other (e.g., women as a discriminated group and the gay community). At the same time, minority groups can also be hostile toward each other. An example is some of the tension between African Americans and Hispanics, who, because of their unequal treatment, feel a sense of competition for power, however little it might be. Thus, there is a sense of exclusivity to most groups, but particularly those that have been mistreated or denied equal status in society. Because of a minority group's position in society, its members feel a need for affiliation with others of the same group.

In prisons, for example, inmates often segregate themselves by ethnicity. For example, let's say that a White male inmate is new to the prison but does not wish to join the Aryan Brotherhood gang, preferring to remain on his own. The norm of gang solidarity is so strong that members from every gang in the prison will attempt to victimize that inmate until he makes the decision to join a particular gang. If the inmate does join the Aryan Brotherhood, his contact with African American or Hispanic gangs will be limited because they are perceived as a threat to him. However, all gang members in the prison, regardless of race, generally oppose the correctional staff and the administration. In this example, being a member of a group not only increases the cohesion between members and demonstrates the tension between the groups, it also identifies the commonality of the groups as they come together against a common adversary.

In-Group Marriage

As a general rule, most people marry people a lot like themselves in terms of religious background, educational levels, occupational levels, and ethnicity. A member of a dominant group is often unwilling to join a supposedly inferior minority group by marrying one of its members. Moreover, the group's sense of solidarity encourages marriages within the group and discourages out-group marriages.[10] This is why for so many years interracial marriage, particularly between Blacks and Whites, was considered unacceptable to many Americans.[11]

⚔ Types of Minority Groups

In making the distinction between different types of minority groups, there is an immediate problem: Where are the boundaries between the criteria? While race as a concept is defined by the physical distinctions between one group of people and another, there are instances in which physical features are insufficient. For example, Hispanics/Latinos have some clearly defined physical features, but they are generally considered an ethnic rather than a racial group. Similarly, although one might be tempted to categorize Jews as a religious group, because their culture is such an essential component to their identity, experts tend to classify them as an ethnic group. This is why, as mentioned earlier, using the term "ethnicity" seems more reasonable. However, the thing to remember is that this typology is used as a general way of categorizing minorities and should not be taken as definitive and complete.

Racial Groups

This term is reserved for those minorities who are classified according to obvious physical differences. The crucial words are *obvious* and *physical*. What is obvious? Hair color? Shape of earlobes? As mentioned earlier, each society defines that which is obvious. In the United States, skin color is perhaps the main characteristic in determining the difference between one race and another, and minority races include Blacks, Native Americans, and Asian Americans.

Ethnic Groups

Minority groups who are designated by their ethnicity are distinguished from the dominant group on the basis of cultural differences such as language, attitudes toward marriage, food habits, and so on. Ethnic groups are distinguished by their national origin or distinctive cultural patterns. Ethnic groups in the United States include a grouping that we refer to collectively as Hispanics or Latinos. This includes Puerto Ricans, Cubans, Mexicans, and other Latin Americans. European ethnic groups include Irish, German, Polish, Norwegian, and Italian, among others.

Religious Groups

The third basis for minority status is association with a religion other than the dominant faith. As mentioned before, Jews are excluded from this category and are placed among ethnic groups because, in their case, culture is a more important defining trait than religious ideology. Jews share a cultural tradition that goes beyond theology. In this sense, it is appropriate to view them as an ethnic group rather than as members of a religious faith.

Gender Groups

The final attribute that divides dominant and subordinate groups in the United States is gender: Males are the social majority and females, although more numerous, are relegated to the position of social minority. Women are a minority even though they do not exhibit all the characteristics outlined earlier. For instance, women encounter prejudice and discrimination and are physically visible. Group membership is involuntary, and women who are members of racial and ethnic minorities face special challenges to achieving equality. They suffer from a form of double jeopardy because they belong to two separate minority groups: a racial or ethnic group plus a subordinate gender group.[12]

✂ Creating Subordinate Groups

Know

You might be wondering how all of this happens. How did society get to a point where there are all of these groups and some of them are mistreated? You also may be wondering why such groups might stay in this country, given the way they have been treated. These are good questions and some of the answer is found in how some minority groups came to this country in the first place. There are three situations that are likely to lead to the construction of a minority group: migration, annexation, and colonialism.

Migration

Migration is the general term to describe any transfer of population. There are actually two types of migration whereby people come into a country. **Voluntary migration** occurs when people immigrate to a new country willingly, looking for a better life. Upon arrival, however, they often find themselves in the position of social minority. The immigrant is set apart from members of the dominant group by cultural or physical traits or religious affiliation.

Although many people may come to the new country voluntarily, leaving the home country is often due to a lack of options. Wars, political unrest, or economic disasters in native countries (such as the potato crop failure in Ireland and Germany of the 1840s) are often the catalyst behind migration. In contrast, **involuntary migration** occurs, for instance, when individuals have been brought into a new land as slaves.

Annexation

There are times when countries attach land as part of a war or conquest. An example is the treaty that ended the Mexican-American War in 1848, giving California, Utah, Nevada, most of New Mexico, and parts of Arizona, Wyoming, and Colorado to the United States. When annexation occurs, the dominant group usually makes a considerable effort to force a change in the attitudes, values, and beliefs of the minority groups.

Colonialism

This is the most frequent way for one group of people to dominate another. Colonialism is the cultural, political, economic, and social domination of a people by a foreign power for an extended period of time. Unlike annexation, it does not involve actual incorporation into the dominant people's nation. Relations between the colonial nation and the colonized people are similar to those between a dominant group and exploited subordinate groups. The colonial subjects are generally limited to menial jobs, and the profits from their labor and from natural resources benefit members of the ruling class. Interestingly, while most of the countries that made up colonies prior to World War I have achieved political independence, many of them have not been able to develop their own industries and technology. As a result, they have remained dependent on their dominators long after they separated from them politically. This dependence and domination is known as **neocolonialism.**[13]

✖ Consequences of Subordinate Group Status

Now you have an idea how minority groups are formed. But what consequences do members feel as being a part of a minority group? Essentially there are six outcomes for minority groups: extermination, expulsion, secession, segregation, cultural fusion, and assimilation.

Extermination is the most extreme way of dealing with a subordinate group. Today the term **genocide** is used to describe the deliberate, systematic killing of an entire people or nation. While it has been associated with Nazi Germany, other forms of ethnic cleansing have occurred in other parts of the world. *Expulsion* is another extreme consequence of being a minority group. As will be discussed in the chapter on Native Americans, essentially, the U.S. government drove them out of their tribal land and forced them to live in uninhabitable locations. This resulted in the decline of many Native Americans, which might be considered a form of extermination.

Secession is another strategy whereby minority groups can depart from their country or at least create their own society. For example, Pakistan was created in 1947 when India was partitioned. The predominantly Muslim areas in the north became Pakistan, making India predominantly Hindu.

Segregation of minority groups usually occurs when the other strategies are not possible or effective. This usually occurs when the dominant group is forced to coexist with the minority group. However, the way the problem is addressed is to simply limit contact between the dominant group and minority members. In the United States, the extent of racial isolation at one time was significant, especially between Whites and African Americans. An analysis of the 1990 U.S. Census showed that neighborhood segregation was just as pervasive as in 1960. It is not limited to impoverished inner cities, there are segregated all-Black middle class or affluent suburban neighborhoods as well. Moreover, residential segregation exists for other minorities such as Hispanics and Asian Americans, but it is usually less profound than that for African Americans.[14]

This Greyhound bus stop provided separate but equal dining accommodations for African Americans during the 1950s.

Cultural fusion is the goal of multiculturalism, whereby minority and majority groups come together to form an entirely new group. An example of cultural fusion occurred during the first part of the 20th century, when the predominant belief was that the United States was a cultural melting pot. The public became convinced that America should meld all of its unique cultures into one unifying ideology. This, people said, would eliminate racism, bigotry, discrimination, and intergroup conflict. However, as mentioned earlier, despite the use of the term in popular culture, it is a mistake to think of the United States as an ethnic mixing bowl. While there are superficial signs of fusion, more significant trends indicate that Americans think little of the contribution of subordinate groups.[15]

Finally, *assimilation* is the process by which the subordinate group takes on the characteristics of the dominant group and is eventually accepted as part of that group. In the United States, assimilation is difficult because individuals must give up their cultural traditions to become a part of a different and often condescending culture. Members of minority groups often discover that even when they assimilate, the dominant culture still casts them in a secondary position. This leaves minority members in a position of marginality: They do not belong to the dominant culture nor are they accepted completely by their native one.[16]

⚔ Prejudice and Discrimination

Prejudice and discrimination are closely intertwined, so much so that people are likely to view them as the same thing. In reality they are quite distinct. **Prejudice** is a negative attitude toward certain people based solely on their membership in a particular group. Individuals are "pre-judged" on the basis of whatever undesirable characteristic the whole group is assumed to have. **Discrimination** refers to behavior, particularly the unequal treatment of people because they are members of a particular group.[17]

The relationship between prejudice and discrimination is complex. Although they are likely to go together, sometimes they do not, as Robert K. Merton, a sociologist, demonstrated in the following typology. In fact, there are four different ways, or permutations, people may combine prejudice and discrimination. The first two are as follows:

The unprejudiced nondiscriminator. This permutation is the most desirable from the point of view of American political and social values. These individuals accept other racial or ethnic groups in both belief and practice. They embrace the idea of difference, of cultural diversity as a healthy concept, and do not try to impose their own cultural and social ideas on others.

The prejudiced discriminator. An individual in this category has negative feelings toward a particular group or groups and translates these sentiments into unequal and negative treatment of people in that group. Examples include members of the Neo-Nazi party or Ku Klux Klan. White supremacists in general typically have strong attitudes against Blacks and other minority groups, and they advocate segregated schools and neighborhoods.

These two types are relatively easy to understand and grasp. One is like a cultural Mr. Rogers, while the other is the most common when one thinks of people who discriminate against others. Hate groups are smaller in size but intense in their feelings toward anyone other than people like themselves. More subtle forms of discrimination and prejudice emerge with the other two permutations. For instance, *the prejudiced nondiscriminator* is the type of person who might be called a closet bigot—someone who is prejudiced against members of some groups but does not translate these attitudes into discriminatory practices. A landlord, for example, may be prejudiced against Asian Americans yet still rents apartments to them because of laws forbidding housing discrimination. Because there are now many laws against discrimination, the incidence of this kind of relationship between prejudice and discrimination is likely to decrease.

Perhaps the most difficult to grasp is *the unprejudiced discriminator*. A person in this category treats members of some groups unequally not because they have any personal animosity toward them but because it is advantageous to do so.[18] In the 1970s, for example, it was common for real estate agents to engage in "steering" of minority clients. This involved efforts to convince minorities to buy homes in predominantly minority neighborhoods, as homeowners in all-White communities feared a decline in property values if African Americans moved in. Because real estate agents wanted return business from affluent Whites who would likely buy more property in the future, agents would try to avoid showing homes in some neighborhoods or highlight the advantages to a minority couple of living in a mixed community. This trend still continues as evidenced by a report by a civil rights organization in 2006.[19]

While Merton's typology helps us gain a better sense of the relationship between prejudice and discrimination, it does not account for what is referred to as **institutional discrimination,** the type of discrimination built into the structure of society. This is particularly distasteful because it is the type of mistreatment of certain groups whereby the people engaging in the behavior do not realize they are doing it. Further, people who engage in institutional discrimination might even think that they are treating everyone fairly. For example, at one time in the United States, many police departments and fire departments had height and weight requirements for their candidates. Because they treated all potential candidates similarly, civil service commissions felt that they did not discriminate against any particular group. However, what if the criteria were biased? What if a person's height and weight had nothing to do with carrying out the duties and responsibilities of a police officer or firefighter? Obviously, women, Hispanics, Asians, and others were being systematically excluded from those jobs even though there was no legitimate reason for doing so. Institutional discrimination is dangerous because it can be deceptive and give the appearance that everyone is treated fairly. As a result of lawsuits, many police and fire departments were required to remove any criteria that were not clearly related to the performance of duty.[20]

⚔ Racism

What about racism? It is perhaps one of the most commonly used terms in the discussion of minority groups and is the basis for much of American social policy with regard to their treatment. **Racism** is the belief that people are divided into distinct

ENVIRONMENTAL RACISM

A chemical manufacturing company wishes to relocate its new factory in your small town. You initially think of the social and economic benefits that will accompany the relocation, including better schools and more jobs. However, the chemical waste produced by the company may have detrimental impacts on your community, including harmful impacts on the river in which you and your children swim and on the water you drink. You begin to realize that you can't enjoy the social and economic benefits without your health. Your initial optimism wanes, and you and your neighbors protest against the relocation of the company. The company offers financial incentives for all residents if permission to relocate is granted. The majority of your neighbors have little money; eventually they cease protesting and begin supporting the relocation.

Historically, the United States and most other countries have shown considerable neglect of environmental protection. Recent societal concerns regarding global warming have drawn attention to protecting the environment. Part of the neglect of the environment involved the underregulation of environmental waste sites. Perhaps the most famous incident of environmental neglect is Love Canal, in Niagara Falls (N.Y.), where extensive dumping of hazardous waste led to numerous health problems among residents in the area in the 1970s.

The location of hazardous waste sites has been controversial. For instance, ask yourself how you would feel if the federal government decided to place a hazardous waste site in your neighborhood. Unfortunately for many minorities and lower-class citizens, hazardous waste sites have historically been placed in their neighborhoods. With limited financial and political power, poor minorities have disproportionately been the target of what is called "environmental racism." Environmental racism involves the underregulation of environmental laws and the disproportionate placement of hazardous materials in minority neighborhoods. Similarly, "environmental justice" refers to attempts to treat all groups, regardless of race, ethnicity, or income, equally with regard to environmental protection and laws. Efforts toward environmental justice also include meaningful involvement on behalf of individuals who are potentially or currently affected by environmental harms.

The environmental justice movement began in the 1960s during the Civil Rights Movement; however, it wasn't until the 1990s that the federal government took substantial action to correct injustices. The Office of Environmental Equity within the U.S. Environmental Protection (EPA) was created in 1992. In 1994 the name was changed to the Office of Environmental Justice. The federal government, specifically the EPA, has made notable progress in correcting environmental injustices; however, there is still concern among researchers that the least powerful groups in society continue to be the target of harmful environmental underregulation.

hereditary groups that are innately different in their behavior and abilities.[21] This also means that groups can be ranked as superior or inferior on the basis of those abilities and behavior. The presumed superiority of some groups is used to legitimate the unequal distribution of resources as well as the mistreatment of groups thought to be inferior to other groups. Because these traits are innate, they are unchangeable, and those groups at the top are given their position by some sort of natural selection process. Evidence of superiority is found in the success of some groups' abilities to gather economic, social, and political power. Consequently, members of a group who are not successful are used as examples of the group's inferiority.

While inherently **ethnocentric,** which is the tendency to judge other cultures by the standards of our own, thinking that ours is superior,[22] racist thought is not confined to those groups in which the physical differences and social abilities are distinct, such as the differences between Whites and Blacks in the United States. Rather, racist beliefs are those that describe any behavior that attributes hateful behavior or exploitation based on hereditary beliefs or justifications of superiority. In this way, racism is not confined to racial groups but can apply to any ethnic group as well. Racism can pertain to Italian Americans, French Canadians, Jewish Americans, or Polish Americans just as easily as it can apply to African Americans or Asian Americans. In light of this, some experts have called for omitting the term "racism" for the same reasons that the term "race" is too vague. Rather, these experts contend the use of the term **ethnicism** is more appropriate because racism applies to all types of ethnic groups.[23]

✤ Where Does Multiculturalism Fit into the Discussion?

At this point you may be confused about all the terms that define certain groups, and you may be wondering how they relate to the differences in arrests, sentences, and other aspects of the criminal justice process. You may even be wondering, as Rodney King once said, why we cannot seem to "just get along." You might even wonder why we should be thinking about multiculturalism and why people in America have trouble living here. After all, shouldn't people from different cultures simply adapt to our standards and culture? Is multiculturalism bad since it means there is no one standard to follow, or is it a good thing to be exposed to different perspectives on the same issues? After all, the world is a pretty boring place if everyone thinks, believes, and acts the same way. These are great questions and we will try to contrast this debate for you, although it is part of a much larger discussion. The remainder of this book highlights the issues stemming from the treatment of certain groups and how it impacts not only crime and criminal justice, but our time, energy, and resources dedicated to dealing with them. Thus, it is in everyone's interest to at least know what the problems are, how extensively they affect people, and the predictions for solving them in the future. We hope that by the end of this text, you will have a greater understanding of these issues.

Is Multiculturalism in America a Good Thing?

While some experts argue that cultural diversity enhances the social harmony that exists in society, other experts contend that the diversity does not serve as a uniting point for Americans but, rather, is the source of racial tension and conflict. One of the challenges we face in the United States is the tendency to engage in ethnocentrism—Americans tend to believe that their culture is far superior to all other cultures in the world. Americans tend to be ethnocentric within their own borders as well, believing their group to be superior to all others.

On one hand, ethnocentrism can be a unifying mechanism, as was the case after the September 11, 2001, terrorist attacks on the World Trade Center and the Pentagon. As a result, most Americans united against the terrorists, and a strong sense of compassion and cohesion was created in the United States. However, at the same time, the September 11th attacks created problems when many Americans began to believe that anyone who was from the Middle East (or even looked like they were from there) suddenly became suspected of being a terrorist. It is interesting to note that prior to 9/11, racial profiling of African Americans by police officers was one of the most controversial topics in criminal justice. However, after the terrorist attacks, the profiling of people of Middle Eastern descent appeared to be acceptable to many Americans.

Thus, the discussion of the value of **multiculturalism,** which can be defined in many ways but includes the embracing of cultural diversity, a willingness to coexist with people from different backgrounds and cultures, and the celebration of difference, centers on whether multiculturalism divides a society or unifies it.

Multiculturalism Divides People

In many countries, such as the United States, there exists a strong national identity or national character. This means that as Americans, people can identify with being part of the larger society. While there are people from many different backgrounds and preferences, there remains a theme that unites them. It is similar to baseball fans: People may support different teams and/or players, but they are all united by the love of the game. However, some people feel that as a society grows more diverse, that national character or identity loses its influence over people. This is especially true for people who are already afraid that the country's character is being diluted for the sake of diversity and individualism.

Critics of multiculturalism argue that when a society becomes more heterogeneous, cultural standards, the very essence that gives a country its character and identity, begin to fall. They argue that in the interest of protecting different backgrounds and abilities of its members, educational standards are reduced, resulting in a decline in talent and innovative thinking. Critics of multiculturalism also argue that this threatens the economic and political viability of the United States, as mediocrity becomes the norm rather than demanding excellence from everyone. Only when minority groups are taught to accept and validate the majority culture can any type of success be achieved. This is particularly important as the discussion turns to language, one of the most important components of a country's culture.[24] In sum, critics of multiculturalism argue that the celebration of cultural differences does little to foster a sense of cultural identity, leads to the reduction of important educational, economic, and political standards of accountability, and weakens the overall collective conscience or morality of a society.

Acts such as the destruction of the World Trade Center towers led to the acceptability of some types of racial profiling.

Multiculturalism Fosters Discrimination

A second and related area that critics of multiculturalism point to is that discrimination between groups is more likely in multicultural societies. As multiculturalism celebrates differences in backgrounds and experiences, it also segregates people into categories or groups. While the intended goal, of course, is to strengthen and validate minority groups and their values, attitudes, and belief systems, the result is that making distinctions between groups may hasten hatred rather than appreciation of the differences between groups. At the very least, it creates a climate where inequality and discrimination based on membership in those groups is more likely. Critics of multiculturalism argue that if society attempts to reduce discrimination, prejudice, and inequality, such a reduction comes not by celebrating the differences but by galvanizing around the similarities.

Related to discrimination against minority groups is the problem of reverse discrimination. As societies attempt to remedy past mistakes in the treatment of minority groups, one solution is to have current members provide some sort of restitution or compensation for deeds of the past. This form of payback can easily create a climate of tension rather than of restoration. An example of such practices includes programs like affirmative action, which were designed to remedy the historical mistreatment of some groups by providing preferential treatment to the descendants of those groups. While the current practice of affirmative action is not what was originally intended, the result has led some people to feel they are being punished for something over which they had no control. In effect, they are being asked to remedy the behavior of their ancestors, and this breeds hostility rather than harmony and equality toward minority members.

Related to discriminatory treatment is the fact that multiculturalism also creates a climate in which minority groups can adopt a victim's mentality. This means that as society calls for more equity and the fair distribution of economic, social, and political power, some minority group members may use that as a justification for failing to meet their responsibilities. For example, an individual or group might contend that the reason they have not found adequate employment is due to the legacy of slavery when, in fact, it is a result of their unwillingness to look for jobs. Such an attitude can cause even the most ardent defenders of past injustices to feel they are now being exploited.

Multiculturalism Prevents Equality

A third argument against multiculturalism is that it places too heavy an emphasis on the differences between groups compared to their similarities. This discourages assimilation by minority groups and encourages them to remain isolated from the larger society, which can result in people being less willing or able to get along with people from other ethnic, racial, or religious backgrounds. As isolationism increases, it leads certain groups to feel as though they need less from the larger society in terms of skills, talents, education, and opportunities. As a result, members do not pursue these opportunities and remain locked into certain professions or jobs and do not become upwardly mobile. This not only creates an ethnic distinction between minority groups and others, but also promotes class distinctions, which is significant because there are many experts who argue that social class, not race or ethnicity, is the key to achieving social, economic, and political equality.[25]

The Value of Multiculturalism

The preceding discussion can easily be taken out of context to mean that everyone should think, look, and act like everyone else, lest society go into a cultural tailspin that results in its destruction. Of course, there are challenges to living in a culturally diverse society, but this is a far cry from saying that unless we limit differences, we are doomed to an identity-less culture.

The other side of the debate about multiculturalism is that it creates a climate in which difference is not something to fear or reject as a bad thing—it actually promotes innovative thinking. Let's face it: America is and continues to be a culturally diverse society. This leaves us with only a few options: to remove everyone who does not think, look, and act like the majority, which is unrealistic and socially dangerous (e.g., who gets to decide?), or to find a way to use people's different backgrounds and talents to create a society that embraces these differences. While it can be tempting to sit around and complain about what's bad about diversity, it is not constructive. Rather, the more productive way appears to be to accept that diversity exists and find ways to use it to society's advantage.

In reality, there are many experts who believe that America's national identity is the composition of a collection of regional and local cultures. What makes America unique, they say, is that while there may be something of a national identity, it is made up of so many different backgrounds and cultural preferences, to diminish certain parts would be virtually impossible. Perhaps more importantly, cultural diversity is central to the tenets of living in a democratic society. How can people claim to be free if they are constrained in terms of what they think and believe simply because it is different from what the majority think? Further, there is a historic precedent in this country for tolerating ethnic diversity. While we also have a history of the mistreatment of certain groups, we have, at least in theory, always accepted people from different cultures.

In its purest form, the arguments in favor of multiculturalism center on integration and social cohesion. While it is true that many Americans, especially those living in large American cities, can feel isolated and lacking in a sense of community, one of the things that binds people together is their commonality. One of those strands might be religion and another is ethnicity. Ethnic ancestry is said by some experts to give minorities a feeling of community—making ethnic identities a method by which a national identity can evolve. Thus, not only does ethnic group membership help individuals to feel more connected to their larger community, it also can bind them into a larger sense of what some call "peoplehood." For example, a person with an Italian background might feel better connected to her neighbors if she lived near a neighborhood comprised mostly of Italian Americans, such as the Little Italy enclave in New York City. By being better integrated at a local level, the person might also begin to affiliate with other groups, such as the local Catholic Church, which further expands her circle and sense of identity. The person then begins to consider her place in the larger society as an American, which further stimulates her integration to the larger society. The process begins, however, at the micro level, where the person uses her cultural heritage as a starting point to affiliate with others and to begin to feel as though her place in the world matters.[26]

In the end, the process of multiculturalism has a host of implications for society. While at extremes it can become problematic, in this age of globalization in which every country is connected politically, socially, and economically to every other one, society in general will continue to diversify. This can be healthy growth, with Americans learning to celebrate differences and to evaluate others not on their differences but on their commonality, or Americans can fear change and differences and compartmentalize their lives because they feel threatened by some groups. The misuse of power or the tendency to exploit or take advantage of others begins with an initial perception of other groups. Many times, impressions of people are based on small bits of information or on stereotypes of what is known about members of particular groups.

The next chapter discusses group dynamics and how we interpret people's behavior, which influences our interactions with them. As we will see, and as will be shown in the subsequent chapters on the treatment of other minority groups in the criminal justice system, often our initial perceptions lead us to believe that certain groups have attitudes, values, and beliefs regardless of whether any evidence exists to verify that perception. Unfortunately, when such perceptions translate into social policy and judicial and police practices, or affect how juries decide facts of a case, the consequences are significant and can even be life-threatening for minorities.

For those students interested in criminology or the study of the causes of crime, many of the theories not only can be used to explain why a particular person engages in unlawful acts, but also can be understood in terms of the way minority groups are treated. That is, some theories argue that because they are exploited or denied opportunities to achieve success, some minority groups engage in criminal acts either to achieve some level of success (e.g., strain or disorganization theories) or out of frustration for the way they have been identified by others (e.g., labeling theory).

Other theories offer insight into the way people's perceptions influence their lack of understanding of cultural differences (e.g., cultural conflict theory) or argue that the person rejected mainstream society and made a poor choice when he or she decided to commit a crime (e.g., Hirschi and Gottfredson's general theory of crime). Still other explanations for the involvement of minorities in the criminal justice system may be due to the perceptions of minorities by participants in the system, such as the police, judges, or even the public when they serve as jurors. Thus, our goal in this text is not to contend that criminals are not responsible because they were oppressed or mistreated over the sweep of history nor to say that the criminal justice system is hopelessly racist. Rather, we believe that there are a host of factors that explain the trends in crime data, including racism and social history, and that these factors get us closer to understanding the interplay between crime, minorities, and criminal justice.

Do minorities get arrested because they commit more crimes? Maybe, but this could also be due to the fact that the police spend more time looking for criminals and that minorities fit the profile officers have been trained to identify. Do African Americans get different sentences for similar crimes as Whites? In some cases, but the reasons for that may not simply be that judges are racist and intentionally hand out tougher sentences because they do not like African Americans. Human behavior is very complex, and the reasons people act as they do are difficult to determine. Unlike other scientific disciplines, in which the laws regulating the universe have been discovered, social behavior remains a mystery in many ways. What is known is that a variety of factors play into a person's decision to engage in certain acts and that some of these factors have historical, economic, political, and social influences. As the next chapter describes, one of the most important factors in understanding social behavior is found in the way people communicate with each other. As you will see, interaction often consists of symbolic cues that must be interpreted correctly in order for communication to be effective. However, a crucial component in that process is an understanding of the *meaning* of those cues and gestures. Misunderstandings, miscommunications, and preconceived ideas about what a person means not only are the basis of poor relationships, but also are at the heart of problems such as discrimination, racism, and the mistreatment of certain groups.

One final important point is needed. Americans live in an information-saturated age. Scholars, reporters, practitioners, and the general public are much more educated about issues and problems than at any time in our history. As a result, they increasingly demand "proof" or "data" to support claims of a practice, a trend, the effectiveness of a particular strategy, or to justify a change in resource allocation. Consequently, researchers have spent a great deal of time studying the criminal justice system and the problems within it.

However, as you will see in some of the chapters, we use the most current data available to describe trends and patterns, but in some cases, the research is limited or dated. It may come as some surprise to students to learn that there are times when the information on a particular topic is sparse or has not been updated in recent years. This is particularly true with some government publications. However, know that we have reviewed the literature and what we offer is based on what is currently known.

Summary

The issue of race and ethnicity in the United States remains an important factor in understanding social interaction, relationships, and the fabric of American culture. While many people like to think that racism, discrimination, and prejudice are a thing of the past, there is ample evidence to suggest that these problems remain a critical component of social life. It is also the case that many people misunderstand or misuse certain terms when discussing race-related issues. This chapter outlined the way social scientists operationalize terms such as prejudice, discrimination, minority groups, racism, race, and ethnicity. It also explained how minority groups are created, how and why they are mistreated, and the debate about the value of multiculturalism in American society. On one hand, some experts believe that too diverse a society dilutes its national identity and the social cohesion that comes from people seeing the world similarly. On the other hand, multiculturalism celebrates people from different backgrounds and offers insight into human nature as well as how groups can coexist peacefully and equitably. For students of criminal justice, the treatment of minority groups is central to understanding how criminal behavior is understood and addressed as well as how the administration of justice affects people without power. Many of the theories offered explain how crime can be used in part to describe the motivation of some offenders, but they also are framed in light of criminals' minority status. Thus, any discussion of crime in American society must contain some attention to the way certain groups are treated by the dominant culture.

Key Terms

collective conscience (p. 4)

discrimination (p. 13)

ethnicism (p. 16)

ethnocentrism (p. 15)

genocide (p. 11)

heterogeneous societies (p. 5)

homogeneous societies (p. 4)

institutional discrimination (p. 14)

involuntary migration (p. 11)

melting pot (p. 4)

minority group (p. 7)

multiculturalism (p. 17)

neocolonialism (p. 11)

operationalization (p. 5)

prejudice (p. 13)

racism (p. 14)

social construction of race (p. 7)

voluntary migration (p. 11)

Discussion Questions

1. What role does diversity play in the strength of the collective conscience or morality of a society?
2. Why is it so difficult to identify examples of institutional discrimination? If rules apply to everyone, shouldn't that be enough to prevent unfair treatment? Can you give examples of institutional discrimination?
3. Are Americans inherently ethnocentric? Do Americans always believe their culture is better than everyone else's? Why or why not?
4. Is multiculturalism really a bad thing, as some experts have suggested? Does it really dilute the "American identity"? Why or why not?

Endnotes

1. U.S. Department of Commerce, U.S. Census Bureau 1990.
2. Durkheim, E. 1851. *The Division of Labor in Society.* New York: The Free Press.
3. Ibid.
4. Schaefer, R. T. 2004. *Racial and Ethnic Groups,* 9th ed. Upper Saddle River, NJ: Prentice Hall.
5. Shulman, R. 2007. "Sharpton's Ancestor Was Owned by Thurmond's." *Washington Post,* February 26, p. A01.
6. Marger, M. N. 2002. *Race and Ethnic Relations,* 6th ed. Belmont, CA: Wadsworth.
7. Ibid.
8. Ibid.
9. Schaefer 2004.
10. Ibid.
11. See, for instance, McNamara, R. P., Tempenis, M., and Walton, B. 1999. *Crossing the Line: Interracial Couples in the South.* Westport, CT: Praeger.
12. Ibid.
13. Marger 2002.
14. Schaefer 2004.
15. Ibid.
16. Schaefer 2004.
17. Macionis, J. 2005. *Sociology,* 10th ed. Belmont, CA: Wadsworth.
18. Merton, R. K. 1949. "Discrimination and the American Creed." In Robert MacIver (ed.), *Discrimination and National Welfare*, pp. 99–126, New York: Harper and Row.
19. Civil Rights.Org. 2006. Report: Racial Steering into Segregated Neighborhoods Most Prevalent Form of Housing

Discrimination. www.civilrights.org/ issues/housing/remote-page. jsp?itemID=28378031 (accessed July 25, 2007).

20. See, for instance, *Smith v. City of East Cleveland*, 363 F. Supp. 1131 (N.D. Ohio 1973).

21. Marger 2002.

22. Macionis 2005.

23. Ibid.

24. Tepperman, L., and Blain, J. 2006. *Think Twice: Sociology Looks at Current Social Issues,* 2nd ed. Upper Saddle River, NJ: Prentice Hall.

25. Wilson, W. J. 2002. *When Work Fails.* Chicago: University of Chicago Press. See also Wilson, W. J. 1978. *The Declining Significance of Race.* Chicago: University of Chicago Press.

26. Tepperman and Blain 2006.

Group Dynamics, Communication, and Social Interaction

Chapter Objectives

After reading this chapter, you should be able to

❖ Recognize Erving Goffman's contribution to our understanding of social interaction.

❖ Understand what constitutes a group.

❖ Understand the basics of communication and the communication process.

❖ Discuss the significance of verbal and nonverbal communication in the criminal justice system.

❖ Identify the potential outcomes of minority-nonminority interactions.

Part of the problem with discrimination, prejudice, racism, and other forms of mistreatment of people is a result of a poor or limited understanding of the values, attitudes, and beliefs of the members of different groups. Limited or no contact with various groups can lead to stereotypical ideas about the motives, beliefs, and behaviors of these groups. Conversely, if the interaction that takes place between different groups tends to be negative, this can lead to problems in understanding behavior. Recall that in the first chapter we mentioned that a great deal of social interaction is ambiguous: We do not always know what people are thinking or intending; all we see is their behavior. This means that the lens with which we filter those actions becomes critical to how we understand and respond to their behavior.

An important thing to remember is that how people act may be misunderstood. Most of the time we are trying to convey a symbolic message with our words, facial expressions, and body language. However, there are a host of instances when what we want to convey and how that is interpreted are incongruent or misunderstood. While we can easily understand the problems that occur when groups from different cultures interact, we should note that all of us have trouble at times interacting with each other, even those we know. We begin this chapter with recognition of the work of sociologist Erving Goffman, who undoubtedly changed the way we recognize and understand human interaction. His work helps us to understand the interactions between the criminal justice system and those who enter the system.

Erving Goffman and the Nature of Social Interaction

In trying to explain the nature of social interaction, Erving Goffman, in his classic book *The Presentation of Self in Everyday Life* (1959), tried to shed light on the nature of social interaction, particularly in a group setting. In order to maintain a stable self-image, people perform for their social audiences. As a result of this interest in performance Goffman focused on **dramaturgy,** or a view of social life as a series of dramatic performances like those performed on stage.[1]

He assumed that when individuals interact, they want to present a certain sense of self that will be accepted by others. However, even as they present that self, actors are aware that members of the audience can disturb their performance. For that reason actors need to control the audience, especially those behaviors or actions that might be disruptive. They hope that the sense of self they present will cause the audience to voluntarily act as the actors intend. Goffman characterizes this central interest as *impression management,* which involves techniques that actors use to maintain certain impressions in the face of problems they are likely to encounter and methods they use to cope with the problems.

Following this analogy, Goffman spoke of a "front stage," as compared to a "backstage." The front stage is that part of the performance that generally functions in rather fixed and general ways to define the situation for those who observe the performance. Several key components of the front stage include **setting,** which refers to the physical scene that ordinarily must be there if the actors are to perform. For instance, a correctional officer requires a prison, just like an ice skater needs ice. **Personal fronts** consist of those items of equipment that the audience identifies with the performers and expects them to carry with them onto the setting. For instance, a police officer is expected to wear a uniform and carry weapons, much as a surgeon is expected to dress in a medical gown and have certain instruments. Pertinent to one's personal front are appearance and manner. **Appearance** includes those items that tell us the performer's social status (e.g., the police officer's uniform). **Manner** tells the audience what sort of role the performer expects to play in the situation (e.g., physical mannerisms, demeanor). A brusque manner and a meek manner may indicate quite different kinds of performance. In general, we expect appearance and manner to be consistent.

Goffman's most interesting insights lie in the domain of the interaction. Goffman argued that because people generally try to present an idealized picture of themselves in their front stage performances, they inevitably feel that they must hide things in their performance. Accordingly, he also discussed a "backstage," which is usually adjacent to the front stage, but it is also cut off from it. Performers expect that no members of their front audience will appear in the back. For instance, roll call in a police department is often conducted behind the scenes, away from the public. The information shared during roll call is typically reserved for police officers and consists of brief training periods and briefings on issues such as crime problems and community concerns. Officers tend to view roll call as "their time" away from the public. The backstage involves several processes, including

1. **Concealing secret pleasures**, which includes activities engaged in prior to the performance or in past lives that are incompatible with their performance.

For instance, a judge may wish to prevent others from knowing that he uses recreational drugs.

2. **Concealing errors** that have been made in the preparation of the performance as well as steps that have been taken to correct these errors. For example, a police officer may seek to hide the fact that she wrongfully stopped someone.

3. **Showing only the end product** and concealing the process of producing it. Officers may wrongfully stop someone, but justify the stop upon finding illegal drugs.[2]

Goffman also argued that the audiences themselves may try to cope with the falsity so as not to shatter their idealized image of the actor. This reveals the interactional character of all performances. A successful performance depends on the involvement of all parties. Actors also try to make sure that all parts of any performance blend together. In some cases a single flaw can disrupt a performance. However, performances vary in the amount of consistency required. For instance, a slip by a priest on a sacred occasion would be very disruptive, but a taxi driver making a wrong turn wouldn't damage his or her overall performance.

Impression Management

Goffman closed *The Presentation of Self in Everyday Life* with some additional insights on the art of impression management (IM). In general, IM is oriented to guarding against a series of unexpected actions, such as unintended gestures and inopportune intrusions, as well as intended actions such as making a scene. Goffman was interested in the various methods of dealing with such problems. Two important components of IM are dramaturgical discipline and dramaturgical circumspection. **Dramaturgical discipline** is defined as concise preparation of the performance. This includes such things as having the presence of mind to avoid slips, maintaining self-control, and managing facial expressions and the tone of voice of one's performance. Related to this is **dramaturgical circumspection,** which involves the logistical planning involved in carrying out the performance. Examples include planning for emergencies, making only brief appearances (which limits the potential mistakes and errors), and preventing audiences access to private information (which might be used to discredit the performance in some way).[3]

One of Goffman's most interesting books is *Stigma* (1963). He was interested in the gap between what a person ought to be, or what he calls "virtual social identity," and what a person actually is, or "actual social identity." Anyone who has a gap between these two identities is "stigmatized." The book focuses on the dramaturgical interaction between stigmatized people and "normals."[4] The nature of that interaction depends on which of the two types of stigma an individual possesses. In the case of **discredited stigma,** the actor assumes that the differences are known by the audience members or are evident to them. An example is a paraplegic or someone who has lost a limb. Here the dramaturgical problem is how to hide the fact of the obvious stigma and demonstrate that the person is just like everyone else. The IM techniques here are called "covering," often accomplished by "proving" the person can do everything a normal person can do. In the case of someone confined to a wheelchair, the person may go to great lengths to demonstrate independence.

A **discreditable stigma** is one in which the differences are neither known by audience members nor perceivable by them. An example might be a homosexual trying to hide his sexual orientation in a heterosexual environment. This is often referred to as "passing," as in passing oneself off as something the person is not. For someone with a discredited stigma, the basic dramaturgical problem is managing tension produced by the fact that people know of the problem. A problem for someone with a discreditable stigma is managing information so that the problem remains unknown to the audience.

Goffman devotes much of *Stigma* to people with obvious, often grotesque stigmas. However, as the book unfolds, one begins to realize that Goffman is really saying that we are all stigmatized at one time or another or in one setting or another. His examples include Jews "passing" in a predominantly Christian community, the obese person in a group of people of normal weight, and the individual who has lied about his past and must be constantly sure that the audience does not learn of his history.

The significance of Goffman's work is found in the nature of social interaction. We spend a great deal of time trying to present ourselves in a much more favorable light, and we tend to evaluate people on the basis of how *they* present themselves. It should be obvious, then, that many of our interactions are not smooth or successful because we are using very little information with which to determine who someone really is. It is also the case that we make mistakes in evaluating others that can have serious consequences for some individuals.[5]

Social Interaction and the Criminal Justice System

In light of Goffman's account of social interaction, consider the following scenario as it relates to the criminal justice system:

> A young, African American man is escorted into a courtroom for his initial appearance, dressed in state-issued attire (i.e., prison garb). Handcuffed and shackled, the young man appears before a judge who informs him of his rights and the charges against him. The young man discouragingly listens with his head down, staring at the ground as the judge reads the charges. The judge begins to get frustrated by the suspect's seeming disinterest in the proceedings and suggests that the individual "look the court in the eye." The young man grudgingly lifts his head and looks at the agitated judge. "Your disinterest in this case reflects your apparent disinterest in the law," says the judge. He adds: "I've read you your rights and informed you of the charges against you. I suggest you take things seriously or you'll find yourself spending a good portion of your life in state prison."

This account of one man's experience in a courtroom exemplifies the power of verbal and nonverbal communication in today's criminal justice system. Let's deconstruct this situation to identify the presumptions made by the two participants. We'll begin with the presence of a young, African American male in the courtroom. In his book *The Rich Get Richer and the Poor Get Prison,* Jeffrey Reiman discusses how, despite the more severe harms resulting from the actions of white-collar offenders, society recognizes young, urban, poor, African American males as the "typical criminal." Reiman notes

The American public's perception of the criminal population is biased towards African Americans.

that the image of the typical criminal, who instills fear in most law-abiding Americans, is created and perpetuated by government practices (e.g., focusing on street crime) and media and government reports suggesting that this group commits an unreasonable amount of crime.[6] The individual entering the court in our scenario undoubtedly fits the mold of the "typical criminal."

The individual in our scenario enters the court handcuffed and shackled in state-issued attire. This look, fitting for a dangerous individual who could violently react in a moment's notice, is ascribed to an individual who is legally "innocent until proven guilty." Remove yourself from this situation and consider walking around the general public, for instance in a mall, dressed as the young man in our example. What impressions would the public have of you? Would they recognize you as "innocent"? On the other hand, do we want allegedly violent individuals to remain unconstrained in a stressful environment such as the courtroom? Needless to say, the appearance of many who enter our courts suggests they are indeed guilty as opposed to "innocent until proven guilty."

We could also question the accuracy of the judge's belief that the suspect was disinterested in the case, and ultimately the law, simply because he was not making eye contact with the judge. The significance of multicultural studies is evident in this particular exchange, as it is possible that the suspect was showing the judge respect by *not* looking him in the eye. It is considered rude in some cultures (e.g., in many Asian cultures) to look someone in the eye, and some cultures consider it respectful to maintain limited eye contact. Americans, however, view eye contact as a sign of respect. For instance, Americans maintain almost three times as much eye contact as Japanese persons.[7] The judge was clearly speculating and engaging in an ethnocentric manner when commenting on the motives behind the suspect's behavior. As you will recall from Chapter 1, ethnocentrism involves believing that one's culture or group is superior to others.[8] The judge seemingly interpreted the suspect's behavior according to personal cultural beliefs, which is not uncommon. Sociologist Robert Young suggests, "Precisely because everyday patterns of behavior are culture specific, culture serves the function of binding us to those who share our culture and alienating us from those who do not." He adds, "Those who are part of the same culture will tend to behave in similar ways and have tastes and preferences similar to each other and at the same time different from those of different cultural backgrounds."[9]

The situation in our scenario could be interpreted differently from the perspective of the judge. For instance, the judge is likely familiar with nonverbal communication given the amount of time judges spend interacting with various individuals in a court-room. It is possible that judges can, with accuracy, recognize the differences between cultural practices and disinterest. It is also possible for judges to misinterpret actions. Further, should we expect the judge to understand all cultures and respond to each, or should the judge expect all who enter the courtroom to conform to the culture the judge finds most appealing? Responding to each culture requires judges (and all criminal justice practitioners) to familiarize themselves with, and accept, the many cultural back-grounds of the people who enter our criminal justice system. While we hope that we can reach complete understanding and acceptance of cultural differences, the limitations of human behavior regularly enter into criminal justice practices and lead to differential treatment of various groups. Recognizing and responding to the expectation of one cultural community often leads us to violate the expectations of another.[10] Finding common ground can be difficult.

The same challenges and opportunities for misinterpretation, or miscommunication, discussed in our scenario could easily be applied to all facets of criminal justice. We could easily replace the courtroom scenario with a police officer reacting notably punitively upon encountering a group of young adults who don't speak English—or with a prison officer who fails to respect the rights of prisoners by disrupting the privacy of those who wish to pray several times a day. To understand our criminal justice system, we must recognize that the system is composed of individuals who act within specific guidelines established by individuals.

⚔ The Criminal Justice "System"?

The compilation of practices that involve identifying and responding to crime and delinquency is often termed a "system." Some experts argue that our criminal justice system is indeed a true system in its current form, although it may not be a fine-tuned system. In other words, our system does something . . . , maybe not the most effective thing, but something. Others suggest it is a fine-tuned system. Still others suggest it is not a system at all. In light of accepted definitions of the term "system," which includes mention of terms such as "correlation," "coordination," and "orderly," our system of justice looks nothing like a system. Our decentralized practice of dispensing criminal justice often results in uncorrelated, uncoordinated practices at local, county, state, and federal levels. While there is greater cooperation and correlation among the levels of criminal justice practices today than there has ever been, much work remains before we could call ours a true system.

On paper our system of justice seems well designed and well planned (Figure 2.1 depicts the steps of the criminal justice system). One merely needs to examine the recorded steps of the criminal justice system to see that protocol is in place for those accused and convicted of breaking the law. Simply using the term "system" conjures images of a smoothly working entity that encounters problematic situations on rare occasions and maintains proper corrective actions for mishaps. One typically thinks of material objects as systems (e.g., an automobile or an air conditioning unit), which typically function in a more mechanical, predictable manner than does an abstract system composed of individuals. The fact that our system of criminal justice is decentralized and composed of human interactions provides several challenges for those who believe it is a true system.

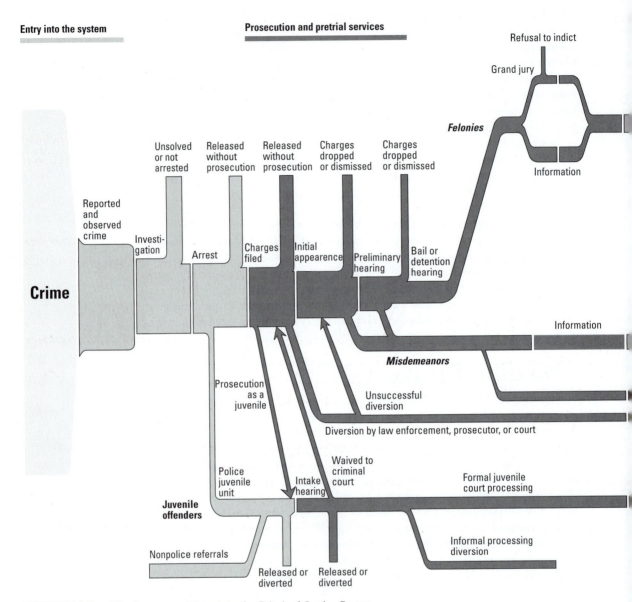

Entry into the system

Prosecution and pretrial services

Refusal to indict

Grand jury

Felonies

Information

Unsolved or not arrested

Released without prosecution

Released without prosecution

Charges dropped or dismissed

Charges dropped or dismissed

Reported and observed crime

Crime

Investigation

Arrest

Charges filed

Initial appearance

Preliminary hearing

Bail or detention hearing

Information

Misdemeanors

Prosecution as a juvenile

Unsuccessful diversion

Diversion by law enforcement, prosecutor, or court

Waived to criminal court

Police juvenile unit

Intake hearing

Formal juvenile court processing

Juvenile offenders

Nonpolice referrals

Released or diverted

Released or diverted

Informal processing diversion

FIGURE 2.1   *The Sequence of Events in the Criminal Justice System*

The effectiveness of the system, despite how fluid it looks on paper, is influenced by human practices. Humans participate on both sides of the law in the criminal justice system. Accordingly, the system is vulnerable to limitations and/or problems associated with human behavior. To clarify, it is often asked whether or not the criminal justice system is racist or biased. The answer, clear and simple, is "no." The system, *as diagrammed,* does not have arrows pointing one way for minorities and another way for nonminorities. The system does not formally treat groups differently. However, humans create laws that are then enforced by police

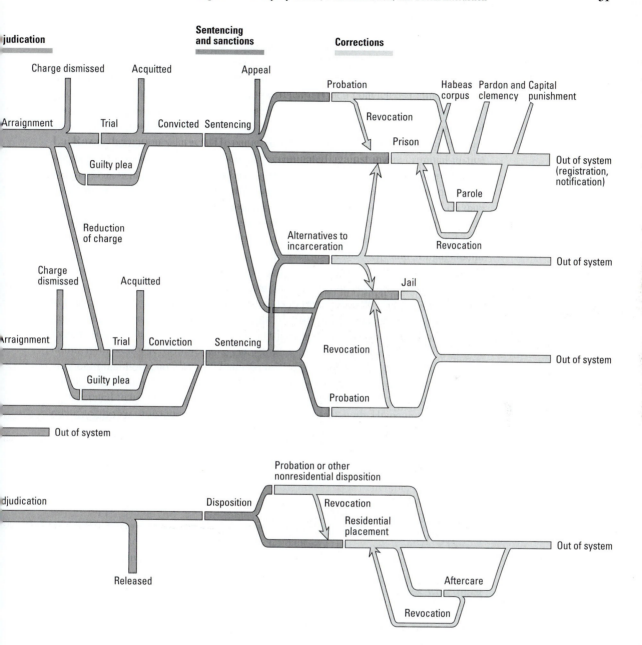

officers and interpreted by courtroom personnel and enforced again by corrections personnel. Individuals influence how justice is determined throughout these and related processes. The system is not biased. Some individuals impacting the system are biased. Fortunately, their impact is not as strong as it once was because one could make a strong argument that today's criminal justice system is more culturally sensitive than at any time in history.

Biases in criminal justice hamper the effectiveness of the system and can result in injustices. Injustices have been abundant in the criminal justice system, as evidenced in the U.S. Supreme Court's landmark decision in the 1972 case *Furman v. Georgia.*[11] In *Furman,* the Court ruled that the death penalty, as it was being administered, constituted cruel and unusual punishment and was in violation of the Eighth and Fourteenth amendments. The majority of justices ruled that the procedures used at that time in applying the death penalty were arbitrary and unfair. The Court didn't rule that death as punishment in and of itself was unfair; instead, the Court found problems with the manners in which the penalty was being applied. Thirty-five states introduced new capital punishment statutes following *Furman.* As evidenced, the criminal justice system often takes steps to correct injustices. Other examples of corrective actions include the introduction of truth-in-sentencing laws, mandatory-minimum sentencing practices, and the use of sentencing guidelines. Nevertheless, the introduction of these actions demonstrates that the system occasionally needs corrective action given the differential treatment of groups, although some critics of the criminal justice system have questioned the fairness involved in each of these "corrective" approaches and sentencing practices in general.[12] Criminal justice policies have both direct and indirect impacts on the daily lives of ethnic and racial groups.[13]

Just how do humans *prevent* the criminal justice system from operating as a true system? One primary obstacle in producing a bias-free criminal justice system occurs when people misunderstand the varied cultural backgrounds of those entering and working in the system. How does the multicultural society in which we live impact simple, everyday exchanges between individuals, specifically within the criminal justice system? The remainder of this chapter addresses this question and others by specifically focusing on three critical topics: "groups," "communication," and "social interaction and multiculturalism." Comprehension of this material helps set the stage for the discussions in the chapters that follow. These issues clearly relate to one another and help to explain how the criminal justice system is not necessarily a smooth-functioning system, per se, as much as it is a behemoth entity filled with justice-seeking personnel, the accused, and the convicted. This chapter will help you understand how and why multiculturalism is one of the most controversial issues within criminal justice.

✂ Groups

We all belong to groups. Whether it's our family, our close network of friends, a church group, an athletic group, or whatever, we all associate with other individuals in varying contexts. Participants in the criminal justice system are not different. We categorize into groups those who engage in criminal justice, whether it is police officers, prosecutors, prison wardens, or the like. Yet, what specifically constitutes a group and what factors influence group behavior? Are the students who sit in the back of the classroom considered a group? Are the three individuals communicating with each other as they walk out of a department store a group?

What Constitutes a Group?

Prominent among the varied definitions of groups include references to group size, whether or not there exists interdependence of members, group identity, the group goals, and group structure.[14]

Cross-cultural relations have improved as the United States has become increasingly tolerant of diversity.

Sociologists Linda Lindsey and Stephen Beach define a **social group** as two or more individuals "who regularly interact and feel some sense of solidarity or common identity. People in groups normally share some values and norms and often work to achieve common goals."[15] Other researchers suggest that groups must have three members. For instance, Joann Keyton, a professor of communication studies, notes that a group must have, at minimum, three members, for the primary reasons of (1) providing the opportunity for members to establish coalitions in which two members side against the third, (2) enabling the opportunity for hidden communication to take place, and (3) determining how roles are assigned.[16] Regardless of the minimum size of groups, the maximum size of a group is dependent on the context of the group. For instance, athletic teams are limited to a set number of participants, whereas some groups (e.g., pro-environmental groups) seek all the support they can muster. The appropriate size of a group is largely determined by the group's ability to achieve its goals.[17]

Interdependence of members is also vital to establishing a group. Members of a group must rely on group or individual actions for the group to accomplish its task(s). People join groups for two primary reasons: (1) to enjoy the company of others and to avoid loneliness and (2) to accomplish goals unattainable individually.[18] Group members rely on one another for direction, support, and interaction. Groups must also include an identity through which members identify themselves. Group members who identify with one another and the group's goals accept the values and norms of the group, which subsequently increases the motivations and abilities of group members to interact and proceed effectively.

The final characteristics central to the definition of groups are group goals and group structure. As the name suggests, **group goals** are agreed-upon tasks or

TABLE 2.1
Characteristics of Groups
Group size
Interdependence of members
Group identity
Group goal
Group structure

activities that the group seeks to complete or accomplish. Goals are varied in nature (e.g., short-term vs. long-term; financial vs. nonfinancial), and not all members of the group have to appreciate the goal. However, there must be a shared understanding of the goal, and group members must perceive it as being worthwhile.[19] Groups must also involve structure, which can be informal (e.g., classmates) or formal (e.g., a police department). **Group structure,** which is largely determined by group roles, typically evolves in accord with, or from, group norms and rules.[20] The structure is vulnerable to change as norms, goals, and other factors impacting the group change. Table 2.1 summarizes the characteristics of a group.

As noted, groups come in all sizes and shapes, and there is some subjectivity in determining a group. Often, we hear of "group member counts," which are sometimes used to gauge support for a particular group and its goal(s). However, simple counts do not suggest that all who are counted are active members of the group. Subjectivity enters when one makes determinations of group membership, for instance, through members paying dues, being active participants, or being listed on a current roster.

Subgroups often emerge as groups become larger and group goals become distorted. Subgroups, or factions of group members that exist within the larger group, sometimes emerge and maintain the possibility of breaking off from the larger group to form an independent group. The existence of subgroups can both help and hinder the larger group as goals are sometimes more easily achieved when individuals work together with limited input and interference. Subgroups, however, may ultimately detach from the larger group, for instance, if they believe their identity or goals differ significantly from those of the larger group or if the subgroup is not receptive to direction from the larger group.

Groups in the Criminal Justice System

Given the elements necessary for the existence of a group, what groups exist within the criminal justice system? To be sure, there are many groups existing at various levels working toward different goals. For starters, we could loosely identify the nearly 2.4 million individuals working in our nation's justice system as a group, which has the ultimate goal of ensuring justice.[21] We could also recognize each component of the criminal justice system as a group (i.e., police, courts, and corrections), and further identify groups as we observe different levels of justice (e.g., local, state, and federal). We could take it further to group individuals working particular beats, in particular courtrooms, or in specific cellblocks.

An example of a group within the criminal justice system is the **courtroom workgroup,** a group of individuals who work on a regular basis in a courtroom setting. The familiarity of courtroom personnel contributes to the local legal culture in the sense that there's a shared understanding of norms, practices, and expectations among courtroom practitioners. The courtroom workgroup emerges as individuals, including judges, prosecutors, and defense attorneys, who work within a jurisdiction come to understand and anticipate particular behaviors from other members of the workgroup. For instance, those regularly acting within a courtroom typically have a clear understanding of the "**going rate,**" or the penalties one can expect to be associated with particular offenses. A defense attorney can share with his or her client any information culled from previous interactions with other members of the workgroup. In turn, suspects have an understanding of what to expect upon entering the courtroom. Among other things, the familiarity among members of the courtroom workgroup helps plea bargain negotiations, which is typical of proceedings in the courtroom as over 90% of criminal cases are resolved in state courts via a plea agreement.[22]

Recognition of suspects as members of particular groups undoubtedly affects criminal justice practices, as identified in the criminal justice research literature and throughout this book. While suspects in general do not meet the criteria of the definition of a group, primarily due to the lack of cohesiveness or organization of suspects, they undoubtedly belong to some group (e.g., based on affiliation with a gang membership or a culture-based group) and are typically pre-judged and treated in various manners in the criminal justice system.

✂ Communication

Communication is at the core of human interaction. It guides, conveys, directs, suggests, and so on. Effective communication is vital to the effective functioning of any group, and it has saved more than one police and correctional officer's life. Communication is perhaps the most important, yet often overlooked, aspect of the criminal justice system. Take, for instance, a police officer who bases her decision to draw and shoot her firearm on interpersonal communication. Consider the prison officer who interprets an inmate's behavior as unruly and proceeds to forcefully remove the inmate from his cell. With regard to parole, criminal justice author/editor Marsha Bailey suggests, "In dealing with Hispanic offenders, parole officers should be direct and to the point when instructing, and should expect to see more reaction from parolees [as] Hispanics generally are more immediate and vocal in communication; sometimes the dialogue sounds more intimidating than it really is."[23] Miscommunication is the basis for some interpersonal conflict and the cause for some criminal injustice.

Communication comes in two forms: verbal and nonverbal. Verbal communication consists of the words we speak. Nonverbal communication entails all nonvocal acts that convey a message. The judge in the scenario at the beginning of this chapter based his assumptions of the suspect upon nonverbal cues and offered his input via verbal communication. The visible power differential in the courtroom, for example, with the judge dressed in a robe and sitting above the courtroom actors, is also a form of nonverbal communication (e.g., the judge expects respect).

DON IMUS' CONTROVERSIAL COMMENTS

In April 2007, popular radio talk-show host Don Imus was featured on the cover of *Time* magazine with a note over his mouth stating "Who Can Say What?" Imus received the attention after he was fired by CBS Radio following his controversial on-air comments regarding the Rutgers University women's basketball team. As a member of the National Broadcaster Hall of Fame and once named by *Time* magazine as one of the "25 Most Influential People in America," Imus referred to the female basketball team players as "some nappy-headed hos" on April 4, a day after the team competed for the national championship. The comments generated reaction across the country, particularly among females and minority-interest groups.

Don Imus has had a long, successful career in radio talk. He generated substantial profits for CBS and has raised over $40 million for various causes. His comments, however, instigated significant backlash and led to the cancellation of his radio show. Sponsors of his show such as General Motors, Proctor & Gamble, Staples, and American Express withdrew their sponsorship following the comments. Prominent leaders in the African American community and various women's rights groups voiced their concern and were significantly influential in Imus' demise. African American leader Al Sharpton spoke for many concerned leaders and citizens when he called the comments racist and sexist.[24]

Don Imus met with the Rutgers team members and apologized. The players and coach accepted his apology, yet noted that the forgiving period will take some time. Imus' comments demonstrate the power of communication. Don Imus is not alone among radio talk-show hosts or, more generally, members of the media who have failed to accept diversity and demonstrate tolerance. His offensive remarks cannot be misinterpreted and came at a time when censorship in the media is of concern and the need for tolerance is an even greater concern. His actions, at the very least, demonstrate that even professional communicators, who have spent much of their lives communicating, sometimes verbally incite anger, hate, and hurt.

The Communication Process

To understand the impact of communication in the criminal justice system, one could deconstruct the communication process. Deconstructing verbal communication provides a starting point for understanding nonverbal communication. Understanding verbal communication begins with the thought process of the individual sending the verbal message (the sender). At the most basic level, the sender interprets or analyzes a situation and generates thoughts. Part of the interpretation and analysis involves determining what message the sender wishes to transmit and how he or she wishes to send it. There is a filter involved as we all sometimes think about saying things, yet refrain from doing so. Some of us have a more restrictive or porous filter than others, which explains why some folks are quiet, others speak their mind, and some are constantly putting their foot in their mouth.

Once the message is created in the sender's mind, the individual targets others (receivers) whom he or she wishes to hear the message. Sometimes we wish to convey a message to some individuals present, yet exclude others from the message, which is why we sometimes whisper or speak coyly. Upon locating proper targets, the sender conveys the message via some channel, typically either verbally or in writing. Failing to properly organize thoughts has prompted many misunderstandings and controversies. Aside from the spoken words, the pitch and tone of a verbal message certainly influence verbal communication.

Receivers encode the message through receiving, interpreting, and analyzing the message. Proper listening is key to verbal communication. Although the act of hearing is physical in nature, listening is a mental exercise. Effective listeners often maintain the ability to lead the conversation. Americans, however, are not effective listeners, as they tend to talk more than they listen.[25]

Upon hearing and listening to the message, receivers generate a response regarding how they received, interpreted, and understood the message. For instance, the message could generate a series of verbal and nonverbal reactions, including a return message, smile, frown, punch, and/or gunshot. The communication process continues until one or all participants find a suitable point for conclusion. Of particular importance in this exchange are one's ability to generate thoughts into words or actions (including the filtering process) and the ability of others to receive, interpret, and adequately respond to the message. Former President Ronald Reagan was deemed the "Great Communicator" for his ability to inspire many with his words and actions. Figure 2.2 depicts the communication process.

Effective communication requires effective listening.

Nonverbal Communication

Nonverbal communication also involves reception, interpretation, and reaction. One merely needs to view commercial advertising to understand the power of nonverbal communication and symbolic cues. Advertisements including people driving vehicles in idealistic environments or individuals drinking beer on an exotic island suggest to consumers that purchase of a particular product will enable them to live such lifestyles. Much research and consideration goes into commercial advertising, so at some point during the advertising development phase a marketing group determined that nonverbal cues such as a hammock and a beach would entice consumers to drink their client's beer.

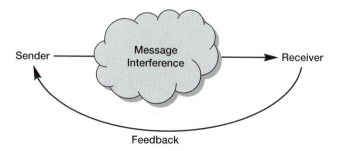

FIGURE 2.2   *The Communication Process*

Nonverbal cues such as clothing, body posture, eye contact, and physical aggression are significant forms of communication that generate and dictate much action within the criminal justice system. Nonverbal communication begins with the nonverbal message transmitted by a sender, which can be in the form of body movements, facial expressions, and gestures. The message is then received and interpreted by the receiver, who evaluates the message and sender and reacts. Similar to verbal communication, the message being sent isn't always the message received.

Interpretation and analyses of nonverbal communication pose particular obstacles due to the greater amount of subjectivity involved, especially since a nonverbal message isn't being directly conveyed like verbal exchanges. This obstacle is evident in the earlier scenario when the judge interprets the suspect's behavior of failing to make eye contact as a sign of disrespect. The significance of nonverbal cues is also recognized in police departments that use a **continuum of force** to guide officer decision-making when encountering potentially violent situations. Officers are expected to consider the continuum of force in their attempts to adequately interpret and respond to suspect behavior. For instance, officers are legally permitted to use deadly force only when they perceive suspects as posing deadly threats to the officer and/or others. The perception aspect of the laws surrounding deadly force involves officers interpreting nonverbal (and sometimes verbal) cues. Failure to react accordingly could result in death(s), civil and criminal litigation, and the officer's dismissal from the force.

Of particular importance in any discussion of communication are kinesics, vocalics, and proxemics.[26] **Kinesics** refers to body language, including gestures, facial expressions, eye behavior, and body movements. **Vocalics,** or paralanguage, refers to vocal characteristics such as inflection, tone, accent, rate, pitch, volume, and vocal interrupters. **Proxemics** refers to the space between the communicator and his or her audience. The actions within the criminal justice system take place at all levels of space. For instance, police officers are sometimes required to physically detain suspects through invasion of the individual's intimate space, while communications between prison officers and prisoners may occur within personal space. Judges sitting in a courtroom typically conduct business from a public distance. The varying levels of acceptable or expected interaction among cultures sometimes leads to misunderstandings and perhaps violence between criminal justice practitioners and the individuals they encounter.

Perhaps you'll recall scenes from the television show *Seinfeld* that used issues pertaining to vocalics and proxemics as part of the humor. One scene involved a guest character who was deemed a "soft talker" (nobody can hear her when she speaks), and the other scene involved a "close talker" who continuously invaded the receiver's intimate space when speaking.

Obstacles Affecting Communication

Many obstacles exist in the communication process, as effective communication involves an expectation that all parties clearly understand each other. One must bear in mind that we often use words, which are human creations, to convey a message and rely on the perception of others to correctly interpret the message. The meanings of words exist in people, not in the actual spoken words.[27]

Perception refers to the act of becoming aware or apprehending something via the senses. As such, word selection is vital to effective communication as there is an assumption that all receivers have the same interpretation of the word. For instance, individuals, specifically suspects, are sometimes deemed "dangerous" or "threatening." Such a classification generally prompts a rapid, punitive response; yet, we must ask several questions before we act rashly. For instance, we must ask, "How are they dangerous?" and "To whom are they dangerous or threatening?" For example, there was a great sense of insecurity in the United States following the terrorist attacks of September 11, 2001. In response, the criteria for perceptions of "dangerous" and "threatening" differed following the attacks, and it is argued that a substantial number of individuals were inaccurately deemed "dangerous." Ethnic profiling has become increasingly recognized in the United States since the attacks.[28]

Prominent among the obstacles involved in communication is the fact that the human body is limited in its intake capacity, and interference can certainly play a role in miscommunication. The limited capacity of the human brain prevents us from fully ingesting and interpreting all societal cues.[29] Physical challenges such as color blindness, deafness, blindness, and speech impairments also restrict successful communication.

Of particular significance to criminal justice is the expectation that conveyed messages will be received and interpreted in the proper context. The multicultural society in which we live poses significant challenges given the numerous languages spoken and the varied values, beliefs, expectations, and interactions of individuals from various cultures. The ability to speak a second (or third) language is becoming increasingly important for criminal justice professionals, particularly since language is a primary identifying feature of a culture.[30] Table 2.2 depicts results from the U.S. Census Bureau's survey of the languages spoken in U.S. households.

TABLE 2.2

Language Spoken at Home in the United States, 2005

Language	Total
Population age 5 years and older	268,110,961
Speak only English	80.6%
Speak a language other than English	19.4%
Speak a language other than English	51,934,850
Spanish or Spanish Creole	62.0%
Other Indo-European languages	19.1%
Asian and Pacific Island languages	15.0%
Other languages	4.0%

Source: U.S. Census Bureau, 2005 American Community Survey

The limitations inherent in communication are sometimes addressed through restating or reemphasizing the message, as we often hear senders state, "Let me clarify . . . ," or "Put simply . . . ," or "For example . . . ." Understanding how individuals react to miscommunication and how to resolve miscommunication should be of utmost importance to criminal justice practitioners and scholars. Understanding our reactions to miscommunication is perhaps as important as recognizing the reasons why we miscommunicate.

Differential Treatment and Symbolism

The criminal justice literature is filled with studies examining differential treatment of groups based on symbolic cues. **Symbols,** or items used to represent something else, are evident throughout the criminal justice system. For instance, the police officer's badge, the judge's gown, and the scales of justice are but a few of the many symbols used by criminal justice personnel to represent something else. The use of symbols, of course, requires that all who encounter the symbol understand what is being symbolized.

Criminal justice personnel not only display symbols, they interpret them as well. Two well-documented examples of symbolism influencing police discretion include the concept of "symbolic assailants" and, more recently, racial profiling. Years ago social scientist Jerome Skolnick used the term "**symbolic assailant**" to refer to particular individuals, as perceived by police officers, who appear as potential sources of violence or as enemies to be reckoned with. Skolnick described symbolic assailants as "persons who use gesture, language, and attire that the policeman has come to recognize as a prelude to violence."[31]

Racial profiling, also discussed in Chapter 13, is a controversial topic in policing and society in general. **Racial profiling,** which involves recognizing individuals as suspects based merely upon race, has existed in society since groups of different backgrounds began interacting. The relatively short history of the United States is rife with accounts of racial profiling, not the least of which involves the Anglo settlers confronting Native Americans prior to and following the Revolutionary War. It has only recently been the topic of much discussion from a research and policy standpoint, particularly in light of accounts of African American motorists being targeted by law enforcement and the differential treatment of those of Middle Eastern descent following the terrorist attacks of September 11, 2001.[32] Racial profiling exemplifies how images and stereotypes of various racial, cultural, and ethnic groups influence formal social control efforts.[33]

Racial profiling is not always targeted toward minority groups and is not always based on race. Police officers often note that crime detection is sometimes an advanced version of the children's game "Which One Doesn't Belong Here?" Specifically, officers identify individuals or objects that don't "fit" within the context of the situation. Examples include expensive automobiles in low-income areas, a minority person loitering in a predominantly nonminority neighborhood, or a nonminority person loitering in a predominantly minority neighborhood. In other words, officers use symbolic cues as a basis for their actions. Proponents of racial profiling argue that categorizing individuals based on appearance is necessary for solid police work, whereas opponents argue that appearance alone should not dictate perceptions of one's behavior.

This base-level account of verbal and nonverbal communication is elaborated upon in the communications studies literature. We've only scratched the surface of the intricate nature of interpersonal communication in an understanding of how individuals communicate, how communications can become distorted, and the significance of miscommunication.

⚔ Social Interaction and Multiculturalism

Social interaction is the process through which individuals act and react in relation to other individuals.[34] Volumes have been written on the complex nature of social interaction, and many more works are forthcoming. Our discussion of social interaction is restricted to the dynamics and complexities involving human interaction in a multicultural society, with particular emphasis on the criminal justice system.

A primary challenge of a multicultural society involves group members' ability to effectively coexist. To understand social interaction in a multicultural society requires recognition of what constitutes culture. Historically, a White, male, European worldview has defined and controlled the majority culture in the United States.[35] However, the world is becoming increasingly diverse as society grows and national borders continuously open. Sociologist John Macionis stated that "multiculturalism represents a sharp turn from the past, when our society downplayed cultural diversity, defining itself in terms of its European (and especially English) immigrants."[36]

Social interaction is regulated by norms that are primarily determined by our culture. However, people act out norms in various ways.[37] Cultural norms provide guidance for our behavior. **Culture** refers to beliefs, values, behaviors, and material goods that collectively constitute a people's manner of life. Culture shapes what we do and our personalities.[38] It is often divided into two categories: material and nonmaterial. **Material culture** consists of objects that are real to the senses (e.g., a baton, handcuffs, a judge's gavel). **Nonmaterial culture** is largely composed of our shared beliefs and values and the social expectations individuals have for one another. Because nonmaterial culture cannot be seen, it is particularly problematic when cultures interact.[39]

Despite the conflicts that develop, people in the United States take great pride in its status as a "melting pot," in which individuals from all cultures are welcome and expected to contribute to the greater good. In turn, the United States is a notably diverse and heterogeneous society consisting of individuals from many different backgrounds and cultures. The extensive diversity in the United States continues to increase. Annually, roughly one million people from other countries come to the United States. In contrast, historic isolation has made Japan the least multicultural of all high-income nations. Intense immigration has contributed to the United States becoming the most multicultural of all high-income countries. A century ago, most people who emigrated to the United States were from Europe, but today most immigrants arrive from Asia and Latin America.[40]

Status and Roles

Understanding social interaction requires recognition of both status and role. **Status** involves the social position maintained by an individual. **Role** refers to the behavior

that is expected of an individual who maintains a particular status.[41] Status is part of our everyday behavior and helps dictate our relationships with those with whom we interact. We each hold a status set that entails the different statuses we maintain at a given time. Statuses are subject to change over time. For instance, one could be a student, then a correctional officer, and later on a father. The multiple statuses that we maintain at a given time dictate the roles we play in everyday life. We could play the role of judge, jury member, probation officer, or therapist.

We sometimes encounter role conflict. For instance, consider the dilemma of the off-duty police officer who is hanging out at a bar with a group of friends. The officer notices that one guy in the group may be unfit (i.e., too drunk) to drive home, even though he says he's "fine" and the others in the group see no problem letting him drive. The officer is faced with role conflict in that he took an oath to serve and protect, yet he wants to remain "one of the guys," not the "police officer friend" in the group. How should the officer handle this situation?

Statuses and roles are noticeably evident in the criminal justice system. For example, prison officers expect, based on their status, to be treated with respect by inmates. Inmates often expect the same treatment; however, their status as "offenders" leaves them in a position to receive limited respect. There are clear hierarchies in many criminal justice agencies that specifically designate one's status in the system.

Socially Constructing Reality

Some researchers argue that individuals don't understand society in a truly objective manner. Instead, they argue, people mentally construct ideas about phenomena and thus create a reality, in what is recognized as the **social construction of reality**.[42] Through interacting with one another, we creatively mold a reality that could vary according to the interpretations of participants. Social interaction involves complex negotiations of reality. Most of us can agree about what occurs in everyday life; however, we may all have different perceptions of happenings.[43] Such differences, particularly as they exist in the criminal justice system and with regard to various cultures, could lead to significant miscommunication and uncomfortable interactions.

It is often argued that issues are socially constructed with particular ideologies in mind. For instance, the war on drugs has disproportionately impacted young, minority males, leading some researchers to question the identified intentions of the war. More generally, one could argue that society's preoccupation with street crime, as opposed to white-collar crime, stems from the status and power differentials of the groups primarily involved in each type of crime. Street crime arrests typically involve lower-class minority males, whereas white-collar crimes are recognized as predominantly involving wealthy nonminorities. Some experts argue that the constructed images of the "typical criminal" and the "war on (street) crime" enable the more powerful in society to maintain status quo with regard to the discrepancy in power.

Sports-talk radio provides an example of competing constructions of the world. Consider, for example, discussions of college football rankings. Put simply, college football rankings are highly subjective. The manner by which teams are evaluated and ranked is highly suspect, at times political, and sometimes responsible for schools earning or losing millions of dollars. To say that one team should be

ranked higher than another ("higher" meaning "better"), when in fact the teams have not played each other or a common opponent, leads to much discussion and argument. Sports-talk radio hosts and their guests debate how the teams should be ranked, all the while sharing their constructed reality that often differs from the reality created by others.

Subjectivity is inherent in communication, and in a multicultural society subjectivity becomes critical in human interaction. Consciously or subconsciously, we all incorporate subjectivity during social interaction. Sometimes, unfortunately, the subjectivity involves characteristics that hamper the coexistence of various groups and acceptance of others. Social interaction is grounded in the belief that messages conveyed will be interpreted in the manner intended. We know, however, that social interaction is often clouded by mis-hearings, mis-speaks, misinterpretations, and various other misunderstandings.[44]

✖ Interaction, Communication, and Multiculturalism in the Criminal Justice System

The significance of cultural diversity in the criminal justice system is evidenced in a recent Bureau of Justice Statistics report, which notes that 95% of state and local law enforcement training academies offer training in cultural diversity, while 85% train cadets with regard to hate/bias crimes.[45] The median number of hours for cultural diversity training is eight, while the median number of hours devoted to hate/bias crimes is four. The need for more effective interaction with the various cultural groups entering the criminal justice system is well documented. Many solutions have been offered in response, including promotion of multiculturalism in criminal justice education.

Researcher William Calathes argues that "criminal justice education has missed much by promulgating a 'melting pot' philosophy. Our students think in terms of white monoculturalism, the assumption that we all belong to one system, which is that of white Anglo-Europeans."[46] The changing nature of society encourages greater recognition of multiculturalism in criminal justice curriculums, as today's criminal justice students are tomorrow's justice professionals.

At any stage during the "suspect turned offender's" journey through the criminal justice system, that person could very easily encounter someone who doesn't view society in the same manner as he or she does. For instance, cultural differences may result in a jury rendering an unfavorable verdict based on preferences or prejudices. The opportunity for miscommunication increases as the number of contacts throughout case processing increases. In turn, there's a greater chance of misunderstanding and misguided behaviors because the suspect/offender encountered a greater number of individuals. An overriding goal of the criminal justice system, then, should be to eliminate, or at least reduce, the likelihood of injustices occurring from improper personal interactions.

Addressing cultural differences as they exist throughout the system is a vital first step toward addressing the issue as evidenced, for example, in the training provided correctional officers at the New Mexico Corrections Training Academy. The Academy requires cadets to recognize and practice facial expressions, posture,

positioning, and distance. Such training, which is not restricted to the New Mexico Corrections Training Academy, helps cadets understand various aspects of nonverbal communication.[47]

The criminal justice system is, by nature, supported by human interaction. Consider the various contexts of human interaction found at all steps involved in criminal case processing. To begin, a crime is committed and someone contacts the authorities. The police investigate primarily through interviewing witnesses and suspects. An arrest may ultimately be made, and the suspect is turned over to the courts where he or she will interact with judges, prosecutors, defense attorneys, and possibly jurors. If convicted, the offender is turned over to the supervision of some correctional group and will encounter many different situations involving individuals from various backgrounds.

The manner in which social interaction takes place in the criminal justice system is influenced by the technological revolution society is currently experiencing. For instance, computers eliminate much of the busywork previously associated with running background checks on individuals and vehicles. The need to communicate with a dispatcher is reduced as mobile computer units are found in many police cars. In corrections, global positional satellite (GPS) monitoring is used to track some offenders serving their penalties in the community. For instance, in June 2006, South Carolina Governor Mark Sanford signed a bill that mandates GPS monitoring for sex offenders convicted of certain offenses. This form of electronic monitorring will likely increase in the criminal justice system, as the number of face-to-face contacts required as part of probation and paroles plans is likely reduced. Email has significantly changed the manner in which many of us interact, as it is easier for many of us to send an email as opposed to making a phone call or personally visiting our target recipient. In the end, understanding and comprehending technology-base communications is becoming increasingly important.

Summary

Effective communication, interaction, and interpretation of conveyed messages are vital for the criminal justice system to function effectively. Misunderstandings, conflict, and undue stress are but a few of the negative outcomes associated with ineffective social interaction. Erving Goffman earlier commented on the intricacies of social interaction. Among other contributions, Goffman stressed the importance of self-awareness, stigmas, and the significance of impression management in social interactions. Goffman has contributed largely to the study of human interaction.

Those working within the criminal justice system face continuous challenges in understanding, interpreting, and responding to individuals from various groups. These groups are not limited to those accused of breaking the law; the criminal justice system is composed of employees from all walks of life. Needless to say, those working within the criminal justice system must maintain a true appreciation for cultural, racial, and ethnic diversity. Anything less could result in misunderstandings and/or conflict.

Communication occurs in many ways. For instance, facial expressions, body posture, verbal expressions, and hand gestures are part of many communication exchanges. Professionals, especially those working in the criminal justice system, must maintain the ability to effectively control various aspects of their communication efforts if they wish for others to accurately interpret the meaning of their message. Further, accurately interpreting the messages sent by others requires skills and abilities that extend beyond merely hearing words and understanding their literal meaning.

Symbolism is present throughout the criminal justice system, from the badges worn by police officers to the gowns worn by judges in the courtroom. Symbolism extends beyond material objects when, for instance, some individuals are stereotyped and/or categorized based on their physical features. The term "symbolic assailant" is used to describe how some police officers believe particular individuals pose a threat simply based on the individual's physical appearance.

A person's cultural background, status, and the roles he or she plays in everyday life largely impact how the person will be treated by the criminal justice system. The research literature is rife with accounts of differential treatment of various groups of offenders. Further, the research identifies differences in how those from varied cultural backgrounds, and with different statuses and/or various roles, face particular challenges while working within the criminal justice system. While the negative impacts of being from different cultural backgrounds, or having atypical statuses or conflicting roles, have subsided to some degree within the criminal justice system, there remains much room for improvement.

You Make the Call

Symbolism and Policing

Consider the following scenario. Debate the pros and cons of all options and decide what you would do.

You're a rookie police officer teamed with an experienced officer on patrol. You're both White males on patrol in a predominantly Asian neighborhood. Racial tensions between the police and the residents were enhanced last week when a White officer was accused of using excessive force on a young Asian suspect. As you patrol, you and your partner notice a young Asian male wearing a shirt that states "I hate pigs" and has a picture of a gun pointing at a police officer. You let it roll off your back, as you've been trained to do. Your partner, however, tells you to pull over. He suggests that the "punk needs to show a little respect." Your partner approaches the Asian youth and tells him to get into the car. The youth complies and your partner tells you to drive off. While driving around, your partner threatens to violently beat the youth and make sure that nobody knows about it. You're taken aback by what's going on, as you expected a better attitude from your colleague. The youth is crying, fearful for his life. He says his older brother made him wear the shirt. After a while, your partner tells you to pull over and let the youth out. He's about two miles from where you picked him up and is left to find a ride home. While pulling away, the officer tells the boy that if anything is said of this encounter, the officer will follow through on his threats.

Questions

1. Should our laws regarding freedom of expression permit individuals to wear hate-based, threatening clothing? Or does such symbolism discourage tolerance?
2. What type of social interaction and nonverbal communication instigated this incident?
3. Should the officers have responded at all to the symbolism found on the youth's shirt?
4. What steps should you have taken to address this troubling situation? How would your actions have impacted your role and status as a police officer?

Key Terms

appearance (p. 25)
concealing errors (p. 26)
concealing secret pleasures (p. 25)
continuum of force (p. 38)
courtroom workgroup (p. 35)
culture (p. 41)
discreditable stigma (p. 26)
discredited stigma (p. 26)
dramaturgical circumspection (p. 26)
dramaturgical discipline (p. 26)
dramaturgy (p. 25)
going rate (p. 35)
group goals (p. 33)
group structure (p. 34)
kinesics (p. 38)
manner (p. 25)

material culture (p. 41)
nonmaterial culture (p. 41)
perception (p. 39)
personal front (p. 25)
proxemics (p. 38)
racial profiling (p. 40)
role (p. 41)
setting (p. 25)
showing only the end product (p. 26)
social construction of reality (p. 42)
social group (p. 33)
social interaction (p. 41)
status (p. 41)
symbolic assailant (p. 40)
symbols (p. 40)
vocalics (p. 38)

Discussion Questions

1. Discuss how those who enter the courtroom as "innocent until proven guilty" may not be recognized as such.
2. Identify and discuss the five characteristics of a group. Would you consider the members of a football team a group? Why or why not?
3. How is assimilation different from multiculturalism? Do you believe multiculturalism is more prominent within society than assimilation? Why or why not?
4. Describe the verbal communication process and note how miscommunication occurs.
5. Describe the similarities between the "typical criminal" and the "symbolic assailant." Do you believe it is effective police practice for officers to identify individuals as threats based on demographic profiles? Do you believe it is fair for officers to do so?

Endnotes

1. Goffman, E. 1959. *The Presentation of Self in Everyday Life*. New York: Doubleday.
2. Ibid.
3. Ibid.
4. Goffman, E. 1963. *Stigma*. Englewood Cliffs, NJ: Prentice Hall.
5. Ibid.
6. Reiman, J. 2007. *The Rich Get Richer and the Poor Get Prison: Ideology, Class, and Criminal Justice*. Boston: Allyn & Bacon. P. 64.
7. Graham, J. L., and Yoshihiro, S. 1984. *Smart Bargaining: Doing Business with the Japanese*. Cambridge, MA: Ballinger.
8. Young, R. L. 1999. *Understanding Misunderstandings: A Practical Guide to More Successful Human Interaction*. Austin: University of Texas Press.
9. Ibid., p. 102.
10. Ibid.
11. *Furman v. Georgia,* 408 U.S. 238 (1972).
12. See, for example, Crawford, C., Chiricos, T., and Kleck, G. 1998. "Race, Racial Threat, and Sentencing of Habitual Offenders." *Criminology* 36 (3): 481–511.
13. Rodriquez, N. 2006. "The Nexus Between Race and Ethnicity and Criminal Justice Policy." In C. R. Mann, M. Zatz, and N. Rodriguez (eds.), *Images of Color, Images of Crime: Readings,* 3rd ed., pp. 243–251. Los Angeles: Roxbury. P. 249.
14. Keyton, J. 2006. *Communicating in Groups: Building Relationships for Group Effectiveness*, 3rd ed. New York: Oxford University Press.
15. Lindsey, L. L., and Beach, S. 2002. *Sociology,* 2nd ed. Upper Saddle River, NJ: Prentice Hall. P. 90. Macionis also suggested only two are needed to constitute a group: Macionis, J. J. 2004. *Society: The Basics,* 7th ed. Upper Saddle River, NJ: Prentice Hall.
16. Keyton 2006.
17. Ibid.
18. Lindsey and Beach 2002.
19. Ibid.
20. Ibid.
21. Hughes discusses employment totals in the U.S. in Hughes, K. A. 2006, April. *Justice Expenditure and Employment in the United States, 2003*. Bureau of Justice Statistics, U.S. Department of Justice, NCJ 212260.
22. Rainville, G., and Reaves, B. A. 2003. *Felony Defendants in Large Urban Counties, 2000*. Bureau of Justice Statistics, U.S. Department of Justice, NCJ 202021.
23. Bailey, M. 1991. "Georgia Parole Officers Confront Language and Cultural Barriers." *Corrections Today,* December, pp. 118, 120–121. P. 121.
24. "CBS Fires Don Imus Over Racial Slur." 2007, April 12. www.cbsnews.com/stories/2007/04/12/national/main2675273.shtml (accessed August 24, 2007).
25. Hunter, R. D., Barker, T., and Mayhall, P. D. 2004. *Police-Community Relations and the Administration of Justice,* 6th ed. Upper Saddle River, NJ: Prentice Hall.
26. Keyton 2006.
27. Hunter, Barker, and Mayhall 2006.
28. Welch, M. 2003. "Trampling Human Rights in the War on Terror: Implications to the Sociology of Denial." *Critical Criminology* 12: 1–20.
29. Jeffery, C. R. 1990. *Criminology: An Interdisciplinary Approach*. Englewood Cliffs, NJ: Prentice Hall.
30. Cesarz, G., and Madrid-Bustos, J. 1991. "Taking a multicultural world view in today's corrections facilities." *Corrections Today,* December, pp. 68–71.
31. Skolnick, J. H. 1966. *Justice Without Trial: Law Enforcement in a Democratic Society*. Berkeley: University of California. P. 45.
32. See, for example, Welch 2003, and Lundman, R., and Kaufman, R. L. 2003. "Driving While Black: Effects of Race, Ethnicity, and Gender on Citizen

Self-Reports on Traffic Stops and Police Actions." *Criminology* 41 (1): 195–220.

33. Rodriguez 2006.

34. Macionis 2004.

35. Miller, L. S., and Hess, K. M. 2002. *The Police in the Community: Strategies for the 21st Century,* 3rd ed. Belmont, CA: Wadsworth.

36. Macionis 2004, p. 48.

37. Lindsey and Beach 2002.

38. Macionis 2004.

39. Young 1999.

40. Macionis 2004.

41. Ibid.

42. Berger, P. L., and Luckmann, T. 1966. *The Social Construction of Reality: A Treatise in the Sociology of Knowledge.* New York: Anchor.

43. Macionis 2004.

44. Young 1999.

45. Hickman, M. J. 2005. *State and Local Law Enforcement Training Academies, 2002.* U.S. Department of Justice, Bureau of Justice Statistics. NCJ 204030.

46. Calathes, William. 1994. "The Case for a Multicultural Approach to Teaching Criminal Justice." *Journal of Criminal Justice Education* 5 (1): 1–14. P. 1.

47. Cesarz and Madrid-Bustos 1991.

Cultural Specifics in the Criminal Justice System

African Americans and the Criminal Justice System

Chapter Objectives

After reading this chapter, you should be able to

- ❖ Identify the role slavery and Reconstruction played in the history of the African American experience in this country.
- ❖ Understand the current state of African Americans, particularly the rise of the Black middle class.

- ❖ Describe the ways in which African Americans perceive the police.
- ❖ Understand the overrepresentation of African Americans in the criminal justice system, including arrests, use of force, deadly force, sentencing, and the death penalty.

The African American experience in the United States is perhaps best understood by examining African Americans' present position in American culture as well as the historical context in which this diverse group of people came to this country. While many experts recognize the varying degrees of difference among Hispanics or Latino Americans, the diversity of African Americans is often overlooked. This is particularly true as many African Americans have transcended social class, educational, and political boundaries. This chapter will explore the presence of African Americans in the social, political, and economic development of the United States as well as offer insight into how and in what ways they become involved in the criminal justice system.

✳ Historical Background

There is little disagreement among historians, sociologists, and anthropologists that African Americans played a significant role in the development of the United States. Black people accompanied the first explorers to this country in the early 1600s, and a Black man was among the first to die in the American Revolution.[1] In fact, over 5,000 Blacks fought in the American Revolution and over 200,000 fought during the Civil War.[2] In the 1960s, the mistreatment of African Americans resulted in numerous riots and other violent episodes in many cities across America.[3] However, perhaps the most significant event in American history as it relates to the African American experience was slavery.

Slavery

The significance of slavery in the United States is argued by many experts to be the basis for most of the racism, discrimination, and prejudice experienced by

African Americans today. Thus, slavery was not simply a single tragic event in the development of a country; rather, slavery has been an essential part of this country's social, political, and economic fabric for nearly four hundred years. In fact, for nearly half of America's history, slavery not only was tolerated, but also was legally protected by the Constitution and the United States Supreme Court.[4] As slavery developed in colonial America, **slave codes,** or laws regulating slave behavior, were created to clarify the position of slaves. Because they were legal, binding, and carried the support of the law, slave codes controlled and determined all aspects of the lives of enslaved Africans, including how slaves were to think, act, and believe.[5]

In an effort to quell potential uprisings by slaves, owners often used religion as a tool to foster compliance. While African religions were forbidden, slave owners introduced slaves to a distorted version of Christianity that taught that complete obedience to one's master and to Whites in general would lead to salvation and eternal happiness. To do otherwise (such as questioning slavery) would be to question God's will, resulting in everlasting damnation.[6] While clearly designed by slave owners to gain compliance and to reduce conflict, religion served another valuable purpose: nightly prayer meetings and singing gave slaves a sense of unity and made their lives more bearable.[7]

The Postslavery Era

For a generation after the American Revolution, restrictions on slaves increased as Southerners accepted slavery as a permanent feature of the economic and social landscape. In order to appease the South, writers of the Constitution legitimized slavery's existence by allowing a slave to be counted as three-fifths of a person in determining representation in the House of Representatives.[8] Abolitionists contended that slavery was morally objectionable, and slaves made the problem worse by not participating in protests. Many Southern states responded to this passive acceptance of slavery by enacting **fugitive slave acts,** which required slaves who had escaped, even to a free state, to be returned to their owners.[9]

In 1863 the **Emancipation Proclamation** was signed; however, the proclamation freed slaves only in the Confederacy. Two years later, abolition became a reality when the Thirteenth Amendment abolished slavery nationwide.[10] From 1867 to 1877, a period known as **Reconstruction,** a new social, political, and economic portrait of the South was created. Because the federal government recognized that Southern states would not likely comply with the parameters of Reconstruction, the Reconstruction Act of 1867 was passed to require compliance. According to the act, each Southern state was controlled by a military governor until a new state constitution could be written.[11] This meant that until each state created a constitution that recognized Blacks as equal, the federal government would retain control over that state. Added to the problems of Reconstruction was the resistance Blacks felt from Whites after Reconstruction ended. Evidence of this resistance was found in the **Jim Crow** era. Jim Crow was a slave who entertained people through song and dance. White performers imitated him in singing and dancing style, and some used makeup to look like Jim Crow. The term "Jim Crow" eventually became a label for the social, political, and legal separation of Whites and Blacks in all aspects of society.[12]

The *Plessy v. Ferguson* case made separate but equal facilities constitutionally protected.

By the end of the 19th century, the legalization of segregation and dis-crimination against Blacks became more evident. In 1896 the U.S. Supreme Court ruled in *Plessy v. Ferguson* that state laws requiring separate but equal accom-modations, such as drinking fountains and restrooms, for Blacks were a reason-able use of state government power.[13] In 1898 the Supreme Court ruled in *Williams v. Mississippi* that the use of poll taxes, literacy tests, and residential requirements were constitutional. Clearly these measures were used to discourage Blacks from voting, but even these measures did not prevent voting completely.[14] The South created a one-party system, which excluded Blacks from voting. This was considered constitutional because the party was defined as a private organiza-tion free to define its own membership.[15]

In response to the way they were treated in the South, many Blacks—nearly one million between 1914 and 1920—moved to the North in hopes of a better life.[16] However, those who thought life would be better in the North were met with a similar form of discrimination and prejudice by Whites until the Civil Rights Movement began in the 1960s.

The Civil Rights Movement

Perhaps in the hopes of achieving equality or at least some level of respect from Whites, over one million Blacks served in the armed forces during World War II.[17] However, Blacks soon found that discrimination also existed in the military. Training for Blacks was minimal, troops were separated by color, and most of the tasks given to Blacks were menial.[18] After the war ended, there were many opportunities for jobs

Crowds of Civil Rights supporters surround the Reflecting Pool in Washington, D.C., on their march toward the Washington Monument.

due to the growth of a number of industries. As a result, many people moved to the cities for work causing schools to become overcrowded and housing to become limited. As problems stemming from congestion escalated, the courts decided cases related to segregation issues, arguably the most important of which focused on the education of Black children.

The **Civil Rights Movement** was essentially the culmination of many attempts by African Americans to secure equality following World War II. Several U.S. Supreme Court decisions during this period suggested a shift in thinking away from tolerating racial inequalities. The White primary and one-party system in the South was finally challenged and declared unconstitutional in the 1944 case of *Smith v. Allwright*. However, many states simply passed laws that used other measures to frustrate African American voters.[19] One such measure was **restrictive covenants,** private contracts between neighborhood property owners, which stipulated that property could not be sold or rented to certain minority groups, thus ensuring minorities could not live in the area. In 1948, in *Shelley v. Kraemer*, the Supreme Court ruled that such covenants were unconstitutional.

While there were demonstrations and lawsuits between 1942 and the early 1950s, perhaps the most noted event for the start of the Civil Rights Movement was the 1954 U.S. Supreme Court's decision in *Brown v. Board of Education of Topeka*. However, this case was not the only attack on White supremacy. There are many examples of rebellion by African Americans as early as 1942, but by 1954, unequal treatment for African Americans was a common feature of the social landscape.[20]

For the majority of Black children, public education meant attending segregated schools. Some school districts assigned children to school by race rather than by neighborhood, which is the practice that was challenged in the *Brown* case. Seven-year-old Linda Brown was not permitted to enroll in the grade school four blocks from her home in Topeka, Kansas. The policy of the local school board dictated that she attend the Black school almost two miles from her home. The NAACP Legal Defense Fund filed a lawsuit on behalf of Linda and 12 other Black children.

The NAACP argued that the Fourteenth Amendment should rule out segregation in public schools. Thurgood Marshall argued the case for the NAACP, and he went on to become the first Black justice of the U.S. Supreme Court, in 1967.[21] The issue for the NAACP was simply that Blacks should be allowed to go to school with Whites. Given their conditions, funding, and size, all-Black schools could never be equal to all-White schools. The result was that Black children were denied the protections of the due process clause of the Fourteenth Amendment.[22]

The reaction to the *Brown* decision to desegregate public schools "with all deliberate speed" was angry and swift. Some state legislators in the South called for the impeachment of all the Supreme Court justices, others petitioned Congress to declare the Fourteenth Amendment unconstitutional, and some cities even closed schools rather than comply with the ruling. In Little Rock, Arkansas, in 1957, Governor Orval Faubus enlisted the National Guard to prevent Black students from entering previously all-White high schools.[23]

The most enduring resistance to *Brown* was found in the formation of White Citizen's Councils. Founded in Mississippi, these councils spread throughout the South and claimed up to half a million members. The groups began opening private all-White **Freedom Schools** that enrolled an estimated 300,000 White children by 1970. All of this effort was done with the sole intent of evading the *Brown* decision.[24]

In 1962 school desegregation took another fascinating turn when Mississippi National Guardsmen and federal authorities clashed over the admission of James Meredith, who was the first African American admitted to the University of Mississippi. A year later, Governor George Wallace "stood in the schoolhouse door" to block two Blacks from enrolling in the University of Alabama. In response to such outlandish opposition to federal law, President John Kennedy federalized the Alabama National Guard in order to guarantee that the students would be admitted to campus.[25]

Civil Disobedience

On December 1, 1955, Martin Luther King Jr. began his campaign of civil disobedience after the arrest of Rosa Parks when she refused to give her seat to a White man on a bus in Montgomery, Alabama. In response to her arrest, King and his followers boycotted the bus system in Montgomery. The bus boycott was the first of many instances in which nonviolent direct action was employed as a means of obtaining rights for Blacks. While the *Brown* decision may have awakened America to the level and scope of racial injustice experienced by African Americans, the Montgomery bus boycott marked a significant shift away from the historic reliance on the NAACP court battles and focused on concrete action to effect social change.[26] Under King's leadership, civil disobedience gained a measure of acceptability among some prominent Whites, including John F. Kennedy. King hoped that by emphasizing nonviolence, southern Blacks would express their hostility to racism and undercut any violent reactions by Whites.

Martin Luther King Jr. and the Riots

In 1963, President Kennedy submitted legislation to Congress to secure voting rights and broaden government protection of African Americans' civil rights. In August 1964, more than 200,000 people participated in the March on Washington for Jobs and Freedom, which is considered the high point of the Civil Rights Movement. It was at this march that King delivered his famous "I Have a Dream" speech.[27]

In January 1964, the Twenty-fourth Amendment to the U.S. Constitution was ratified, outlawing the poll tax that had prevented Blacks from voting. The 1964 enactment of the Civil Rights Act, which provided equal rights to African Americans, was hailed as a major victory and provided the illusion of equality.[28] The Voting Rights Act, passed in 1965, encouraged Blacks about their role in the political process. However, the significance of this event was overshadowed by violence in the Watts section of Los Angeles.[29] The worst riot since 1943, the Watts riot in Los Angeles in 1965 was shocking in its intensity and left 34 people dead. Many Americans believed that racial harmony had been addressed through the passing of federal legislation; however, the events in Watts were a marker of the tension felt all over the country.[30]

In fact, many scholars point to the series of riots that devastated certain cities across America as the end of the Civil Rights Movement. Between 1965 and 1967, major riots broke out in Cleveland, Newark, and Detroit. A presidential commission on the causes of violence estimated that, for 1967 alone, there were 257 civil disorders in 173 cities, killing 87 and injuring 2,500, leading to 19,000 arrests. In April 1968, after the assassination of Martin Luther King Jr., more cities witnessed violence.[31]

The Rise of Black Power

In 1966, following the passage of the Voting Rights Act, James Meredith marched from Memphis, Tennessee, to Jackson, Mississippi, in an effort to encourage fellow Blacks to vote.[32] During the march, activist Stokely Carmichael proclaimed to a cheering Black crowd, "What we need is Black power!" By advocating **Black Power,** Carmichael encouraged Blacks to create new institutions and emulate the political path followed by many European immigrant groups, such as the Italians and the Irish, in previous generations. Prominent Black leaders opposed the concept because they feared that Whites would retaliate even more violently than before. While the Civil Rights Movement tried to end segregation, it was fairly evident that White society was not interested in equality in any meaningful sense. In contrast, Black Power contended that the only way for African Americans to ever gain a political, economic, or social influence was to be more assertive.[33]

The Nation of Islam and Black Identity

Few recent social movements have gained as much attention and reaction as **Black Nationalism,** the philosophy that encourages Blacks to see themselves as Blacks first rather than as Americans. An important part of this movement for the individual is a transformation that leads Blacks to control their own destiny and to resist any attempts to continue their own subordination.

As mentioned earlier, Southern slave owners encouraged and often required their slaves to attend church and to embrace a distorted version of Christianity. Black Nationalism, as a general rule, rejects this ideology. An example of Black Nationalism is found in the **Nation of Islam,** which became known as the Black Muslims, and has attracted a large number of followers. The Muslim religion was first introduced to Black America in 1930 by W. Fard Muhammad in Detroit, Michigan.[34]

Under the leadership of Elijah Muhammad, W. Fard Muhammad's successor, the Black Muslims became a well-known and controversial organization. Malcolm X became the most powerful voice of this group in the 1960s.[35] In 1977 a Muslim sect led by Louis Farrakhan broke with the current leadership of the Nation of Islam and created his own group, adopting the more orthodox ideals of Elijah Muhammad such as Black moral superiority.[36]

⚔ African Americans Today: The Rise of the Black Middle Class

Some critics of African American history have attacked the generalizations of African American families, arguing that historians overemphasize the poorest segment of the Black community. Instead, many scholars focus on the growth of the **Black middle class** as a testimony to the success many African Americans have achieved in overcoming a legacy of racism. However, this description of African Americans today would be equally inaccurate. Rather, a true understanding of the African American experience must include a balanced view of both the success and failure of this group to achieve some semblance of the American Dream.[37]

A clearly defined Black middle class has emerged. According to the 2000 U.S. Census, nearly one-third of African Americans earned more than the median income for Whites. Yet many African Americans are more likely than Whites to be first-generation middle class, who depend on two or more sources of income and live precariously close to the lower class.[38]

In 2005, in testimony before the U.S. Commission on Civil Rights, David Besharov, a research fellow at the Enterprise Institute, a think tank in Washington, D.C., argued that since 1980, while the numbers have increased, the Black middle class has hardly grown as a percentage of African Americans. As evidence, Besharov points to data on median family income for Whites and Blacks. He found that between 1980 and 2003, the percentage of Black households with incomes greater than the 1980 median income of all American households increased by one-third, from about 29% to about 40%. However, at the same time, White incomes have increased, leaving the gap between Black and White median income about the same. Thus, while there are an increasing number of African Americans who might fit into the middle-class category, the number of Whites who are in that category has also increased. The reason for this continued stagnation has a great deal to do with the lack of educational progress for many African Americans.[39]

As some scholars have pointed out, the migration of the middle-class Blacks out of the ghetto in the 1970s and 1980s left a vacuum. Middle-class Blacks may still care about the problems of the poor, but they are no longer present as role models. As social class becomes more salient in the lives of African American families, particularly those that have gained some measure of economic and even political success, the relationship of social class, race, and poverty becomes important.[40]

Social scientists have long recognized the importance of class. It is a difficult concept to define, as many disagree on the boundaries of where one class category begins and another ends, not to mention the problems of determining a sufficient number of class categories. However, few experts argue that social class is not an

ABORTION AS A CRIME-REDUCTION STRATEGY FOR AFRICAN AMERICANS

The relationship between race and crime, particularly for African Americans, is often seen in comments made by policy makers and political figures. While many people lament the high percentage of African Americans involved in the criminal justice system, there are many people who propose controversial solutions. One such example, briefly mentioned at the beginning of Chapter 1, occurred in 2005 by former secretary of education William Bennett, who also served as President Reagan's chairman of the National Endowment for the Humanities from 1981 to 1985 and the nation's "drug czar" in George H. W. Bush's administration.

Bennett told a caller on his radio show that "if you wanted to reduce crime, you could—if that were your sole purpose—you could abort every black baby in this country and your crime rate would go down. That would be an impossibly ridiculous and a morally reprehensible thing to do, but your crime rate would go down." A day later, Bennett stood by his comments. He said that his comments were taken out of context. He said, "I was putting forward a hypothetical proposition. Put that forward. Examine it. And then said about it that it's morally reprehensible. To recommend abortion of an entire group of people in order to lower your crime rate is morally reprehensible. But this is what happens when you argue that the ends can justify the means."

In response, Nancy Pelosi, currently the Speaker of the House in Congress, said, "What could possibly have possessed Secretary Bennett to say those words, especially at this time? What could he possibly have been thinking? This is what is so alarming about his words." Bruce Gordon, president and CEO of the NAACP, demanded an apology from Bennett on his radio program. He said, "In 2005, there is no place for the kind of racist statement made by Bennett. While the entire nation is trying to help survivors, black and white, to recover from the damage caused by Hurricanes Katrina and Rita, it is unconscionable for Bennett to make such ignorant and insensitive comments."

Clearly the comments and subsequent reactions by Bennett inflamed the issue and gave the appearance that racism continues to play a role in people's understanding of crime, specifically as it relates to African Americans. As this chapter has shown, the fact that African Americans are overrepresented in the crime statistics may be due to a number of factors, not simply because they commit more offenses. To even suggest that abortion is related to crime reduction suggests Bennett believes that the only reason African Americans are disproportionately arrested is due to the fact that they commit more crime. This stereotypical thinking is one of the main reasons many members of the African American community do not trust the police or White policy makers and politicians.

important variable in the discussion of issues such as poverty, employment, health care, housing, and criminal justice.[41]

The complexity of relative influence of race and class was apparent in the controversy surrounding William Julius Wilson's (1978) *The Declining Significance of Race*. Pointing to the increasing influence of African Americans, Wilson concluded that class has become more important than race in determining life chances or opportunities for Blacks' success in the modern world. His conclusions suggest that programs must be developed to confront class issues rather than ethnic and racial discrimination. Wilson argues that the legacy of discrimination is still alive, as reflected in the disproportionate number of Blacks who are poor and less educated and who live in inadequate housing. However, he contends that the evidence shows that many segments of the African American population are able to effectively compete with segments of the White population.[42]

⚔ The Historical Treatment of African Americans in the Criminal Justice System

Any discussion of the African American experience in this country is incomplete without including what some experts have referred to as a by-product of the legacy of slavery. That so many African Americans are under the supervision of the criminal justice system, with many others touched by its extensively long hand, illustrates the social position of African Americans in the United States.

In his book *No Equal Justice: Race and Class in the American Criminal Justice System* (1999), social scientist David Cole argues that, historically, African Americans were mistreated by the criminal justice process. This exploitation began with the ratification of the U.S. Constitution in 1788, where, prior to its ratification, women could not vote and enslaved Africans counted as three-fifths of a person and had no fundamental rights of citizenship. The institution of slavery simultaneously was built on the tenet that Africans brought to America "had no rights which the White man was bound to respect," as articulated by the U.S. Supreme Court in the landmark case of *Dred Scott v. Sanford* in 1857 (60 U.S. 393).

The ratification of the Thirteenth, Fourteenth, and Fifteenth Amendments and the Reconstruction Act of 1867, which was purported to offer a glimmer of hope for equality and citizenship, led many African Americans to believe that equality was within their grasp. However, violence by groups such as the Ku Klux Klan kept most African Americans away from the polls.[43] Cole makes an interesting argument concerning the way the Thirteenth Amendment was written to increase the likelihood that African Americans would continue to be legally exploited despite the abolition of slavery. He states that as a legal loophole, the Thirteenth Amendment provided for the continued enslavement of an individual based on his or her status as a *criminal offender*.[44]

Cole also points out that during the Jim Crow era of the late 19th century, African Americans were convicted of crimes at a much higher rate than Whites. As evidence of this, Cole points to statistics from Georgia, where, in 1908, Black prisoners outnumbered White prisoners 10-to-1 and the majority of the Black prisoners were convicted of nonviolent property crimes.[45]

Other scholars raise similar concerns about decisions by the U.S. Supreme Court.[46] Two of the most well-known Supreme Court decisions on criminal justice do not in practice protect African Americans. In 1963, in the case of *Gideon v. Wainwright* (372 U.S. 335), the Court held that states must provide a lawyer at state expense to all defendants charged with a serious crime who cannot afford to hire one. In 1966, in *Miranda v. Arizona* (384 U.S. 436), the Court required the police to provide poor suspects with an attorney at state expense and to inform all suspects of their rights before questioning them in custody.

Some experts argue that in these landmark decisions, the Court sought to ameliorate societal inequalities that undermined the criminal justice system's promise of equality. As the Court stated in *Miranda,* "While authorities are not required to relieve the accused of his poverty, they have the obligation not to take advantage of indigence in the administration of justice."[47] These decisions were decided by the Supreme Court under Chief Justice Earl Warren, at a time when the Court was solidly liberal and strongly committed to racial and economic equality. Harris also argues that at virtually every juncture since *Gideon* and *Miranda,* the Supreme Court has undercut the principle of equality reflected in those decisions.[48]

These same scholars contend that *Gideon* is a symbol of equality unrealized in practice; poor defendants are entitled to the assistance of counsel at trial, but the Supreme Court has failed to demand that the assistance be meaningful. Cole says, "Lawyers who have slept through testimony or appeared in court drunk have nonetheless been deemed to have provided their indigent clients 'effective assistance of counsel.'"[49] These experts argue that today's Court has so diluted *Miranda* that the decision has had little effect on actual police interrogation practices.[50]

More generally, the problems of exploitation and inequality in the criminal justice system are driven by the need to balance two fundamental and competing interests: the protection of constitutional rights and the protection of law-abiding citizens from crime. For example, without a constitutional requirement that police have probable cause and a warrant before they conduct searches, police officers would be far more effective in rooting out and stopping crime. Without jury trials, criminal justice administration would be much more efficient. But without these safeguards, we would live in a police state, with no meaningful privacy protection. Absent jury trials, the community would have little check on overzealous prosecutors.[51]

Much of the public and academic debate about criminal justice focuses on where we should draw the line between law enforcement interests and constitutional protections. Liberals and conservatives agree, at least in principle, that the line should be drawn in the same place for everyone. However, some experts suggest that there appears to be an inconsistency when and where that line is drawn, which results in an unfair burden placed on African Americans.[52]

African Americans and the Criminal Justice System Today

The Police

Perhaps the most controversial interaction that African Americans have with the criminal justice system relates to the police. Much has been said and written about police–minority relations, the use of force by police officers against African Americans, and racial profiling. As described below, there are a number of sensational cases in which the police have mistreated members of minority groups. There also appears to be a long record of such activity involving African Americans. The following accounts, the first of which was mentioned briefly at the beginning of Chapter 1, are illustrative.

On November 26, 2006, hours before he was to be married, Sean Bell, a 23-year-old African American, was leaving his bachelor party at a strip club in Queens, New York, that was under police surveillance, when he was shot and killed. At the time, Mr. Bell was accompanied by two of his friends, both of whom were wounded, one critically. According to police and witness accounts, Mr. Bell and his friends walked out of the club and got into their car. Mr. Bell then drove the car half a block, turned a corner, and struck a black unmarked police minivan bearing several plainclothes officers. Mr. Bell's car then backed up onto a sidewalk, hit a storefront's rolled-down protective gate, and nearly struck an undercover officer before racing forward and slamming into the police van again. In response, five police officers fired over 50 rounds at the car, hitting it at least 21 times. The bullets ripped into other cars and slammed through an apartment window nearby. Mr. Bell was shot in the neck, shoulder, and right arm and was taken to Jamaica Hospital Medical Center, where he was pronounced dead. The two wounded men, Joseph Guzman, 21, and Trent Benefield, 23, were taken to a nearby hospital and released.[53] The district attorney in the case subsequently prepared evidence to present to the grand jury with an eye toward indicting the officers involved.[54]

Early in the morning on February 4, 1999, a young immigrant named Amadou Diallo from Guinea was returning to his Bronx apartment when he was approached by four plainclothes New York City police officers. According to some accounts, Mr. Diallo fit the description of a serial rapist who had assaulted some 40 women in areas around Manhattan. What happened as the officers approached Mr. Diallo is unclear. The officers contend they identified themselves and said Mr. Diallo's behavior led them to believe he was reaching for a weapon. Eyewitnesses disagree with this interpretation of events. What *is* known is that officers drew their weapons and fired a total of 41 shots, resulting in the unarmed Mr. Diallo's death.[55]

In 1997, Abner Louima, a 30-year-old immigrant from Haiti, was arrested when he tried to intervene in a fight outside a Brooklyn, New York, nightclub. When Mr. Louima arrived at the police station, he was dragged into a restroom and sodomized by officers with the handle of a toilet plunger, which was then forced into his mouth. Eventually, he was taken to the hospital after having been charged with resisting arrest and disorderly conduct. Mr. Louima was critically injured, suffering a perforated colon, a lacerated bladder, and several missing teeth, among other injuries.[56] In July 2001, Mr. Louima received an $8.7 million settlement from the New York City police department.[57]

Studies in Maryland and New Jersey indicate profiling by police agencies that target African Americans. In April 1999, the attorney general of New Jersey issued a report stating that state troopers had engaged in racial profiling along the New Jersey Turnpike. The data used in this report showed that people of color constituted nearly 41% of the stops made on the turnpike and, although few stops resulted in searches, 77% of those searched were people of color. This is in contrast to searches of Whites, which constituted approximately 11% of the total searches.

A report issued by the New York attorney general also indicated that racial profiling occurred in New York City with regard to stop and frisk practices. A review of 175,000 incidents in which citizens were stopped by the police over a 15-month period in 1999 found that African Americans were stopped six times more often than Whites and that Latinos were stopped four times as often. African Americans make up 25% of New York City's population, yet 50% of the people stopped.

On almost any given day, we hear of instances like the ones just described. These dramatic episodes raise questions about the role of the police in our society, particularly in their interactions with minority groups. Some minority leaders, as well as others, have asserted that the police, and to some extent the entire criminal justice system, are prejudiced and racist. These individuals argue that situations like the ones described above are indicators that the police target minorities and treat

Ethnic and racial tensions have fueled many conflicts between the police and the public.

them differently. Is there any truth to these assertions? Are the police racist? Do they treat minorities differently? How does the public perceive the police?

Public Opinion and the Police

According to a Department of Justice report, an estimated 45 million people in the United States—about 15% of the population—have some form of face-to-face contact with the police every year. In a review of the literature on the public's attitudes toward the police, one study found that while race and ethnicity are the most important factors in shaping attitudes toward the police, the vast majority of Whites have very favorable attitudes toward police.[58] According to the *Sourcebook of Criminal Justice Statistics,* 85% of the people surveyed by the Department of Justice in 1985 said they were very satisfied with the police who served their neighborhoods. Whites expressed the most satisfaction, with 90% being very satisfied or satisfied, whereas only 76% of African Americans felt that way.

There is also a difference in the way people feel about how the police treat other groups. According to the *Sourcebook of Criminal Justice Statistics,* in response to the question "Do you think the police in your community treat all races fairly or do they tend to treat one or more of these groups unfairly?" 59% felt the police treated all groups fairly, 33% felt they treated one or more groups unfairly, and 7% did not know. When the race of the respondent is included, a dramatically different picture emerges. Sixty-seven percent of Whites felt the police treated all races fairly, whereas only 48% of Hispanics and only 30% of African Americans felt that way.

These figures indicate that, in general, a significant proportion of the population thinks the police are doing a good job; however, compared to Whites, minorities generally feel less confident in the police and are generally less satisfied with police services. Another important factor is the characteristic of the neighborhood. One study found that people living in high-crime neighborhoods and low-income communities tend to have more contact with the police and report less overall satisfaction than those living in low-crime and high-income communities. Furthermore, because minorities tend to live in these types of neighborhoods, it is not surprising that their confidence in the police is lower than that of Whites.[59]

A 2003 study found that neighborhood characteristics and interactions with police officers are the most influential factors in assessing the public's opinion of the police. The study, conducted in four diverse neighborhoods in Los Angeles, found that residents from neighborhoods perceived to be crime ridden, dangerous, and disorderly were less likely to approve of the police. In contrast, residents who had informal personal contact with police were more likely to express approval.

While race and ethnicity had been cited as influential factors in other studies, neither was as important as the level of social and physical disorder in the community in determining the public's satisfaction with police. Where race and ethnicity did matter was the perception of how the police treated minorities. For example, African Americans were more likely to say that officers acted unprofessionally toward them than toward Whites. The 2003 study mentioned earlier also found that the media had little influence on public opinion of the police. While limited in its ability to make an overall assessment of the public's opinion of the police, this study nevertheless raised a number of questions about how to change the public's perception of police officers.[60]

Why do police officers have more contact with low-income and minority neighborhoods? Part of the answer is that people in these neighborhoods make greater use of police services than those in other neighborhoods. Police departments assign more patrol officers to these neighborhoods because of greater calls for service and because minority groups in these areas have higher crime rates. Another reason is that minorities and low-income people are more likely to call the police to solve a variety of noncriminal matters. Compared to middle-class Americans, for instance, people in the low-income category are more likely to call the police for assistance with medical emergencies and family problems. This means that the police are more actively and intrusively involved in the daily lives of people who live in low-income neighborhoods. Greater contact also means that the decisions made by officers may not be what the members of these neighborhoods prefer, resulting in lower levels of satisfaction. In sum, evidence suggests differential treatment of minorities by police on a variety of indicators, including response to violent crime, arrests, use of force, deadly force, and other minor forms of abuse.[61]

Response to Violent Crime

Perhaps due to the distortion of crime and criminals in the media, as well as their own experiences with crime, many people, including the police, believe that African Americans and other minorities are more involved in violent crime than Whites. Moreover, this perception affects how officers respond to violent crimes. For instance, using data from the National Crime Victimization Survey, one study examined the relationship between the victim and the offender's race on three police responses to robbery and aggravated assault. The variables considered were the response time to the scene, the amount of effort made by officers to investigate these crimes at the scene, and the likelihood of arrest.[62]

Officers were quicker to respond and invested more effort in the investigation (i.e., searches) when the incident involved African American offenders and White victims. This relationship held even when variables such as poverty, victim's gender, and whether or not the victim was injured were taken into account. With regard to aggravated assault, particularly incidents involving strangers, officers were more likely to do a thorough investigation at the scene if it involved a White victim and an African American offender. Officers were also more likely, all other aspects of the crime being the same, to respond more quickly and to put forth a more determined effort if there was an injury to the White victim, particularly by an African American offender. None of these findings applied when the victim was an African American and the offender was White. Thus, evidence suggests that the race of the victim and the race of the offender play a role in how the police respond to violent crime. If the crime involves a White victim and an African American offender, officers seem to respond more quickly to the scene of the crime and investigate it more thoroughly, and arrests are more likely to occur.[63]

Arrests

Is race a factor in the arrest of a suspect? The answer appears clear as minorities are arrested out of proportion to their representation in the population. According to the *Uniform Crime Reports,* in 2005, African Americans represented about 13% of the population but approximately 28% of all arrests and 39% of arrests for violent crime. However, there is a great deal of controversy surrounding this issue. What are the reasons for this apparent differential treatment? Do police officers arrest African Americans more frequently than Whites due to racial bias or because Blacks commit more crimes? What variables are considered in the decision to arrest?

Sociologist Donald Black (1971), in his famous article "The Social Organization of Arrest," found that, in general, the decision to arrest was predicated on a number of factors, including the strength of the evidence, the seriousness of the crime, whether or not the complainant or victim wanted the suspect arrested, and whether the suspect was disrespectful toward the officer. The decision to arrest was also based on the relationship between the victim and the offender. If the suspect was a stranger to the victim, the officers were more likely to arrest him or her.[64]

Interestingly, Black found that race was not a factor in the decision to arrest. He did find that African Americans were arrested more often than Whites, but this was mainly due to the fact that Whites were more likely to show deference to the officer. As he describes, this creates a vicious cycle, whereby the African American men who are arrested more often have negative feelings toward the police. When these feelings are demonstrated, there is more likely to be an arrest, which increases the hostility felt by African Americans toward the police.[65]

Much research following Black's earlier work found that race does matter. In the 1980s, for instance, race was considered in terms of the decision to arrest. One study found that in those instances where the suspect was African American and the victim was White, officers were more likely to make an arrest.[66] Similar to Black's findings, in these situations, officers were also more likely to arrest the suspect upon the victim's request to do so.[67]

Another study found that African Americans and Hispanics were more likely to be arrested on less evidence than Whites. The study also found that Blacks and Hispanics were more likely to be released without the case going to the prosecutor. While at first glance this may appear to be advantageous, arrest still represents a form of punishment even though formal charges may not be filed.[68]

Another study examined 718 police officers in Ohio and examined the extent to which a suspect's race influenced an officer's behavior. The results of the study showed that officers did not feel race was a significant factor in determining the officer's behavior. What was significant was the suspect's demeanor—how he or she acted toward the officer. However, care should be taken in interpreting this finding since it may be related to race in that African Americans may be more likely to have a negative attitude toward the police, which can lead to a similar outcome. The evidence seems to suggest, then, that the race of the victim and the race of the offender play an important role in the decision to arrest.[69]

Use of Force

The 1991 beating of Black motorist Rodney King by White police officers is perhaps the most visible and memorable reminder of excessive use of force by police officers. However, there was considerable academic interest in the use of force topic prior to the King incident.[70] In his classic study of the police in 1971, researcher Albert J. Reiss found that race per se was not a determining factor in the use of excessive force. Instead, "Class rather than race determines police misconduct."[71] The typical victim of excessive force is a lower-class male, regardless of race. Other experts, however, disagree and see excessive use of force as particularly prevalent against African American men. According to a 1999 Bureau of Justice Statistics report on police–citizen contacts, there are substantial racial and ethnic disparities in police use of force. African Americans are three times as likely to experience force or threatened force than Whites. Hispanics are more likely than Whites but less likely than African Americans to experience police use of force.[72]

The implications of this trend are particularly significant for African Americans. Even if the overall rate of the use of force comprises 1% of all police–citizen encounters, if those incidents are concentrated in low-income neighborhoods and consist of lower-class men, who are likely to be African American, the effects of these incidents accumulate over time to create a perception that the police routinely harass African Americans.[73] The symbolic significance of the excessive use of force should not be overlooked. As representatives of the larger system, police officers who engage in excessive use of force serve as a reminder of the larger problems of discrimination and exploitation felt by African Americans.[74]

Deadly Force

Despite the notoriety when such events occur, there has been a general decline in the incidence of deadly force by the police.[75] However, a great deal of attention has been given to the frequency with which police officers use deadly force against minorities.[76] When compared with their numbers in the population, African Americans are disproportionately killed by the police. However, these findings also suggest that when compared with rates of police–citizen contacts, arrest rates and resistance to or attacks upon the police, there is no apparent racial disparity in the use of deadly force by the police.[77]

By the mid-1980s, when many departments adopted a "defense of life rule," which allows officers to use deadly force only when attempting to protect themselves or the lives of others, the number of persons shot and killed by the police decreased significantly. Part of the reason for the general decline in the use of deadly force has come from more restrictive policies at the departmental level as well as from the Supreme Court decision in *Tennessee v. Garner*.[78] One study found that from 1970 to 1984, the police use of deadly force declined substantially, particularly against African Americans.[79] More recently, the data indicate that the racial disparity in the number of people shot and killed by the police has decreased from about seven African Americans for every White to about three for every one.[80]

Another situation in which deadly force is justified occurs when the officer prevents the escape of a person who is extremely dangerous.[81] *Tennessee v. Garner* (471 U.S. 1; 1985) involved a case in which two officers used deadly force against an African American juvenile who was fleeing the scene of a burglary. At that time, the officers were justified in using deadly physical force against a fleeing felon. However, the Court ruled in *Tennessee v. Garner* that this was no longer acceptable. As a result, many departments were required to modify their policies concerning use of force against fleeing felons. Thus, while there was a time when officers were given wide latitude in using deadly force, since 1980 departments all over the country have changed their policies regarding the use of force and the number of incidents have declined considerably.

Profiling and Other Minor Forms of Abuse

The issue surrounding discriminatory treatment of African Americans extends beyond serious offenses. In fact, one might argue that it is the minor forms of abuse that create a climate of fear and hostility between the police and minorities. These indignities, or what sociologist Elliot Liebow has referred to as the "little murders of everyday life,"[82] characterize the attitudes the police have toward minorities in some circumstances. The difference between this type of abuse and the others discussed, however, is that there is no tangible reminder that the incident occurred.

Minor forms of abuse such as profiling usually end with the interaction between the officer and the suspect. These forms of abuse usually occur on the street and typically involve no witnesses. This makes sustaining allegations very difficult and results in continued tension between the police and minorities.[83]

In the mid-1990s, the New Jersey State Police were under investigation for allegedly ordering officers to concentrate on stopping Black drivers. Three state troopers stated they were instructed by their superiors to single out African American drivers for traffic stops. Additionally, a 1992 study of traffic stops in Florida found that while only 5% of the drivers on the road were African American or Hispanic, nearly 70% of those stopped and 80% of those searched were African American or Hispanic. Further, nationally, from January 1993 to August 1995, almost 90% of the individuals subjected to search and seizure operations on buses and trains were people of color. Another study of all reported federal decisions from 1993 to 1995 involving bus and train sweeps found that nearly 90% of those targeted were minorities.[84]

A controversy was created when, in April 2005, a report on racial profiling was scheduled to be released by the Department of Justice's Bureau of Justice Statistics. Based on interviews with 80,000 people in 2002, the study found that White, Black, and Hispanic drivers nationwide were stopped by the police that year at about the same rate, roughly 9%. But the Department of Justice report also stated that once they were stopped, Hispanic drivers were searched or had their vehicles searched by the police 11.4% of the time and Blacks 10.2% of the time, compared to only 3.5% for White drivers. The study found that officers were more likely to threaten or use force against Blacks and Hispanics more often than against Whites, and the police were much more likely to issue tickets to Hispanics than to simply give them a warning.

The authors of the Department of Justice report said they were not able to draw any conclusions about the reason for the differing rates, but they said the gaps were notable. The research "uncovered evidence of Black drivers having worse experiences—more likely to be arrested, more likely to be searched, more likely to have force used against them—during traffic stops than White drivers," the report concluded. The inflammatory nature of these findings allegedly led the Department of Justice to try to suppress some of the information or to change the findings. While strenuously arguing that the results should not be altered for political purposes, the director of the Bureau of Justice Statistics was demoted.[85]

Another study explored the extent to which there are racial differences in getting hassled by the police as well as what the researchers identify as *vicarious hassling*—knowing someone who has experienced this type of treatment by the police. The main finding of the study was that African Americans are more likely than Whites to perceive they are being hassled by the police individually and vicariously. Nearly one-half of African Americans in the study had experienced a negative police interaction and two-thirds knew someone who had had a similar experience, compared to the 10% of Whites who experienced this type of treatment in the same way. While such a discrepancy could be a result of different patrol practices, which focus on minority neighborhoods, it could also be that some of these perceptions may be a result of frequent police contact. A third explanation may be that there exists a perception by officers that African Americans and other minorities are more likely to commit crimes and thus are potential offenders that warrant police attention.[86]

Finally, there is verbal abuse. Many complaints are filed each year against officers who verbally abuse citizens. The Christopher Commission, created in 1990 to investigate allegations of abuse in Los Angeles following the beating of Rodney King by White officers, found that officers frequently use abusive language. This may occur during the interaction with citizens, or it may happen between officers. For example, the commission's investigation discovered that computer messages containing racially offensive comments had been sent between officers.

Research on police behavior suggests that derogatory comments and the stigmatizing labeling of people are ways for officers to control suspects. Profanity serves several functions: to gain the individual's attention when interacting with officers, to keep officers at a social distance while the interaction occurs, and to psychologically dominate the individual.[87]

What does all of this tell us? It should remind us that the relationship between the police and African Americans is complex. African Americans may be arrested disproportionately, in part, because of their more pronounced involvement in criminal activities; it may also have to do with the way African Americans respond to police contact. Structural issues such as poverty and overcrowding in urban areas may contribute to greater police contact in that the problems experienced in those areas require a more frequent police presence. Minority involvement with the police may also have something to do with the attitudes of police officers—some officers believe minorities are more likely to become involved in criminal activities, so they merit greater police attention. Finally, African American overrepresentation in criminal activities may also have something to do with the perceptions of the police, which tend to inflame the nature of the interaction between the two groups.

In response to problems stemming from police interactions in low-income African American communities, and after being accused of racially motivated excessive use of force, some officers in Cincinnati, Ohio, and other cities around the country have employed de-policing as a strategy. **De-policing** is a tactic employed by some officers who answer only 911 calls instead of engaging in routine patrol. This is done to avoid contact with minorities and to prevent routine situations from escalating into charges of racial profiling or discriminatory treatment of minorities. Answering only emergency calls limits such contact, but crime rates also increase dramatically. A Seattle, Washington, police officer recently noted: "Parking under a shady tree to work on a crossword puzzle is a great alternative to being labeled a racist and being dragged through an inquest, a review board, an FBI and U.S. Attorney's investigation and a lawsuit."[88]

The Courts and African Americans: Sentencing Issues

Not only is there evidence to suggest that Blacks are more likely than Whites to be stopped, searched, arrested, and killed by police officers, they are also more likely to receive harsher treatment once they arrive in court. In fact, there are many who contend that the war on drugs is really a war on African Americans.[89] For instance, there is evidence to suggest that African Americans are more likely to receive harsher penalties and sentencing than Whites for similar crimes. This is most apparent in the different penalties for selling crack cocaine compared to powder cocaine, designer drugs, or even steroids. The federal sentencing guidelines are substantially harsher than the penalties provided by many state statutes, suggesting that state prosecutors are more likely to refer crack cases involving racial minorities to the federal system for prosecution.[90]

A related disparity in sentencing appears in murder cases. Researchers found that when the level of seriousness is controlled for—meaning that it is not taken into consideration, such as the degree of severity and the number of persons killed—prosecutors and juries are more likely to demand the death penalty if the victim is White and the offender is Black than in any of the other possible racial combinations (e.g., White victim/Black offender; White offender/Black victim; Black offender/Black victim; White offender/White victim).[91] Part of the explanation for the dramatically different punishment for cocaine and crack is likely a result of the fear of drugs and those who sell drugs rather than pure discrimination and prejudice. Because of the perception by members of mainstream culture that crack cocaine represents a more serious and immediate threat to way of life than powder cocaine, particularly when crack cocaine left the inner city and appeared in the suburbs, more punitive measures were easily justified. Given that African Americans were already perceived to be responsible for the "drug problem" nationwide, the perceptions that the problem was being brought into middle-class suburbia resulted in panic and more punitive actions.[92]

Further, a number of studies indicate that Whites receive a higher proportion of plea bargains than Blacks. One study found that Whites were more successful in getting charges reduced or dropped, and in getting diversion, probation, or fines instead of incarceration.[93] However, other studies indicate inconsistent results with regard to the effects of race on plea bargaining and prosecution strategies.[94]

A number of studies demonstrate racial bias in sentencing. A study in 39 states found that Blacks typically serve longer sentences than Whites for robbery, rape, and murder.[95] A growing body of research indicates that in many cases the key factor is the race of the victim. Preliminary evidence suggests that when the victim of rape or robbery is White, the sentence is likely to be more severe.[96]

In 1991 the 17-member New York State Judicial Commission on Minorities composed of judges, lawyers, law professors, and an official from the state Department of Education concluded that the state court system showed signs of racism. The commission concluded that minority group members are less likely than

African Americans are more likely to be involved in the criminal justice system than are other types of offenders.

Whites to receive favorable actions from the courts; that judges and prosecuting attorneys, more than other court employees, are more hostile and racially biased toward minorities; and that minority lawyers are often subjected to opposing attorneys' racial stereotyping and racist jokes.[97]

The Death Penalty and African Americans

African Americans' overrepresentation in sentencing and incarceration is also found among offenders sentenced to death. According to the Bureau of Justice Statistics, in 2004 about 42% of inmates on death row were Black. This percentage has been consistent since 1968, and 53% of all people executed since 1930 have been African American.[98]

Perhaps the most graphic illustration of the relationship between race and criminal justice involves the use of capital punishment. When the *Furman v. Georgia* (408 U.S. 238; 1972) decision was first handed down by the Supreme Court, many scholars interpreted the finding as the abolition of capital punishment in the United States. However, in 1976 the Court heard three cases, the most important of which was *Gregg v. Georgia* (428 U.S. 153; 1976). In this case, the state of Georgia provided the Court with a set of procedural safeguards designed to guide the discretion of the judge or jury when faced with a capital case. For instance, the Georgia statute provided an automatic appeal of all death penalty cases. It was argued that separate trials, one trial to determine guilt and another for punishment, guarded against irrelevant evidence that might influence sentencing decisions. The Georgia statute made it mandatory that the death penalty could not be imposed unless a jury unanimously (and beyond a reasonable doubt) found that there were aggravating circumstances—that the offender used excessive force or engaged in behavior that escalated the severity of the crime. The Court argued in *Gregg* that capital punishment does not necessarily amount to cruel and unusual punishment as long as certain procedural safeguards are carried out that are designed to curb arbitrary and capricious application of the death penalty. In short, where discretion is reasonable and controlled, capital punishment is constitutionally permissible for the crime of murder.

Studies have revealed that, despite the significance of this case, the guidelines established in *Gregg* have not eliminated racial disparities in capital cases. One study examined patterns of death sentencing in Florida, Texas, Ohio, and Georgia. In each of these states, killers of Whites were sentenced to death more consistently than killers of Blacks. Also, Black defendants with White victims were more likely to receive the death penalty than White defendants with Black victims. The implication, of course, is that the decision to execute in these states reflects the same arbitrariness that has characterized the imposition of the death penalty in the past.[99]

Another study found a clear pattern of racial disparity in South Carolina death penalty cases when the race of the offender and the race of the victim were considered together. This study found that Blacks who kill Whites had over 4.5 times greater risk of having the death penalty sought by the prosecutor than did Black killers of Blacks. Whites who killed Blacks were 1.1 times more likely to have the death penalty sought by the prosecutor than Whites who killed other Whites. This study concluded that the race of the victim may be a more important consideration of public prosecutors than the race of the offender.[100]

In *McCleskey v. Kemp* (481 U.S. 279; 1981), Warren McCleskey, a Black man, was convicted in Fulton County, Georgia, of murdering a White police officer during an armed robbery of a furniture store. The conviction was consistent with the Georgia statute concerning aggravating circumstances. At trial, McCleskey failed to present any mitigating evidence to the jury and was subsequently sentenced to death.

On appeal to the U.S. Supreme Court, McCleskey claimed that the Georgia capital sentencing process was administered in a racially discriminatory manner that violated the protections provided by the Eighth Amendment to the U.S. Constitution. He also argued that the discriminatory system violated the Fourteenth Amendment's equal protection clause. To support his claim, McCleskey offered the results of an empirical study documenting evidence of a racial bias against African Americans. The study showed that from 1973 to 1979 there were 2,484 murder and non-negligent manslaughter cases in Georgia. Defendants who killed Whites were sentenced to death in 11% of the cases, whereas defendants who killed Blacks were sentenced to death in only about 1% of the cases.[101]

This study also discovered that the death penalty was imposed in 22% of the cases where an African American defendant was convicted of murdering a White; 8% of the cases with a White defendant and a White victim; 3% of the cases with a White defendant and a Black victim; and only 1% of the cases involving a Black defendant and a Black victim. In this detailed analysis, the researchers controlled for some 230 nonracial variables and found that none could account for the racial disparities in capital sentences among the different racial combinations of defendant and victim. People who killed Whites were 4.3 times more likely to be sentenced to death than those who killed Blacks.[102]

McCleskey claimed that race had infected the administration of capital punishment in Georgia in two ways. First, offenders who murdered Whites were more likely to be sentenced to death than offenders who murdered Blacks. Second, Black murderers were more likely to be sentenced to death than White murderers.

In 1987 the Supreme Court handed down its 5–4 decision. The essential question before the Court was whether a complex statistical study that indicates a risk that racial consideration enters into capital sentencing determinations is unconstitutional under the Eighth and Fourteenth Amendments. The Court held that the study does not prove that the administration of capital punishment in Georgia violates these amendments.

The essence of the Court's ruling is that there are acceptable standards of risk of racial discrimination in imposing the death penalty. The Court held that the study simply shows that discrepancies appear to correlate with race in imposing death sentences, but that, according to the Court, "[T]he statistics do not prove that race enters into any capital sentencing decisions or that race was a factor in the petitioner's case." The Court was also concerned that a finding for the defendant would open other claims that "could be extended to other types of penalties and to claims based on unexplained discrepancies correlating to membership in other minority groups and even to gender." The dissenters in the ruling argued that whether McCleskey can prove racial discrimination in his particular case is totally irrelevant in evaluating his claim of a constitutional violation because the Court has long recognized that a pattern of substantial risk of arbitrary and capricious capital sentencing suffices for a claim of unconstitutionality.

Corrections and African Americans

It seems fairly evident, by any measure, that African Americans are disproportionately incarcerated. While they represented approximately 13% of the overall population in this country in 2004, African Americans represented almost 39% of those incarcerated in state and federal prisons. Whites represented about 75% of the population, yet they constituted only 32% of the inmate population. Hispanics represented about 13% of the population, but only about 18% of those incarcerated in 2004. Clearly, African Americans are overrepresented in prisons and jails in this country.

According to the Bureau of Justice Statistics, at the beginning of 2004, American federal and state adult prisons contained about 1,421,911 inmates. Overall, the United States incarcerated 2,267,787 persons at year-end 2004, an increase of about 2% over 2003. Although the total number of sentenced inmates rose 32% between 1995 and 2004, the racial and ethnic composition of the inmate population changed only slightly. Among male inmates with a sentence of more than one year in 2004, 551,300 were Black, 449,300 were White, and 260,600 were Hispanic. More than 40% of all sentenced males were Black.[103]

According to the Bureau of Justice Statistics, in 2004 Black males in their twenties and thirties were found to have higher rates of incarceration compared to other groups. Almost 9% of Black males aged 25 to 29 were in prison in 2004, compared to 2.5% of Hispanic males and about 1.2% of White males in the same age group. While it is relatively common to discover that incarceration rates decrease with age, the percentage of Black males aged 45 to 54 in prison was still nearly 3.3% in 2004, which is more than twice the highest rate of 1.2% among White males aged 25 to 29.[104]

Incarceration rates for females, though lower than those for males, still reflect this racial and ethnic disparity. Black females, who have an incarceration rate of 170 per 100,000 population, were more than twice as likely as Hispanic females (75,000 per 100,000) and four times as likely as White females (42 per 100,000) to be in prison in 2004. These differences among White, Black, and Hispanic females were consistent across all age groups.[105]

Type of offenses also varied by race and ethnicity. In 2004 about half of White, Black, and Hispanic state inmates had been convicted of violent offenses. However, White offenders were more likely serving time for a property offense (26%) compared to Blacks (18%) and Hispanics (16%). Drug offenders made up the largest portion of Hispanic inmates (27%), followed by Black inmates (25%) and White inmates (15%).[106]

African Americans' interaction and involvement in the three primary components of the criminal justice system (police, courts, and corrections) are further discussed later in this book. To be sure, controversy exists with respect to African American and other minority group involvement in the criminal justice system. Below we comment on factors that generate and perpetuate the controversy and discrepancy.

Race, Fear, and Crime

Given evidence that clearly suggests that African Americans are more likely than Whites to be stopped, frisked, arrested, prosecuted, convicted, sentenced to long prison terms, and given the death penalty, how can such a distinctive set of trends be explained?

One theory is that African Americans are more likely to engage in criminal activity, more likely to get caught, and, given their repeated patterns of behavior, receive harsher treatment at every level of the criminal justice system. This is perhaps the most popular theory since it focuses the blame squarely on the people who are adversely affected. Arguably, African Americans are punished more harshly because they commit more acts against society, and this is reflected in the arrest, conviction, and incarceration statistics.

Another theory places the blame for the misrepresentation of African Americans in the criminal justice system on the structure of society and on the system itself. Arguments on this side contend that the system is racist and that African Americans are treated unfairly largely because of public fears. As a result, a self-fulfilling prophecy develops. Motivated by the perception that African American offenders represent a greater threat than White offenders, police, judges, and other court officials treat African Americans more harshly. Blacks, in turn, perceive this treatment as biased and are likely to become a more substantial threat than they would have been without exposure to racism in the criminal justice system. This reinforces the public's fears that African American offenders pose a greater threat to safety than White offenders.

Wilbanks and the Myth of a Racist Criminal Justice System

Criminal justice scholar William Wilbanks, in his book *The Myth of a Racist Criminal Justice System* (1987), presents a somewhat different argument about the relationship of race to the criminal justice system. He contends that Whites and Blacks differ sharply over whether the criminal justice system is racist. The vast majority of Blacks appear to believe that the police and the courts discriminate against Blacks, whereas a majority of Whites reject this charge. This disparity also appears to exist among those who work in the system.

According to Wilbanks, some Blacks have suggested that the criminal justice system is so characterized by racism that Blacks are outside the protection of the law. A sizable minority of Whites, in contrast, think that the system actually discriminates *for* Blacks out of fear of being charged with racism from the Black community. White police officers have reported often ignoring criminal activity by Blacks out of a fear of criticism from the department, the Black community, and/or the media.

Wilbanks contends that these contrasting perceptions regarding the fairness of the system have at least four important consequences. First, research shows that Blacks may turn to criminality or engage in more crime because of a perception that the criminal law and its enforcement are unfair and even racist. Thus, in a way, Blacks believe they are justified in breaking the law. The second consequence relates to civil disturbances. Many riots occur because of a perception that the system is unfair and unjust. The Kerner Commission, which investigated the civil disturbances in American cities in the 1960s, found a widespread belief among Blacks that the criminal justice system was racist and concluded that Blacks' negative perceptions were a major cause of the violence.

A third consequence of these opposing perceptions is a heightened sense of hostility toward the police. As mentioned, many Blacks view the criminal justice system as racist and the police as prejudiced. The greater intrusiveness by police officers into the lives of people in low-income areas often leads to heightened tensions and resentment of the police. It also creates an impression that the police are intentionally harassing people in these neighborhoods, looking for a reason to arrest them.[107]

The fourth consequence is that the recent White backlash to civil rights programs such as affirmative action and racial quotas may be due in part to a White perception that Blacks complain about racism, when, in fact, Whites provide excessive preferential treatment to African Americans. Wilbanks takes the position that the perception of the criminal justice system as racist is a myth. He argues that the question of whether the criminal justice system is racist must not be confused with Blacks committing crimes at a higher rate than Whites because of discrimination in employment, housing, education, and so on. It may be that racial discrimination produces a gap in offending between Blacks and Whites, but that this gap is not increased as Black and White offenders move through the system. If the gap does not increase after the point at which offenses occur, the system cannot be held responsible for the gap that results at the end of the system (e.g., prison).

Wilbanks says that Blacks believe the system is racist for several reasons, the most important of which he calls *negative attribution*. This suggests that, in response to the history of how Blacks have been treated, African Americans have developed a negative view of Whites that attributes evil motives and traits to them. Whites are an "out group" intent on denying Blacks equal rights and opportunities. This attribution leads to the tendency to look for "facts" to confirm this view of Whites.

Second, Wilbanks explains that the suspicions of African Americans of the entire criminal justice system are not an abstract or intellectual argument. The mistrust of the system in general, and of the police in particular, comes from their direct personal experiences with police officers. For example, one study reported that one in four adult Blacks in Detroit claimed to have been stopped and questioned by the police without good reason and that one in five adults claimed to have been searched unnecessarily. Such personal experiences tend to confirm what people commonly hear in the Black community; thus, Blacks often express the view that they do not need statistical proof of racial discrimination since they have experienced it.

Summary

This chapter has explored the historical experience of African Americans in the United States and how this group has found itself in a disadvantaged position for some time. From the early days of slavery to discrimination as they fought in world conflict to the Civil Rights Movement, the African American has played an important role in the history of the United States. Reconstruction also played a role in the current position of African Americans as many formal and informal norms and laws were created to distance African Americans from Whites even when they were forced to live in close proximity to one another. The legacy of slavery, Jim Crow, segregation, and the denial of equal protection under the law, as found in the decisions of U.S. Supreme Court cases, has fundamentally shaped the position of

African Americans in the United States. A by-product of this treatment and legacy of slavery is seen in the disproportionate representation of African Americans in the criminal justice system.

While the topic remains controversial, there can be little doubt that African Americans are overrepresented in crime statistics. This is true despite the fact that there is a growing Black middle class of educated, professional, and politically savvy African Americans. Whether it involves arrest, use of force, searches, convictions, sentences, or executions, Blacks are disproportionately represented in the criminal justice system. Not only do Blacks have different experiences with the criminal justice system than Whites, they also have a general sense of mistrust of the system in general and of the police in particular.

In many low-income neighborhoods there is a significant amount of tension between African Americans and the police. Part of the reason for this mutual mistrust is due to the fact that police officers intervene in the lives of many African Americans perhaps more so than in the lives of Whites in suburban neighborhoods. As a result, not only do African Americans perceive the police as intrusive, this frequent contact can also make it more likely that they become involved in the criminal justice system.

The reasons for the overrepresentation of African Americans in the criminal justice system range from individualistic theories, which contend that African Americans commit more crimes, get caught more often and are punished more harshly, to structural explanations, which suggest there are factors outside the control of individuals that result in their involvement in the system. Finally, as Wilbanks points out, there also exists a debate concerning the racism embedded in the criminal justice system itself.

You Make the Call

Excessive Force?

Consider the following scenario. Debate the pros and cons of all options and decide what you would do. One thing to consider is whether someone who holds negative attitudes against a group of people is likely to translate them into his or her behavior.

You are a White, middle-class, male police officer with less than one year's experience in law enforcement. You have been assigned to a high-crime, low-income neighborhood. There are many calls for service and a significant amount of violent crime in this area. In fact, several times this year the SWAT team has been called to rescue officers who have been attacked by armed residents. Your partner is an eight-year veteran officer who has been involved in many disturbances in this neighborhood and dislikes many of the citizens who live here. In fact, during the course of several conversations, your partner uses racial epithets against African Americans and talks about "nuking the entire area" and starting all over with a group of "civilized" people. In the 11 months since you've been a police officer, you have heard rumors that this officer has engaged in acts of excessive violence toward citizens and has even "planted" evidence on suspects in order to arrest them.

While working late one night, the two of you answer a call from a resident that a domestic disturbance is taking place. Your partner says, "I know these people, we get called here all the time. I'll handle this." You enter the home of an African American family and your partner rushes into another room. Three shots are fired and when you come into the room, you find a Black man lying on the floor with gunshot wounds to his chest. Your partner is standing over him with his weapon drawn, smoke coming from the barrel of his pistol. He tells you that the dead man reached for a gun, but none is found. The man's family begins to scream that your partner shot an unarmed man.

Later, when detectives take your statement, they ask if your partner used excessive force against the victim. The investigators also tell you that the deceased family members claim they did not own a gun and one was not found at the scene.

Questions

1. Is your partner a racist?
2. Do your partner's attitudes toward African Americans factor into his behavior?
3. What do you say to the detectives who take your statement about the incident?

Key Terms

Black middle class (p. 57)
Black Nationalism (p. 56)
Black Power (p. 56)
Civil Rights Movement (p. 54)
de-policing (p. 68)
Emancipation Proclamation (p. 52)
Freedom Schools (p. 55)

fugitive slave acts (p. 52)
Jim Crow (p. 52)
Nation of Islam (p. 56)
Reconstruction (p. 52)
restrictive covenants (p. 54)
slave codes (p. 52)

Discussion Questions

1. Why do you think African Americans are overrepresented in the crime statistics? Is it because they commit more crimes, or is it due to greater police presence in their communities?
2. What role, if any, does the legacy of slavery play in the involvement of African Americans in crime?
3. Do you think the criminal justice system is racist toward African Americans, or is it individual people within the system who discriminate against African Americans?
4. What role does the media play in assessing the importance of the race factor in the criminal justice system?
5. What role do you think the Black middle class should play in resolving some of the problems in low-income neighborhoods?
6. Assume you are a U.S. Supreme Court justice and are hearing a case on the death penalty. Do you think studies examining the race factor in executions should be used to determine if discrimination against minority groups exists in applying the death penalty? Why or why not?

Endnotes

1. Shaefer, R. T. 2004. *Racial and Ethnic Groups,* 9th ed. Upper Saddle River, NJ: Prentice Hall.
2. Tarver, M., Walker, S., and Wallace, H. 2002. *Multicultural Issues in the Criminal Justice System.* Boston: Allyn & Bacon.
3. Franklin, J. H., and Moss, A. A. 2000. *From Slavery to Freedom: A History of African Americans,* 8th ed. New York: McGraw-Hill.
4. Dubois, W. E. B. 1970. *The Negro American Family.* Cambridge, MA: MIT Press.
5. Shaefer 2004; Dubois 1970.
6. Frazier, F. 1964. *The Negro Church in America.* New York: Schocken; Stammp, K. 1956. *The Peculiar Institution: Slavery in the Ante-Bellum South.* New York: Random House.
7. Rawick, G. P. 1972. *From Sundown to Sunup: The Making of the Black Community.* Westport, CT: Greenwood Press.
8. Franklin and Moss 2000.
9. Oaks, J. 1993. "Slavery." In M. K. Clayton, E. J. Gorn, and P. W. Williams (eds.), *Encyclopedia of American Social History,* pp. 1407–1441. New York: Scribners.
10. Shaefer 2004; Killian, L. M. 1975. *The Impossible Revolution, Phase 2: Black Power and the American Dream.* New York: Random House.
11. Ibid.
12. Abrahams, R. D. 1992. *Singing the Master: The Emergence of African American Culture in the Plantation South.* New York: Pantheon; Free, M. D. 1996. *African Americans and the Criminal Justice System.* New York: Garland.
13. Bennett, L. 1966. *The White Problem in America.* Chicago: Johnson.
14. Lacy, D. 1972. *The White Use of Blacks in America.* New York: McGraw-Hill.
15. Lewinson, P. 1965. *Race, Class, and Party: A History of Negro Suffrage and White Politics in the South.* New York: Universal Library; Lacy 1972.
16. Free 1996.
17. Tarver Walker, and Wallace 2002.
18. Shaefer 2004.
19. Oberschall, A. 1968. "The Los Angeles Riot of August 1965." *Social Problems* 15: 322–341.
20. Ibid.
21. Kluger, R. 1998. *Simple Justice.* New York: Random House.
22. Ibid.
23. Killian 1975.
24. Kluger 1998.
25. Butler, J. S. 1996. "The Return of Open Debate." *Society* 39 (March/April): 11–18.
26. Franklin and Moss 2000.
27. Ibid.
28. Shaefer 2004.
29. Oberschall 1968.
30. Ibid.
31. Ibid.
32. Shaefer 2004.
33. Cleaver, K. 1982. "How TV Wrecked the Black Panthers." *Channels,* November/December, pp. 98–99.
34. Watnabe, T. 1999. "Righting Islam's Image in America." *Los Angeles Times,* May 18, p. B2.
35. Ibid.
36. Ibid.; Allen, E. 1996. "Religious Heterodoxy and Nationalist Tradition: The Continuing Evolution of the Nation of Islam." *Black Scholar* 26 (3/4): 2–34.
37. Crank, J. P. 1998. *Understanding Police Culture.* Cincinnati, OH: Anderson.
38. Shaefer 2004.
39. Besharov, D. J. 2005. "The Economic Stagnation of the Black Middle Class." Testimony before the U.S. Commission on Civil Rights (July).
40. Wilson, W. J. 1987. *The Truly Disadvantaged.* Chicago: University of Chicago Press; Anderson, E. 1990. *Streetwise.* Chicago: University of Chicago Press.

41. Crank 1998.

42. Wilson, W. J. 1978. *The Declining Significance of Race.* Chicago: University of Chicago Press.

43. Cole, D. 1999. *No Equal Justice: Race and Class in the American Criminal Justice System.* New York: The Free Press.

44. Ibid.

45. Ibid.

46. Ibid.

47. Harris, J. 2002. *Fathers Behind Bars and On the Street.* St. Louis, MO: Family and Corrections Network.

48. Ibid., p. 24.

49. Ibid.

50. Ibid.

51. Ibid.

52. Cole 1999; Harris 2002.

53. McFadden, R. 2006. "Police Kill Man After a Queens Bachelor Party." *New York Times,* November 26.

54. Chase, A. 2007. "Sean Bell Supporters Protest as Case Goes to Grand Jury." *SOHH.com,* January 22.

55. "Only a Minority: Police Brutality." *The Economist* 344 (8031): 19, August 23, 1997.

56. Chebium, R. 2000. "New Report Chronicles Criminal Justice System's Racial Bias." *CNN.com,* February 16. www.archives.cnn.com/2000/law/05/04/civil.rights/index.html.

57. Smith, D. A., and Visher, C. 1991. "Street Level Justice: Situational Determinants of Police Arrest Decisions." *Social Problems* 29: 167–177.

58. Decker, S. H. 1981. "Citizen Attitudes Toward the Police: A Review of Past Findings and Suggestions for Future Policy." *Journal of Police Science and Administration* 9: 80–87.

59. Smith and Visher 1991.

60. Maxon, C., Hennigan, K., and Sloane, D. 2003. *Factors That Influence Public Opinion of the Police.* Washington, DC: National Institute of Justice.

61. Walker, S., Spohn, C., and Delone, M. 1996, 2000, 2004. *The Color of Justice: Race, Ethnicity and Crime in America.* Belmont, CA: Wadsworth.

62. Bachman, R. 1996. "Victims' Perceptions of Initial Police Responses to Robbery and Aggravated Assault: Does Race Matter?" *Journal of Quantitative Criminology* 12 (4): 363–390.

63. Ibid.

64. Black, D. 1971. "The Social Organization of Arrest." *Stanford Law Review* 23: 1087–1111.

65. Ibid.

66. Smith and Visher 1991.

67. Ibid.

68. Petersilia, J. 1983. *Racial Disparities in the Criminal Justice System.* Santa Monica, CA: Rand.

69. Son, I. S., Davis, M., and Rome, D. M. 1998. "Race and Its Effect on Police Officers' Perceptions of Misconduct." *Journal of Criminal Justice* 26 (1): 21–28.

70. Friedrich, R. J. 1980. "Police Use of Force: Individuals, Situations, and Organizations." *Annals of the American Academy of Political and Social Science* 452: 82–97; Adams, K. 1995. "Measuring the Prevalence of Police Abuse of Force." In W. Geller and H. Toch (eds.), *And Justice for All.* Washington, DC: The Police Executive Research Forum; Cohen, H., and Sherman, L. 1986. "Exploiting Police Authority." *Criminal Justice Ethics,* Summer/Fall, pp. 23–31.

71. Reiss, A. J. 1971. *The Police and the Public.* New Haven, CT: Yale University Press.

72. Adams 1995.

73. Walker, Spohn, and Delone 2004.

74. Ibid.

75. Ibid.

76. Shoop, J. G. 1998. "National Survey Suggests Racial Disparity in Police Use of Force." *Trial* 34 (1): 97; Fyfe, J. J. 1988. "Police Use of Deadly Force: Research and Reform." *Justice Quarterly* 5: 165–205; Dunham, R., and Alpert, G. 1992. *Critical Issues in Law Enforcement.* Cincinatti, OH: Waveland; Westley, W. 1970. *Violence and the Police: A Sociological Study*

of Law, Custom, and Morality. Cambridge, MA: MIT Press.

77. Fyfe 1988; Geller, W. A., and Scott, M. S. 1993. "Deadly Force: What We Know." In C. B. Klockars and S. D. Mastrofski (eds.), *Thinking About Police,* pp. 446–476. New York: McGraw-Hill.

78. Walker, Spohn, and Delone 2004.

79. Cohen and Sherman 1986.

80. Walker, Spohn, and Delone 2004.

81. Roberg, R. R., and Kuykendall, J. 1993. *Police and Society.* Belmont, CA: Wadsworth.

82. Liebow, E. 1999. *Tell Them Who I Am.* Chicago: University of Chicago Press.

83. Walker, Spohn, and Delone 2004.

84. Cole 1999.

85. Lichtblau, E. 2005. "Profiling Report Leads to Demotion." *New York Times,* August 24, p. B1.

86. Browning, S. L., Cullen, F. T., Cao, L., Kopache, R., and Stevenson, T. J. 1994. "Race and Getting Hassled by the Police: A Research Note." *Police Studies* 17 (1): 1–11.

87. White, M. F., Cox, T. C., and Basehart, J. 1991. "Theoretical Considerations of Officer Profanity and Obscenity in Formal Contacts with Citizens." In T. Barker and D. L. Carter (eds.), *Police Deviance,* 2nd ed., pp. 275–297. Cincinnati, OH: Anderson.

88. Williams, D. 2007. *African Americans and Crime.* www.gmu.edu/departments/economics/wew/articles/o1/ideology.html.

89. Tarver, Walker, and Wallace 2002.

90. Walker, Spohn, and Delone 2004.

91. Ekland-Olson, S. 1988. "Structured Discretion, Racial Bias, and the Death Penalty: The First Debate after *Furman* in Texas." *Social Science Quarterly* 69 (December): 853–873.

92. Crawford, C., Chiricos, T., and Kleck, G. 1998. "Race, Racial Threat and Sentencing of Habitual Offenders," *Criminology* 36 (3): 481–511.

93. Weitzer, R., and Tuch, S. A. 1999. "Race, Class and Perceptions of Discrimination by the Police." *Crime and Delinquency* 45 (4): 494–507.

94. Tarver, Walker, and Wallace 2002.

95. Hacker, A. 1989. "Affirmative Action: The New Look." *New York Review of Books* 36 (October 12): 63–68.

96. LaFree, G. 1980. "The Effect of Sexual Stratification by Race on Official Reactions to Rape." *American Sociological Review* 45 (October): 842–854.

97. Gray, J. 1991. "Panel Says Courts Are Infested with Racism." *New York Times,* June 5, p. B1.

98. Walker, Spohn, and Delone 2004.

99. Bowers, W. J., and Pierce, G. 1980. "Deterrence or Brutalization: What Is the Effect of Executions?" *Crime and Delinquency* 26: 453–484.

100. Paternoster, R. 1984. "Prosecutorial Discretion in Requesting the Death Penalty: A Case of Victim-Based Racial Discrimination." *Law and Society Review* 18: 437–478.

101. Baldus, D., Woodworth, G., and Pulaski, C. A. 1990. *Equal Justice and the Death Penalty: A Legal and Empirical Analysis.* Boston: Northeastern University Press.

102. Ibid.

103. Maguire, K., Pastore, A. L., and Flanagan T. J. (eds.). 1998, 2004. *Sourcebook of Criminal Justice Statistics.* Washington, DC: U.S. Government Printing Office.

104. Ibid.

105. Ibid.

106. Ibid.

107. Walker, Spohn, and Delone 2004.

Hispanic Americans and the Criminal Justice System

Chapter Objectives

After reading this chapter, you should be able to

❖ Understand the significance of the Hispanic/ Latino influence in the United States.

❖Understand the historical importance of immigration for Chicanos, Cubans, Puerto Ricans, and those from Central and South America.

❖ Describe the current position in American society for Chicanos, Cubans, and Puerto Ricans.

❖ Describe the overrepresentation of Hispanic Americans in the criminal justice system, including arrests, use of force, deadly force, and sentencing.

The group label *Hispanic Americans* includes a population of people who share a common language heritage but have many significant differences. More than one in eight people in the United States are of Spanish or Latin American origin.[1] Collectively this group is called Hispanics or Latinos, a term we will use interchangeably in this chapter. The U.S. Census Bureau estimates that by 2050 Hispanics will constitute about a quarter of the U.S. population. According to the 2000 Census, there are 35.3 million Latinos, which outnumber the 34.7 million African Americans in the United States. The majority of the Latino population, about 21 million, are Mexican Americans or Chicanos. Puerto Ricans and Cubans make up the largest groups representing the remainder of the Latino population.[2]

The problems of identity are evident from the outset of the discussion. How does one define this group of diverse people—are they Hispanic, Latino, or something else? People of Spanish or Latin origin share the group label Hispanic or Latin and a common ancestral home, Central and South America. The Hispanic label combines the offspring of colonized natives, the *Hispanos,* with the descendants of foreigners, and with political and economic refugees.[3] The term *Hispanic* is not universally used and some people, particularly from Latin America, prefer the term **Latino.** Also, significant differences exist among the cultures of Latin America.[4]

In addition to the countries of origin, some sense of the Hispanic population can be made by examining where different groups tend to live. Chicanos, for example, are found primarily in the Southwest, whereas Puerto Ricans tend to live in the New England area, and Cubans tend to congregate in Florida. Given their diversity in both background and regionalism, groups in the West tend to use the term *Latino* whereas the term *Hispanic* is more often used in the East.[5]

There is even diversity found in the one area thought to be common for all Hispanics: language. Because of different dialects and nuances in pronunciation, while Spanish might be the way to generally identify the group, perhaps it is more accurate to say that Hispanics or Latinos are a non–English speaking group.

⚔ Chicanos and Mexicans

Chicanos, who are Americans of Mexican origin, are the largest ethnic group in the United States. Numbering more than 12 million, Chicanos have a long history in the U.S. dating back to the early days of European exploration. The Chicano people trace their ancestry to the merging of Spanish settlers with Native Americans of Central America. In fact, evidence of Chicano history can be traced to the Mayan and Aztec civilizations.[6] Thus, the Spaniards conquered the land and merged with Native Americans over several centuries to form the Mexican people.

In 1821 Mexico obtained its independence from Spain, but domination from the United States began less than a generation later. After the conclusion of the Mexican-American War in 1848, treaties were signed that gave Texas, California, and most of Arizona and New Mexico to the United States for $15 million. In exchange, the U.S. granted citizenship to about 75,000 Mexicans.[7]

The beginning of the Chicano experience was varied, but the one thing Chicanos had in common was that they were regarded as a vanquished people. Although maltreatment and discrimination existed, more serious issues arose when Whites began to encroach on Chicano land. Prior to 1869, Chicanos in California owned all parcels of land valued at more than $10,000. By the 1870s they owned only 25% of the land. A widely accepted, and ironic, explanation for this trend was that many Whites felt justified in taking Chicano land because of the landgrabbing that some Mexican governors perpetrated against American Indians. That Whites perpetuated this same type of behavior against American Indians somehow is lost in the justification in the treatment of Chicanos.[8]

Immigration

Immigration from Mexico is unique in several respects. From about 1901 to 1913, large numbers of Mexicans came into the United States to work in the growing agricultural industry. The Mexican population grew significantly after the Mexican Revolution of 1909–1922, which brought even more refugees into the U.S. When World War I began, fewer people from Europe came to this country, which opened the proverbial door in the labor market for Mexicans. More Mexicans emigrated to the U.S. after the Mexican Revolution due to the political conflicts in their native country.[9]

The influx of Mexicans into the United States slowed after 1929 as the Great Depression was felt all over the country. Consequently, Mexicans were not needed for labor, and the ones already in the U.S. were considered competition for existing jobs. In an attempt to reduce the labor force, the government embarked upon a deportation program, referred to as **repatriation,** to effectively send Chicanos back to Mexico.[10]

The legal justification for repatriation was that deportation applied only to illegal immigrants. However, one of the problems created by this program stemmed from the poorly kept records concerning immigrants prior to 1930. Because the

While illegal immigration is a controversial topic, many legal migrant workers struggle to obtain fair treatment.

United States had little interest in whether Mexicans entered with the proper credentials, preferring their labor to their papers, many Mexicans who could be classified as illegal aliens had resided in the U.S. for decades. However, because many Mexicans had children who were citizens at birth, technically they could not be legally deported. Regardless, many Chicanos were deported because they could not produce sufficient documentation that they were U.S. citizens.[11]

As a result, about half a million people were deported to Mexico. For the Chicanos and Mexicans who were allowed to remain, they could not find work and many lost the property they owned because they were unable to pay taxes. As a result, many Chicanos flocked to growing concentrations of segregated areas, called **barrios,** of the Southwest.[12]

When the Depression ended, Mexican laborers again became attractive to industry. In 1942 the United States and Mexico agreed to a program called **Los Braceros** that allowed migration across the border by contracted workers. Minimum standards were maintained for the transportation, housing, wages, and health care of the Braceros. Ironically, these safeguards placed the Braceros in a better economic situation than Chicanos, who often worked alongside the protected Mexican nationals.[13]

Chicanos Today

Perhaps the two most significant areas that demonstrate the current status of Mexican Americans in this country relate to education and health care. Both Mexican Americans and Puerto Ricans have seen some progress in terms of educational achievement; however, both groups lag behind Whites in this area. Part of the reason for this is the sense of segregation and isolation many Mexican American and Puerto Rican students feel. Almost three-quarters of Hispanics attend predominantly minority schools. This figure is higher than that for African American students.[14]

A second, and related, factor has been the loss of emphasis on the desegregation of schools. At one time, particularly in the 1960s and 1970s, strong campaigns were launched to ensure that Whites and Blacks were provided equal educational opportunities. The momentum for equality has lessened at a time when more Hispanics are entering congested, minority-dominated schools.[15]

ILLEGAL IMMIGRATION, FENCING, AND THE MINUTEMAN DEFENSE CORPS

Illegal immigration is one of the most pervasive and controversial social issues among U.S. citizens. People are primarily concerned about the rise in illegal immigration, particularly from Mexico into the United States. Strategies to contain illegal immigrants consist of stricter enforcement of immigration laws or, more recently, the construction of a fence across the border between Mexico and the U.S. This fence, estimated to stretch over a 70-mile area and cost nearly $55 million, will be built along the border using the fiber optic mesh produced by FOMGuard, USA, also currently in use on U.S. military installations, the Demilitarized Zone in Korea, and the West Bank in Israel. Perhaps most important, the fence will be built on private ranch land through private donations.

Another strategy to deal with illegal immigrants is referred to as The Minuteman Project (TMP). Beginning in April 2005, TMP was created as a way for citizens to actively take part in addressing the immigration problem from Mexico and Canada. The name of the group comes from the minutemen who fought in the American Revolution. Essentially, The Minuteman Project is a citizen patrol group, which is a form of a community crime prevention program. The law enforcement community typically does not support citizen patrol groups, such as the Guardian Angels, because of concerns about the lack of adequate training and the threat of vigilante or "mob" justice. The U.S. Border Patrol, the primary agency responsible for the control of illegal immigration into the United States, supports The Minuteman Project.

Supporters of TMP also include union leaders, who see illegal immigrants as a threat to job security, and California Governor Arnold Schwarzenegger, who, in 2005, said he thought that the group had been doing a good job and was an asset to the community.

Critics of TMP include former Mexican President Vicente Fox, President George W. Bush, and the Anti-Defamation League. Their concern about TMP is that the program has been infiltrated with White supremacist groups, such as the American Nazi Party and the Ku Klux Klan. An added problem is that some TMP members have carried weapons while on patrol, lending to the perception that they are confrontational and do not supplement the Border Patrol. In response, TMP members argue that some members bring weapons while on patrol to kill snakes and other animals that present a threat to their personal safety. TMP members also point out that they have provided medical treatment to people they encounter while waiting for the Border Patrol to arrive. Most important, TMP members often engage in activities with Border Patrol agents. A spokesperson for the Tucson, Arizona, sector of the Border Patrol says there have been no incidents in which Minuteman volunteers used their firearms to harm illegal immigrants.

The Minuteman Project is controversial for many reasons, but it does demonstrate the willingness of some citizens to recognize the limitations of the Border Patrol as well as their willingness to address the issue of illegal immigration. There is a fine line between citizen responsibility and vigilante justice, and the debate about The Minuteman Project is at the heart of the issue.

Not surprisingly, Mexican Americans and Puerto Ricans are underrepresented in higher education. As an illustration, according to the 2000 U.S. Census, only 51% of Mexican Americans and 64% of Puerto Ricans aged 25 and over had completed high school, compared to 88% of non-Hispanic Whites. Further, less than 5% of all college professors were Hispanic.[16]

Hispanics are also adversely affected by issues surrounding health care. According to the U.S. Census Bureau, approximately one-third of Hispanics have no health insurance, compared to about 11% for African Americans and about 10% for Whites. Not only is the quality of health care limited for Hispanics, but there is no continuity of care since they must rely on clinics for their medical needs. It also means preventive health care is limited; for example, fewer Hispanics than any other race or ethnic group are immunized.[17] This problem is complicated by the limited number of Hispanic health professionals, who accounted for less than 4% of dentists, nurses, and physicians in 2000, according to the U.S. Census Bureau. An added problem is the language barrier. Even with translators, communication with Hispanic patients is difficult since many medical terms are not easily translatable, particularly for interpreters who are not familiar with medical terminology.[18]

⚔ Cubans

Third in population only to Chicanos and Puerto Ricans, Cuban Americans represent a significant ethnic minority in the United States. The Cuban influence in this country was seen as early as 1831, with small, close-knit communities organized around a single enterprise such as a cigar manufacturing factory.[19]

Immigration

Until recently, the number of Cuban Americans was relatively small. In 1960, 79,000 people who were born in Cuba lived in the United States. By 1990, this number had grown to over one million. This increase followed Castro's rise to power after the 1959 Cuban Revolution. Since then, immigration to the U.S. has come in four distinct waves. First, there was an initial exodus of approximately 200,000 following Castro's claim to power. The first wave lasted for a period of about three years and ended as a result of the Cuban missile crisis in 1962.[20]

The second stage of immigration was informal, but important. Between 1962 and 1965, there was no direct sanctioned transportation, but nearly 30,000 Cubans came via private planes, boats, and other forms of transportation. The third stage occurred between 1965 and 1973, when the Cuban government permitted approximately 300,000 immigrants to arrive in the United States.[21]

The fourth wave has been the most controversial. In 1980 more than 124,000 refugees fled Cuba to Key West, Florida, seeking asylum in the United States. President Jimmy Carter, reflecting the nation's hostility toward Cuba's communist government, welcomed the refugees "with open arms and an open heart." Castro saw President Carter's claim as an opportunity to deport a host of inmates, criminals, and drug addicts. However, while refugees from this last wave of immigration have been somewhat historically stigmatized, it should be noted that the majority of refugees were not social deviants.[22]

While many Cubans are opposed to Castro, few feel that his death will result in substantial changes in the political structure of that country.

Unfortunately, this group of refugees was given the name **Marielitos.** The word, meant to suggest that they were undesirable, refers to Mariel, the fishing port west of Havana where Cuban authorities herded people onto boats. The negative reception by the Cubans who were already here, coupled with the group's lack of formal education, resulted in a great deal of difficulty for many Marielitos in adjusting to life in America.[23]

Cubans Today

Compared to other recent immigrant groups, and Hispanics as a whole, Cuban Americans have made a successful transition to American culture. Unemployment rates are low, especially for Cuban American women, who are less likely than other groups to seek employment. The close-knit structure of Cuban American families encourages women to follow traditional roles of homemaker and mother.

Probably no ethnic group has had more influence on the fortunes of a city in a short period of time than the Cubans have had on Miami. It is the only city in the country where more than 50% of the inhabitants, an estimated one million Cuban Americans, are foreign-born.[24] The early immigrants were generally well educated, and many had professional or managerial backgrounds. Consequently, many Cubans used their talents and skills in the United States to achieve economic success.

Like the city of Miami, which continually undergoes changes, Little Havana is no longer exclusively a Cuban neighborhood. Cubans have begun to move to suburban areas, such as Coral Gables, Coconut Grove, Kendall, and Hialeah. In their place, immigrants from Nicaragua, Venezuela, Colombia, and Argentina have established roots in Little Havana.[25] Still, Little Havana remains the symbolic center for the vibrant Cuban community.

The long-range prospects for Cubans in the United States depend on several factors. Of obvious importance is the health of Cuba's dictator, Fidel Castro. Many Cuban immigrants might be tempted to return to their native land should Castro's reign end in the near future and democracy replace the communist regime. More dramatic than efforts to change Cuba politically has been the transformation of Miami politics. Miami was once a liberal Democratic stronghold, but Republican Cuban Americans outnumber Democrats 2-to-1 and have been instrumental in electing a number of conservatives to major offices.[26]

Cubans have selectively accepted White culture; they do not feel that they need to forget the Spanish language as other immigrant children have done. As a result, Miami has become the most bilingual of any city in the United States that is not on the Mexican border. But the Cuban experience has not been completely positive. In the late 1990s, Miami's Cubans expressed concern over what they felt was the indifference of Miami's Roman Catholic hierarchy. Cubans, like other Hispanics, are underrepresented in the leadership positions throughout the church. While there is one White priest for every 855 English-speaking Catholics, there is only one Hispanic priest for every 5,000 parishioners.[27]

Some of this concern may be less important to Cubans now than in the past, however. Cubans are less religious than Latinos from other countries, with only 59% claiming that religion is the most important or a very important thing in their lives compared to 70% of Mexicans, 69% of Puerto Ricans, and 73% of Central Americans. Furthermore, Cubans are less likely than all the other Latino groups to attend religious services. Less than one-third of all Cubans (28%) said they go to religious services once a week or more compared to 47% of Mexicans, 46% of Puerto Ricans, 48% of Central Americans, and 44% of South Americans.[28]

Puerto Ricans

Puerto Ricans represent an interesting case because they are a group left in limbo with regard to their status in the United States. The island of Puerto Rico was taken by the U.S. during the Spanish-American War in 1898. During the time Spain controlled the island, for about four centuries, slavery was prominent as many Puerto Ricans were enslaved by the Spanish and there was an influx of Africans to the island. This legacy of slavery and intermarriage can be seen in the skin tone of many Puerto Ricans, who appear darker than other Hispanic or Latino groups.

The subsequent economic, social, and political colonization, which was enhanced in 1948 when Puerto Rico became a commonwealth of the United States, left the people in a state of ambiguity in terms of status. While they are U.S. citizens and elect their own governor, Puerto Ricans cannot vote in presidential elections and have no representation in Congress. However, they are subject to military service and all federal laws.[29]

Historically, many Puerto Ricans came to the mainland during World War II to work on railroads and in food manufacturing. New York City represented a haven for many Puerto Ricans because there was a large group who had already settled there.

More recently, while many Puerto Ricans remain in New York City, others have migrated to New Jersey, Florida, Connecticut, and Pennsylvania. This latter group of Puerto Ricans is much more familiar and comfortable with American culture, making the migration easier. Perhaps most significant has been the loss of manufacturing jobs in many cities, necessitating a move to another area.[30] Puerto Ricans who return to the island after spending time away, typically in New York, have come to be called **Neoricans.** Neoricans as a group represent a better-educated, more affluent segment of the population who returned to Puerto Rico.[31]

The main issue for Puerto Ricans relates to independence—this is the easiest way for the island to retain and strengthen a sense of cultural and political identity. While there are advantages and disadvantages to statehood, independence, or remaining as a commonwealth, it is not clear that even islanders agree on what needs to be done. In 1998 a nonbinding referendum was taken with 50% favoring continuing commonwealth status and 47% preferring statehood. Less than 3% favored independence. A similar survey of Puerto Ricans in the United States found the population evenly split, with a third favoring each option.[32] Until there is unification among the people of Puerto Rico, it is unlikely that any changes will be made to its economic and political status.

Economically, migration to the United States was a safety valve for Puerto Rico's population, which has grown annually at a rate 50% faster than the U.S. population. Typically, migrants from Puerto Rico are more likely to be laborers and semi-skilled workers than are the people of the island as a whole. Yet the most recent studies found that 69% of migrants leaving Puerto Rico were unemployed.[33] In virtually all social areas, such as housing, health care, and education, Puerto Rico falls far short of acceptable minimal standards.[34]

✍ The Influence of Central and South America

When most people think of Hispanics and Latinos, they usually think only of the groups mentioned thus far in this chapter. However, an essential part of the Hispanic and Latino presence in this country is occupied by immigrants and citizens with a background from Central and South America. In fact, as mentioned earlier, the influence of this group on the culture of Little Havana in Miami or even the changing face of New York City is considerable.

For instance, people from Chile and Costa Rica have very little in common with other Hispanic and Latino groups other than the Spanish language and geographic location. In the case of Brazil, natives do not speak Spanish; the official language is Portuguese. For some reason, Americans tend to lump groups from Central and South America into a single category despite a wide range of cultural differences. In addition, instead of making distinctions between group membership based on light or dark skin tones, as is done in this country, Latin Americans make distinctions in terms of group membership based on a light- to dark-skin continuum sometimes called a **color gradient.** These differences are significant in terms of identifying social class and religious differences between South American and Central American groups. Thus, besides not fitting into a simple category of "Hispanic" or "Latino," people from these regions of the world have enough differences to render any type of generalization difficult.[35]

⚔ Hispanics and the Criminal Justice System

Like their African American counterparts, not only are Hispanics likely to commit more crimes and engage in other forms of unacceptable behavior than Whites, they are significantly overrepresented in many of the crime statistics in this country as well. The same arguments that are used to explain why African Americans are over-represented in the crime figures can be applied to Hispanics/Latinos. That is, on one hand, the treatment of Hispanics and Latinos demonstrates the fact that the system discriminates against minority groups. A counterargument is that Hispanics and Latinos have fewer opportunities to obtain a well-paying job, have poorer educational experiences, and have fewer overall chances to succeed than Whites. All of these factors, in turn, are reasons why some segments of the Hispano/Latino population turn to crime.

Involvement in Crime

While Hispanics and Latinos engage in a wide assortment of crimes, three of the most noted crimes involve illegal immigration, the development of gangs, particularly in California, and drug use. This is not to say that Hispanics and Latinos have a "corner on the market" with regard to these activities; however, there does appear to be a high percentage of the group's involvement in these behaviors. Additionally, the aforementioned structural barriers to legitimate success may play a role in explaining why these crimes occur. We will discuss each briefly.

Illegal Immigration

What are the characteristics of illegal immigrants? The extent and characteristics of illegal immigration are discussed in a 2005 report by the Pew Hispanic Center, in Washington, D.C. In 2004 naturalized citizens represented just under one-third of the estimated 35.7 million foreign-born population in the United States. About 10% of all immigrants living in this country are called "legal permanent resident" aliens (LPRs or "legal immigrants") and have yet to become permanent citizens. Almost a third of the foreign-born population (29%) in the United States is identified as "unauthorized," meaning they either have entered the country without going through conventional or legal channels (such as applying for a visa and beginning the process of becoming a citizen) or have entered the country with forged documents. More commonly, unauthorized immigrants have remained in this country after their visas have expired.[36]

    The unauthorized population has been steadily increasing in size since the mid-1990s. Similarly, the naturalized citizen population has grown rapidly in recent years as increasing numbers of legal immigrants have taken advantage of the opportunity to naturalize. The LPR alien population, on the other hand, actually decreased for several years as the number who naturalized (or left the U.S. or died) exceeded the number being admitted. As of March 2004, there were an estimated 10.3 million unauthorized migrants living in the United States, of which about 57% are from Mexico. The rest are mainly from Central America, which accounts for another 25% of the total. The remaining 20% is made up of immigrants from countries all over the world.[37] Virtually all of the unauthorized are either visa **overstayers,** persons admitted on temporary visas who either stay beyond the expiration of their visas or otherwise violate their terms of admission, or EWIs ("entries without inspection" or clandestine entrants). Visa overstayers probably represent 25% to 40% of the unauthorized migrants.[38]

Another large group not included in the estimate of legal residents are persons in the legal immigration backlog. There are more than 600,000 persons in the United States who have applied for green cards but are waiting for them to be issued. In addition there are perhaps another 100,000 persons who are immediate relatives of, or engaged to, legal resident waiting for their final papers. Most people in these groups will eventually acquire green cards. All told, there are probably about 1.5 million unauthorized residents known to the Department of Homeland Security whose cases are pending.[39]

Almost two-thirds (68%) of the unauthorized population lives in just eight states: California (24%), Texas (14%), Florida (9%), New York (7%), Arizona (5%), Illinois (4%), New Jersey (4%), and North Carolina (3%). In the past, the foreign-born population, both legal and unauthorized, was highly concentrated. In 1990, 45% of the unauthorized population, or about 1.6 million persons, lived in California; by 2004, that had dropped to 24%. The rapid growth and spreading of the unauthorized population has been the main reason the immigrant population has moved to new settlement states such as Arizona, North Carolina, Georgia, and Tennessee.[40]

What is perhaps most significant about the explosive growth of illegal immigration is the increase in criminal activity committed by this segment of the population. Perhaps even more fascinating has been the way the United States has tried to address illegal immigrant crime in major cities. According to Heather MacDonald, a senior researcher at the Center for Immigration Studies,[41] "Not only do illegal criminals represent a significant threat to public safety, but in places like Los Angeles, CA, police policy to arrest illegal immigrants has run into a political windstorm."

The construction of a border fence to thwart illegal immigrants.

MacDonald cites a few statistics concerning the crime problem related to immigration. She says, "Police commanders may not want to discuss, much less respond to, the illegal alien crisis, but its magnitude for law enforcement is startling." For example, in 2004, in Los Angeles, 95% of all outstanding warrants for homicide (which total 1,200 to 1,500) target illegal aliens, and up to two-thirds of all fugitive felony warrants (17,000) are for illegal aliens.[42]

In response to the increase of illegal aliens, Special Order 40 was enacted in Los Angeles in 1979. The order prohibits officers from "initiating police action where the objective is to discover the alien status of a person." In practice, this means that the police may not even ask someone they have arrested about his or her immigration status until after criminal charges have been entered. Additionally, the police may not arrest someone for immigration violations. Officers may not check a suspect's immigration status prior to arrest nor may they notify the Bureau of Immigration and Customs Enforcement (ICE) about an illegal alien picked up for minor violations. Officers can inquire about a suspect's immigration status or report the offender to immigration only after he or she has been booked for a felony or multiple misdemeanors.[43]

Laws like this one, often referred to as **sanctuary laws,** contradict much of what has been learned about crime reduction strategies. One of the most significant discoveries in law enforcement in the last decade has been the potential effectiveness of community policing. The broken windows theory, on which much of community policing is based, suggests that arrests for minor offenses often lead to reductions in serious crimes.

In a similar way, some experts believe that enforcing immigration violations against known felons is arguably effective in reducing crime committed by illegal immigrants, but sanctuary laws inhibit this type of preventive enforcement. Only if the felon has given the officer some other reason to stop him or her, such as the officer observes a crime being committed, can the offender be detained, and only for that non-immigration-related reason. The officer cannot arrest for the immigration felony. Critics argue that such a policy is extraordinarily inefficient and puts the community at risk.[44]

The rationale behind enacting sanctuary policies is to encourage illegal alien crime victims and witnesses to cooperate with the police without fear of deportation and to encourage all illegal aliens to take advantage of city services like health care and education. Critics argue that there has never been any empirical verification that sanctuary laws actually increase cooperation with the police or other city agencies. Critics of sanctuary laws also say the real reason cities prohibit police officers from immigration reporting and enforcement is a fear of alienating the population of illegal aliens, on whom the country relies so heavily.[45]

In trying to come to grips with the illegal immigrant–crime connection, cities such as Los Angeles have found that not only are the laws designed to limit the scope of investigative abilities, but even when local police officers require the assistance of ICE agents, immigration officials are so overwhelmed that officers often do not get the assistance they need. This lack of assistance, coupled with sanctuary laws, sends a message to the offender population that they are not likely to be punished or deported.

Additionally, a confidential California Department of Justice study reported in 2004 that 60% of the 18th Street Gang in California is illegal (with an estimated membership of 20,000). This gang collaborates with the Mexican Mafia, the dominant force in California prisons, on a variety of illegal activities. The gang has dramatically expanded its numbers over the last two decades by recruiting recently arrived youngsters from Central America and Mexico.

Hispanic Gangs

The post–World War II era brought Hispanic street gangs to places like Los Angeles, California. The 1950s were to be a decade of rapid growth for gangs. To further compound the issue, many families were moving away from cities like Los Angeles to the smaller surrounding cities to avoid inner-city gang violence. Unfortunately, relocated children brought the gang mentality and philosophy to their new neighborhoods, creating new gangs that were extensions of the ones they were associated with in Los Angeles.[46]

Throughout the 1950s, many Hispanic gang members were sent to prison. Between 1956 and 1957, several *Eslos,* short for East Los Angeles, were doing time at the Deuel Vocational Institute in Tracy, California, and formed the Hispanic prison gang known as *La Eme,* the Mexican Mafia, the first prison gang in California. Initially, La Eme was formed for protection against other inmates and prison staff. From the beginning there was a rivalry between northern and southern Hispanics in California. The Hispanics from northern California formed Nuestra Familia (NF), another prison gang, to protect them from La Eme, whose membership was made up primarily of southern Californians.[47]

By 1970, incarceration had become a status symbol for many gang members. There was also a concerted law enforcement effort to curb gang violence, which resulted in many gang leaders going to prison. Having served as mentors for younger members and enforcers of gang rules, many elders lost their influence when incarcerated. Consequently, in many gangs the younger members were free to do as they pleased without recognizing treaties or rules of conduct for the gang.

By the mid to late 1980s, the traditional ways of the Hispanic street gangs had all but been abandoned. Members had begun to commit crimes in their own neighborhoods—traditionally a tactic frowned upon by gang members—and non–gang members, particularly undocumented immigrants, had become a new class of victim for Hispanic street gangs. In response, immigrant youth started to form their own gangs for protection against established gangs, which only increased inter-gang conflicts, with gang violence becoming commonplace.[48]

By the early 1990s, Los Angeles was considered by many experts as the "gang capital" of the country. Although there was an attempt to educate community members on dangers related to gang membership, Hispanic gangs continued to grow in size and violence. In 1991, Los Angeles County reported an estimated 100,000 gang members and 750 different street gangs in L.A. County alone, with Hispanic street gangs accounting for a majority of the street gangs.[49]

By the mid-1990s, law enforcement agencies had begun to document a change in the gang culture. Respect no longer seemed to be based on age, experience, or knowledge. In the street code, respect was increasingly based on fear due to the loss of older gang leaders and the rapid increases in the size of individual street gangs.[50]

Recently, Hispanic street gangs have become the fastest-growing type of gang in the country. There continue to be turf-oriented Hispanic gangs located in regions of the

Hispanic street gangs have become the fastest-growing type of gang in the United States.

United States, but the concept of turf for some gangs has changed in that they operate in an entire city, not just one neighborhood. These gangs do not always use graffiti to mark their turf's boundaries in the same manner of traditional Hispanic gangs.[51]

Drug Use

According to the U.S. Census Bureau, one in three Hispanics is under the age of 18. In a 2005 study by the National Institute of Health, called the National Survey on Drug Use and Health, one in ten Hispanic youth 12 to 17 years old reported using illicit drugs in the past month. Among the racial/ethnic groups surveyed in the 2002 Monitoring the Future school-based study, Hispanic eighth-graders tend to have the highest rates of past-year drug use for most illegal drugs, including marijuana, cocaine, and heroin. Data from the same survey indicate that Cuban adolescents have the highest reported 12-month illicit drug use rates of any ethnic group in the United States.

Research over the past two decades has revealed a number of alarming trends about Latino drug use. For instance, data from the National Household Survey of Drug Abuse for 2000 and 2001 show that rates of past-month illicit drug use in the Latino population ranged from 9.2% for Puerto Ricans to 5.8% for Mexicans to 3.7% for Cubans and 3.6% for Central and South Americans aged 12 and older. This compares to similar rates for Whites and African Americans, 6.8% and 6.9% respectively. The group with the highest past-month use for those 12 and older was clearly American Indian/Alaska Natives, with 9.9%. However, it is worth noting that while drug use among Cubans and Central Americans remains low, the rate of drug use among Puerto Ricans is very similar to that of American Indian/Alaska Natives, who lead the country in that category.[52]

Another study found that the rate of drug use among Latina females has historically been significantly lower than that of Latino males.[53] Latina women also report lower rates of substance abuse compared to non-Latina women.[54] However, some evidence suggests that once drug abuse begins, there are no differences between Latina women and non-Latina women or between Latina women and Latino men. This suggests that while it may be initially lower in terms of prevalence rates, with the onset of dependency, Latina women are no different from other types of abusers.[55] In fact, some evidence suggests that Latinas are using drugs at a rate similar to that of Latinos[56] and, in some cases, even higher.[57]

Perhaps the best way to digest this information is to state that research indicates that Latinos have high rates of substance abuse, have the highest reported symptoms of dependency, and the highest need for alcohol and drug treatment compared to Whites and African Americans.[58] The consequences for dependency and substance abuse have far-reaching implications. It is not accidental that there is a connection between Latino alcohol and drug abuse and HIV/AIDS transmission. Research has shown that risk behaviors such as sharing needles may be more predominant among Puerto Ricans than among other Hispanics. Recent research also notes that among men, Latinos were significantly more at risk for HIV/AIDS than other groups.[59]

Risk Factors and Drug Use

Researchers over the past two decades have identified risk factors for Hispanic youth and found that Hispanics are more likely than non-Hispanic Whites to live in poverty. In 2002, 21.4% of Hispanics were living in poverty, compared to 7.8% of non-Hispanic Whites. Further, more than 40% of Hispanics over the age of 25 had not graduated high school, increasing their likelihood of being poor.

Another explanation for the high rate of drug use among Hispanics focuses on individual factors. Some studies have found a relationship between adolescent drug abuse and low religiosity and negative attitudes toward academic achievement.[60] Psychiatric disorders are also associated with the development of drug dependence, but this occurs in both Latino and non-Latino populations.[61] Family discord also plays an important role in drug abuse among Latino youth. Given the importance of family as a defining trait of Latino culture, the lack of family or the effects of a disrupted family have a significant impact. Latino youth have a greater likelihood of becoming alcohol or drug abusers compared to African Americans or Whites.[62] Additionally, when Latino parents fail to participate in conventional activities with their children, it increases the probability of Latino youth abusing drugs.[63] While peers and family influence is important, cultural factors are perhaps the most important variable in explaining high rates of drug abuse among Latinos. U.S.-born Latino youth, particularly those of Cuban descent, have higher rates of experimental drug use, abuse, and dependence than other immigrants.[64] Other studies have found a link between cultural pride and lower rates of abuse—those immigrants who have assimilated into mainstream American society have higher drug abuse rates than those who retain a strong sense of cultural heritage.[65]

In sum, the data on the prevalence of substance abuse among Latinos suggest that beginning in early adolescence, Latinos lead the nation in alcohol and illicit drug use. They also have the highest need for alcohol and drug treatment compared to Whites and African Americans, yet there are fewer efforts made in terms of U.S. policy or programs to dedicate time, resources, and energy to this group than to other groups.

✖ Hispanic Involvement in the Criminal Justice System

The impact of the criminal justice system on the Hispanic population has been studied since the 1970s. Several significant studies have been conducted including the following: a report by the U.S. Commission on Civil Rights entitled *Mexican Americans and the Administration of Justice in the Southwest* (1970); a report from the National Minority Advisory Council on Criminal Justice entitled *The Inequality of Justice: A Report on Crime and the Administration of Justice in the Minority Community* (1982); and a report by the Population Research Institute at Penn State University entitled *Hispanics Penalized More by Criminal Justice System than Whites and Blacks* (2001). In these reports, the involvement and treatment of Hispanics in the criminal justice process have been highlighted and have shown a consistent trend of discrimination.

In 2002, Charles Kamasaki, senior vice president of the National Council of La Raza, testified before the United States Sentencing Commission on the impact of drug sentencing on the Latino community. He argued that there is increasing evidence that Hispanics are being held to a standard of accountability far exceeding that of any other segment of the population in the criminal justice system. For instance, according to the 2000 Census, Latinos represented 12.5% of the U.S. population but, according to the U.S. Sentencing Commission, constituted 43.4% of the total drug offenders. Of those, approximately 51% were convicted of possession or trafficking powder cocaine and about 10% for crack cocaine. While some experts might argue that these figures indicate Hispanics commit more drug offenses or use drugs at a higher rate than Whites, Kamasaki argued that federal health statistics indicated drug use per capita for Whites and minorities was very similar.[66]

Additionally, Kamasaki argued that Hispanics are discriminated against at every stage of the criminal justice process. For example, Hispanic and Black federal defendants are more likely than White defendants to be charged with drug offenses. According to the 2000 Census, compared to 29% of Whites charged with drug offenses in U.S. district courts, 46% of Hispanic offenders and 48% of Black offenders were charged with drug offenses. Perhaps most important, three times as many Hispanic men aged 25 to 29 were sentenced to prison than Whites. Additionally, Hispanic men were 33% less likely to be released before trial than Whites—approximately 23% of Hispanics were released before trial compared to 63% of White defendants. This occurred at a time when Hispanic defendants had less-extensive criminal histories than White defendants, making them less of a risk to the community than their White counterparts.

As further evidence of this disparity, half of Hispanic federal prison inmates had no previous criminal history, compared to 29% of Blacks and 38% for Whites. Finally, of all federal inmates to receive some type of substance abuse treatment, Hispanics were least likely to receive treatment. Compared to 54% of Whites and 48% of African Americans, only 36% of Hispanics received any type of substance abuse treatment. In sum, Kamasaki argued that despite the fact that Latinos are no more likely than other groups to use illegal drugs, they are more likely to be arrested and charged with drug offenses and less likely to be given pretrial release. Once convicted, Latinos receive harsher sentences even though the majority of offenders have no criminal history.

More recently, in October 2004, a report issued by the **National Council of La Raza,** the nation's largest Hispanic civil rights organization, found additional ways that Hispanics are systematically discriminated against in the criminal justice system. The report, entitled *Lost Opportunities: The Reality of Latinos in the U.S. Criminal Justice System,* was heralded as the first comprehensive examination of Hispanics in every facet of the criminal justice system. The study is based on data from government sources, including the Bureau of Justice Statistics and the U.S. Census Bureau, and is coauthored by the Center for Youth Policy Research and Michigan State University's Office of University Outreach and Engagement. According to Nancy Walker, president and senior research fellow of the Center for Youth Policy Research, "This study conclusively documents the criminal justice system's discriminatory practices against the nation's largest and fastest growing minority population. . . . This indictment of the system comes from the government's own statistics. Our nation cannot afford to ignore the compelling case that these numbers make for reforming our system."[67]

Among the many key findings from the report is that Hispanics experience discrimination during arrest, prosecution, and sentencing and are more likely to be incarcerated than Whites when charged with the same offense. Some of the findings relate to the circumstances surrounding police contact with Hispanics, which can often lead to arrest, but Hispanics are also disproportionately represented by public defenders, who are often overwhelmed with cases. Compared to defendants with private attorneys, 71% who were represented by public counsel, compared to 54% with private attorneys, were sentenced to incarceration. The report also highlights problems stemming from harsh mandatory minimum sentences, which give prosecutors the upper hand in plea negotiations and are inconsistent with the severity of the offense. The report is also critical of courts that do not provide documents written in Spanish or fail to provide translators to defendants.

Another important finding of this study is that Hispanics were disproportionately charged with nonviolent, low-level drug offenses. Similar to a report in 2002, in which health statistics showed similar rates of drug use, Hispanics were three times more likely to be arrested for drug offenses than Whites and accounted for nearly half of all offenders convicted of drug offenses in 2000.

A third area of concern for Hispanics relates to the zero tolerance policy used to deport minorities. Arrests for immigration offenses increased 610% between 1990 and 2000. A list of more than 50 crimes, including fighting at school, was used to facilitate deportation; however, according to the Federal Bureau of Prisons, U.S. citizens are 10 times more likely than immigrants to be incarcerated for violent crimes. Thus, the National Council of La Raza argues that a double standard is being used in holding Hispanics accountable for their behavior.

Finally, the report suggests that public policy regarding the punishment of Hispanic offenders is counterproductive. In fact, the report argues that there are a variety of non-incarceration strategies that are more effective than prison and cost less, yet officials seem unwilling to take advantage of them. For instance, particularly for non-violent, low-level drug offenders, the most expensive option is incarceration, with an estimated cost of approximately $24,000 per inmate per year. One of the recommendations in the report is to take advantage of drug courts and residential and outpatient treatment programs that cost on average less than $5,000 per person per year. A RAND Corporation study found that for every dollar spent on drug and alcohol treatment, a state can save seven dollars in reduced crime costs. States cannot avoid spending on crime costs; either they spend a dollar or they spend seven dollars. Several states have found success with the treatment approach; for example, Texas saved nearly $30 million by sending offenders to a state drug treatment program rather than to jail. Using a related strategy, Texas drug court participants had significantly lower two-year recidivism rates for arrest and incarceration. However, as it relates to Hispanics, the preference remains focused on punishment through incarceration.[68]

The Police and Hispanics

While the subject of police treatment of minorities has been discussed in a variety of ways, such as the aforementioned arrest rates,[69] abusive practices,[70] and the use of deadly force,[71] most of the studies have not considered Hispanics as a minority group. One study compared perceptions of police abuse of minorities by Whites and Hispanics in a U.S.-Mexico border community. The findings showed that young, male Hispanics, and those living in the barrio, were more likely than their White counterparts to report having seen abusive practices. This group poses perhaps the greatest challenge to police authority (and potential risk of injury to officers) due to the age of those involved as well as their attitudes about the police in general.[72]

Similarly, the police in these communities were more likely to view individuals living in those areas with suspicion. Other research supports this finding. For instance, one report found that a higher proportion of Hispanics believed the police use excessive force.[73] Thus, it appears that like their African American counterparts, Hispanics are more likely to be perceived as threatening to the police, and this creates a climate of fear, suspicion, and hostility from both groups.

Why Hispanics Are Overrepresented

The inequities in the system stem from a variety of sources, including mandatory minimum sentences, the war on drugs, and the war on crime, that have resulted in high levels of incarceration for low-level drug offenses. Additionally, the perception that Hispanics are largely responsible for the drug problem has resulted in a more strict enforcement of immigration laws. Another factor reflecting the trends in the system for Hispanics is the practice of "overcriminalizing" certain behaviors—treating what would otherwise be minor offenses as major violations. The zero tolerance practice increases the likelihood of arrest and incarceration for offenders. Finally, the media portrayal of Hispanics can play a role in Hispanics' involvement with the criminal justice system. Distorted images, an inaccurate assessment of motives, and stereotypical images of Hispanics might lead some people to think Hispanics are more involved in criminal activity than is warranted.

Summary

This chapter explored the changing face of American society as an increasing number of Hispanics, both legal and illegal, become a fixture of the social landscape. Estimates by the U.S. Census Bureau suggest that Hispanics will constitute the largest minority group by 2050. The Latin and Hispanic influence on American culture can be seen in a host of ways. Perhaps the best example exists in Miami, which has been transformed by the influx of Cuban immigrants over the years. Moreover, the way that Hispanics and Latinos have been historically treated in this country has resulted in many subgroups remaining mired in a life of poverty and crime. As we have seen, part of the problem for Chicanos stems from the isolation they experience with regard to education as well as the limited access to quality health care in this country. For Puerto Ricans, the main issue is independence, but they will remain a commonwealth of the United States until the people on the island and on the mainland decide whether they want to be an independent country or remain a subsidiary of the United States.

Hispanics, as a general category, are overrepresented in virtually every area of criminal justice. Whether it is treatment by the police, sentences relating to drug crimes, or the increase in the number of Hispanic inmates in prison, clearly the trend with this group's experience in the criminal justice system looks remarkably like that of their African American counterparts.

 # You Make the Call

On the Border

Consider the following scenario. Debate the pros and cons of all options and decide what you would do.

You are a Hispanic American Border Patrol agent working along the border in Arizona. You were born in El Paso, Texas, and joined the Border Patrol (BP) five years ago. One night while on patrol, you spot a "coyote," or smuggler, attempting to bring illegal immigrants across the border. As you call for backup, you and your partner, a White, middle-class, male police officer with over 20 years' experience in the BP, attempt to intercept the group. While en route, you see that a group of Minutemen, a civilian group of volunteers dedicated to preserving the borders between the U.S. and Mexico, arrive. They begin abusing the immigrants as well as the coyote, kicking and punching the men in the group. As you arrive, your partner tells you to "hold back" for a minute to assess the situation. This is a relatively common strategy in such situations, but something about your partner's tone suggests that this is not the reason for delaying.

You finally intervene and separate the groups. One of the Minutemen has injured a number of immigrants, some of whom require medical attention. As you take his statement, you learn that he is also originally from El Paso; in fact, the two of you went to high school together. He begins to pressure you to let him go, saying he has been doing his civic duty and is trying to prevent more problems from occurring. Your partner agrees with him, and both he and the suspect begin to suggest that you let everyone go and forget the entire incident occurred. The immigrants and the coyote are happy to comply, your partner feels sufficient "justice" has been served, and you are the only one who thinks arrests should be made of the trafficker as well as of the Minutemen for their actions.

Your supervisor radios in that he is tied up with another call and asks you to handle the situation.

Questions

1. What do you do?
2. Are you allowing a crime to occur against an innocent victim simply because the person is already engaging in illegal activity?
3. Should the Minuteman volunteer be arrested for his assault on the immigrants?
4. Would your personal feelings as a Hispanic play into the decision? After all, you could have been one of those immigrants sneaking across the border.
5. What if one of the illegals was a family member? Would that change your mind about how to proceed?

Key Terms

barrios (p. 82)
Chicano (p. 81)
color gradient (p. 87)
Latino (p. 80)
Los Braceros (p. 82)
Marielitos (p. 85)

National Council of La Raza (p. 95)
Neorican (p. 87)
overstayers (p. 88)
repatriation (p. 81)
sanctuary laws (p. 90)

Discussion Questions

1. Why have Cubans been so successful in assimilating into American society yet retaining elements of their native culture?
2. How can the high rates of illegal immigration be curtailed? Is the solution simply to grant citizenship to those who have entered illegally? Why or why not?
3. Why is drug use so high among Hispanic adolescents?
4. Why do you think some Hispanic groups continue to struggle economically, politically, and socially in the United States? Is it the language barrier or some other set of factors?
5. What do you think is needed for Hispanic/Latino groups to assimilate and be accepted by mainstream society? Why does it appear that Americans are reluctant to treat them fairly?
6. Are the experiences of African Americans similar to or different from those of Hispanics in this country? Give several examples depending on your point of view.

Endnotes

1. Logan, J. 2001. *The New Latinos: Who They Are—Where They Are.* Albany, NY: Lewis Mumford Center for Comparative Urban and Regional Research.
2. Guzman, B. 2001. *The Hispanic Population.* Washington, DC: U.S. Census Bureau.
3. Schaefer, R. 2004. *Racial and Ethnic Groups*, 9th ed. Upper Saddle River, NJ: Prentice Hall.
4. Gonzalez, D. 1992. "What's the Problem with 'Hispanic'? Just Ask a 'Latino.'" *New York Times,* November 15, p. E6.
5. Schaefer 2004.
6. Doob, C. 1993. *Racism: An American Cauldron.* New York: HarperCollins.
7. Meier, M., and Rivera, F. 1972. *The Chicanos: A History of Mexican Americans.* New York: Hill and Wang.
8. Moquin, W., and Van Doren, C. (eds.). 1971. *A Documentary of the Mexican Americans.* Westport, CT: Praeger.
9. Guerin-Gonzalez, C. 1994. *Mexican Workers and American Dreams.* New Brunswick, NJ: Rutgers University Press.
10. Stoddard, E. R. 1973. *Mexican Americans.* New York: Random House.
11. Meier and Rivera 1972.
12. Guerin-Gonzalez 1994.
13. Schaefer 2004.
14. Ibid.
15. Moore, H. A., and Iadicola, P. 1981. "Resegregation Processes in Desegregated Schools and Status Relationships for Hispanic Students." *Aztlan* 12 (September): 39–58; Rodriquez, C. E. 1989. *Puerto Ricans: Born in the USA.* Boston: Unwin Hyman.
16. Schaefer 2004.
17. Mills, R. 2001. "Health Insurance Coverage: 2000." *Current Population Reports.* Washington, DC: U.S. Government Printing Office.
18. McNamara, R. P., and McNamara, K. M. 2001. *Hispanic Healthcare Needs in Greenville, South Carolina.* Center for Social Research, Furman University.
19. Abrahamson, M. 1996. *Urban Enclaves: Identity and Place in America.* New York: St. Martin's Press.
20. Perez, L. 2001. "Growing Up in Cuban Miami: Immigrants, the Enclave, and New Generations." In R. G. Rumbaut and A. Portes (eds.), *Ethnicities,* pp. 91–125. Berkeley: University of California Press.
21. Ibid.
22. Ibid.
23. Clary, M. 1997. "Black, Cuban Racial Chasm Splits Miami." *Los Angeles Times,* March 23, pp. A1, A20.
24. Miami-Dade Department of Cultural Affairs. 2005. *The City of Miami.*
25. Ibid.
26. Martin, L. 2006. "A Question of Tolerance." *Miami Herald,* July 14, pp. 11, 71.
27. Schaefer 2004.
28. Levitt, P. 2003. "I Feel I Am a Citizen of the World and of a Church Without Borders." In R. de la Garza, L. De Sipio, and H. Pachon (eds.), *Becoming Latinos, Latinos Becoming,* pp. 344–360. New York: Simon and Schuster.
29. Aran, K., Herman, A. Colón, R., and Goldberg, H. 1973. *Puerto Rican History and Culture.* New York: United Federation of Teachers; Christopulos, D. 1974. "Puerto Rico in the Twentieth Century: A Historical Survey." In J. Lopez and J. Petras (eds.), *Puerto Rico and Puerto Ricans: Studies in History and Society,* pp. 123–166. New York: Wiley; Schaefer 2004.
30. Navarro, M. 2000. "Puerto Rican Presence Wanes in New York." *New York Times,* February 28, pp. A1, A20.
31. Muschkin, C. G. 1993. "Consequences of Return Migrant Status for Employment in Puerto Rico." *International Migration Review* 27 (4): 13; Muschkin, C. G. 1998. "With a Vote for 'None of the Above' Puerto Ricans Endorse Island's Status Quo." *New York Times,* December 14, p. A12.

32. Navarro 2000.

33. Doob 1993.

34. Hemlock, D. A. 2006. "Puerto Rico Loses Its Edge." *New York Times,* September 21, pp. 17, 30.

35. Orlov, A., and Ueda, R. 1980. "Central and South Americans." In S. Thernstrom (ed.), *Encyclopedia of American Ethnic Groups,* pp. 210–217. Cambridge, MA: Belknap Press.

36. Pew Hispanic Center. 2005. *Unauthorized Migrants: Numbers and Characteristics.* Washington, DC.

37. Ibid.

38. Ibid.

39. Ibid.

40. Ibid.

41. MacDonald, H. 2004. *Crime & the Illegal Alien: The Fallout from Crippled Immigration Enforcement.* Washington, DC: Center for Immigration Studies.

42. Ibid.

43. Ibid.

44. Ibid.

45. Ibid.

46. Valdez, A. 1998. *A History of California's Hispanic Gangs.* National Alliance of Gang Investigators Association.

47. Ibid.

48. Ibid.

49. Ibid.

50. Ibid.

51. Ibid.

52. Department of Health and Human Services, Substance Abuse and Mental Health Services Administration, Office of Applied Studies. 2004. *Results of the 2001 National Household Survey on Drug Abuse. Vol. I: Summary of National Findings.* Washington, DC: U.S. Government Printing Office.

53. Anthony, J. C., Warner, L. A., and Kessler, R. C. 1994. "Comparative Epidemiology of Dependence on Tobacco, Alcohol, Controlled Substances, and Inhalants: Basic Findings from the National Comorbidity Survey." *Experimental and Clinical Psychopharmacology* 2 (3): 244–268.

54. Young, V. D., and Harrison, R. 2001. "Race/Ethnic Differences in the Sequences of Drugs Used by Women Among Mexican American Youth." *Adolescence* 33: 391–403.

55. Valdez 1998.

56. Warner, L. A., Canino, G., and Colón, H. M. 2001. "Prevalence and Correlates of Substance Use Disorders Among Older Adolescents in Puerto Rico and the United States: A Cross-Cultural Comparison." *Drug and Alcohol Dependence* 63: 229–243.

57. Sloboda, Z. 2002. "Changing Patterns of Drug Abuse in the United States: Connecting Findings from Macro- and Microepidemiologic Studies." *Substance Use and Misuse* 37: 1229–1251.

58. De La Rosa, M., Holleran, L. K., Rugh, D., and MacMaster, S. A. 2005. "Substance Abuse Among U.S. Latinos: A Review of the Literature." *Journal of Social Work Practice in the Addictions* 5 (1/2): 1–20.

59. Zule, W. A., Desmond, D. P., Medrano, M. A., and Hatch, J. P. 2001. "Acculturation and Risky Injection Practices Among Hispanic Injectors." *Evaluation and Program Planning* 24 (2): 207–214.

60. Brook, J. S., Whiteman, M., Balka, E. B., and Cohn, P. 1997. "Drug Use and Delinquency: Shared and Unshared Risk Factors in African American and Puerto Rican Adolescents." *Journal of Genetic Psychology* 158 (1): 25–39.

61. Kessler, R. C., Aguilar-Gaxiola, S., Berglund, P. A., Caravelo-Anduaga, J. J., Dewit, D. J., and Greenfield, S. F. 2001. "Patterns and Predictors of Treatment Seeking After Onset of a Substance Abuse Disorder." *Archives of General Psychiatry* 58: 1065–1071.

62. Krohn, M. D., Lizotte, A. J., Thornberry, T. P., Smith, C., and McDowell, D. 1996. "Reciprocal Causal Relationships Among Drug Use, Peers, and Beliefs: A Five Wave Panel Model." *Journal of Drug Issues* 26: 405–428.

63. Krohn, M. D., and Thornberry, T. P. 1993. "Network Theory: A Model of Understanding Drug Abuse Among African American and Hispanic Youth." In M. De La Rosa and J. L. Adrados (eds.), *Drug Abuse Among Minority Youth: Advances in Research and Methodology*, vol. 130, pp. 102–128. Rockville, MD: U.S. Government Printing Office.

64. Vega, W. A., Aguilar-Gaxiola, S., Andrade, L., Bijil, R., Borges, G., and Caravelo-Anduaga, J. J. 2003. "Prevalence and Age of Onset for Drug Use in Seven International Sites: Results from the International Consortium of Psychiatric Epidemiology." *Drug and Alcohol Dependence* 68: 285–297.

65. Gil, A. G., Wagner, E. F., and Vega, W. A. 2000. "Acculturation, Familism and Alcohol Use Among Latino Adolescent Males: Longitudinal Relations." *Journal of Community Psychology* 28: 443–458.

66. Kamasaki, C. 2002. "Testimony on Drug Sentencing and Its Effects on the Latino Community." United States Sentencing Commission, February 25.

67. National Council of La Raza. 2004. *Lost Opportunities: The Reality of Latinos in the U.S. Criminal Justice System.* Executive Summary, p. ix.

68. Ibid.

69. Sampson, R. J. 1986. "Effects of Socioeconomic Context on Official Reaction to Juvenile Delinquency." *American Sociological Review* 51: 876–885; Smith, D. A., and Visher, C. 1991. "Street Level Justice: Situational Determinants of Police Arrest Decisions." *Social Problems* 29: 167–177.

70. Reiss, A. J. 1971. *The Police and the Public.* New Haven, CT: Yale University Press; Westley, W. 1970. *Violence and the Police: A Sociological Study of Law, Custom, and Morality.* Cambridge, MA: MIT Press.

71. Fyfe, J. J. 1982. "Blind Justice: Police Shootings in Memphis." *Journal of Criminal Law and Criminology* 73: 707–722; Sorenson, J. R., Marquart, J. W., and Brock, E. 1993. "Factors Related to Killings of Felons by Police Officers: A Test of Community Violence and Conflict Hypotheses." *Justice Quarterly* 10: 417–440.

72. Holmes, M. D. 1998. "Perceptions of Abusive Police Practices in a U.S.-Mexico Border Community." *Social Science Journal* 35 (1): 107–118.

73. Maguire, K., Pastore, A. L., and Flanagan, T. J. (eds.). 1998, 2004. *Sourcebook of Criminal Justice Statistics.* Washington, DC: U.S. Government Printing Office.

Asian Americans and the Criminal Justice System

Chapter Objectives

After reading this chapter, you should be able to

❖ Understand the differences between Far East Asians, Southeast Asians, and Pacific Islanders, and why these differences are important.

❖ Understand the historical importance of immigration for Chinese, Japanese, Korean, Filipino, and other Asian groups.

❖ Understand the current position in American society for Japanese, Chinese, Koreans, Southeast Asians, and Pacific Islanders.

❖ Understand the representation of Asian Americans in the criminal justice system, as well as their involvement in different forms of criminal activity such as drugs, gangs, human smuggling, and transnational crime.

The U.S. Census uses the label Asian Americans to refer to people from the Far East (such as China, Japan, and Korea), Southeast Asia (such as Thailand, Cambodia, Vietnam, Laos, Malaysia, and Indonesia), and the Indian subcontinent (such as India, Pakistan, Burma, Sri Lanka, Bangladesh, and Nepal). The term Pacific Islander refers to people who have origins in Hawaii, Guam, or Samoa, or to other Pacific Islander groups.[1]

Asian Americans, like Hispanics/Latinos and Native Americans, represent a vast array of people who are diverse in their customs, language, and culture. However, as with most minority groups in this country, those differences tend to be simplified, and groups are often put into a generic and overly broad category. In fact, the term Asian American covers a wide breadth of people, who, in some cases, are nothing like each other. This collection of individuals from different backgrounds is one of the fastest-growing segments of the U.S. population. One of the topics this chapter will explore is the differences between these groups and the groups' impact on American culture. Like other groups, Asian Americans have made a concerted and successful effort at assimilating into mainstream America. Unfortunately, there are many Americans who have stereotypical perceptions of Asian Americans, and this has overshadowed the hard work and determination of many members of these populations.

In some ways, then, Asian Americans are different from other minority groups in the sense that they have made the transition, retained much of their native culture, and while some are involved in criminal activity, Asian Americans are generally underrepresented in crime statistics. This underrepresentation not only means they do not appear to represent a large portion of the data collected on crime; it also means that Asian Americans have not been studied in as much depth as other minority groups in their involvement in crime. Asian Americans have less of a presence than, say, African Americans, Whites, or Hispanics. This chapter will discuss Chinese Americans, Japanese Americans, Southeast Asians (specifically Vietnamese Americans), and Asian Indians. Because they represent the largest group of Pacific Islanders in this country, Hawaiians and Filipinos will also be discussed.

In 2005, according to the U.S. Census Bureau's American Community Survey, there were an estimated 12,868,845 people listed under the category of Asian/Pacific Islander, which constitutes about 4.4% of the U.S. population. Of this group, 397,030 were Pacific Islanders. The Census Bureau expects that the Asian American population will double by 2020 and reach about 38 million by 2050, which will constitute about 9% of the total U.S. population.[2] Some of this growth will be attributed to immigration by certain groups, while another source of this increase will be due to higher birth rates. Statistically, Asian Americans have higher birthrates than Whites, with 23% of married couples having three or more children, compared to only 13% of married White couples.[3]

The influx of Asians in the United States can be divided into two distinct periods. The first occurred roughly from the middle of the 1800s to the early years of the 20th century. The Chinese were the first Asian group to arrive, followed by the Japanese, with Koreans and Filipinos arriving in much smaller numbers afterward. The first wave of immigrants were mostly recruited for the construction of railroads and work in the agricultural industry.

The second wave of immigration is different from the first in that most of the new immigrants have come from a higher socioeconomic status. Changes in immigration laws prevented many Asians from entering this country until after 1965.[4] This second group of immigrants has also been more diverse in national origin, coming from all areas of Asian society.[5]

✖ Issues of Concern for Asian Americans

While there are a number of promising trends for some Asian Americans, for others the transition to the United States has resulted in difficult circumstances. A number of issues have arisen for all Asian Americans, particularly those who have achieved some level of societal success. These issues include the model minority myth, lower family incomes, the glass ceiling in the labor market, hate crimes, and racial profiling.

Model Minority Myth

According to the **model minority myth,** Asian Americans constitute an ideal minority because they have endured political, economic, and social obstacles. Some experts even argue that Asian Americans are no longer considered a marginal minority.[6] However, to effectively determine whether the apparent success can be extended across all Asian American groups, we must examine the data.

Some experts argue that Asian Americans are no longer considered a marginal minority.

In terms of education, it appears at first glance that Asian Americans as a group have exceeded Whites in terms of academic achievement. According to the 2000 U.S. Census, 44% of Asian Americans 25 years and older held bachelor's degrees, compared to 28% of the White population. In 2005 this figure was 49% for Asians compared to 30% for Whites, demonstrating an outpacing of Whites when it comes to secondary education.[7]

Although the term "model minority" might seem to be complimentary, many Asian Americans see it as condescending and as a damaging stereotype. Some Asian Americans have pointed out that this positive image tends to minimize or ignore some of the social and economic problems that continue to prevent many Asian Americans from succeeding. This is particularly true of Southeast Asian refugees, who remain poor, uneducated, and relatively unsuccessful.[8] Evidence of the model minority myth is also seen in statistics which show that the high school dropout rate for Asian Americans is actually increasing.[9] Additionally, approximately 9% of Asian American families live below the federal poverty line (in 2007, $21,027 for a family of four), compared to 7.5% of White families. Clearly, the problems of poverty hit other minority groups harder than Asian Americans, but the poverty rate for Asian Americans suggests that this group has its share of problems as well as success stories. Thus, in many ways, when President Ronald Reagan called Asian Americans the model minority, he set in motion a series of expectations that ignored the wide diversity of educational talent among this segment of the population.

DOES EDUCATION PAY OFF FOR ALL ASIAN AMERICANS?

While most Americans agree that education is the path out of poverty and is the best way for minorities to achieve success, some evidence exists that problems occur even when minority groups embrace education. As recently as 2001, Asian Americans have been identified as an ethnic minority group that has successfully overcome racism and achieved the American dream, primarily through education. It's true that 42% of all Asian American adults have at least a college degree, the highest of all the major racial/ethnic groups. It's also common for Asian American students to have the highest test scores and/or GPAs within any given high school or college cohort. However, for every Chinese American or South Asian in the United States who has a college degree, the same number of Southeast Asians are still struggling to adapt to their lives in this country. For example, Vietnamese Americans have a college degree attainment rate of 16%, only about one-quarter the rate for other Asian American ethnic groups. Further, Laotians, Cambodians, and Khmer have rates around 5%. Many Southeast Asians have the highest high school dropout rates in the country. Those Asian Americans who are struggling tend to be immigrants who have limited English proficiency. Currently about 60% of all Asian Americans are immigrants. Most are relatively fluent in English but a large portion are not. Therefore, similar to other immigrant minority groups, Asian Americans have a need for bilingual education that is culturally sensitive to their immigration experiences and family situations.

Even for Asian Americans who make it to college, there have been challenges. Since the 1980s, many more Asian Americans have been applying to college than in earlier years. Soon, it became common for 10%, 15%, or more of a given university's student population to be of Asian ancestry at a time when Asians were only about 3% of the general population. Many universities responded by rejecting Asian students once their Asian student population reached 10–15% of the student body. Soon, Asian Americans were accusing universities such as UC Berkeley, UCLA, Stanford, Harvard, Princeton, and Brown of imposing a quota, or upper limit, on their admission numbers. After several protests and investigations, these universities admitted that there were problems with these admission procedures but never admitted any deliberate wrongdoing. Thus, Asian Americans may appear to be succeeding in assimilating into American society, but the reality is that many still face a host of problems.

Lower Family Incomes

Another sign of the apparent success of Asian Americans is the figure concerning median family incomes. Some experts contend that Asian American family incomes approach those of Whites because of greater academic achievements. However, the evidence shows that for each additional year of education, Asian Americans' average earnings are significantly less than average earnings for Whites ($2,300 compared to $3,000). Thus, while Asian Americans as a group have significantly more formal schooling, they actually have lower median family incomes.[10] Additionally, while the median family income of Asian Americans might seem significant to many outsiders, the total number of family members who work should be factored into the analysis because median family income considers only total family income, not the number of people working within that family. It is one thing if a family consists of a single parent earning most of the money, such as a corporate executive, which should suggest a certain socioeconomic position for that family. However, in many Asian American families, the total family income requires several people, all working full-time, to earn that same amount. This suggests a different economic picture for that family.

The Glass Ceiling

There is also the issue of the "glass ceiling" in business. The **glass ceiling** is understood as a phenomenon whereby certain groups can achieve only a certain level of upward mobility. In other words, they can see the next level of success in their careers, but cannot reach that level due to their minority status. While it appears promising that Asian Americans work in the same professions as Whites, Asian immigrants are found disproportionately in the lower-paying service occupations. Human resource managers and recruiters offer their observation that many entry-level candidates are of Korean, Chinese, and Japanese heritage, but, even in managerial positions, few Asian Americans ever reach the top of the corporate ladder. One study found that less than 2% of corporate officers for *Fortune 500* companies were Asian Americans.[11] There are a few notable exceptions, such as Andrea Jung, the chief executive officer of Avon cosmetics, but for the most part, there is a noticeable absence of Asians at this level of the labor market.

In an effort to explain this trend, Jane Hyun, in her book *Breaking the Bamboo Ceiling: Career Strategies for Asians* (2005), offers her insight into why so few Asian Americans obtain top management positions. She says that part of the reason is cultural. Many Asian American employees are taught to respect authority.

Human resource managers and recruiters suggest that many entry-level candidates are of Korean, Chinese, and Japanese heritage.

Consequently, they remain quiet in meetings, and this is interpreted by their White colleagues as aloofness, arrogance, or inattention, when it is simply the Asian habit of respecting authority.[12] Thus, while Asian Americans have done well in small businesses, because of the long hours the income from these businesses may be below prevailing wages. Examples include Chinese restaurants, Korean American convenience stores, and Asian Indian–owned motels and gasoline stations.[13] In sum, while it might appear that Asian Americans are doing well, this is an oversimplification of the diversity of the group and its experiences. Further, this simplification also changes the public's perceptions of the need to help many Asian Americans in terms of social programs.[14]

Hate Crimes and Racial Profiling

The perception that Asian Americans are accepted in the United States is not completely congruent with their experiences here. For instance, reports by the National Asian Pacific American Legal Consortium demonstrate an anti-Asian sentiment in this country. Moreover, the hostility against Asian Americans is not limited to violent episodes or individual hate crimes. Part of the problem stems from the apparent success of many Asian Americans in education, business, and professions, which creates a backlash of resentment from Whites. Another reason for Whites' resentment of Asian Americans has been due to the economic growth of some Asian countries, such as Japan in the early 1990s. So strong was the resentment that ad campaigns were launched that encouraged people to buy "American," meaning American-made products, in order to save American jobs.

A 1995 study indicated a 35% increase in anti-Asian hate crimes in the United States from the previous year. Like many crimes, these figures must be viewed with caution since some immigrants might be reluctant to report crimes for a variety of reasons, including language problems, distrust of the police, and the embarrassment of becoming a victim of crime.[15]

More recently, the trend of hate crimes against Asian Americans can be seen in official statistics. According to the *Uniform Crime Reports* in 2005, approximately 56% of the hate crimes in this country are motivated by racial bias. In 2005 law enforcement agencies reported 8,380 hate crimes, of which about 5% were due to an anti–Asian/Pacific Islander bias. Of these, 5,190, or 62%, were crimes against persons. Most of these included acts of intimidation or assault, although about 20% were considered aggravated assault. Most of the time, hate crimes are person-specific, meaning the offender attacks an individual or the individual's property. However, there are occasions when organizations are attacked. In terms of offenders, of the 8,380 total hate crimes committed in 2005, 43% of the offenders were White, while only 11% were African American. Asian offenders comprised less than one-half of one percent of hate crime offenders, the lowest of any group.[16]

Many Asian Americans also report evidence of a new form of racial profiling. In one survey just after the 1999 scandal in the Los Alamos National Laboratory, in which a Chinese American nuclear physicist was falsely accused of being a spy for China, a survey by the Department of Energy found that almost half of the people surveyed (46%) said they were worried about Chinese Americans passing secrets to China.[17] This scandal sounded strikingly familiar to the attitudes of many Americans during World War II concerning the "threat" of Japanese Americans to our economic interests.

Thus, while it may appear that Asian Americans have succeeded in their attempts to assimilate into mainstream American society, there are noticeable differences between the groups as well as a tendency to overgeneralize the level of success they have achieved. Perhaps the place to begin is to examine a selection of these groups that make up Asian Americans and explore their history as well as their current situations.

⚔ Far East Asians

Chinese Americans

Early immigration from China into the United States was initiated largely because of economic and political unrest in China coupled with discovery of gold in California in the 1840s. Added to this was the construction of the transcontinental railroads, which drew many Chinese immigrants to the U.S.[18] At the time, Chinese immigrants were welcome because they provided a sizable group of hardworking employees. In a very short time, however, the influx of Chinese workers created a backlash of anti-Chinese sentiment. Based partly on the perceived threat by White workers, the hostility toward Chinese immigrants led to the passage of the **Chinese Exclusion Act** by Congress in 1882. This act outlawed Chinese immigration for ten years and also denied naturalization rights to immigrants already in the United States. There was little debate in Congress, in part because of the general belief in the threat the Chinese posed to American workers.[19]

In 1892 Congress extended the Exclusion Act for another ten years and added that Chinese laborers had to obtain certificates of residence within a year or face deportation. The ban against the Chinese was made permanent in 1907 and marked a significant moment in U.S. history, when, for the first time, a specific group was formally prohibited from entering the country.[20]

When the Exclusion Act was initially passed in 1882, there were approximately 125,000 Chinese immigrants in the United States. By 1910 the number of immigrants had dropped to about 70,000 and did not really change until after 1965. Part of the reason for this had to do with the fact that most of the people coming into this country at that time were males. By one estimate, before 1882, more than 100,000 men but fewer than 9,000 women had emigrated to the U.S. from China.[21] Because of this imbalance between the sexes, it was difficult for Chinese immigrants to create ethnic communities. As a result of this sense of isolation, both from feeling discriminated against by the larger society and from feeling disconnected ethnically, many were forced to live in urban ghettos or Chinatowns. In fact, many immigrants did not leave Chinatowns in great numbers until after the end of World War II.[22]

After the Exclusion Act was repealed in 1943, Chinese nationals were gradually permitted to enter the United States, first as spouses of servicemen and

Chinatowns have provided many economic, cultural, and social opportunities for Chinese Americans.

later as college students, who were allowed to complete their education. Immigration continued slowly until the 1965 Immigration Act was passed, allowing more Chinese citizens to emigrate to the U.S. The influx has recently become fairly robust, with numbers approaching 100,000 annually. In fact, in the 1990s the number of Chinese immigrants entering the U.S. actually exceeded the total number that were here in 1980.[23]

At least on the surface, Chinese Americans appear to have lower unemployment rates than other groups and are represented in many professional occupations. However, most of the jobs held by Chinese Americans are found in Chinatowns in large urban areas. The reason for this is that Chinese Americans were prohibited for generations from working anywhere else. While Whites did not object to Chinese immigrants in domestic occupations, largely because White men were unwilling to participate in such menial jobs, for the most part, Chinese Americans had few opportunities to work outside of the Chinatowns.

Japanese Americans

The Japanese American experience in the United States is a fascinating case of how minority groups appear to be a threat to the mainstream way of life even when they have made efforts to assimilate. While it appears that the "threat" of minority groups often drives much of our fears about allowing them into this country, what is more fascinating is the source of those fears and how they dictate our perception of certain groups. As we will see, the **yellow peril,** largely based on Whites' fear of Asians, actually resulted in strict immigration laws and the imprisonment of Japanese American citizens.

The First Wave of Anti-Japanese Resentment

The Japanese who emigrated to the United States in the 1890s took jobs as laborers at low wages with poor working conditions. Their industriousness in these situations made them popular with employers but unpopular with unions and other employees. The Japanese had the misfortune of arriving just as bigotry toward the Chinese had been formalized in the Chinese Exclusion Act of 1882. While this legislation limited opportunities for Chinese workers, Japanese workers, at least initially, replaced the dwindling number of Chinese laborers in some industries, especially agriculture. Over time, however, once the "threat" and presence of Chinese workers disappeared, it was replaced with an anti-Japanese sentiment.

In 1913 California enacted the **Alien Land Act,** which prohibited anyone who was ineligible for citizenship to own land and limited leases to three years. This drove many first-generation Japanese into cities. However, government and union restrictions prevented Asian immigrants from taking jobs. As a result, many Japanese immigrants embarked upon self-employment to earn a living, opening more grocery stores and other types of small businesses than any other immigrant group. The Japanese differed in many respects from the Chinese in terms of how they were treated. For instance, Japanese Americans had the benefit of witnessing what happened to the Chinese and were able to understand what changes had to occur for their treatment to be different from that of the Chinese.

Second, Japanese Americans were much more vocal than Chinese Americans about the unfair treatment they received. First- and second-generation Japanese Americans often organized demonstrations, held boycotts, and enlisted the support of sympathetic Whites. Finally, compared to China, Japan took a more active interest in what was happening to its citizens in the United States. The knowledge of how Japan felt about the treatment of their immigrants in this country, coupled with the fear of retaliation for the way Japanese Americans had been treated, led many Americans to be concerned about Japanese Americans' loyalty once Japan attacked Pearl Harbor on December 7, 1941.

The Second Wave: Internment

Almost immediately after the attack on Pearl Harbor, fear and concern about the war led people to feel threatened by Japanese Americans living on the West Coast. Many feared that Japanese Americans would fight on behalf of Japan, resulting in a successful invasion of the United States. Rumors mixed with racist bigotry rather than facts explain the events that followed. Japanese Americans in Hawaii were alleged to have cooperated in the attack by using signaling devices to assist pilots in locating their targets. Newspapers covered in detail FBI arrests of Japanese Americans allegedly assisting the attackers. They were accused of poisoning drinking water, cutting sugarcane fields to form arrows directing enemy pilots to targets, and blocking traffic along highways to the harbor. None of these charges were substantiated despite thorough investigations.[24]

The Executive Order signed by President Roosevelt in 1942 authorized the removal of anyone considered a threat to national security in defined strategic military areas. All people on the West Coast of at least one-eighth Japanese ancestry were taken to assembly centers for transfer to **internment camps,** places for refugees to be held until their release by the government was granted. This order covered

Many of those sent to internment camps were American citizens, who lost ownership of business and property.

90% of the 126,000 Japanese Americans on the mainland. Of those evacuated, two-thirds were American citizens and three-quarters were under the age of 25. Ultimately, 120,000 people were interned in the camps: 113,000 from the mainland, 1,100 evacuated from Hawaii, about 200 voluntary residents (Caucasian spouses), and 5,900 who were born in the camps.[25]

What is interesting is that the evacuation order did not arise from any court action. No trials took place, no indictments were issued. Merely having a Japanese great-grandparent was enough to mark an individual for involuntary confinement. Perhaps even more fascinating was the fact that many Japanese Americans did not fight the order. The governing body for Japanese Americans and immigrant groups, the Japanese American Citizens League, believed that if any of those interned tried to flee or defied the order, it would likely confirm that Japanese could not be trusted.

Those who were to be interned were instructed to carry only personal items. No provision was made for shipping their household goods. The federal government took a few steps to safeguard the belongings internees left behind, but the evacuees assumed all risks and agreed to turn over their property to the government for an indeterminate length of time. Internment caused merchants, farmers, and business owners to sell their property at any price they could get. Precise figures of the loss in dollars are difficult to obtain, but the Federal Reserve Bank estimated it to be approximately $400 million by 1941 standards. Today that amount would easily be billions of dollars.[26]

A few Japanese Americans resisted the evacuation and took legal action. Several cases arising out of the evacuation and detention reached the U.S. Supreme Court during the war. The Court upheld lower court decisions on Japanese Americans without even raising the issue of the constitutionality of the internment. Finally, in *Mitsuye Endo v. the U.S.* (1944), the Supreme Court ruled that the defendant, and presumably all evacuees, must be granted their freedom. Two weeks later, Japanese Americans were allowed to return to their homes for the first time in three years.[27]

As the *Endo* case demonstrates, our attitudes about the appropriateness of internment remained steadfastly strong. No legal action granting compensation to the evacuees for property lost was taken until 1948, with the Japanese Americans Evacuation Claims Act. Even when Americans recognized the injustice, little was done to remedy the problem. Two years after the Evacuation Claims Act's passage, only 73 people had received any money. Eventually there were approximately 23,000 claims and the government paid $38 million, less than 10% of the Federal Reserve Bank's estimate of the financial loss Japanese American internees had suffered. All claims were settled with no interest or consideration of the increase in land values. Moreover, the settlements were delayed so that by 1967, when the final payments were made, many of the claimants had died.[28]

In the late 1970s, President Carter created the Commission on Wartime Relocation and Internment of Civilians. The final Commission recommendation in 1983 was for a formal apology from the government and a tax-free payment of $20,000 to each of the approximately 66,000 surviving internees. Congress began hearings in 1986 on the bill, and President Reagan signed the Civil Liberties Act in 1988, which authorized the payments.[29] Still the payments were slow in coming, and the internees were dying at a rate of 200 per month. In 1990 the first checks were finally issued, accompanied by President George H. W. Bush's letter of apology.[30]

Korean Americans

In the early part of the 20th century, a few thousand Koreans were recruited to work on the sugarcane plantations in Hawaii. They were needed, in fact, to replace the Chinese workers who had been prohibited from remaining in the United States by the 1882 Chinese Exclusion Act. Still, the number of Korean immigrants remained small until after the Korean War in the early 1950s, when many came either as refugees or as spouses of American servicemen returning home. However, the growth of the Korean American population exploded in the 1970s, increasing from 70,000 to 355,000 between 1970 and 1980. According to the 2000 U.S. Census, Korean Americans numbered over one million.[31] However, in the late 1990s many Korean Americans chose to return to Korea. Part of the reason had to do with the political and economic growth in Korea, while for others who had difficulty adapting to American culture, the chance to feel "at home" was very appealing. For still others, operating a small business in the United States was considered too risky as tensions between Koreans and African Americans rose during the Los Angeles riots in 1992.[32]

In L.A.'s poor areas, the only shops in which to buy groceries or liquor or gasoline were owned by Korean immigrants. They had largely replaced the White-owned businesses that closed when scores of White business owners left the ghetto area after the 1965 Watts riots. African Americans were well aware of the dominant role Korean

The tension between African Americans and Korean Americans reached a boiling point during the L.A. riots.

Americans played in their local retail market. Many African Americans expressed resentment that had been previously fueled by the 1991 shooting of a 15-year-old Black girl by a Korean grocer. The resentment grew when the grocer, convicted of manslaughter, had her prison sentence waived by a judge in favor of five years probation.[33]

During the 1992 L.A. riots, 1,000 Korean businesses valued at $300 million were destroyed. In a post-riot survey of African Americans who were arrested, 80% felt that Korean Americans were disrespectful, compared to 56% who felt similarly about Whites. Korean Americans' desire to succeed led them to the inner city, where they did not face competition from Whites, but it also meant that they had to deal on a daily basis with the frustration of African Americans.[34]

⚔ Southeast Asian Americans

The people of Southeast Asia, the Vietnamese, Cambodians, and Laotians, were once citizens of the former French Indochinese Union. Southeast Asian is only a term of convenience, especially since the people of these areas are ethnically and linguistically different. Numbering more than 2 million in 2000, Vietnamese Americans are the largest group with 1.2 million, which is approximately 11% of the total Asian American population.

The catalyst to understanding this group of people for many Americans has been the Vietnam War. Historically, Southeast Asia consisted of many different tribes and countries such as Vietnamese, Hmong tribes, Cambodians, and ethnic Khmer. These and many other tribal groups came together in the early 1860s under the label "Indochina" as the French colonized the region. Because of the dissatisfaction with the political, cultural, economic, and social dominance by the French, civil wars broke out and communist influence began to take hold in the mid-1950s. In 1954 the United States sent 16,000 military advisors and support personnel in an effort to prevent communism from taking over South Vietnam. By 1962, military involvement had escalated in the form of air strikes and the use of Special Forces units to infiltrate the area. By 1964, most Americans believed that the U.S. had an obligation to free the people of Vietnam from communism.[35]

By 1965, over 550,000 U.S. troops had been sent to Southeast Asia. At about the same time, the communist government in Laos attempted to eliminate any support for U.S. efforts in that country. The civil unrest that followed led to over three million Cambodians being killed by the Khmer Rouge government between 1975 and 1979. The U.S. withdrew from Southeast Asia in 1975 leaving 58,000 American soldiers dead and thousands more wounded. While the U.S. withdrawal left the region under communist control, thousands of refugees were brought into this country.[36]

The problems for Vietnamese Americans, like those for all immigrant groups, were essentially based on the perceived threat they represented to Americans. This is true even though the initial U.S. involvement in the Vietnam War was intended to protect the South Vietnamese from the spread of communism. When the war ended and the idea of many refugees coming to America became a reality, public opinion about Vietnamese presence was negative and hostile. Some people thought that allowing more immigrants from different cultures would cause the U.S. to lose its identity as a country. This same attitude was found in the mid-1970s with regard to Southeast Asians. Some experts believed that the news media created an unflattering image of the South Vietnamese, which led Americans to believe the Vietnamese were not worth saving.[37]

Approximately one million refugees fled Vietnam after the war in an attempt to escape religious persecution. In a scene similar to what was experienced in the 1980s and 1990s in Cuba, many of the people attempting to leave their native country took to the ocean in overcrowded vessels, hoping that some ship would pick them up and offer sanctuary. Hundreds of thousands were placed in other nations or remained in overcrowded refugee camps administered by the United Nations.[38] In fact, similar to Cuban immigration, there were four distinct waves of immigration to the U.S. from Vietnam.

The first wave, which occurred between 1975 and 1977, resulted in over 130,000 refugees, the vast majority of whom were Vietnamese. For the most part, these were people from upper- and middle-class backgrounds. Educated and professional, this group had perhaps the easiest time making the adjustment to life in a new country. The second wave occurred between 1978 and 1979, bringing nearly 60,000 Vietnamese, Chinese from Vietnam, Cambodians, and Hmong to the United States. Because this group of immigrants was more diversified in terms of their social class and educational backgrounds, they had considerable difficulty transitioning to America.

The third wave, which occurred between 1980 and 1981, had perhaps the greatest impact on American society. This group of immigrants consisted of peasants, farmers, and others who had no formal education or experience with Western culture.[39] Included in this wave of immigrants were nearly 200,000 Hmong tribal members. This is a group that lived in the highlands of Laos, Vietnam, and Cambodia and was intimately involved in the U.S. efforts in Laos. In fact, some estimates indicate that the Hmong experienced nearly a 50% casualty rate during the war. Because they tend to migrate and had no written language until the 1950s, the Hmong experienced a significant problem in adjusting to American culture.[40]

The fourth wave of immigration is associated with people who lived in refugee camps in Thailand and other relocation centers. Between 1987 and 1993, the number of refugees admitted from Vietnam was 173,116; from Laos (including the Hmong), 75,554; and approximately 9,000 from Cambodia.[41] Fortunately, Hmong children in these camps were exposed to English and American culture at an early age, which made the transition to America easier.

Despite the fact that it has been over 30 years since the end of the Vietnam War, Americans still seem to have mixed feelings about Southeast Asians. Surveys in the late 1980s and early 1990s show that although few Americans regarded this group as undesirable, about 50% still worried that they would be a drain on the U.S. economy. Even though most Southeast Asian children spoke no English upon arrival here, they have done extremely well in school. Many families place a heavy emphasis on education for their children. It remains to be seen whether or not this focus on education will translate into greater job opportunities for Southeast Asian children. What is known is that many adult immigrants have experienced **downward social mobility,** which means that the jobs Southeast Asian immigrants take are often occupationally below what they were doing in their native country. However, U.S. Census Bureau data suggest that refugees from Vietnam have increased their family incomes when compared to what their incomes were back home. Part of the reason for this, however, may be due to working longer hours or having more members of the family working full-time than when they were in Vietnam.[42]

⚔ Pacific Islander Americans

Hawaiians

Historically, Hawaiians were very tolerant of missionaries and plantation operators. Hawaiians were united under a monarchy and respected by European immigrants, and this developed into a spirit of goodwill. In the late 1800s, a revolution occurred and the monarchy was overthrown. The United States got involved and, five years later, Hawaii was annexed as a U.S. territory. During that time, citizenship had a mixed impact. Laws were passed that granted civil rights to all those born on the islands, but the anti-Asian laws still applied, which excluded the Chinese and Japanese from voting or running for office.

Hawaii has become a strategic military outpost although that role has had only a limited effect on race relations. Even the attack on Pearl Harbor had relatively little influence on Japanese Americans in Hawaii. While most demographers contend that people marry others with similar backgrounds, sometimes known as endogamy, a high incidence of marrying outside one's group, called exogamy, can be taken as an indicator of acceptance of other groups. In Hawaii, there is a general acceptance of intermarriage, or exogamy. The rate of intermarriage varies by group, but it is about 45% of all marriages in Hawaii, 62% of which include at least one Chinese American spouse.[43]

Hawaii has its share of social problems. The pineapple and sugarcane plantation legacy persists, and native Hawaiians tend to struggle financially, often working land they do not own. The economy is dominated by Japanese Americans. Chinese Americans have had some success in business in Hawaii, but almost all the top positions are filled by Whites. The conclusion from these trends suggests that, in an absolute sense, Hawaii is not a racial paradise. The future of race relations in Hawaii is uncertain, but relative to the mainland and much of the world, its race relations more closely resemble harmony than bigotry.[44]

Filipinos

Few people think of Filipinos when they consider Asian Americans. Yet this group is one of the largest segments of the Asian American population. During the past 30 years, only Mexicans have outnumbered Filipinos as immigrants to the United States.[45] After the Spanish-American War the U.S. took possession of the Philippines. Following the country's independence in 1946, political ties with the U.S. remained close. As evidence, English is one of the country's major languages and is spoken by most educated Filipinos. Moreover, like the early Koreans, Filipinos were brought to Hawaii as agricultural workers to replace the excluded Chinese, and many emigrated to the mainland in the 1920s.

Interestingly, because the Philippines was a U.S. territory at the time, immigrants were considered American nationals, and as such, they were not subject to the same kind of restrictions and resentment as other Asian groups.[46] Added to the gentler attitude toward Filipinos was the fact that the Philippines became an important ally in the Pacific war against Japan. Consequently, Americans were much more tolerant of immigrants from this country than from perhaps any other country. The long history and cultural compatibility, not to mention the U.S. military presence in the Philippines over the last 40 years, has resulted in a great deal of overlap between the two cultures.[47]

Surprisingly, U.S.-born Filipinos often have less formal schooling and lower job status than recent immigrants from the Philippines. They tend to come from poorer families and have been relegated to unskilled work, including migrant farming. Their poor economic background has resulted in their owning fewer small businesses than Korean Americans or other Asian groups.[48]

✕ Indian Subcontinent

Asian Indians

Like the Asian American category as a whole, people classified as **Asian Indian** represent a wide range of populations. India itself is a diverse nation with dozens of languages and ethnic enclaves. While most observers of India might note the religious divisions of Hindus, Muslims, and Sikhs, there are many other distinctions as well. The majority of Asian Indian immigrants have come from India, but sizable numbers come from Pakistan, Bangladesh, and Sri Lanka as well as other countries, such as Trinidad, Tobago, and Guyana.[49]

As with other Asian groups, changes in immigration policies in the 1960s allowed many Asian Indians to enter the United States legally. Those who have come in recent times have been highly educated and from professional classes in their native countries. In fact, many Asian Indian immigrants have been students at American universities who find employment in the U.S. after graduation. This is particularly true in the computer industry.[50]

Like some other immigrant groups, Asian Indians have witnessed two types of experiences once arriving in this country. On one hand, Asian Indians have played a significant role as entrepreneurs in the small business sector. For instance, by one estimate, more than half of all motels in the United States are owned by Asian Indians.[51] On the other hand, there is a segment of this population that has not fared as well, being relegated to lower-paying jobs such as restaurant workers, taxi drivers, and truck drivers. As one study concluded, Asian Indians are as likely to be cab drivers or managers of convenience stores as they are to be physicians or college professors. Many of the jobs in the service sector place Asian Indians at higher risk to be victims of crime.[52]

✖ Asian Americans and the Criminal Justice System

Crime Statistics

According to the *Uniform Crime Reports* for 2005, Asian Americans represented 105,996 of the 10,189,691 arrests made by the police. This represents 1% of all arrests, even less than Native Americans, who represent 1.3% of all arrests for that year. The percentage of arrests of Asian American or Pacific Islander juveniles was similar to that for all arrests, approximately 1.3% of all arrests for those 18 years and under. This low representation in crime statistics has been a consistent trend for many years. Further, while Asian Americans represent about 4% of the total population in this country, they represent only about 1% of those arrested.[53] Unlike African Americans, Hispanics/Latinos, or even Native Americans, Asian Americans are underrepresented in the crime statistics. This trend has been consistent since 1999 (see Table 5.1).

TABLE 5.1

Arrest Trend for Asian Americans

Year	Total Arrests	Arrests	Percentage
2005	10,189,691	105,996	1.0%
2004	9,940,671	106,846	1.1
2003	9,529,469	110,168	1.2
2002	9,797,385	109,727	1.1
2001	9,306,587	103,750	1.1
2000	9,068,977	104,411	1.2
1999	9,100,050	102,541	1.1

Since 1990 the literature on crime and offenders has changed its focus from the commonly known minority groups, such as African Americans and Hispanics, to less noticed minorities, such as Native Americans and Asian Americans. While there is still a great deal less information, scholars and experts have begun examining the criminal behavior patterns among Asian Americans,[54] and some of the evidence from these studies shows that certain Asian groups are more likely to be involved in criminal activity than others.

One study examined the odds of arrest for various offenses of seven different Asian groups. The findings revealed that Southeast Asian immigrants were more likely to engage in criminal activity than Whites. Vietnamese immigrants were overrepresented in every arrest category, while Cambodians, Laotians, and Vietnamese were more likely to be arrested for property crimes such as larceny and auto theft.[55]

A few trends also appear when examining the data on Asian Americans as victims of crime. However, one of the problems in assessing the victimization rates among Asian Americans is that the indicator used, primarily the National Crime Victimization Survey (NCVS), collapses all the categories of Asian Americans into one group. As we have seen, there is a great deal of difference in the types of groups under this heading, and aggregating the cases obscures their differences and minimizes the overall impact of any single group. In fact, the NCVS collapses all racial groups into three categories: White, Black, and Other. It also includes a separate category comparing Hispanics to non-Hispanics. Because of the aggregation of the data, any real analysis of Asian Americans is virtually impossible, but the data do suggest that Asians are not victimized to the same extent as other groups.

Thus, while Asian Americans as a group are underrepresented in crime statistics, both as offenders and as victims, some attention has been given to the types and extent of criminal activity by some Asian American groups.

Asian Gangs

Growing concern about Asian crime stems from several factors, such as the legal and illegal immigration of Asians into the United States over the past 20 years. This has provided new opportunities for immigrants to engage in criminal activities, particularly through being involved with youth gangs.[56] Some research suggests that younger Chinese Americans, unlike their elders, are not content to be grateful for what they have been given in exchange for their labor but expect the full rights and privileges of citizenship. More than their parents, they refuse to tolerate continued discrimination and unemployment.[57] Upward mobility is not in the future of many of these alienated and angry youth who, with the prospect of low-wage work in restaurants and laundries, turn to gangs to achieve some level of success.

Chinese Gangs

In perhaps one of the most thorough examinations on the subject, Ko-Lin Chin, a professor at Rutgers University in New Jersey and an expert on Chinese culture, describes what is known about Chinese gangs.[58] While there is some research to contradict Chin's findings, Chin argues that Chinese gangs are closely associated with, and are controlled by, powerful community organizations. In other words, they are an integral part of community life. These gangs are also influenced, to a great extent, by Chinese secret societies and the norms and values of the Triad subculture.[59] The Triad subculture is very similar in many ways to the Italian mafia, which stresses a code of honor in dealing with each member and affiliation to a larger, secret society.

The primary activity of Chinese gangs is making money. Members invest a considerable amount of money in legitimate businesses and spend a lot of time negotiating business deals. Chinese gangs develop in communities in which adult criminals serve as role models and mentors for gang members. Although involved in drug trafficking, gang members rarely use drugs. In fact, if a member begins using drugs, he is expelled from the gang. Thus, unlike Black and Hispanic gangs, the establishment of Chinese gangs is not based on illicit drug use or fads.

Additionally, Chin found that Chinese gangs do not experience the harsh living conditions and poverty that other types of gangs do. Rather, Chinese gangs grow and become economically prosperous by maintaining ties with the economic and political structure of their communities. In other words, there is a cultural component to the success of Chinese gangs: They have a certain legitimacy within the community based on the historical experience of the Triad subculture.[60]

More recently, a study in New York City found that, like Chin's findings, Chinese gangs are characterized by a highly structured and disciplined manner. However, unlike the conclusions drawn by Chin, while Chinese gangs maintain close ties to adult organizations, they are not controlled by them. Adult criminals also provide opportunities for gang members to advance within the larger criminal organization and to become apprentices of crime.[61]

Chinese gangs also typically engage in nonviolent forms of extortion of local merchants. The pervasiveness of extortion comes from a cultural understanding that extortion is a part of regular business activity. When gang violence is evident, it usually involves inter-gang rivalries. Popular wisdom about gang wars stemming from drug trafficking or gangs being used to leverage political control is not supported by empirical research. Also popular but unsupported by the research is the organized nature of human trafficking. While the activity is fairly common, it is not controlled by gangs. Rather, human smuggling is often a loosely organized, entrepreneurial activity.[62]

Vietnamese Gangs

While still part of an overall Asian American category, Vietnamese youth gangs, especially in southern California, are quite different in their characteristics from Chinese gangs. This group of immigrants, having experienced racism and discrimination both in the job market and in the classroom, has had a number of significant problems assimilating into mainstream American culture. Essentially, there are three themes that best characterize Vietnamese gangs: mistrust, low profile, and self-control.

A pervasive cultural theme of mistrust runs through Vietnamese communities, one that gang members exploit. For example, many members of the Vietnamese community distrust American banks and, as a result, keep their valuables and money at home. This creates a host of opportunities for gangs to rob Vietnamese citizens. As a result, robbery is a primary activity for gangs. Drug dealing in Vietnamese gangs is perceived as too risky; thus, very few Vietnamese gang members are involved in drug dealing. Drug use, however, is heavy. The drug of choice is cocaine, while heroin is avoided because it is perceived to make one unreliable and crazy.

Vietnamese gang members continue their low-profile approach to social life by avoiding conspicuous gang tattoos and hand signs. Those that are used as indicators of gang affiliation (such as tattoos) are designed so that they can be easily concealed. Moreover, in regard to dress, Vietnamese gangs tend to opt for clothing similar to that of other youth in southern California. In this way, they are able to blend in to the social landscape and more easily avoid the attention of the police. Finally, the structure of Vietnamese gangs tends to be unorganized and fluid. Membership changes constantly, and the rituals and practices of traditional gangs are noticeably absent.[63]

A recent study of Laotian/Hmong gangs in California reveals that these groups have become one of the latest threats to social life in southern California. Laotian and Hmong gangs are an understudied area in the gang literature, yet they appear to have a greater willingness to engage in violence. Accordingly, they are a cause for considerable concern.[64]

Human Smuggling

As mentioned earlier, one of the main areas of criminal activity for Asian Americans involves illegal immigration. For Chinese immigrants in particular, the problems are similar to illegal entry into the United States by Mexicans. However, given the distance that must be traveled, as well as the unique nature of the activity, some attempts have been made to learn more about human smuggling organizations, particularly in China.[65] While human smuggling into the U.S. has been going on for more than 20 years, its prevalence is based on the overwhelming numbers of Chinese who wish to enter this country. As a result, when legitimate avenues were blocked, illegitimate opportunities were created. People who leave China illegally are often called **human snakes.** Chinese human smugglers who lead illegal immigrants across the borders are called **snakeheads.** This has become an industry term to describe human smugglers either in China and elsewhere.

There are three main smuggling methods with estimated costs ranging from $35,000 to $65,000 to transport each illegal Chinese immigrant into the United States. Often, these methods are used in combination. One method is to travel to Mexico or Canada and then illegally cross the border into the U.S. This method would be similar in many respects to what illegal immigrants in Mexico do to enter the country; there, the term *coyote* is used to describe the guides or facilitators who bring Mexican immigrants into the country. A second method is to have immigrants obtain false documents certifying they are citizens of another country, and then fly into the United States through transit points outside China. A third method, the one best popularized in the media and Hollywood movies, is to use fishing trawlers or freighters to smuggle immigrants into the U.S.[66]

While conventional wisdom suggests that this type of activity would be sponsored and carried out by organized crime syndicates, largely because of the logistics involved, the research seems to suggest that human smuggling is run by individual entrepreneurs. That is, snakeheads come from a host of different backgrounds and occupations and do not affiliate with any particular organized crime group, and individual teams of smugglers may work together, usually in groups of no more than five, largely based on their particular skills or networks at different points in the smuggling process.[67] In addition to the loose affiliation many snakeheads have in terms of cooperation, they generally do not remain involved in smuggling for longer than six years, making discovery, study, or even prosecution of snakeheads exceptionally difficult.[68] Finally, the absence of a figurehead or leader of this activity, what some researchers have called a "godfather," prohibits the police from any meaningful intervention to minimize this type of criminal activity.

Transnational Organized Crime

In 2004, in an attempt to assess the impact of Asian transnational organized crime in the United States, as well as to lay the foundation for a research agenda that will help the U.S. better understand the potential threats of international crime, the National Institute of Justice conducted a study to explore the extent of Asian transnational organized crime.[69] While agreement on the particular problems as well as the scope of activities relating to organized crime is difficult, leading experts on organized crime in eight Asian countries (Cambodia, China, Hong Kong, Japan, Macau, the Philippines, Taiwan, and Thailand) have agreed that there are a few common issues.

In China, for example, law enforcement officials and other authorities consider drug distribution to be the most serious problem in that country. The increase in the number of heroin addicts in China has led officials to believe that local drug syndicates are importing heroin from the Golden Triangle area (Burma, Thailand, and Cambodia) and distributing it locally. Gambling is also considered a serious problem in China. According to officials, even though the problems of gambling and prostitution were thought to be eradicated in China when communist reign began in 1949, today these two industries appear to be thriving. Finally, Chinese authorities are concerned about the escalating levels of violence in their country. Perhaps more important, the violence extends beyond criminal gangs or organized crime syndicates and is affecting ordinary citizens and business owners.[70] Chinese officials are also concerned about the problems stemming from the human smuggling industry.[71]

In Japan, the most serious organized crime is the **Yakuza.** Its members' involvement in gambling, prostitution, drug trafficking (particularly amphetamines), and extortion is cause for considerable concern. Yakuza criminal activities inevitably have an impact on U.S. markets due to the products and services they provide.

Additionally, because of the large number of wealthy businessmen in Japan, the country has become a major destination for women in the sex industry.[72]

In the Philippines, the main concerns relate to human trafficking and kidnapping for ransom, the drug trade, illegal gambling, and firearms smuggling. While the country recently passed an anti-trafficking law, little priority is given to enforcing the law despite the sexual exploitation that occurs there. Thus, while the official position is that something needs to be done about these crimes, the reality is that little is being done to stop them.

With regard to the drug trade, in response to improved law enforcement interdiction efforts to control the influx of amphetamines from China, Filipino authorities have discovered local laboratories that have been established to manufacture the drugs. Thus, the problems in the Philippines relating to drugs have shifted from an international focus to a local concern. Authorities contend that much of this trade, like a great deal of criminal activity in general, is controlled by organized crime syndicates who are protected by local politicians.[73]

Summary

This chapter explored several of the most common Asian American groups in the United States. Far East Asians include Chinese, Japanese and Koreans, while Southeast Asians consist of Cambodians, Vietnamese, Malaysians, and Indonesians. There is also the Indian subcontinent, which includes India, Pakistan, Sri Lanka, and Nepal, among other countries. Finally, there are Pacific Islanders, who are from Hawaii, the Philippines, Guam, and Samoa. Many of these groups listed under the general heading "Asian American" have different attitudes, values, beliefs, and languages, making the category more of convenience than actual understanding. Additionally, diversity is evident in Asian Americans' experiences and success in assimilating into mainstream American culture. Historically, most of these groups, particularly the Chinese and Japanese, were initially perceived as beneficial since they provided cheap labor in expanding industries. However, as these immigrants demonstrated their willingness to work hard and work for very little money, they became perceived as threatening to American workers. As a result, legislation was passed to limit their immigration into the United States.

The willingness to work hard and persevere has resulted in some success for groups of Asian Americans, particularly in the area of education. In fact, in recent times, Asian Americans were given the label "model minority" to describe how well they assimilated into American culture. This label is a myth largely because it does not address the wide range of experiences for Asian Americans. While some have achieved a level of societal success, other groups remain mired in poverty and discrimination. Thus, for some groups of Asian Americans, many have been able to successfully assimilate; for others, however, the problems of poverty and crime are readily self-evident. Thus, while it appears from an examination of the crime statistics as well as victimization surveys that Asian Americans are underrepresented in terms of their involvement in crime, there remains a portion of the population that is actively involved in criminal activity.

You Make the Call

An Asian Gang Case

Consider the following scenario. Debate the pros and cons of all options and decide what you would do.

You are a young prosecutor with only two years' experience trying criminal cases. A gang fight erupts in an Asian neighborhood that results in the death of two rival gang members. Upon interviewing residents of the area who might have seen what happened, police officers cannot find anyone willing to make a statement. They do, however, recover substantial physical evidence that links two particular suspects to the crime. While you are trying to decide what to do, local Asian Americans protest the treatment citizens receive by police officers, causing a major uproar at City Hall. As a result, your supervisor tells you to drop the case since it will likely result in a political disaster. Given that the gang problem has become a topic of interest for the police and is of some concern to the courts as well, what do you do? Assume, also, that you have what you think would be enough evidence to obtain a warrant for the arrest of the suspects.

Questions

1. Do you proceed despite your supervisor's orders? What is the dilemma for you?
2. What repercussions might you experience if you decide to continue with the case? What would they be if you decided to drop the case?
3. Why would the police chief, the district attorney, and the mayor want you to drop the case?
4. Can a group such as Asian Americans, which typically represent a small percentage of the crime statistics and are usually less vocal than other minority groups, really have an impact on local politics? If so, in what ways?

Key Terms

Alien Land Act (p. 110)

Asian Indians (p. 116)

Chinese Exclusion Act (p. 108)

downward social mobility (p. 115)

glass ceiling (p. 106)

human snakes (p. 120)

internment camps (p. 110)

model minority myth (p. 103)

snakeheads (p. 120)

Yakuza (p. 121)

yellow peril (p. 109)

Discussion Questions

1. What do Chinese, Japanese, and Koreans have in common in terms of their immigration into the United States?
2. How does the media contribute to the model minority myth for many Asian American groups?

3. Do you think Asian Americans are underrepresented in the crime statistics because they commit fewer crimes or because they are simply better at avoiding the police?
4. Do you think that hate crimes against Asian Americans are common? Why is it that when people think of hate crimes, they usually think of African Americans?

Endnotes

1. Humes, K., and McKinnon, J. 2000. *The Asian and Pacific Islander Population in the United States: Population Characteristics*. U.S. Census Bureau, Current Population Reports. Washington, DC: U.S. Government Printing Office.
2. United States Census Brief. 2000. *From the Mideast to the Pacific: A Profile of the Nation's Asian Foreign-Born Population*. U.S. Department of Commerce, Census Brief 100-4. Washington, DC: U.S. Government Printing Office.
3. Ibid.
4. Marger, M. N. 2003. *Race and Ethnic Relations: American and Global Perspectives*, 6th ed. Belmont, CA: Wadsworth.
5. Ibid.
6. Fong, S. 2002. *The Contemporary Asian American Experience: Beyond the Model Minority*, 2nd ed. Upper Saddle River, NJ: Prentice Hall.
7. U.S. Department of Commerce, U.S. Census Bureau, 2000, 2006. *American Community Survey Data Iterated by Race, Hispanic Origin, Ancestry and Age*. Washington, DC: U.S. Government Printing Office.
8. Marger 2003.
9. Shaefer, R. T. 2004. *Racial and Ethnic Groups*, 9th ed. Upper Saddle River, NJ: Prentice Hall.
10. Wu, F. 2002. *Yellow Race in America: Beyond Black and White*. New York: Basic Books.
11. Catalyst. 2005. *Catalyst Census of Women Corporate Officers and Top Earners of the Fortune 500*.
12. Hyun, J. 2005. *Breaking the Bamboo Ceiling: Career Strategies for Asians*. New York: HarperCollins.
13. Shaefer 2004.
14. Ibid.
15. U.S. Commission on Civil Rights. 1992. *Civil Rights Issues Facing Asian Americans in the 1990s*. Washington, DC: U.S. Government Printing Office.
16. Department of Justice. 2005. "Incidents and Offenses: Hate Crime Statistics." *Uniform Crime Reports*. Washington, DC: U.S. Government Printing Office.
17. Wu 2002; U.S. Department of Energy. 2000. *Final Report: Task Force Against Racial Profiling*. Washington, DC: U.S. Government Printing Office.
18. Marger 2003.
19. Ibid.
20. Ibid.
21. Lyman, S. 1974. *Chinese Americans*. New York: Random House.
22. Marger 2003.
23. Shaefer 2004.
24. Ibid.
25. Weglyn, M. 1976. *Years of Infamy: The Untold Story of America's Concentration Camps*. New York: Quill.
26. Shaefer 2004.
27. Ten Brock, J. Barnhart, E. N., and Matson, F. 1954. *Prejudice, War and the Constitution*. Berkeley: University of California Press.
28. Shaefer 2004.
29. Department of Justice. 2000. "The Civil Liberties Act of 1988: Redress for Japanese Americans." www.usdoj.gov/crt/ora/main.html (accessed December 1, 2007).
30. Commission on Wartime Relocation and Internment of Civilians. 1982. *Recommendations*. Washington, DC: U.S. Government Printing Office; Shaefer 2004.

31. Marger 2003.
32. Ibid.
33. Shaefer 2004.
34. Ibid.
35. Marger 2003.
36. Tarver, M., Wallace, S., and Walker, H. 2002. *Multicultural Issues in the Criminal Justice System.* Boston: Allyn & Bacon.
37. Luce, C. B. 1975. "Refugees and Guild." *New York Times,* May 11, p. E19.
38. Shaefer 2004.
39. Tarver, Wallace, and Walker 2002.
40. Ng, F. 1998. "Towards a Second Generation Hmong History." In F. Ng (ed.), *Adaptation, Acculturation, and Transnational Ties among Asian Americans,* pp. 99–117. New York: Garland.
41. Portes, A., and Rumbaut, R. G. 1996. *Immigrant America: A Portrait,* 2nd ed. Berkeley: University of California Press.
42. Shaefer 2004.
43. Hawaii Department of Health. 2001. Annual Report.
44. Tarver, Wallace, and Walker 2002.
45. Marger 2003.
46. Ibid.
47. Ibid.
48. U.S. Bureau of the Census 2001; Shaefer 2004.
49. Marger 2003.
50. Boxall, B. 2001. "Asian Indians Remake Silicon Valley." *Los Angeles Times,* July 6.
51. Varadarajan, T. 1999. "A Patel Motel Cartel?" *New York Times Magazine,* July 4, pp. 36–39.
52. Ibid.
53. Department of Justice, Federal Bureau of Investigation. 2005. "Crime in the United States 2005." *Uniform Crime Reports.* Washington, DC: U.S. Government Printing Office.
54. Penn, E. B., and Gabbidon, S. L. 2005. "Race and Justice." *Criminal Justice Studies* 18 (1): 1–121.
55. Kposowa, A. J., and Tsunokai, G. T. 2003. "Offending Patterns Among Southeast Asians in the State of California." *Journal of Ethnicity in Criminal Justice* 1 (1): 93–113.
56. Wang, J. Z. 2004. "Asian Gangs: New Challenges in the 21st Century." *Journal of Gang Research* 8 (1): 51–62.
57. Ibid.; see also Chin, K. 1990. "Chinese Gangs and Extortion." In C. R. Huff (ed.), *Gangs in America,* pp. 129–145. Newbury Park, CA: Sage.
58. Chin 1990.
59. Joe, D., and Robinson, N. 1980. "Chinatown's Immigrant Gangs." *Criminology* 18: 337–345; Joe, K. 1994. "Myths and Realities of Asian Gangs on the West Coast." *Humanity and Society* 18 (2): 3–18; Takagi, P., and Platts, T. 1978. "Behind the Gilded Ghetto." *Crime and Social Justice* 9 (2): 2–25.
60. Chin 1990.
61. Wang 2000; Chin, L. 1996. *Chinatown Gangs: Extortion, Enterprise and Ethnicity.* New York: Oxford University Press.
62. Ibid.
63. Long, P. D., and Ricard, L. 1996. *The Dream Shattered: Vietnamese Gangs in America.* Boston: Northeastern University Press; Vigil, J. D. 1990. "Cholos and Gangs: Culture Change and Street Youth in Los Angeles." In C. R. Huff (ed.), Gangs in America, pp. 106–128. Newbury Park, CA: Sage; Vigil, J. D., and Chong Yun, S. 1990. "Vietnamese Youth Gangs in Southern California." In Huff (ed.), pp. 146–162. Newbury Park, CA: Sage.
64. Wang, J. Z. 2002. "A Preliminary Profile of Laotian/Hmong Gangs: A California Perspective." *Journal of Gang Research* 9 (4): 1–4.
65. Zhang, S., and Chin, K. 2002. *Characteristics of Chinese Human Smugglers.* Washington, DC: National Institute of Justice.
66. Ibid.
67. Ibid.
68. Ibid.
69. Finckenauer, J. O., and Chin, K. 2004. *Asian Transnational Organized Crime.* Netherlands: Van Stockum.
70. Ibid.
71. Zhang and Chin 2002.
72. Finckenauer and Chin 2004.
73. Ibid.

Native Americans and the Criminal Justice System

Chapter Objectives

After reading this chapter, you should be able to

❖ Identify the significance of the historical treatment of American Indians in this country.

❖ Understand the importance of federal intervention in the form of laws and agencies in regulating life both on and off the reservation.

❖ Describe the current condition of many Native Americans in this country.

❖ Understand the involvement of Native Americans in the criminal justice system, particularly in light of the tension between self-governance of tribes and the influence of federal laws.

As with the other groups discussed thus far, it is impossible to describe the many American Indian cultures of North America, let alone those in Central and South America and the islands of the Caribbean. The term "Indian culture" includes a vast array of cultures and ways of life of the group we call "American Indians." For simplicity's sake, the terms Native Americans and American Indian will be used interchangeably, but, as we saw with the discussion of Hispanics and Latinos, know that there are a host of differences that make any sweeping generalizations impractical.

❖ Historical Presence of Native Americans

The United States has had a stormy history with Native Americans. In 1500 there were an estimated 7 million American Indians north of the Rio Grande. This number gradually decreased as food sources disappeared or they died from diseases such as measles and smallpox. Between 1800 and 1900, the Native American population decreased from about 600,000 to approximately 250,000.[1]

The U.S. government's policy toward Native Americans has historically been one of expediency. If the needs of the tribes interfered with Whites' needs or desires, the sentiment was that Native Americans should capitulate to Whites. The tribes were viewed as separate nations to be dealt with by government treaties. While one may think this is a civilized approach, history clearly shows that American Indians were either exploited by cooperating with the federal government or eliminated if they refused to give up their land.[2] For instance, as settlers moved west, the need for land increased. The government believed that Indians had no right to interfere with societal progress. To that end, the **Indian Removal Act of**

1830 called for the relocation of all eastern tribes to west of the Mississippi River. The act not only disrupted Native American culture but also did not move the tribes far enough to stay ahead of the growing population of settlers. In an effort to elicit cooperation, peace commissioners were sent in 1867 in an attempt to create reservations for Native American tribes.[3]

The 19th century proved to be a difficult time for Native Americans as the United States continued to claim land that belonged to tribes. The treatment of the Sioux Nation serves as an example of this insensitivity. In 1868 the U.S. government signed the Fort Laramie Treaty with the Sioux. The government agreed to keep Whites from hunting or settling on the newly established Great Sioux Reservation, which included all of the land that is now South Dakota. In exchange, the Sioux relinquished most of the remaining land they occupied at that time.[4]

Urged on perhaps by General George Custer's claims of gold in the Black Hills, a flood of White people eventually infiltrated the Great Sioux Reservation. As one might expect, conflict between the Sioux and Whites occurred. In response, the U.S. violated the parameters of the Fort Laramie Treaty and demanded that the Sioux move out of the Black Hills. When the Sioux failed to move, Custer was sent into the area to remove them. He underestimated the strength of the Sioux warriors, which led to the **Battle at Little Big Horn** in 1876, where Custer and his men were defeated. Afterward, Custer's army redoubled its efforts to eliminate the Sioux. The tribe eventually sold the Black Hills to the federal government and agreed to the reduction of the Great Sioux Reservation to five smaller reservations.[5]

The Sioux had a difficult time adjusting to life on the reservation. They sought escape through the **Ghost Dance religion,** which included dances and songs proclaiming the return of the buffalo and the resurrection of dead ancestors in a land free of the White people. Although the Ghost Dance was essentially harmless, Whites feared that the social solidarity it encouraged would lead to renewed warfare. As a result, more troops were summoned to areas where the Ghost Dance had become popular.[6]

In late December 1890, anticipating that a massive Ghost Dance would occur, a U.S. cavalry division arrived at a reservation of Sioux at Wounded Knee Creek on the Pine Ridge, South Dakota. While an exact account of what happened is not known, a battle ensued that left about 300 Sioux and 25 U.S. soldiers dead. This conflict, known as the **Battle of Wounded Knee,** was not the deadliest for Native Americans but is heralded by historians as significant because it extinguished the hope of the Sioux Nation of ever returning to a life of freedom.[7]

The Battle at Little Big Horn was the last great victory for the Sioux under Sitting Bull.

Early Attempts at Assimilation

As the Sioux death toll mounted and the conflict between Native Americans and White settlers continued, the federal government attempted a different strategy: assimilation. The idea was that if cultural differences were the source of the problem, meaning that the attitudes, values, and beliefs of the tribes were in conflict with the progressive ideas of the government and settlers, then the solution was to weaken the influence of tribal culture. If tribal institutions were weakened, then Native Americans would be more likely to assimilate and subscribe to the ideas the federal government proposed. Evidence of assimilation strategy was seen in the General Allotment Act of 1887, also known as the Dawes Act of 1887.[8]

The General Allotment Act was advocated largely by community activists who sought to empower tribal members by helping them to become more like Whites. The act proposed to make landowners of individual tribe members without consulting tribal leaders. Each family was given 160 acres of land. However, like programs for the poor that attempt to empower families as homeowners but do not properly equip them with the skills necessary to maintain a home, the General Allotment Act made no effort to acquaint Native Americans with the skills necessary to make the land productive. As a result, eventually much of the land initially deeded under the act came into the possession of Whites when Native Americans became victims of fraudulent land transfers. By 1934 Native Americans had lost approximately 90 million of the 138 million acres in their possession prior to the General Allotment Act.[9]

John Collier was appointed to head the Bureau of Indian Affairs during President Franklin D. Roosevelt's first term. The **Bureau of Indian Affairs,** formed in 1832, is the primary regulatory arm of the federal government as it relates to Native Americans. Collier proposed major changes in Indian policy that included the preservation of Native American culture. Perhaps most significant was his proposal to end the allotment of land to Native Americans. In 1934 Congress passed the Indian Reorganization Act, which, among other things, prohibited further allotments of tribal lands and encouraged Native Americans to create self-governing systems within their tribes.[10]

Termination of Tribes

In the mid-1940s, Whites realized the significance of mistreating Native Americans, especially the mistreatment of Native Americans who lived on reservations. However, instead of improving the quality of life on reservation land, many Americans mistakenly thought that part of the solution was to force Native Americans to assimilate into mainstream society.[11] This was accomplished by simply eliminating official recognition of tribes. The **Termination Act,** passed by Congress in 1953, led to the termination of 13 tribes between 1945 and 1962. The act also meant that certain tribes would lose tax-exempt status for their lands. As a result, many tribal members who lost their status had to sell their land to pay the taxes on it and to pay for health and educational services for their communities.[12] Consequently, nearly 35,000 displaced former landowners were forced to relocate in urban areas.

The Bureau of Indian Affairs Employment Assistance Program offered reimbursement for transportation, low-cost housing, and incidental expenses to Native Americans who agreed to resettle in cities. Soon, Indian populations in cities exceeded those of some reservations. According to the U.S. Census Bureau, in the 1960s more than half of all Native Americans lived in cities. Most Native Americans strongly resisted the Termination Act, realizing that tribes would lose their lands as well as their native culture.

Preservation of Rights

During the 1970s the **Red Power Movement,** which was similar to the Black Power Movement for African Americans in that Native Americans tried to gain economic, social, and political equality, pressured the federal government to address Native Americans' concerns and to reaffirm tribal rights as set out in the Indian Reorganization Act. The effect was a renewed effort by the U.S. government to give more control back to the tribes.

The more radical **American Indian Movement** (AIM), which began in 1968, became the most visible reminder of the Red Power Movement. Its original purpose was to monitor the police and to document evidence of police brutality. Eventually, AIM turned its attention to solving problems within the Native American community by initiating programs that focused on reducing the high incidence of alcoholism among Native Americans as well as educational programs for Native American children to improve academic performance.

The 1970s, a time of great protest in the United States, were also a time when Native Americans made dramatic efforts to have their rights preserved. Perhaps the most dramatic confrontation between Native Americans and the federal government

Many Native Americans have rallied against the treatment they have received from the federal government.

occurred in 1973. Known as the Battle of Wounded Knee II, the leader of AIM and nearly 300 supporters began a 70-day standoff with authorities in Wounded Knee, South Dakota, the site of the first battle with General Custer in 1890. While the event drew a great deal of media attention, it had little effect on the federal government's policy on Native Americans.[13]

Government Involvement in Indian Affairs

In recent years, many of the policies instituted by the Bureau of Indian Affairs have been designed with the idea that the federal government should be less involved in Indian life. In an attempt to relinquish control over Indian affairs, the federal government formed the **Indian Claims Commission** (ICC) in 1946 to handle land disputes. Before 1946, Native Americans could not bring any land claim against the federal government without a special act of Congress. Although not an official U.S. court, the ICC operates somewhat like one in that lawyers present evidence for both sides. If the commission agrees with the tribe, it then determines the value of the land at the time it was illegally seized. This is of critical importance since the value of the land at the time of loss could be pennies an acre. Payments are then decreased by what are called **setoffs,** which are deductions from the money due equal to the cost of federal services provided to the tribe. It is not unusual to have a case decided in favor of the tribe only to have its settlements exceeded by the setoffs.[14] In other words, while the tribes may have won a moral and legal victory by having a case decided in their favor and being entitled to compensation, the costs of using government services often left tribes in a deficit because the value of the land was not calculated at current market value.

More recently, but particularly in the 1980s, which is recognized as a decade of progress in Indian law, Native Americans have increasingly succeeded in winning their lawsuits. The U.S. Supreme Court ruled on nearly 80 cases between the 1960s and 1980s, most of which have been decided in favor of the tribes and have reasserted such basic principles as tribes as separate governments. The 1990s were heralded as a time of new tribal sophistication, where tribal courts were increasing in quantity and in political standing, spawned perhaps by the economic wealth of some tribes due to casino gambling.[15] **Tribal courts** are courts of jurisdiction designed to allow tribes the authority to hear and decide cases relating to life on the reservation without interference of traditional U.S. courts.

✷ Native Americans Today

We must again emphasize the diversity of Native Americans. Besides the variety of tribal heritages, there is a distinction between Native Americans who live on and off reservations, as well as between tribal members who live in small towns and in central cities, and between those living on the West Coast and the East Coast. Native American life has generally shifted from several hundred reservations to small towns and big cities. Life in these places is quite different, but there are enough similarities to draw a few broad conclusions about the status of Native Americans in the United States today. Let's look at a couple of dimensions.

The 2000 Census indicates there were 4.1 million American Indians, or 1.5% of 281 million people, living in the United States. Problems emerge, however, when the categories are examined. In 2000 the Census Bureau implemented a new method for collecting data on race and ethnicity. Respondents were given the option of selecting one race to indicate their identity or selecting a number of categories. Thus, a look at the American Indian and Alaska Native category shows that 2.5 million listed only one race and 1.6 million listed American Indian in combination with one or more other races.[16]

In terms of identifying with a particular tribe, with 43% of Native Americans living on reservations, the Cherokee, followed by the Navajo and Sioux, are the largest tribes today. The increase in population size over the past 20 years is primarily due to a greater willingness of Native Americans to claim their heritage, either by moving back to reservations or by simply claiming their heritage within an official survey. The reasons for the increased size of the population may be several, but some experts contend that it is based on the growth of the casino gambling industry.[17]

Employment and Income

By the U.S. standard of living, Native Americans are quite poor. In an absolute sense of dollars earned or quality of housing, they are no worse off now than in the past. However, when making comparisons between minority groups and the larger society, most experts use a relative standard, not an absolute one. In other words, poverty is not defined by the percentage of people who have no food, clothing, or housing. Poverty is determined by a standard that is relative to some larger group. In a relative sense, Native Americans are far behind on all standards of income and occupational status when compared to Whites. In the 1980s, for example, according to the U.S. Census, Native American families were three times more likely than Whites to live below the federal poverty line and much less likely to have anyone in the family working full-time.

More recently, when Congress passed the Personal Responsibility Work Reconciliation Act in 1997, now more commonly known as welfare reform, a major part of the act focused on chronic poverty, which many Native Americans experience. For example, in South Dakota, where American Indians make up 7% of the population, they account for over half of the welfare recipients. As the time limits stipulated by welfare reform become a reality for these families, one can only imagine what their lives will be like. As part of welfare reform legislation, recipients are mandated to find and keep jobs; however, for many Native Americans, particularly those living in rural areas or on reservations, employment opportunities are few.[18]

According to the Bureau of Indian Affairs, at least half of the reservation population lives below the federal poverty line, surviving on welfare checks, food stamps, and Medicaid. In 1990 the Indian Health Service, a division of the Public Health Service, reported that 43% of Indian children under 5 years old lived in poverty. In 1995 more than 20% of Native American reservation households had annual incomes below $5,000, compared with 6% for the overall U.S. population. Only 8% of reservation households had annual incomes greater than $35,000, compared with 18% for the overall U.S. population. These general trends have continued in the new millennium. According to the U.S. Census Bureau, in 2005 the median household income for Native Americans was $32,866, compared with a median household income of $43,318 for the overall U.S. population.[19]

Despite the perception of wealth stemming from casino gambling, many Native Americans live in poverty.

People living on reservations also have the highest rates of unemployment in the United States—up to 70% or higher on some reservations in 2006. Some of the most commonly cited reasons for high unemployment among Native Americans are lack of education, discrimination, and the scarcity of jobs and industry on and near reservations. In fact, many American Indians move to cities in search of better schooling, improved housing, and higher-paying jobs. While urban areas provide better opportunities for some Native Americans as evidenced by the lower unemployment rates for those who live in cities compared to those on reservations, moving to cities often entails other costs. Native Americans in cities do not always improve their standard of living because housing, food, clothing, and health care are more expensive in urban areas.[20]

Casino Gambling

One area that has served as a respite for some tribal members has been the increase of gambling casinos on reservations. For many tribes, commercial gambling is the only viable source of employment and revenue. Under the 1988 Gaming Regulatory Act, states must negotiate gambling agreements with reservations and cannot prohibit any gambling already allowed under state law. In 2001, 201 tribes in over 21 states were operating a variety of gambling operations, such as blackjack, roulette tables, sports betting, slot machines, and high-stakes bingo. The booming gambling industry netted almost $11 billion in 2000 and $22 billion in 2006. This is overshadowed, however, by the fact that about two-thirds of the tribes have no casinos or other gambling ventures.[21]

INSULTS, MASCOTS, AND NATIVE AMERICANS IN SPORTS

There is little question that racism affects all aspects of American society. On one hand, Americans seem willing to avoid the use of derogatory terms because they evoke such a strong and offensive reaction on the part of the targeted group. Americans have also become more sensitive to racial slights in sports and advertising. Depictions of African Americans and Hispanics that, in the past, seemed funny or entertaining are now no longer used. For example, no one today would even consider naming a sports team the Frito Banditos or the Little Black Sambos. Nor would any team consider using these characters as mascots.

However, the same sensitivity seems lacking for Native Americans. Many colleges and universities as well as professional sports teams frequently use Native American terms and depictions. This is particularly true in professional baseball and football. Examples include the Cleveland Indians and the Atlanta Braves, who are famous for their tomahawk chop to rally the team. Professional football uses Native American logos for the Kansas City Chiefs and the Washington Redskins.

It would be unconceivable to purposely insult the racial and religious values of African Americans, Hispanics, or women. However, according to the National Coalition on Racism in Sports and Media, very little progress has been made to educate teams, fans, coaches, and the general public about the offensive nature Native American logos and mascots present. The public has historically been conditioned by the sports industry, educational institutions, and the media to trivialize indigenous culture as common and harmless entertainment. These groups somehow fail to recognize that using Native American names and depictions to identify teams, particularly caricatures, shows a lack of respect for the history of Native Americans and diminishes the importance of certain social positions, such as the tribal leader or "chief."

Apparently this inconsistency is being noticed as at least six universities have stopped using Native American logos and/or mascots for the university athletic program, including the University of Illinois. Perhaps Americans are realizing that the historical insensitivity toward Native Americans has to stop and that they should be treated like other minority groups in this country.

A few tribes have had staggering success, such as the 493 members of the Connecticut Mashantucket Pequot Indians, whose Foxwoods Resort Casino provides generous benefits to anyone who can establish that he or she is at least one-sixteenth Pequot. In fact, the impact of the Pequot casino extends far beyond individual tribal members. The casino is now one of the largest taxpayers in Connecticut and also one of its largest employers.[22] The tribe has also donated money to a variety of charities and paid for many improvements in the state's infrastructure, such as roads leading to the casino, and it has been indirectly responsible for a host of ancillary industries surrounding the area.

In other states, Native American casinos have contributed money to create childcare programs, housing, roads, scholarships, health clinics, and water systems for Native Americans. Revenues also fund tribal law enforcement, firefighting, and other services. Another example of the success of some Native American casinos was witnessed in 2006, when the Seminole Tribe in Florida announced the purchase of the Hard Rock Café franchise for $965 million.[23]

While the success of casinos owned by Native Americans seems readily apparent, the National Indian Gaming Association states that the tribes that make substantial profits from gambling amount to less than 1% of the total Native

Casinos have had a significant impact in several Native American communities.

American population. The more typical picture is of moderately successful gambling operations associated with tribes whose social and economic needs are overwhelming. In fact, only an estimated 25% of the jobs from the gaming industry are held by Native Americans.[24]

The main criticism of Indian casinos is the concern that organized crime will infiltrate the industry and that casinos will become a magnet for other criminal activities. While only limited research exists on a direct relationship between Indian gaming and criminal activity on reservations, there is some evidence that shows a relationship between Indian gaming and organized crime.[25]

Allegations of corruption, money laundering, and loan-sharking have been made against various tribes. For example, Asian-based organized crime has been linked to loan-sharking and other forms of exploitation of Asian customers at the Mohegan Sun and Foxwoods Casinos in Connecticut.[26] An added problem, critics point out, is that Indian casinos are self-regulated and the supervision offered by the National Indian Gaming Commission, the Internal Revenue Service, and other regulatory agencies is limited due to funding and jurisdictional issues.[27] Despite these claims, no definitive evidence exists of a connection between Indian gaming and organized crime.[28]

What is significant about the research linking Native American gaming and crime on reservations relates to the delay between the startup of a tribally owned casino and a large increase in crime and gambling in counties near an Indian casino.[29] Property crimes, such as auto theft and larceny, increase by about 10% four or more years after a casino opens in a given county. The explanation for this trend is likely found in the increased number of people living and working near the casino. Trends in auto theft and larceny are likely related to the idea that casinos induce gambling problems, and people with such an addiction turn to crime to support their habit.[30] Gangs and delinquency can also be linked to casino gambling because parents work long hours, leaving their children unsupervised. While neglect of children by parents is a phenomenon that existed long before casinos were built, recent research suggests that the relationship between the two is a cause for concern.[31]

Educational Achievement

As it has been with many other aspects of Native Americans' lives, education has been under the control of the federal and state governments. Unfortunately, the lack of understanding of the social, cultural, political, and economic differences between Native Americans and other groups has resulted in poor management of Native American children's educational experiences. Part of the problem has been lack of government funding of Indian education programs. Additionally, there are few Native American teachers, and curriculum decisions do not take into account the unique position of Native American students. U.S. educational policies appear to reflect the insistence that Native Americans should assimilate and ignore the celebration of their heritage. It is not surprising that Native American students have the highest dropout rate of any racial or ethnic group—36% in 1990 and 51% in 2000.[32]

According to a 2004 report by the Urban Institute, nationally, high school graduation rates are low for all students. Only an estimated 68% of those who enter ninth grade will graduate four years later with a regular diploma. However, these rates are substantially lower for most minority groups, especially for males. While Native Americans have graduation rates that are comparable to those for African American and Hispanic/Latino students, all hovering around 50%, the percentage for males drops to about 45% (43% for African Americans, 47% for Native Americans, and 48% for Hispanics/Latinos).[33]

The problems associated with the educational achievement of Native Americans extend beyond elementary and high school. College graduation rates for Native Americans are also low. In 1995 Native American students accounted for less than 1% of all students in higher education. The majority of these students attended two-year rather than four-year institutions. The graduation rate for Native Americans was only 37% in 1995, the lowest among major ethnic minority groups. In 2001 the graduation rate was 51%. The reason for the increase is not known, but it may have to do with revenues generated from casinos, subsequent generations of Native Americans who value education as a means of social mobility, or some other factor.

In response to this problem, federal legislation was enacted to create institutions that recognize the importance of Native American culture. In 1968 the Navajo Nation created the first tribally controlled college, now called Diné College, in Tsaile, Arizona. It is a four-year institution. Other tribal colleges quickly developed. Most of these began as two-year institutions and have open admissions policies. In 2001 most tribal colleges were fully accredited. In 2005, according to the State Department, 75% of American Indians and Alaska Natives aged 25 and older had at least a high school diploma while the percentage who held at least a bachelor's degree was 14%.[34]

Health Care

From the beginning of their interactions with Whites, Native Americans have been susceptible to disease and illness. In the early part of the 20th century, there were a number of epidemics, particularly tuberculosis, that killed thousands of American Indians. By the end of the century, the health of Native Americans had improved due to a higher standard of living and an increase in immunizations.

While physical diseases such as measles and diphtheria were brought under control, social problems have continued to grip this population. Alcoholism, domestic violence, and mental disorders have plagued Native Americans, particularly in the 1980s and 1990s.[35] For instance, in the late 1980s, the Indian Health Service reported that the number of deaths of Native Americans due to alcoholism was four times greater than what was reported for the general population. Additionally, suicide rates among Native Americans were 77% higher than the national average. More recently, diabetes and HIV have become prominent issues for Native Americans. In the mid-1990s, the Indian Health Service reported that Native Americans were about three times more likely to be diagnosed with diabetes than Whites.

Health care is provided by the Indian Health Service, but not all of its facilities meet the health care needs of Native Americans. Moreover, not all reservations or communities have medical clinics or hospitals, and the ones that exist are often small with outdated equipment.[36] Part of the problem stems from a lack of funding. Because of poor salaries and inadequate equipment, there is a shortage of doctors, nurses, and pharmacists in reservation clinics, which affects the quality and continuity of health care for Native Americans. According to the Indian Health Service, there are 74 doctors for every 100,000 Native Americans in the United States, compared to 242 per 100,000 in the general population.[37]

⚔ Native Americans and the Criminal Justice System

In the 2000 Census, people who identified themselves as American Indians were asked to report their principal tribe. American Indians belong to approximately 562 federally recognized tribes. About 79% of American Indians who reported a single race reported a specific tribe. Among those who reported American Indian with more than one race, over two-thirds specified a tribal affiliation. The ten largest Native American tribes accounted for nearly half of the 2.5 million respondents. Of those who identified with one tribal nation, over 20% reported belonging to the Cherokee or Navajo tribes.[38]

An important element of tribal self-government is jurisdiction over incidents that take place on reservations. For instance, there are currently separate laws governing the prosecution of Native American and non–Native American offenders for crimes that take place on reservations. Another area of concern involves the lack of attention paid to the victimization of Native Americans. As the data show, the rate of violent crime against Native Americans is substantially higher than the rates against other minority groups. A third area of concern relates to the type and frequency of crimes committed by Native Americans. Clearly, crime appears to have become a consistent feature of social life for Native Americans.

Crime Rates

There is substantially less information regarding Native Americans and crime compared to African Americans and Hispanics. In a report issued by the U.S. Department of Justice in 1997, the homicide rate for Native American males was almost three times higher than the rate for White males. Between 1992 and 1996, while the rest of the country was experiencing a decline in violent crime, the Native American population witnessed a dramatic increase. According to the *Uniform Crime Reports,* the annual average violent crime rate among Native Americans was twice as high as that for Blacks (50 per 1,000 persons), 2.5 times higher than that for Whites (41 per 1,000 persons), and 4.5 times higher than that for Asians (22 per 1,000 persons).[39]

According to the National Criminal Justice Association, for people between the ages of 12 and 24, the rate of Indians murdered in 2005 directly paralleled the rates of Whites and Asians but was well below the rate of Blacks.[40] One study found that in Montana, the homicide rate on reservations was twice that of New Orleans, one of the most violent cities in the country.[41]

In 2004, according to the *Sourcebook of Criminal Justice Statistics,* American Indians and Alaska Natives committed 131,539 of the estimated 10,021,050 crimes. Of the crimes committed by Native Americans, assaults (12,229), liquor law violations (11,634), larcenies (10,976), and public drunkenness (8,739) were the most common.[42] Clearly all of these crimes relate to alcohol, which will be discussed in a section later in the chapter.

During that time, gang activity in Native American communities was similar to the level of violence perpetuated by many street gangs across the country. While the motivations for engaging in violence are different, with urban street gangs influenced more by economic opportunities and profit, concepts like status, recognition, and a sense of belonging are common features among Native American gangs.[43]

Victimization

According to information collected by the Bureau of Justice Statistics (BJS), American Indians are likely to experience violent crimes at more than twice the rate of all other U.S. residents. The BJS reported that between 1992 and 1996 the average annual rate of violent victimizations among Indians (including Alaska Natives and Aleuts) was 124 per 1,000 residents aged 12 years and older, compared to 61 violent victimizations per 1,000 Blacks, 49 per 1,000 Whites, and 29 per 1,000 Asians. These rates are all the more significant because there are only about 2.3 million Native American residents of the United States, which represents just less than 1% of the total population.[44]

More recently, a BJS report on Native American crime between 1992 and 2002 found that the violent crime rate in every age group below 35 was significantly higher for Native Americans than it was for the general U.S. population. The report also found that among Native Americans aged 25 to 34, the rate of violent crime victimization was more than 2.5 times the rate for all persons the same age. Rates of violent victimization for both males and females were higher for Native Americans than for all races. Further, the rate of violent victimization among Native American women was more than double the rate among all women.[45] Unlike most crimes, where there is a relationship between the victim and the offender, strangers committed most of the robberies (71%) against Native Americans. This group was also more likely to be a victim of assault and rape by a stranger rather than an intimate partner or family member.

In 2004, in all age groups, Native Americans had higher rates of violent victimization than other minority groups. The rate was highest for Native Americans aged 18 to 24, at 155 per 1,000 people, compared to the highest rate in the 12 to 17 age group for all races (94 per 1,000). Among the elderly, Native Americans 55 and older had a violent crime rate that was three times that for all races (22 per 1,000 compared to 8 per 1,000).[46]

As previously mentioned, in terms of the race of the offender and the relationship with the victim, Native Americans who were victims of violent crime were more likely to have been victimized by a stranger than an intimate partner. Strangers committed 42% of the violent crimes against Native Americans from 1992 to 2001, while an acquaintance committed about one-third of all violence against Native Americans. Only about 20% of the victimizations of Native Americans came as a result of a relationship between the victim and the offender.[47]

Crime against Native Americans tends to be interracial, whereas victimization against other races tends to be intraracial. Nearly 88% of the victimizations against Native Americans were committed by White or African American offenders. Victims stated that Asians and other Native Americans were responsible for only 13% of violent acts. National Crime Victimization Survey data show that Native Americans accounted for an average of about 1.3% of all violent victimizations in 2004.

While it was mentioned that alcohol plays an integral role in the life of Native Americans, this also translates into criminal activity. Not only is the arrest rate among Native Americans higher for driving under the influence (479 per 100,000 compared to 332 per 100,000 for all members of the population), arrests for liquor law violations were about four times higher among Native Americans than the rest of the population (405 per 100,000 compared to 143 per 100,000).

The problems relating to criminal behavior by Native Americans are not episodic; rather, they reflect the chronic condition many members of this population experience. For example, the recidivism rate of Native Americans was similar to the rates of all offenders, whether for a new arrest, conviction, or sentence to prison. An estimated 60% of Native Americans are arrested for a new crime, a felony, or a serious misdemeanor within three years of their release from state prison. Related to this is the fact that over a third of Native Americans released from prison are returned to prison due to a parole or probation violation.[48]

Native Americans in the Federal System

Generally speaking, Section 1153 of the U.S. Title 18 Federal Code gives jurisdiction to federal courts over American Indians who commit crimes within the limits of any Indian reservation regardless of whether or not the victim was an American Indian. The U.S. Attorney's Office is the agency responsible for investigating crimes and prosecuting non–Native American offenders for crimes occurring on American Indian reservations. In 2000, of the estimated 6,000 suspects investigated for violent offenses, about 25%, or approximately 1,525 offenses, took place on reservations. As an illustration of the greater incidence of violence on reservations, consider that nationally, or off reservations, the percentage of suspects investigated for violent offenses was approximately 5%. In contrast, the percentage of suspects investigated for violent crimes on reservations was about 75%. The data suggest that a substantial amount of violent crime occurs on reservations, more so than in other places.[49]

Moreover, it appears that the level of violence on reservations is increasing. According to the Bureau of Justice Statistics, the number of federal charges filed against Native Americans for violent crimes on reservations increased 27% from 1997 to 2000. The tendency for Native Americans to be convicted and sentenced to prison for violent episodes is evident in the prison population. According to the Federal Bureau of Prisons, in 2001 almost 3% of all offenders entering federal prison were American Indians. Further, Native Americans represented about 16% of all violent offenders entering federal prison in 2001, a figure that had remained relatively constant since 1996. Over half of American Indians entering federal prison were serving a sentence for a violent crime compared to 4% of White offenders, 13% of African American offenders, and 5% of Asian offenders.[50]

As mentioned earlier, the prison experience does not seem to deter Native Americans from engaging in further criminal activity. According to the Bureau of Justice Statistics, an estimated 60% of Native American offenders are arrested for a new crime, and more than half of Native Americans released from prison in 1994 were back in prison because they violated a condition of their release, such as failing a drug test or failing to meet with their parole officer.[51]

Despite this tendency for violence, capital punishment does not seem to play a significant role in the lives of Native Americans. Out of the total 7,254 persons sentenced to death from 1973 to 2002, only 60 were American Indian. Between 1977 and 2002, a total of 8,290 persons were executed, 8 of whom were American Indian. This represented about 1% of the total number of those executed.[52]

The Role of Alcohol in Native American Crime

Alcohol use among Native Americans is not a recent development. Historically its use was limited to ceremonies and religious rituals.[53] Some tribes, for example, believed that drunkenness brought a purification of one's mind and heart that would also produce rain for crops.[54] However, the impact of alcohol abuse among Native Americans can be seen in physical diseases. One study found that alcoholism kills Native Americans at a rate five times higher than the rates for other Americans. The rate is ten times higher for those between the ages of 25 and 35.[55] The relationship between alcohol consumption and violence is particularly noteworthy among Native Americans. Crimes such as rape, homicide, and suicide occur with a much higher frequency among this segment of the population than they do among other segments. Alcohol is also involved in 75% of all fatal accidents, a rate three times higher than that for non–Native Americans.[56]

Unfortunately, there is no single explanation for alcohol abuse among Native Americans. One of the most prevalent theories is that it is due to the loss of their culture. That is, in an attempt to deal with the psychological problems relating to being isolated by society and unable to achieve their goals, many Native Americans use alcohol to relieve feelings of anxiety and depression. The living conditions for many Native Americans also contribute to the need for self-medication through alcohol.

On the other hand, there are experts who contend that Native Americans do not live in a cultural vacuum. That is, every culture undergoes changes and even though Native Americans might have lost their culture over generations of time, it could also be the case that as they assimilate and move to cities, their identification with American culture can ease the stress they are experiencing because they have some type of cultural mooring.[57] This school of thought argues that alcohol abuse is more a function of poor choices than a way to cope with the loss of one's culture.

According to some researchers, the government's response to alcohol abuse among Native Americans has been minimal despite the physical and social risks related to it. The government often criminalizes the behavior that comes as a result of alcohol abuse, such as homelessness, public intoxication, and liquor law violations.[58] Unfortunately, the solution then becomes arresting and incarcerating people for these symptomatic behaviors instead of addressing the larger issue of alcoholism and its causes.

Questioning the Relationship Between Native Americans and Crime Statistics

A number of researchers question the official statistics regarding Native American crime. In fact, some go so far as to question whether Native Americans are actually overrepresented in the crime data. One group of scholars is critical of a widely cited 1999 report published by the Bureau of Justice Statistics (BJS) entitled *American Indians and Crime.* This report contends that American Indians over the age of 12 are twice as likely to be victims of violent crime than are members of all other racial and ethnic categories combined. Critics of this report contend that the actual rates of arrest for violence among American Indian youth are the same as those for White youth and that the rates of American Indians arrested for murder has remained constant for the past 20 years. Further, one must consider that American Indian victims of violent crime are most likely attacked by non-Indian offenders—which makes the prosecution of crimes against American Indians difficult, especially if the crimes occurred on Indian land. Finally, critics of the BJS report argue that the highest rates of violence occur in urban settings, not on reservations. Nevertheless, the perception that Native Americans perpetuate a higher proportion of crime is a common assertion in the media.[59]

Some experts even believe that federal surveys may not be the most effective tool to measure crime among Native Americans on reservations due to a host of logistical and methodological problems. For instance, the number of crimes known among Native Americans and the size of the population on the reservation used to calculate arrest rates can produce exaggerated crime estimates.[60] This can easily create the impression that crime is more common, and a more serious problem, on reservations than in other places.

In an attempt to remedy the methodological problems stemming from using aggregated data, particularly with small populations, an in-depth analysis of a decade of arrest data for one tribe on one reservation was conducted by a team of researchers. The findings showed that rates of violent and nonviolent juvenile crime were far below the estimates in the BJS report. They also showed that juvenile crime in this community, as in many communities across the country, was the result of a small group of repeat offenders.[61]

Native Americans and the Police

Perhaps the most fascinating, and complicated, issue surrounding Native Americans relates to the jurisdiction and composition of tribal courts. When Congress passed Public Law 280 (PL 280) in 1953, criminal and civil jurisdiction over tribal lands was transferred to local governments. This gave local law enforcement the authority over Indian communities. In places where PL 280 did not apply, either the Bureau of Indian Affairs or the tribal councils were to provide law enforcement officers.[62]

These varying jurisdictional boundaries present problems related to the prosecution of offenders depending on whether or not the offender is a Native American, whether the crime took place on or outside Indian land, and whether local law enforcement, tribal councils, or the Bureau of Indian Affairs has authority over that particular area. Problems emerge, for example, when a non–Native American commits a crime on Indian land. In this situation, a criminal act normally prosecuted by state and local governments is considered an Indian issue, rendering no criminal charges against the offender. When a Native American commits a crime on Indian land and is convicted by tribal courts, the Indian Civil Rights Act of 1968 usually applies, which means tribal criminal sentences can last no more than one year in custody and can impose no more than a $5,000 fine, regardless of the crime.[63] Clearly, both sets of circumstances are not in the interest of justice nor do they send the appropriate message about accountability of offenders' behavior.

While the burden of proof differs between tribal courts and U.S. courts, there is also the problem of law enforcement. According to the *Uniform Crime Reports,* in 2005 in non-Indian communities with populations under 10,000 people, the ratio of police officers to people was 2.9 to 1,000. In Native American communities, the ratio was 1.3 officers to 1,000 people. This was true despite the fact that there are higher crime rates in Native American communities. In more remote areas, the ratio was 1 officer to 1,000 people. The Bureau of Indian Affairs, the federal government's presence on tribal lands, consisted of only 1,600 officers, responsible for 56 million acres of tribal land.[64] Clearly the general problems in law enforcement are found among tribal police officers, such as low pay, poor equipment, and a heavy burden of responsibility. However, these problems are particularly acute in places that already have low police representation. According to a recent report by the Bureau of Justice Statistics, among all Native American tribes, there were 171 law enforcement agencies and 2,303 full-time sworn officers. The largest of these agencies, the Navajo Nation Department of Law Enforcement in Arizona, has 321 full-time sworn personnel and is responsible for 22,174 square miles of reservation land. This translates into 1 officer per 100 square miles. Further, about 88% of the tribally operated law enforcement agencies participate in some form of crime prevention, and about 25% of these agencies operate one or more jails.[65]

The problems relating to policing were addressed to some degree in 1995 with the establishment of the **Office of Tribal Justice,** a division of the Department of Justice, to serve as a liaison between the tribes and the federal government. The Office of Tribal Justice has attempted to coordinate policies, promote funding opportunities to improve the quality of policing on reservations, and build better relationships with the tribes. In addition, the Office of Community Oriented Policing Services has attempted to make inroads into the problems relating to violent crime and quality-of-life issues on reservations. The FBI has also dedicated resources to reducing the violent crime rate on reservations as well as attempting to close legal loopholes that allow some violent offenders to avoid prosecution. Finally, better training is being offered to tribal police officers. For instance, Bureau of Indian Affairs officers attend the Police Academy in Artesia, New Mexico, which provides identical training to what is offered at the Federal Law Enforcement Training Center in Atlanta, Georgia.[66]

Native Americans and the Courts

There are also differences in philosophy between tribal courts and American criminal courts. Over the past 200 years, the federal government has established a pattern of taking over the jurisdiction of an increasing number of crimes committed by Native Americans, removing them from tribal authority, and giving itself the power to punish offenders. This contradicts the parameters of treaties signed by the federal government giving Native tribes the right to have their own separate system of justice.[67]

As mentioned earlier, in 1953 Congress passed Public Law 280, without tribal consent, which offered states the opportunity to assume jurisdiction over reservations within their borders. PL 280 law stipulates that law enforcement for Native reservations is typically handled by state police and county or state courts rather than through the tribe. This law has created concern that courts are treating Native people and Whites unequally.[68]

As sovereign entities, Native tribes have the right to organize and maintain their own laws and law enforcement agencies; however, not every tribe in the United States has the funding for its own tribal court or police system. In states without these, law enforcement can fall instead to the state police or U.S. Marshals Office. Even tribes that have police forces may have jurisdiction only over crimes committed by and against Native people in the community. Native communities that have a tribal court may have jurisdiction only over certain types of cases, such as misdemeanors committed in the community, while state and federal courts will have jurisdiction over other crimes.[69]

Some experts argue that since federal laws are generally harsher than state laws, and because Native reservations are considered federal jurisdiction, most offenders who commit crimes on reservations face harsher sentences simply as a result of where they live. The importance of this trend is that Native Americans are disproportionately imprisoned. This is most evident in places like Montana, where 16% of prisoners are American Indians even though they constitute just 6% of the state's population. In North Dakota, American Indians are only 5% of the state's total population but are 19% of the prison population.[70]

Summary

This chapter examined the history of Native Americans in this country as well as the ways in which they become involved in the criminal justice system. The position of Native Americans is unique in that while they are supposed to have a separate system of justice to address problems relating to crime, increasingly, the federal government is encroaching upon tribal authority to handle a variety of tasks. Historically, the United States seemed to have a sense of entitlement when it came to taking land that belonged to Native Americans. Social progress was seen as more important than preserving the heritage and authority of Native Americans. Even when treaties were signed that stipulated the rights and privileges of Native Americans, Whites ignored the agreements and used force when Native Americans refused to capitulate. More recently, the federal government created the Bureau of Indian Affairs to regulate most of the aspects of life on and off the reservation. Other agencies, such as the Department of Health and Human Services, the Public Health Service, and the Indian Health Service, all attempt to address the many issues surrounding Native Americans.

While Native Americans have made an effort to assimilate, their experiences have resulted in a number of social problems. Many Native Americans still lag behind Whites economically and educationally. Their high school dropout rate is high, and compared to other minority groups, fewer Native Americans graduate from college and even fewer have professional careers. Moreover, a large percentage of Native Americans live at or below the federal poverty line. Native Americans also suffer from a variety of health problems, including tuberculosis, alcoholism, and mental illness.

Many of the limitations and problems faced by Native Americans result in a significant involvement with the criminal justice system, either as victims or as offenders. Thus, while this does not involve a large segment of the population, like their African American and Hispanic counterparts, Native Americans are overrepresented in the crime statistics. As was mentioned, jurisdictional problems confuse the issues of justice. Other issues, for instance, the issue of responsibility for investigating crimes and the apprehension of suspects, continue to be debated: The federal government intends to retain control over reservations while tribal councils want to be able to exercise their own authority in the administration of justice.

 # You Make the Call

Native American Inmate Rituals

Consider the following scenario. Debate the pros and cons of all options and decide what you would do.

Imagine you are the cultural diversity officer with the Federal Bureau of Prisons. Part of your responsibilities center around ensuring that correctional institutions remain sensitive to the cultural and religious needs of inmates. You receive a complaint from a Native American inmate in a federal correctional institution who states that his religious beliefs are being denied. This particular inmate, along with several other Native Americans in the institution, practice what is known as the Pipe Religion. Pipe Religion revolves around the use of the Sacred Pipe in seven specific rituals, in particular, the sweat lodge ceremony, which is the traditional way of cleansing body, mind, and spirit. By sweat and prayer, Native Americans cleanse their bodies of toxins and their minds of negativities, heighten their spirits, and come into a balanced relationship with themselves, the Earth, and everything that surrounds them.

Although other correctional facilities provide a sweat lodge for Indian inmates, the prisoners in this facility are restricted as to when and how long the sweat lodges can be used. As a result, Sacred Pipe ceremonies, which normally span several days, cannot be performed.

Many correctional officials and other experts hold the position that freedom of religion is less important than the state's interest in maintaining security and order within the prison.

Questions

1. How do you respond to the inmate's complaint? Do you allow the religious practice, or do you argue that inmates lose some of their constitutional protections once they are convicted?
2. What liability does the institution bear if someone becomes ill or injured during the course of one of these rituals?
3. Should taxpayer money be used to allow inmates to practice their religion?
4. Are correctional officials as well as the public at greater physical risk by denying inmates the opportunity to practice their religion?

Key Terms

American Indian Movement (p. 129)
Battle at Little Big Horn (p. 127)
Battle of Wounded Knee (p. 127)
Bureau of Indian Affairs (p. 128)
Ghost Dance religion (p. 127)
Indian Claims Commission (p. 130)

Indian Removal Act of 1830 (p. 126)
Office of Tribal Justice (p. 141)
Red Power Movement (p. 129)
setoffs (p. 130)
Termination Act (p. 128)
tribal courts (p. 130)

Discussion Questions

1. What role, if any, does casino gambling have on improving the lives of Native Americans? Is it really a solution to the problems relating to the poverty and unemployment that are characteristic of Native Americans?
2. In the recent era of celebrating individual differences and cultures, why do you think the federal government has forced Native Americans to assimilate into mainstream American culture? What implications do you think this has on the preservation of Native American culture?
3. Should there be a separate system of justice for Native American tribes or should the federal government retain authority to hear all cases? Should there be a distinction between crimes committed on reservations and crimes committed outside those areas?
4. Do you think Native Americans should have their own educational system, such as tribal colleges? Why or why not?
5. What obligation, if any, should the federal government have to improve the lives of Native Americans on reservations? Defend your position.

Endnotes

1. Remini, R. V. 2001. *Andrew Jackson and His Indian Wars*. New York: Viking.
2. Ibid.
3. Ibid.
4. Thorton, R. 1981. "Demographic Antecedents of the 1890 Ghost Dance." *American Sociological Review* 46 (February): 88–96.
5. Brown, D. 1971. *Bury My Heart at Wounded Knee*. New York: Holt, Rinehart and Winston.
6. Ibid.
7. Ibid.
8. Dennis, H. C. 1971. *The American Indian 1492–1970: A Chronology and Fact Book*. Dobbs Ferry, NY: Oceana.
9. Nagel 1996. *American Indian Ethnic Renewal: Red Power and the Resurgence of Identity and Culture*. New York: Oxford University Press.
10. Marger, K. 2003. *Race and Ethnic Relations*, 6th ed. Belmont, CA: Wadsworth.
11. Ibid.
12. Nies, J. 1996. *Native American History: A Chronology of the Vast Achievements of a Culture and Their Links to World Events*. New York: Ballantine Books.
13. Washburn, W. 1984. "A Fifty-Year Perspective on the Indian Reorganization Act." *American Anthropologist* 86: 279–289.
14. Nagel 1996; Drabelle, D. 1997. "The Trade of the Tribes," *Washington Post National Weekly Edition*, September 8, p. 34.
15. Tarver, M., Walker, S., and Wallace, H. 2002. *Multicultural Issues in the Criminal Justice System*. Boston: Allyn & Bacon.
16. United States Bureau of the Census. 2000. *Resident Population Estimates of the United States, 2000*. Washington, DC: U.S. Government Printing Office.
17. Ross, L. 1998. *Inventing the Savage: The Social Construction of Native American Criminality*. Austin: University of Texas Press. Pp. 16–19.
18. Belluck, P. 1997. "A New Window to Run Welfare Is a Tight Squeeze for Many Tribes." *New York Times*, September 9, pp. A1, A15.
19. Perry, S. W. 2004. *American Indians and Crime 1992–2002*. Department of Justice, Bureau of Justice Statistics. Washington, DC: U.S. Government Printing Office.
20. Ibid.
21. Peroff, N. C. 2006. "Indian Gaming and the American Indian Criminal Justice System." In J. I. Ross and L. Gould (eds.), *Native Americans and the Criminal Justice System*, pp. 179–186. Boulder, CO: Paradigm Publishing.
22. Carstensen, F. 2000. *Economic Impact of the Mashantucket Pequot Tribal Nation Operations in Connecticut*. Storrs: Connecticut Center for Economic Analysis.
23. Peroff 2006.
24. Ibid.
25. Rezendes, M. 2000. "Gambling and Crime," *CitizenLink*, December 27. www.family.org; Unseem, J. 2000. "The Big Gamble: Have American Indians Found Their New Buffalo?" *Fortune*, October 2.
26. Burgard, M., and Green, R. 2002. "More Arrests in Loan Scheme: Casino Patrons Are Victimized." *Hartford Courant*, March 13.
27. Rezendes 2000.
28. Buffalo, H. M. 2002. "Indian Gaming Success in the North." In *Oklahoma Supreme Court Sovereignty Symposium 2002: Language and the Law*, III 22-III, p. 40. Oklahoma City: Supreme Court of Oklahoma; Fine, G. A. 2001. *Review of Indian Gaming Crimes*. Office of Inspector General, Report Number 1-2-1-06, July 3.
29. Evans, W. N., and Topeleski, J. H. 2002. "The Social and Economic Impact of Native American Casinos." National Bureau of Economic Research Working Paper 9198. http://wnetc.mcc.ac.uk/WoPEc/data/Papers/nbrnberwo9198.html.
30. Ibid.

31. Peroff 2006.
32. U.S. Bureau of Justice Statistics. 2004. *Sourcebook of Criminal Justice Statistics.* Washington, DC: U.S. Government Printing Office.
33. Orfield, G. (ed.). 2004. *Dropouts in America: Confronting the Graduation Rate Crisis.* Cambridge, MA: Harvard Education.
34. U.S. Department of Justice. 2005. *Uniform Crime Reports.* Washington, DC: U.S. Government Printing Office.
35. Gould, L. 2006. "Alcoholism, Colonialism, and Crime." In J. I. Ross and L. Gould (eds.), *Native Americans and the Criminal Justice System,* pp. 87–102. Boulder, CO: Paradigm Publishing.
36. Perry 2004.
37. Ibid.
38. Ibid.
39. U.S. Department of Justice 2005, *Uniform Crime Reports*.
40. National Criminal Justice Association. 2005. *Native Americans and Crime.* Washington, DC: U.S. Government Printing Office.
41. DiGregory, K. V., and Manuel, H. A. 1997. *Final Report of the Executive Committee for Indian Country Law Enforcement Improvements.* Washington, DC: U.S. Department of Justice.
42. U.S. Bureau of Justice Statistics 2004, *Sourcebook of Criminal Justice Statistics.*
43. Bond-Maupin, L., GoodTracks, T. X., and Maupin, J. R. 2006. "Research on Juvenile Delinquency in Indian Communities." In J. I. Ross and L. Gould (eds.), *Native Americans and the Criminal Justice System,* pp. 187–196. Boulder, CO: Paradigm Publishing.
44. U.S. Bureau of Justice Statistics 2004, *Sourcebook of Criminal Justice Statistics.*
45. Perry 2004.
46. Ibid.
47. Ibid.
48. U.S. Bureau of Justice Statistics 2004, *Sourcebook of Criminal Justice Statistics.*
49. Perry 2004.
50. U.S. Bureau of Justice Statistics 2004, *Sourcebook of Criminal Justice Statistics.*
51. Ibid.
52. Ibid.
53. Snake, R., Hawkins, G., and LaBoueff, S. 1976. *Report on Alcohol and Drug Abuse: Final Report to the American Indian Policy Review Commission.* Washington, DC: U.S. Government Printing Office.
54. Parry, J. H. 1967. "Spanish Indian Policy in Colonial America: The Ordering of Society." In J. J. TePaske (ed.), *Three American Empires,* pp. 109–126. Durham, NC: Duke University Press.
55. Grim, C. 2002. *Responding Through Collaborations.* Report delivered at the Tribal Leader Summit on Alcohol and Substance Abuse. Albuquerque, New Mexico.
56. Gould 2006.
57. Saggers, S., and Gray, D. 1998. *Dealing with Alcohol: Indigenous Usage in Australia, New Zealand and Canada.* Cambridge, UK: Cambridge University Press.
58. Gould 2006.
59. Bond-Maupin, GoodTracks, and Maupin 2006.
60. Silverman, R. A. 1996. "Patterns of Native American Crime." In M. O. Nielsen and R. A. Silverman (eds.), *Native Americans, Crime and Justice,* pp. 58–74. Boulder, CO: Westview Press.
61. Bond-Maupin, GoodTracks, and Maupin, 2006.
62. Tarver, Walker, and Wallace 2002.
63. DiGregory and Manuel 1997.
64. U.S. Department of Justice 2005, *Uniform Crime Reports.*
65. U.S. Bureau of Justice Statistics 2004, *Sourcebook of Criminal Justice Statistics.*
66. Tarver, Wallace, and Walker 2002.
67. Ross 1998.
68. Ibid.
69. Ibid.
70. U.S. Bureau of Justice Statistics 2004, *Sourcebook of Criminal Justice Statistics.*

Women and the Criminal Justice System

Chapter Objectives

After reading this chapter, you should be able to

❖ Understand the differential treatment of males and females in the criminal justice system.

❖ Recognize the differences between male and female criminality and victimization.

❖ Understand how females have overcome some barriers, but continue to face others,

with regard to being accepted as law enforcement officers.

❖ Contrast the role of males and females with regard to courtroom practices.

❖ Understand the particular challenges facing women under correctional supervision.

Women have faced much adversity in their fight for equal rights with men. Toward this end, much progress has been made, yet much work remains. Regarding criminal justice, historically, females have been an afterthought, with a few "evil women" entering the system. The situation is much different today. An increasing number of females are entering the criminal justice system, in turn providing distinct challenges for the system and multiple hurdles for female offenders.

✵ The Fight for Rights

Females were largely taken for granted in the early part of U.S. history. The limited consideration of females is evidenced in their prohibition from voting, serving on juries, holding property, or making legal contracts. Further, the 1776 Declaration of Independence noted that all *men* are created equal, and the only reference to sex in the U.S. Constitution is in the **Nineteenth Amendment,** ratified by Congress in 1920, which gave women the right to vote. Women were not considered persons protected by the Fourteenth Amendment to the Constitution, which provides equal protection of the law.[1]

The advancement of females in relation to these and related restrictions is largely attributable to **feminist movements,** which generally promote the idea that males and females should be politically, socially, and economically equal. The beginning of the first feminist movement of the 19th century is traced to a convention in Seneca Falls, New York, in 1848, attended by roughly 300 women intent on achieving equal rights for women. The group's focus was on property and suffrage. Attendees adopted a women-specific Declaration of Independence highlighting women's concerns. In the end, their efforts went formally unrecognized.[2] However, their voices were heard, in turn, opening the doors for additional women's rights movements and the ultimate advancement of female interests.

Other forms of activism in support of women's rights emerged following the gathering in Seneca Falls. For instance, in 1916, a group of feminists, then known as suffragists, organized into the National Women's Party and picketed the White House. This group of feminists consisted of two factions with differing goals. One faction sought reform of all institutions of society, while the other faction focused on winning the right for females to vote. The latter faction dominated the movement, and with passage of the 1920 Amendment, which gave women the right to vote, the group disintegrated.[3]

Support for women's rights reemerged in the 1960s and continues today. This movement has broad goals ranging from increasing employment opportunities for females to reducing the amount of violence against women. It is focused on meeting the needs of today's women and continues to shape public policy as it relates to gender equality.[4] Women's rights movements have paid off in terms of the advancement of females. Table 7.1 highlights the accomplishments of eight women who significantly impacted the criminal justice system. To be sure, many other women have impacted the development of the criminal justice system. The individuals listed in the table are among those who have made the most significant contributions.

Despite the progress, females continue to face discrimination and challenges involving the criminal justice system. Among the problems they currently face are increased levels of drug addiction, poverty, racism, and incarceration. These troubles are pronounced with regard to the marginalized females in society, including homeless females, single mothers, and women below the federal poverty line.[5]

TABLE 7.1

Influential Women in the History of U.S. Criminal Justice

Jane Addams   Her work improving social and living conditions for the poor was among the contributions that earned her a Nobel Peace Prize in 1931.

Lola G. Baldwin   In 1908 she became one of the United States' first female policewomen.

Dorothea Dix   During the 19th century she was extremely influential in advocating humanitarian reform in American mental institutions, which ultimately reduced the burden on the criminal justice system.

Penny Harrington   In 1985 she became the first woman in the United States to become chief of police in a large city when she was appointed to head the Portland Police Bureau.

Sandra Day O'Connor   In 1981 she began serving as the first female associate justice of the Supreme Court of the United States.

Charlotte E. Ray   In 1872 she became the first African American woman admitted to the bar in the United States.

Mary Weed   The first woman administrator in U.S. corrections, she was the principal keeper of the Walnut Street Jail in 1793.

Alice Stebbins Wells   In 1910 she became one of the United States' first female policewomen.

⚔ Women as a Distinct Culture

In May 1992, John Gray published the best-selling book *Men Are from Mars, Women Are from Venus*. In the book, Gray discusses the differences between males and females, suggesting that men and women are as distant as planets of the solar system, and he offers advice regarding how the differences between males and females can be overcome. Whether one agrees with Gray's assertions that there are substantial differences between men and women is one's own prerogative. However, it cannot be denied that men and women are different in several ways, not only biologically but culturally, psychologically, and sociologically as well.

There is some debate regarding whether or not women's culture is distinct from men's culture. At the most basic level, culture involves the sharing of norms, language, beliefs, values, behaviors, and material objects. Thus, the question is asked, Do females differ from males with regard to culture? Researchers have identified differences between males and females with regard to each of these criteria, yet are the differences significant enough to warrant a women's culture distinct from a men's culture? We believe there indeed exists a distinct women's culture; thus a chapter on females is included in this book. Nevertheless, we recognize the great number of similarities between males and females and appreciate the arguments of those who suggest females are not culturally distinct from males. The deciding factor in our decision to include a chapter on females in this work was the distinct nature, treatment, and plight of females entering the criminal justice system. In many ways, the females who enter the justice system are different from the males who do so.

Gender identity and roles have significant impacts on cultural differences. **Gender** is a master status as it cuts across all walks of life. It is a social characteristic that varies from one social group to another and refers to femininity or masculinity. We are all labeled either male or female and, with that label, come expectations of our behavior and images of what we are like. The labels often guide our behavior. Similar to gender is **sex,** which relates to the biological characteristics that distinguish males and females. You inherit your sex; you are socialized into your gender by the expectations and standards of the culture in which you live.[6]

Females are considered a minority group in the United States despite there being more females than males in the population. How can this be? As mentioned earlier in this book, a minority group is a group of individuals who face discrimination based on members' cultural or physical characteristics.[7] While progress has been made with regard to societal acceptance of women as equal to men, there remains a great deal of discrimination against females solely on the basis of gender.

The distinction between sex and gender generates debate regarding whether human behavior is mostly a product of biological or sociological influences. For instance, are females distinct from males in many ways due to biological factors, or are the differences attributable to the manner in which society treats both males and females? The issue of nature versus nurture is alive and well.

Aside from the obvious biological differences, females differ from males in a variety of ways. The psychological, biological, and sociological research literatures are filled with studies highlighting differences between males and females. Differences between males and females with regard to social factors are evident and

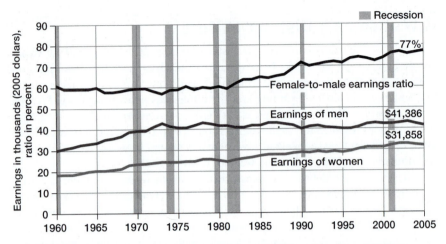

FIGURE 7.1   *Female-to-Male Earnings Ratio and Median Earnings of Full-Time, Year-Round Workers 15 Years and Older by Sex, 1960 to 2005*

Note: The data points are placed at the midpoints of the respective years. Data on earnings of full-time, year-round workers are not readily available before 1960.

SOURCE: U.S. Census Bureau, Current Population Survey, 1961 to 2006 Annual Social and Economic Supplements.

relevant to the study of crime and justice. For instance, along with education levels, a major predictor of poverty is the sex of the individual who heads the family. Females, compared to males, are more likely to be poor and most poor families are headed by a female. Figure 7.1 depicts the income disparities for males and females.[8] Divorce, births to single women, and the lower wages paid to females compared to males largely contribute to the increased level of poverty among females.[9] These factors ultimately contribute to increased incarceration rates.

The criminal justice system has been mixed in its approach to recognizing distinctions between male and female criminals and the different types of crimes they commit. For example, there exists a wealth of research suggesting that, compared to males, females are given preferential treatment by police, prosecutors, and judges. On the other hand, the lack of consideration of female needs in prison and the belief that what explains male crime also explains female crime suggest that criminal justice professionals and criminologists believe females are no different from males.

The continuously emerging field of feminist criminology has aptly changed society's interpretation of differences between males and females regarding criminality. Too often, females are considered as only a control variable in criminological research.[10] While the consideration of male/female differences is appropriate, merely including females as a control variable says little of the distinct nature of female involvement in crime and criminal justice practices. The fields of criminology and criminal justice lag behind many other disciplines with regard to the acceptance of female scholarship as vital to these fields of study. While feminist scholarship has grown in the past three decades, much of the work has been marginalized and relegated to specialty journals.[11] Females have been underrepresented in sociological and criminological journals dating back to 1895, with both male and female researchers more likely to focus on males than on females.[12]

⚔ Female Arrestees and Victims

Females have historically been underrepresented in criminal behavior. Recent evidence suggests increased female involvement in crime; however, males continue to be responsible for the bulk of criminal behavior. Data from the *Uniform Crime Reports* show that females constituted 23.8% of all arrests in 2005. There was a notable difference in arrest patterns with regard to violent crimes and property crimes. Specifically, females constituted 32% of arrests for property crime, yet only 17.9% of arrests for violent crime.[13]

Trends in Arrest Rates

Arrest trend data highlight the increased level of female involvement in crime and the criminal justice system. Nationwide, between 1996 and 2005, the number of males arrested decreased 7.6% compared to an increase of 7.4% in the number of females arrested. During the same time frame, the number of males arrested for violent crime fell 15.1%, yet the number of females arrested for violent crime rose 4.4%. The number of persons arrested for drug abuse violations notably increased for both males and females from 1996 through 2005: an increase of 21% for males and 41.7% for females.[14] Again, despite the substantial increases in arrests of females, it remains that men constitute the bulk of offenders and arrestees. Nevertheless, these findings must be considered in light of the fact that arrests do not necessarily explain criminal behavior. For instance, some researchers believe that despite increased arrests for females who commit violent crimes, the typical female offender has not become increasingly violent in recent history.[15] Arrests are largely influenced by police officer discretion, which certainly influences arrest statistics.

Increased female involvement in the criminal justice system has not happened by chance. To be sure, there are several explanations why females are increasingly represented in arrest statistics, including

- less biased responses by criminal justice practitioners to criminal behavior;
- changes in law enforcement practices targeting less serious offenses;
- gender equality and more desire and opportunity to commit crime;
- increased economic marginalization of women;
- increased inner-city community disorganization;
- expanded opportunities for female-type crimes, for instance, as they relate to increased consumerism;

Recent evidence suggests increased female involvement in crime.

- changes in the criminal underworld, for instance, the reduced supply of male crime partners due to increased incarceration;
- trends in drug dependency, with drug addiction encouraging income-generating crime; and
- crime prevention programs targeted primarily toward males.[16]

Each of these items helps explain the rise in female involvement in the criminal justice system, and each is worthy of greater empirical evaluation to determine the extent to which it has impacted females and the criminal justice system.

Victimization

The distinction between males and females in the criminal justice system is obvious with regard to victimization statistics, as female victimization rates and characteristics generally differ from those of males. For instance, from 2002–2003 to 2004–2005, the rate of violent crimes against females decreased 11.7%, while the rate decreased only 2.6% for males. In 2004–2005, females were less likely than males to be the victims of violent crime, as 17.6 females per 1,000 persons 12 and older were violently victimized, compared to 25.2 males per 1,000 persons. In 2005, females were far more likely than males to be the victim of rape or sexual assault, yet much less likely to be the victim of robbery or any type of assault. Females were slightly more likely than males to be the victim of personal theft.[17]

Females are more likely than males to be victimized by someone known to them rather than by a stranger.

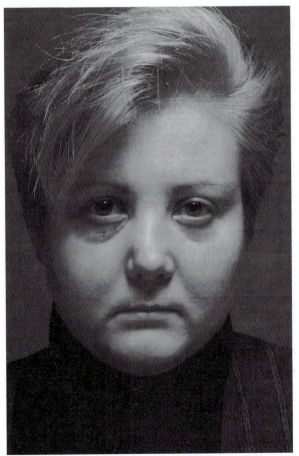

Females are notably more likely than males to be victimized by someone known to them rather than by a stranger. Table 7.2 depicts how females, more often than males, are violently victimized by a nonstranger. The increased likelihood of women being violently victimized during domestic abuse cases largely contributes to these findings. Absent from Table 7.2 is a comparison of male and female victimization with regard to rape and sexual assault. Females are far more susceptible to sex offenses than are males. The small number of males who reported being raped or sexually assaulted in 2005 makes comparisons of rates invalid. However, an estimated 176,090 females were the victim of rape or sexual assault in 2005, with almost three-quarters of the victims being familiar with the offender. Twenty-six percent of rapes or sexual assaults were committed by strangers.[18] **Acquaintance rape,** which involves an individual raping an acquaintance; **marital rape,** in which a man or woman rapes their spouse; and sexual abuse (including

TABLE 7.2

Victim and Offender Relationship, 2005

	Violent Crime	Robbery	Aggravated Assault	Simple Assault
Male Victims				
Nonstranger	43%	23%	42%	48%
Stranger	54	74	54	49
Unknown	3	3	4	3*
Female Victims				
Nonstranger	64%	50%	62%	66%
Stranger	34	48	37	33
Unknown	2	3*	1	1

* Percentages do not total 100% due to rounding.

Source: U.S. Department of Justice, Bureau of Justice Statistics. *Criminal Victimization, 2005.*

children) are of particular concern to females, who are also especially vulnerable to specific types of violent crime, such as domestic violence and stalking.

Crime reporting practices, particularly with regard to violent crimes, are another area where males and females differ. Specifically, females were substantially more likely than males to report violent victimizations in 2005. Roughly 54% of violent acts committed against females were reported to police, compared to only about 42% of violent acts committed against males. Overall, only 47.4% of violent incidents were reported to police. With regard to reporting property crimes, there is very little difference among males (who reported 40% of the property crimes committed against them) and females (39%).[19]

⚔ Women and Policing

There is debate regarding who deserves the title of the first female police officer in the United States. Alice Stebbens Wells arguably became the United States' first policewoman when she began her career with the LAPD in 1910. Others claim Lola Baldwin became the nation's first policewoman following her 1908 appointment as an officer in Portland, Oregon. Regardless of who deserves the distinction, female involvement in policing prior to the time of Wells and Baldwin was restricted to roles as jailers and police matrons. By 1915 female police officers worked in 25 different U.S. cities, and in 1918 Ellen O'Grady became police commissioner of New York City.[20] The pioneering work of these and other female officers has paved the way for enhanced female involvement in policing, yet for several reasons, females remain very underrepresented in policing. Primary among the reasons for underrepresentation of females in policing is the nature of police work. It is likely that many females may not wish to work in policing. Females and other minorities have historically been underrepresented on police forces, although proactive efforts by police departments have increased the representation of both groups.

Increased representation among the ranks of law enforcement has not overwhelmingly led to females assuming positions among the top ranks of law enforcement agencies. Only about 200, or roughly 1%, of police chiefs and sheriffs in the United States are female.[21] Obviously, some cities have been more proactive than others in promoting females to the top ranks of law enforcement and other positions. For example, in 2004 San Francisco Mayor Gavin Newsom appointed women to the top positions in the city's fire and police departments.

Females have made great progress in policing since the **Civil Rights Act of 1964,** which prohibited discrimination in hiring on the basis of color, race, sex, religion, or national origin, and the **Equal Employment Opportunity Act of 1972,** when protections of women and other minorities were extended to local governments. Women have moved beyond primarily assuming administrative assignments and other matron-like duties to increasingly engaging in traditional police officer practices. Nevertheless, much work remains. Females remain underrepresented in all ranks of policing, constituting only 11.6% of the 673,146 local law enforcement officers as of October 2005. Higher percentages of female officers are generally found in larger departments than in small, rural departments. Females are more likely to hold non-officer law enforcement positions (i.e., as civilians) than officer positions.[22]

Policewomen

Despite the misperception of some members of the general public and some male police officers that females are unsuited for the difficulties associated with police work, females have much to offer police work. For instance, the research literature in policing suggests females, compared to males, tend to use less force and thus face fewer complaints of excessive force; have better communications skills; are better able to address situations involving violence against women; and could change the climate of policing to reduce the number of claims regarding sexual harassment and sex discrimination.[23]

Policewomen have often faced difficulty overcoming the barriers associated with being accepted as "legitimate" police officers. For instance, some male officers (and some officers' wives) perceive that females may not provide adequate backup during dangerous encounters. Some officers believe policewomen often are unwilling or unable to provide the appropriate level of enforcement when needed.[24] The police culture, which emphasizes masculinity and toughness, provides a notable obstacle for females wishing to be accepted among the ranks. Women officers are perceived by some in policing and the general society to lack the physical and emotional strength to tackle the rigors of police work.[25] Females are sometimes required to "prove" themselves and mitigate traditional stereotypes early in their careers by using force in the presence of male officers.[26] Research examining officer use of force in St. Petersburg, Florida, and Indianapolis, Indiana, suggests that, compared to male officers, female officers were not reluctant to use physical force, and few differences were found with regard to the extent to which officers used verbal and physical violence and the reasons for doing so.[27] Some barriers females have had to overcome in being accepted as police officers are

- stereotypes, for instance, that females are not strong enough for police work;
- discrimination in the hiring process;

- sexual harassment;
- social isolation;
- a double standard in performance evaluations, as females feel they must outperform their male counterparts;
- receiving less desirable assignments;
- limited opportunities for promotion; and;
- lack of family-friendly policies such as those pertaining to child care.[28]

Female officers from racial/ethnic minority groups sometimes face a sense of **double jeopardy,** for instance, when their race and gender pose particular challenges not faced by many other officers.[29] Hostility, separation, intimidation, and implicit and explicit discriminatory behaviors of male officers contribute to the underrepresentation of African American female officers on many forces.[30] Double jeopardy is not restricted to African American females in policing, as female officers from other minority groups face similar challenges. For instance, researchers found that lesbian police officers in a large municipal police department faced a notable sense of social exclusion and overt sexist and anti-gay behavior from coworkers. Lesbian officers in a small department sensed that their greatest barriers were attributable to their gender rather than their sexual orientation.[31]

The misperception that females are less effective police officers than males hampers females' efforts to become more ingrained in policing. Very few individuals in society would seek to work in an area where their colleagues and customers or clients are skeptical of their abilities to perform the job. The term "misperception" is used as it is well documented that females perform as well as, or better than, males in particular aspects of policing. To be sure, there are aspects of policing that are better suited to males. For instance, males are generally better suited to wrestle offenders given the likelihood of male officers having more muscle mass than females. Yet, wrestling offenders is a small, albeit important, aspect of the job. The inability of females to physically interact with offenders on par with males is tempered by the fact that some male offenders won't engage in physical contact with females, and female officers are better able than male officers to verbally, as opposed to physically, quell a confrontational situation.

Interaction with the Police

It is well established in the criminology literature that males commit the bulk of crime in society. Accordingly, it is expected that males would more often be in contact with the police. In 2005 an estimated 39.2 million males had contact with police, compared to 32 million females. Only 17.2% of females 16 and older in the United States had contact with the police, compared to 21.1% of males. Also, males were more likely than females to have multiple contacts with the police.[32]

Most police–citizen encounters occur while officers are on patrol. Patrol is considered the backbone of policing. Among other functions, patrol enables officers to respond quickly to calls, promotes positive police–community relations, deters would-be offenders, and helps control crime through traffic stops. Although there were roughly the same number of males and females in the driving population in 2005, male drivers were notably more likely than females to be stopped by

THE INTERNATIONAL ASSOCIATION OF WOMEN POLICE

In 1915 the International Policewomen's Association was established to support the advancement of females in policing. The group reorganized and changed its name to the International Association of Women Police (IAWP) in 1956. Among other contributions to supporting women's involvement in policing, the IAWP annually hosts a five-day forum for researchers and practitioners from around the world to share their views and disseminate information on females in policing. Currently, the IAWP has over 2,400 members from more than 45 different countries.

The IAWP, like other professional associations that promote the advancement of females in policing, offers its members educational, networking, and mentoring opportunities. Further, the IAWP seeks to enhance the prestige and professionalism of policewomen, to encourage officers to learn new things about themselves and their career, and to provide a sense of belonging for the officers. Primary among the goals of the IAWP is to promote fairness and equity in workplaces and to encourage a work environment that is free of harassment and discrimination.[33]

The adoption of an international component of a professional policewomen's association demonstrates the awareness of the need to promote cross-national interaction in policing, particularly with regard to females. Understanding the challenges faced by female officers in other countries, and the responses to those challenges, provides numerous benefits to policing in general, including officer mentoring; and strengthening, uniting, and raising the profile of women in criminal justice internationally. Along these lines, the existence of the IAWP and other professional associations designated for policewomen (such as the National Association of Women Law Enforcement Executives, the National Center for Women & Policing, and various state- and regional-level groups) provides invaluable support for female officers and demonstrates the significant advancement of females in policing.

police (10.8% compared to 6.8%). During these stops, punitive actions were more likely to be taken against males than females. Females were more likely than males to be issued a written warning and/or given a verbal warning; males were more likely to be arrested, ticketed, and/or searched. Males were also more likely than females to have force used against them by police.[34] These numbers do not prove differential treatment of males and females, as one must consider the actions and behaviors of the motorists stopped by, and individuals in contact with, the police. Nevertheless, the numbers do suggest that interactions between police and motorists differ based on gender.

✕ Females and the Courts

Discretion is inherent in the criminal justice system, and it is perhaps most obvious in the legal arena, where critical decisions are often made. The decisions to file charges, grant pretrial release (including the nature of the release), engage in plea bargaining, convict or acquit, and impose a punitive or soft sentence are among the most critical decisions made by courtroom personnel. To be sure, consideration of race and ethnicity influences some decisions. For instance, the **"double bind"** faced by minority females in the criminal justice system, based on their status as female and minority, dictates that courts ought to make concerted efforts to release female minority defendants on their own recognizance since they often have low incomes and are unable to post bail.[35] If bail is required, it should be reasonable given that many minority females who enter the criminal justice system are single parents and detention would have secondary effects on their children.[36] Similarly, poor minorities entering our courts also face "double marginality."[37] Such a situation increases the difficulties associated with, among other things, obtaining competent representation and/or securing release from detention.

Gender-based decisions are notably obvious in the legal arena, as evidenced in the criminal justice research literature and our discussion of females and the courts. We focus on several critical areas of gender differences as they exist in the courts. Specifically, we examine decision making and gender as it relates to sentencing and the imposition of capital punishment, and the nature and challenges of females who work in the courtroom.

Sentencing

Historically, female offenders generally received more lenient sentences than their male counterparts. The difference was more pronounced with regard to less serious crimes, as more serious, violent crimes decreased the likelihood of differential treatment. Some research suggests there is no gender neutrality in the sentencing process, as females face much lower odds than males of being incarcerated. Female offenders are sometimes viewed as less culpable, less likely to reoffend, and more amenable to rehabilitation than male offenders, and sentenced accordingly.[38] There is debate, however, regarding whether or not females continue to receive preferential treatment in the courts, and whether or not paternalism or chivalry on behalf of

Females are becoming increasingly involved in all aspects of the courts.

criminal justice officials persists. In light of increasing numbers of females entering the criminal justice system, some researchers suggest females are no longer treated differently from males.

It appears that with regard to judicial decision making and sentencing decisions, judges consider both legally relevant and legally irrelevant factors when sentencing females, yet only legally relevant factors when sentencing males.[39] Judges typically consider legally relevant factors such as dangerousness, blameworthiness, and social costs in their sentencing decisions, with the consideration of social costs most often benefiting female defendants. With respect to legally irrelevant factors, judges are more likely to take child care into consideration in processing females convicted of less serious crimes.[40] For example, judges would be less punitive toward mothers arrested for a misdemeanor than toward their male counterparts. **Sentencing guidelines,** designed to provide consistency and parity in sentencing decisions, are seemingly undermined by judges who deviate from the sentencing schedule while treating females more leniently than males.[41] Nevertheless, sentencing guidelines have largely contributed to the increased rate of female incarceration.

Capital Punishment and Females

In 1998 Karla Faye Tucker generated worldwide attention. Tucker, a born-again Christian, was scheduled for execution in Texas. Prior to the execution, Waly Bacre Ndiaye (of the United Nations Commission on Summary and Arbitrary Executions), Pope John Paul II, Italian Prime Minister Romano Prodi, conservative American political figure Newt Gingrich, and Christian evangelist Pat Robertson offered support of Tucker, who had been convicted of committing murder with a pickaxe. Why the controversy, given that Texas executes many offenders? For starters, Tucker was to be the first female executed in Texas since the Civil War. To be sure, other females in Texas committed offenses worthy of capital punishment between the Civil War and 1998. Karla Faye Tucker was executed on February 3, 1998.

It is suggested that receiving the death penalty (i.e., capital punishment) is akin to a crapshoot which is dependent upon a variety of variables. Judicial discretion, jury makeup, and the state in which the capital offense was committed largely contribute to one's likelihood of being executed. Needless to say, capital punishment remains one of the more controversial issues in society. The small number of females executed or facing execution in relation to the number of males adds to the controversy.

Males undoubtedly commit more violent crime and more capital offenses than females. Thus, it is not surprising that 59 men and only 1 female were executed in 2005. It is expected that more females will be executed in the near future as females become increasingly involved in committing crimes. In 2005 there were 52 women under the sentence of death, an increase from the 47 facing death in 1995. Most of the women on death row as of year-end 2005 were being held in five states: California (14 female inmates on death row), Texas (9), Pennsylvania (5), North Carolina (4), and Alabama (3).[42] Much of the controversy surrounding the execution of females has subsided.

Female Courtroom Personnel

Courtroom personnel have traditionally consisted of White males, although recent trends suggest an increase in the numbers of women assuming law-related careers as public defenders, prosecutors, and judges.[43] For instance, the percentage of female lawyers increased from 23% in 1994 to 29.1% in 2003. Between 1994 and 2002, increases were noted with regard to the percentage of law school entrants who were female; women in tenured positions at law schools; women partners in major law firms; and women in the federal judiciary.[44] Further, females constitute between one-third and one-half of all law school students and over 10% of judges in U.S. courts.[45] An increasing number of females have assumed positions as federal judges beginning with Jimmy Carter's presidency, with females constituting 18% of former president Bill Clinton's nominations to the federal judiciary.[46] Nevertheless, females remain underrepresented as practitioners in the legal system.

The problem is enhanced for minority females, who face the double bind of being female and a minority group member. For instance, in 2004 only 17% of law partners were female and only 4% were of color. Compared to White male attorneys, women attorneys of color felt excluded from informal and formal networking opportunities, were more likely to believe they met with clients only when their gender or race would be advantageous to the firm, and more often felt their accomplishments didn't receive due consideration.[47]

Unfortunately, women of all races who have "broken the barrier" and entered the inside world of working within the courts continue to face particular challenges such as limited advancement opportunities due to stereotyping of females and lack of access to the male socialization process.[48] Gender bias is primary among the concerns addressed by the women's rights movement, and it is certainly evident in our courts as the U.S. legal system is by no means exempt from claims of gender bias. Since the early 1980s, task forces have been created in 36 states to investigate gender bias in the legal system. Such bias can come in the form of decision making based on stereotypes regarding gender—for instance, in believing that domestic violence is a private matter that should be addressed at home. Gender bias also comes in the form of comments and actions toward individuals based on gender. Referring to female attorneys by their first names and making sexist remarks or telling sexist jokes fall in this category and were common among the claims addressed by the task forces. Bias based on gender is also evident in claims that females face more difficulty than males in being hired and promoted, and that they are paid less than their male counterparts.[49]

The increased number of females working in the legal arena may or may not lead to changes in our courtrooms. The possibility and/or extent of these changes is open to debate. For example, gender differences may result in differential treatment of those entering our courts. There is also the possibility that any differences due to gender would be tempered by the background of the females entering the courts and the socialization process found in our courts. Put simply, there is uncertainty regarding if and how biological (i.e., differences due to gender) or sociological factors (e.g., the influences of law school and working directly within the court system) will influence future courtroom practices in light of the increasing number of females working in our courts.

Of particular interest with regard to the increased number of females working within our courts are the changing practices associated with judicial discretion. Speculation and assumptions regarding the behaviors of female judges tend to suggest that female judges are less punitive than male judges, although more likely than male judges to act harsher toward sex offenses and to impose sentences. There is also the belief that male judges are more paternalistic (i.e., they assume the role of a father-figure) than female judges toward female defendants. However, limited empirical research has examined the on-the-job differences between male and female judges. To address the lack of research in the area, social scientists Darrell Steffensmeier and Chris Hebert examined the sentencing practices of male and female judges and found both similarities and differences in the sentencing practices of males and females on the bench. Particularly, they found that female judges were somewhat more punitive and more considerate of defendant characteristics (specifically, race, sex, and age) and prior record than male judges. They also found that female judges were more punitive than male judges when sentencing repeat Black offenders, both males and females.[50]

⚔ Females and Corrections

As the arrest and conviction rates of females increase, it follows that a greater percentage of women will be under correctional supervision. The increased presence of females in correctional facilities and under community corrections provides particular challenges to correctional staff and administration. Females under correctional supervision have special needs distinct from those of male offenders. Female prisons and jail administrators must continue to consider the special needs of female inmates and ensure that the goals of the correctional agency or institution are met. Too often in corrections, it is believed that simply applying male-based correctional practices to female inmates will suffice. This approach is limited at best.

The increased number of incarcerated females has encouraged corrections officials to adjust to a series of issues and concerns as they relate to females. For instance, many female inmates have children they must care for while incarcerated. Traditional correctional practices and procedures are not well suited to address the special needs of females. Addressing, at least in part, the challenges posed by an increasingly female correctional population has changed the face of corrections. At the very least it has forced correctional agencies to consider ways to best adapt to the changing demographics of the prison population.

Female Incarceration

The United States began experiencing a dramatic increase in its incarceration rate in the early 1980s. Increased incarceration of both males and females has impacted females in several ways. For example, the high cost of building prisons takes resources away from the social services from which females often benefit, and which female professionals often offer. In turn, there are fewer professional employment opportunities for women.[51]

One of the more notable developments in society pertains to the increased number of females incarcerated in U.S. prisons and jails. Although many more males are incarcerated than females, the percentage of incarcerated females is increasing at a higher rate than that of males. Three competing hypotheses are offered to explain the increased rate of female incarceration: the demise of chivalry, or the paternalistic treatment of women; women as becoming increasingly "evil"; and the equal treatment of females.[52] Contemporary researchers generally support the equal treatment of females by the criminal justice system as the primary cause of their increased rate of incarceration.[53]

Primary among the reasons for the increased presence of females in the criminal justice system are the substantial impact the war on drugs has had on females and the merging of society's move to become tough on crime with a backlash against women's equality.[54] Other factors influencing the increased number of females being incarcerated include

- increased poverty of women;
- income inequality;
- selective enforcement of drug crimes disproportionately targeting minority groups and the poor;
- an overall more punitive societal and criminal justice system approach to crime;
- increased use of sentencing guidelines and less use of judicial discretion;
- increased drug use and addiction among women;
- a political switch to the right in which criminal behavior is believed to be caused by evil self-will; and
- racism, sexism, homophobia, and class bias.[55]

With regard to prison statistics, men, at mid-year 2006, were roughly 14 times more likely than females to be incarcerated. However, between 2000 and 2006, the female prison population grew an average of 3.3%, compared to an average increase of 2.0% in the male prison population. Females comprised 7.2% of the total prison population at mid-year 2006, compared to 6.1% at year-end 2000.[56]

With regard to race and gender, minority females are more likely than White females to be incarcerated. There were more White women than Black or Hispanic women incarcerated at mid-year 2006; however, the rate of incarceration for Hispanic women (152 per 100,000) and Black women (358) was higher than it was for White women (94).[57] This discrepancy is largely attributable to the war on drugs, which has been very influential in that increasing numbers of minority women are being incarcerated for drug crimes. The war has had a particular influence on Black and Latina women. Along these lines, women of color are more often the mothers of dependent children, and economically marginalized and disadvantaged. The increased level of female incarceration has heavily impacted Black and Latina women in that they are unable to earn a living and care for their children.[58]

Women in Jail

With a relatively transient population, jails offer more limited treatment opportunities and services than prisons. This problem has been compounded by the increasing number of females incarcerated. From mid-2005 to mid-2006, the number of adult females placed in jail increased 4.9% compared to 2.2% for adult males. Similarly, from 2000 to 2006, the number of females placed in local jails increased by 40% compared to 22% for adult males.[59]

Jails have been forced to adapt to a changing inmate population. While several areas of policy and procedure in jails remain constant regardless of inmate gender (e.g., searches, housing, and transportation), special accommodations are needed for females. Inmate mental and physical well-being is of concern, as is the need to consider that many female inmates are single parents who must consider the well-being of their children. These considerations are by no means restricted to jails, as female prison inmates face these and other struggles.

Jails need to consider several issues as related to the increasing involvement of females in the criminal justice system. Particularly, females generally have a more difficult time than males raising money for pretrial release, and may not receive proper medical and mental health attention, as jails have traditionally been structured toward serving male inmates. Also of concern to female inmates are visiting hours with their children, appropriate jail-issued clothing, hygiene supplies, recreational activities, work training programs, and inmate worker positions.[60]

These concerns have not always been addressed. The government has continuously failed to meet the special needs of women and provide adequate medical care. Many of these issues also apply to females in prison; however, these concerns are more likely to be addressed in prison than in jails given that those in prison stay for longer periods of time and the problems may be more noticeable in prison. Unfortunately, females in jail have been referred to as an "afterthought" that pose burdens on the staff.[61] Experienced jail staff who convey to new recruits the stereotype that women in jail are "difficult" perpetuate a culture of bias.[62] It is anticipated that jails will continue to address the particular needs of female inmates.

Women in Prison

Female prisoners were housed in institutions designed for males until the early 19th century. In some institutions, females and males were housed in separate sections. The initial step toward creating prisons specially designed for women didn't occur until 1835, when the Mount Pleasant, New York, Female Prison was attached to Sing Sing, a male prison. The 20th century brought about the incarceration of women exclusively in female prisons, which were less threatening and smaller than male prisons. Unfortunately, their small size resulted in a decreased number of facilities for the inmates.[63]

Prisons contain inmates facing long-term stays (more than one year). Accordingly, the opportunity for inmates to receive specialized treatment and recognition of gender differences is generally of greater consideration in prison than in jails. However, the burden is on prison officials to provide the specialized treatment and recognize and respond to the various gender differences.

The Social Structure of Female Prisons

One of the more notable differences between male and female prisons concerns the social world of prison life. The social structure of male prisons is largely built around the ideas of masculinity, manhood, and homophobia, while female prisons are more structured around kinship, open expression of affection, and family structures.[64]**Prison play-families,** in which inmates assume the roles of different family members, are more often found in female prisons than in male institutions, where such structural arrangements are frowned upon. Latina prisoners are particularly active in play-families given their likelihood of being from families with strong kinship ties outside of prison.[65]

Maintaining Familial Ties

Concern for familial ties extends beyond the prison walls. Of particular concern regarding female prison inmates is care for their children. While female jail inmates must also contend with caring for their children while incarcerated, since prison stays are longer than the time spent in jail, family concerns are amplified among female prisoners. The social, psychological, and economic effects of an increasing number of children who have incarcerated parents will have significant societal impacts for years and generations to come.[66] More children are likely to encounter the incarceration of a father than a mother; however, since the mother is often the primary caregiver, children of female inmates are more likely than children of male inmates to suffer from problems associated with being separated from their parent.[67] Pertinent among the factors influencing the ability of a child with an incarcerated mother to avoid involvement with the criminal justice system include the age of the child at the time of the mother's incarceration, the child's relationship with his or her caregiver at this time, the strength of the mother–child bond, the type of crime committed by the mother, and the length of the mother's sentence.[68]

The most recent data concerning incarcerated parents and their children came from the U.S. Bureau of Justice Statistics (BJS) in 2000. The report noted that in 1999 most state (55%) and federal (63%) prisoners reported having a child under age 18. An estimated 336,300 U.S. households with minor children were affected by the resident parent being imprisoned. Roughly 22% of all minor children of incarcerated parents were under 5 years old. Females (65.3%) incarcerated in state prisons (where most inmates are held) were more likely than their male counterparts (54.7%) to have a child under age 18. Mothers (18.4%) in state prison were also more likely than fathers in state prison (8.5%) to have been homeless, living on the streets, or residing in a shelter in the year prior to their arrest. Between 1991 and 1999, the number of children with a parent in state or federal prison increased from 936,500 to 1,498,800.[69]

The increasing number of parents, particularly mothers, who are incarcerated leads to two concerns: What becomes of the children upon incarceration of their parent(s), and how can prisons facilitate continued parental contact with their children? Most inmates (80%) reported that their children were living with the child's other parent. However, there is a notable difference between male and female inmates with regard to who assumes custody of their children while the parent is incarcerated. Particularly, 90% of male inmates in state prison reported that their children were in the care of the child's mother, compared to 28% of mothers who reported their children were in the custody of their father. Female inmates in state prison most often reported that their children were in the care of the child's grandparent (53%) or other relatives (26%).[70] The large number of incarcerated males leaves behind a greater percentage of troubled children living in single-parent families with marginal economic resources.

The aforementioned BJS report suggested that female inmates are more often in contact with their children than are male inmates. Unfortunately, a majority of male (57%) and female (54%) inmates in state prison report never having a personal visit with their children since their admission to prison. The lack of personal contact between incarcerated parents and their children could be largely explained by the finding that over 60% of parents in state prison were reportedly being incarcerated in institutions over 100 miles from their last place of residence.[71]

Criminal justice officials concerned with promoting close contact between incarcerated parents and their children need to consider placement issues, with the goal of keeping parents as close as possible to their children while maintaining the goals of incarceration. Close family ties during incarceration are related to lower recidivism, improved mental health of inmates, enhanced unification of the family following release, and enhanced success on parole.[72]

Avenues to address the negative impacts upon children of incarcerated parents include

- crisis nurseries to address acute trauma such as a parent's incarceration;
- crisis intervention counseling for children following the arrest of a parent;
- therapeutic interventions to help children address the effects of disturbing situations and promote coping skills;
- therapeutic visitation to reduce the likelihood of domestic violence upon the parents' return home;
- community-based mother–infant correctional programs to foster maternal bonding;
- parent–child visitation programs to encourage positive interactions between child and incarcerated parent; and
- children's support groups, which help children confront the concerns they may face while having an incarcerated parent.[73]

Cultural Concerns in Female Prisons

The varied cultural background of incarcerated females generates several issues of concern. Consideration of cultural concerns regarding Latina, African American, and Asian American female inmates is documented in the criminology and criminal justice literatures. Also, Native American females were identified as having several unmet needs while in prison, despite the fact that females and Native Americans are among the groups with the fastest-growing incarceration rates. Unfortunately, little is known about Native American female inmates. In response, Native American scholar Luana Ross studied the troubles faced by Native American women in a Montana prison, and noted how these inmates resist prison due to the lack of recognition or honoring of Native American culture in prison. Ross found that Native American female inmates lacked access to native spiritual leaders and culturally relevant betterment programs in prison. The desistance of these women led to them receiving more punitive treatment in the facility.[74] To be sure, these and related cultural challenges exist not only within the institution Ross studied, but in many other correctional institutions as well. Further, cultural concerns are not restricted to Native American females, as other groups face a variety of challenges.

Treatment, counseling, and other therapeutic approaches in correctional facilities have historically been designed and targeted toward male offenders. These need to be adapted to meet the needs of female offenders. Further, prison staff should be well versed in multicultural counseling awareness, training, and sensitivity as they pertain to females. Failure to recognize and address the special needs of females, in conjunction with a lack of concern for their well-being after their release from prison, contributes to the reincarceration of female (and other) offenders.[75] Females entering the criminal justice system are more likely than other women to have substance abuse problems, yet correctional institutions often lack adequate substance abuse treatment. In some cases, substance abuse counseling is offered absent additional treatment approaches such as group therapy, family counseling, reunification programs, mental health assistance, and treatment for other ailments faced by female inmates.[76] Greater focus on issues such as violence against females, childhood sexual abuse, and caring for children while incarcerated is needed in today's prisons.

Supervision in the Community

Our discussion of females under correctional supervision has centered primarily on institutional corrections. However, due to the increasing number of females being arrested and convicted, there are an increasing number of females under correctional supervision in the community. The increased presence of females in the criminal justice system is evident in the percentage of females on probation and parole. At year-end 2005, females constituted roughly one in four probationers. The percentage of females on probation increased from 21% in 1995 to 23% in 2005.[77] Further, the estimated 93,000 female parolees at year-end 2005 constituted about one in eight adults on parole. The percentage of females on parole increased from 10% to 12% of all parolees between 1995 and 2005.[78]

Females face particular challenges and issues not only as offenders under community corrections but also as professionals supervising offenders in the community. Consider the particular challenges they face in supervising Hispanic males in the community. The emphasis on machismo in the Hispanic community may pose particular challenges for female probation officers. For example, it is suggested that female probation officers clearly identify their professional role in the relationship due to Hispanic males' often basing their relationship with women according to roles.[79] Further, understanding cultural differences with regard to language can facilitate interactions with clients. Hispanics are typically more immediate in their vocal communications than other racial/ethnic groups, which may, inaccurately, sound intimidating to non-Hispanics. Interactions are enhanced if parole officers, especially female officers, are concise and to the point when communicating with Hispanic clients.[80]

Women Working in Corrections

While not completely absent from correctional facilities, females working in prisons were historically restricted to clerical duties. This changed with Title VII of the Civil Rights Act of 1964, which prohibited sex discrimination by

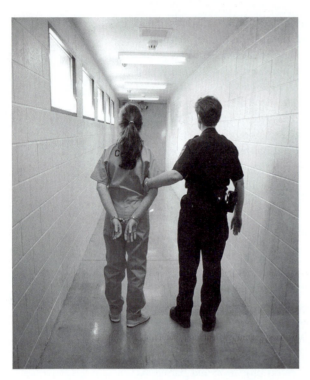

Female correctional officers have had a difficult time gaining acceptance among their male counterparts.

governments in hiring and promotion practices. Among many other accomplishments, this act enabled females to increasingly assume positions in correctional facilities. Currently, roughly 23% of correctional officers are women.[81]

Early Obstacles

Females have had to overcome a series of obstacles to gain acceptance as correctional officers. They were notably underrepresented in the ranks of jail employees until the 1980s and 1990s.[82] Despite the increase in numbers, they have not been particularly well received as employees working in jails. Discrimination, harassment, and the belief that females are unable to fulfill the need for authoritativeness and occasional aggressiveness are but a few of the factors working against females employed in jails. Females have fared somewhat better in prisons.

The introduction of female staff members into male prisons initially generated controversy among inmates and (male) prison staff. Much of the controversy stemmed from the belief that female prison officers were not strong enough to guard male inmates and that they were more sympathetic to inmate causes than male officers.[83] Further, some male officers believe that the long shifts and the need to put in overtime as a correctional officer render females unsuitable as prison officers, primarily because women are viewed as having to be accountable to family needs.[84] Among other effects, the resentment faced by early female correctional officers limited women officers' opportunities to learn from the social networks established by experienced male officers.[85] These, and related concerns, subsided over time, yet corrections remains the most male-dominated, sex-segregated component of the criminal justice system.[86]

When women first became correctional officers in prisons, inmates had their own set of concerns with regard to their presence on the staff. Some male prisoners were sensitive to having to use toilets and showers in plain view of female correctional officers. Sexual harassment of female officers also generated concern, as inmates (and male correctional officers) would have to learn and abide by the laws pertaining to sexual harassment.[87] Today, female and male prison officers are viewed by prisoners as similar with regard to arbitrariness, fairness, and empathy.[88]

Historically, females were absent from the top-level of administration in prisons, but today more females are assuming positions as wardens of men's (and women's) prisons.[89] Tekla Miller, who was appointed warden of the maximum-security Huron Valley Men's Facility in Michigan in 1985, documented the challenges she faced upon assuming the role.[90] Male prison staff, some of whom struggled with female employees in a male prison, viewed the appointment of Miller as warden with disdain. She was able to successfully overcome the opposition of the officers through remaining diplomatic and encouraging a team-oriented approach from her subordinates. In general, females have had success as wardens of male (and female) prisons.[91] However, the number of female wardens will remain low until females are more openly accepted among the ranks of correctional officers—an important stepping-stone for one who wishes to become a warden. Females have had a much easier time being accepted among the ranks of probation and parole officers.

Females Working in Community Corrections

Probation emerged from the treatment model of corrections in the early part of the 20th century and was led by White female probation officers who had a background in social services. Probation took a slight turn in focus during the late 1960s and early 1970s when the emphasis on rehabilitative services turned toward **reintegration,** or helping offenders adjust to society. In the 1980s and 1990s, the focus of probation would change again, this time adopting an emphasis on risk assessment and increased surveillance. The latter change has negatively impacted probation officer morale and involvement.[92]

Through all of these changes, female probation officers have remained active in probation services. For several reasons, they have not faced the same level of rejection and harassment they face in law enforcement and, to a lesser degree, the legal arena. First, male probation and parole officers have not established a culture that excludes females. Second, the historical need for professionally trained social workers in probation and parole fares well for the acceptance of females. Third, probation has never truly been recognized as a male-dominated profession; thus, male officers often have little concern when working with female colleagues.[93]

Increased diversification in correctional staff provides greater encouragement for multicultural training. For instance, correctional agencies were forced to offer specialized training for prison officers upon the increased presence of females in male prisons. Issues such as sexual harassment, supervision of men in prison, and management strategies increasingly became part of correctional officer and administrator training programs.[94] Similar training concerns appeared as more racial and ethnic minorities joined the staffs of our prisons. There has been a notable increase in the overall number of African American females working in criminal justice, particularly in corrections. Among the reasons for the increase are civil rights legislation, welfare reform, national and local changes in public assistance programs, and national movements promoting awareness and support for diversity and inclusion.[95]

Summary

Women may or may not be culturally distinct from males. Regardless of one's view, females are distinct from males when it comes to crime and justice. As both practitioners and "participants" in the system, females face specific hurdles not often faced by their male counterparts, including, for instance, the difficulties of raising children due to irregular working hours (female employees in the system) or being caught up in the system (female inmates).

Criminal justice in the United States is undergoing significant changes that will impact generations to come. Prominent among the changes is the increased involvement of women in all aspects of our justice system. Females are increasingly assuming roles as police officers and police chiefs; attorneys and judges; probation, parole, and correctional officers and wardens; defendants, inmates, and clients. Responding to these changes has been, and continues to be, a work-in-progress that will hopefully result in benefits for all. As practitioners, females have much to offer the criminal justice system. The goal is to recognize and utilize the many benefits they have to offer. Equally important is the need to recognize and respond to the fact that male and female offenders differ and that accommodations for these differences should not be ignored.

 # You Make the Call

Female Correctional Officer

Consider the following scenario. Debate the pros and cons of all options and decide what you would do.

As a female, you are a bit apprehensive about becoming a prison officer. Particularly, you wonder how the inmates will treat you. You know that tension exists between prison officers and prisoners, but you don't expect tension from your colleagues. As you begin your career in corrections, several male officers make off-the-cuff comments about you being a female prison officer. One officer asks you why you want to do a "man's job." Not one to put up with such shortsightedness, you report their behavior to your supervisor. The supervisor notes that the officers are "testing" you, to see if you can handle the ridicule—to see if you are "one of them." He says the comments will cease after you've been on the job for a while—"once you prove yourself."

Word gets out that you complained about the comments about you to the supervisor, and you begin to feel increasingly isolated among the prison officer ranks. The officers stop making comments to your face, but they also stop speaking to you unless communication is absolutely necessary. You can sense that the officers are making derogatory comments about you behind your back. Although you're not a quitter, it becomes increasingly difficult for you to continue working in such an atmosphere.

Questions

1. Do you believe the situation would have improved if you had stood up for yourself and ridiculed the male officers in response?
2. Should the supervisor have reacted differently when you reported the male officers' behavior?

3. What steps, if any, can you take in this instance to improve your working conditions?
4. Was it appropriate for you to complain about the comments to your supervisor, or should you have simply brushed them off?

Key Terms

acquaintance rape (p. 152)
Civil Rights Act of 1964 (p. 154)
double bind (p. 156)
double jeopardy (p. 155)
Equal Employment Opportunity Act
   of 1972 (p. 154)
feminist movements (p. 147)

gender (p. 149)
marital rape (p. 152)
Nineteenth Amendment (p. 147)
prison play-families (p. 163)
reintegration (p. 167)
sentencing guidelines (p. 158)
sex (p. 149)

Discussion Questions

1. Why have females become increasingly involved in the criminal justice system?
2. What barriers do females face with regard to being accepted as police officers? What can be done to address these barriers?
3. Discuss the differences between male and female courtroom personnel.
4. What are the special needs of females who are under correctional supervision?
5. What can prison officials do to reduce the problems children face when their parents are incarcerated?

Endnotes

1. Muraskin, R. 2007. "Ain't I a Woman?" In R. Muraskin (ed.), *It's a Crime: Women and Justice,* pp. 2–12. Upper Saddle River, NJ: Prentice Hall.
2. Ibid.
3. Henslin, J. M. 2003. *Sociology: A Down-to-Earth Approach.* Boston: Allyn & Bacon.
4. Ibid.
5. Price, B. R. and Sokoloff, N. J. 2004. "Preface." In B. R. Price and N. J. Sokoloff (eds.), *The Criminal Justice System and Women: Offenders, Prisoners, Victims, & Workers,* 3rd ed., pp. xiii–xxii. New York: McGraw-Hill.
6. Henslin 2003.
7. Ibid.

8. DeNavas-Walt, C., Proctor, B. D., and Lee, C. H. 2006, August. "Income, Poverty, and Health Insurance Coverage in the United States: 2005." U.S. Department of Commerce, U.S. Census Bureau. P60-231. Washington, DC: U.S. Government Printing Office.
9. Ibid.
10. Sharp, S. F., and Hefley, K. 2007. "This Is a Man's World . . . Or Least That's How It Looks in the Journals" (sic). *Critical Criminology* 15: 3–18.
11. Ibid.
12. Hughes, L. A. 2005. "The Representation of Females in Criminological Research: A Content Analysis of American and British

Journal Articles." *Women and Criminal Justice* 16: 1–28.

13. U.S. Department of Justice, Federal Bureau of Investigation. 2006. "Arrests, by Sex 2005—Table 42." *Crime in the United States, 2005*. www.fbi.gov/ucr/05cius/data/table_42.html (accessed July 19, 2007).

14. U.S. Department of Justice, Federal Bureau of Investigation. 2006. "Ten-Year Arrest Trends, by Sex 1996–2005—Table 33." *Crime in the United States, 2005*. www.fbi.gov/ucr/05cius/data/table_33.html (accessed July 19, 2007).

15. For example, Steffensmeier, D., and Schwartz, J. 2004. "Contemporary Explanations of Women's Crime." In B. R. Price and N. J. Sokoloff (eds.), *The Criminal Justice System and Women: Offenders, Prisoners, Victims, & Workers,* 3rd ed., pp. 113–126. New York: McGraw-Hill.

16. Ibid.

17. Catalano, S. M. 2006, September. *Criminal Victimization, 2005*. U.S. Department of Justice, Bureau of Justice Statistics. NCJ 214644. Washington, DC: U.S. Government Printing Office.

18. Ibid.

19. Ibid.

20. Lyman, M. D. 1999. *The Police: An Introduction*. Upper Saddle River, NJ: Prentice Hall.

21. Schulz, D. M. 2004. *Breaking the Brass Ceiling: Women Police Chiefs and Their Paths to the Top*. Westport, CT: Praeger.

22. U.S. Department of Justice, Federal Bureau of Investigation. 2006. "Full-Time Law Enforcement Employees—Table 74." *Crime in the United States, 2005*. www.fbi.gov/ucr/05cius/data/table_74.html (accessed July 19, 2007).

23. See Paoline, E. A., III, and Terrill, W. 2004. "Women Police Officers and the Use of Coercion." *Women and Criminal Justice* 15 (3/4): 97–119, for elaboration on the ability of women to perform as police officers.

24. Paoline and Terrill 2004.

25. Ibid.

26. Hunt, J. 1999. "Police Accounts of Normal Force." In V. Kappeler (ed.), *The Police and Society,* 3rd ed., pp. 306–324. Prospect Heights, IL: Waveland.

27. Paoline and Terrill 2004.

28. Harrington, P. S., and Lonsway, K. A. 2004. "Current Barriers and Future Prospects for Women in Policing." In B. R. Price and N. J. Sokoloff (eds.), *The Criminal Justice System and Women: Offenders, Prisoners, Victims, & Workers,* 3rd ed., pp. 495–510. New York: McGraw-Hill.

29. Martin, S. E. 1994. "'Outsiders Within' the Station House: The Impact of Race and Gender on Black Women Police." *Social Problems* 41: 383–384, 389.

30. Ibid; Felkenes, G. T., and Schroeder, J. R. 1993. "A Case Study of Minority Women in Policing." *Women and Criminal Justice* 4: 65–89.

31. Miller, S. L., Forest, K. B., and Jurik, N. C. 2004. "Lesbians in Policing: Perceptions and Work Experiences within the Macho Cop Culture." In B. R. Price and N. J. Sokoloff (eds.), *The Criminal Justice System and Women: Offenders, Prisoners, Victims, & Workers,* 3rd ed., pp. 511–525. New York: McGraw-Hill.

32. Durose, M. R., and Langan, P. A. 2007, April. *Contacts Between the Police and the Public, 2005*. U.S. Department of Justice, Bureau of Justice Statistics. NCJ 215243. Washington, DC: U.S. Government Printing Office.

33. International Association of Women. 2006. "Past & Present, 1915–Today." www.iawp.org/history/pastpresent.htm (accessed August 29, 2007).

34. Durose and Langan 2007.

35. Mann, C. M. 1989. "Minority and Female: A Criminal Justice Double Bind." *Social Justice* 16: 95–114.

36. Ibid.

37. Walker, S., Spohn, C., and DeLone, M. 2004. *The Color of Justice,* 3rd ed. Belmont, CA: Wadsworth. P. 147.

38. Spohn, C., and Beichner, D. 2000. "Is Preferential Treatment of Female Offenders a Thing of the Past? A

Multisite Study of Gender, Race, and Imprisonment." *Criminal Justice Policy Review* 11 (2): 149–184. See also Spohn, C. C., and Spears, J. W. 1997. "Gender and Case-Processing Decisions: A Comparison of Case Outcomes for Male and Female Defendants Charged with Violent Felonies." *Women and Criminal Justice* 8: 29–59.

39. Williams, M. R. 1999. "Gender and Sentencing: An Analysis of Indicators." *Criminal Justice Policy Review* 10 (4): 471–490.

40. Spohn and Beichner 2000.

41. Ibid.

42. Snell, T. L. 2006, December. *Capital Punishment, 2005*. U.S. Department of Justice, Bureau of Justice Statistics. NCJ 215083. Washington, DC: U.S. Government Printing Office.

43. Steffensmeier, D., and Hebert, C. 1999. "Women and Men Policy Makers: Does the Judge's Gender Affect the Sentencing of Criminal Defendants?" *Social Forces* 77 (3): 1163–1196.

44. American Bar Association. 2006. "Charting Our Progress: The Status of Women in the Profession Today." Chicago: American Bar Association. www.abanet.org/women/ChartingOurProgress.pdf.

45. Neubauer, D. W. 2005. *America's Courts and the Criminal Justice System,* 8th ed. Belmont, CA: Wadsworth.

46. Spill, R., and Bratton, K. 2001. "Clinton and Diversification of the Federal Judiciary." *Judicature* 84: 256–261.

47. American Bar Association. 2006. "Visible Invisibility: Women of Color in Law Firms—Executive Summary." Chicago: American Bar Association. www.abanet.org/women/VisibleInvisibility-ExecSummary.pdf.

48. Steffensmeier and Hebert 1999.

49. Neubauer 2005.

50. Miller, S. L., and Meloy, M. L. 2007. "Women on the Bench: Mavericks, Peacemakers, or Something Else?" In R. Muraskin (ed.), *It's a Crime: Women and Justice,* pp. 707–722. Upper Saddle River, NJ: Prentice Hall.

51. Danner, M. J. E. 2007. "Three Strikes and It's *Women* Who Are Out." In R. Muraskin (ed.), *It's a Crime: Women and Justice,* pp. 723–733. Upper Saddle River, NJ: Prentice Hall.

52. Belknap, J. 2001. *The Invisible Women: Gender, Crime, and Justice*, 2nd ed. Belmont, CA: Wadsworth.

53. Neubauer 2005.

54. Chesney-Lind, M. 1997. *The Female Offender: Girls, Women, and Crime*. Thousand Oaks, CA: Sage.

55. Price and Sokoloff 2004.

56. Sabol, W. J., Minton, T. D., and Paige, M. H. 2007, June. *Prison and Jail Inmates at Midyear 2006*. U.S. Department of Justice, Bureau of Justice Statistics. NCJ 217675. Washington, DC: U.S. Government Printing Office.

57. McGee, Z. T., Joseph, E., Allicott, I., Gayle, T. A., Barber, A., and Smith, A. 2007. "From the Inside: Patterns of Coping and Adustment (sic) Among Women in Prison." In R. Muraskin (ed.), *It's a Crime: Women and Justice,* pp. 507–527. Upper Saddle River, NJ: Prentice Hall.

58. Ibid.

59. Ibid.

60. McCampbell, S. W. 2005. "Gender-Responsive Strategies for Women Offenders." *American Jails*, September/October, pp. 39–41, 43–46.

61. McCampbell 2005.

62. Ibid.

63. Adler, F., Mueller, G. O. W., and Laufer, W. S. 2006. *Criminal Justice: An Introduction,* 6th ed. New York: McGraw-Hill.

64. Van Wormer, K. S., and Bartollas, C. 2007. *Women and the Criminal Justice System,* 2nd ed. Boston: Allyn & Bacon.

65. Diaz-Cotto, J. 1996. *Gender, Ethnicity, and the State: Latina and Latino Prison Politics*. Albany: New York State University Press.

66. Reed, D. F., and Reed, E. L. 2004. "Mothers in Prison and Their Children." In B. R. Price and N. J. Sokoloff (eds.), *The Criminal Justice System and Women: Offenders, Prisoners, Victims,*

& *Workers,* 3rd ed., pp. 261–273. New York: McGraw-Hill.

67. For example, Bloom, B., and Steinhart, D. 1993. *Why Punish the Children? A Reappraisal of the Children of Incarcerated Mothers in America.* San Francisco: National Council on Crime and Delinquency; Fishman, S. H. 1983. "Impact of Incarceration on Children of Offenders." *Journal of Children in Contemporary Society* 15: 89–99.

68. McGee et al. 2007.

69. Mumola, C. J. 2000, August. *Incarcerated Parents and Their Children.* U.S. Department of Justice, Bureau of Justice Statistics. NCJ 182335. Washington, DC: U.S. Government Printing Office.

70. Ibid.

71. Ibid.

72. For example, Hariston, C. F. 1991. "Family Ties during Imprisonment: Important to Whom and for What?" *Journal of Sociology and Social Welfare* 18 (1): 87–104; Schaefer, N. E. 1991. "Prison Visiting Policies and Practices." *International Journal of Offender Therapy and Comparative Criminology* 35 (3): 263–275.

73. Johnston, D. 1995. "Intervention." In K. Gabel and D. Johnston (eds.), *Children of Incarcerated Parents,* pp. 199–236. New York: Lexington Books.

74. Ross, L. 2004. "Resistance and Survivance: Cultural Genocide and Imprisoned Native Women." In B. R. Price and N. J. Sokoloff (eds.), *The Criminal Justice System and Women: Offenders, Prisoners, Victims, & Workers,* 3rd ed., pp. 235–247. New York: McGraw-Hill.

75. Morton, J. B. 2004. *Working with Women Offenders in Correctional Institutions.* Lanham, MD: American Correctional Association.

76. McGee et al. 2007.

77. Glaze, L. E., and Bonczar, T. P. 2006, November. *Probation and Parole in the United States, 2005.* U.S. Department of Justice, Bureau of Justice Statistics. NCJ 215091. Washington, DC: U.S. Government Printing Office.

78. Glaze and Bonczar 2006.

79. Bailey, M. 1991. "Georgia Parole Officers Confront Language and Cultural Barriers." *Corrections Today,* December, pp. 118, 120–121.

80. Ibid.

81. Camp, C. G. 2003. *The Corrections Yearbook, 2002.* Middletown, CT: Criminal Justice Institute.

82. Pogrebin, M. R., and Poole, E. D. 1997. "The Sexualized Work Environment: A Look at Women Jail Officers." *The Prison Journal* 77 (March): 41–57.

83. Irwin, J. 2005. *The Warehouse Prison: Disposal of the New Dangerous Class.* Los Angeles: Roxbury.

84. Pollock, J. 2002. *Women, Prison & Crime,* 2nd ed. Belmont, CA: Wadsworth.

85. Jurik, N. 1985. "An Officer and a Lady: Organizational Barriers to Women Working as Correctional Officers in Men's Prisons." *Social Problems* 32: 375–388.

86. Byrd, M. V. L. 2004. "African-American Women in Corrections." In C. Smalls (ed.), *The Full Spectrum: Essays on Staff Diversity in Corrections,* pp. 105–116. Lanham, MD: American Correctional Association.

87. Irwin 2005.

88. Ibid.

89. Van Wormer and Bartollas 2007.

90. Miller, Tekla, S. 1991. "Woman Warden's Assignment Offered Rewarding Challenges." *Corrections Today,* December, pp. 110–111.

91. Van Wormer and Bartollas 2007.

92. Ibid.

93. Ibid.

94. Bergsmann, I. R. 1991. "ACA Women in Corrections Committee Examines Female Staff Training Needs." *Corrections Today,* December, pp. 106, 108–109.

95. Byrd 2004.

The Gay Community and the Criminal Justice System

Chapter Objectives

After reading this chapter, you should be able to

❖ Describe the characteristics of the homosexual population in the United States.

❖ Describe the history of the "Gay Power" movement in the United States.

❖ Understand hate crimes and the nature of victimization for homosexuals.

❖ Discuss the issues and challenges in the criminal justice system in dealing with homosexuals, including gay police officers, juror bias against gays, and homosexuality in prisons.

❈ Public Attitudes About Homosexuality

In recent years, one of the most controversial social issues relates to same-sex marriage. In 2003, when a court in Massachusetts ruled that the state had no grounds to deny same-sex couples the right to marry, many states passed laws recognizing these types of unions. Initially, there was a great deal of discussion and controversy surrounding same-sex marriage, fueled primarily by religious conservatives on one side and gay activists on the other.

Public opinion polls reveal that Americans are divided on the acceptance of homosexuality as an alternative lifestyle but seem to support the idea of same-sex marriages. A 2005 USA Today/CNN/Gallup Poll found that, when asked whether same-sex relations between consenting adults should be legal, 48% responded yes while 46% responded no. This represented an increase in the percentage of people who were opposed to same-sex relations between consenting adults from previous years. While Americans are not clear on the idea of gay relationships, they seem to be when it comes to same-sex marriage. Approximately 60% of people surveyed supported legal marriages for gay couples in 2005.

Experts note that some of the factors relating to the general tolerance toward gay couples in general and same-sex marriages in particular involve a U.S. Supreme Court case that struck down anti-sodomy laws (*Lawrence v. Texas,* 539 U.S. 558; 2003).

Additionally, corporations have become more accepting of the homosexual lifestyle. For instance, Wal-Mart has recently expanded anti-discrimination protection to gay workers, and the Walt Disney Company recently changed its policy regarding the Fairy Tale Wedding program to include gay couples. Disney's prior policy was that only couples with a valid marriage license could purchase the service,

Disney has lent support to alternative lifestyles by allowing wedding ceremonies by same sex couples.

which ranges from $8,000 to more than $45,000. Disney Parks and Resorts spokesman Donn Walker said, "We believe this change is consistent with Disney's long-standing policy of welcoming every guest in an inclusive environment. We want everyone who comes to celebrate a special occasion at Disney to feel welcome and respected."[1] Other corporations see the change in acceptability of same sex-marriage as a function of the growing visibility of gays in the media and politics and as cultural leaders.[2]

While Americans might be willing to acknowledge homosexuals and same-sex marriages in general, there appears to be a reluctance to giving gay couples equal rights in all aspects of society. The 2005 USA Today/CNN/Gallup Poll found that only 40% of those surveyed thought that same-sex relationships should be treated the same as opposite-sex relationships. This represents the most opposition since the poll first asked the question in 2000.[3]

Still another issue relating to homosexuality is the position of the United States military. When President Bill Clinton signed the "Don't ask, don't tell" policy into law in 1993, he billed it as a compromise between basic principles of justice and claims of military necessity. The idea was to respect the privacy of gay soldiers while avoiding threats to military readiness that would emerge if the ban on gay soldiers was eliminated. The problems stemming from this policy were highlighted in 2007, when Marine Corps General Peter Pace, chairman of the Joint Chiefs of Staff, was interviewed by the *San Francisco Chronicle* newspaper. During the course of the interview, General Pace likened homosexual acts to adultery and said the military should not allow gays to serve in the armed forces. However, Pace did say he supported the policy that prohibits commanders from asking about a person's sexual orientation, which became federal law in 1994.[4] A few days later, in response to the controversy, General Pace did not apologize for his remarks, but said he regretted that he offered his personal views and did not confine his comments to the Defense Department's policy about gays in the military.

Many critics of the law argue that the "Don't ask, don't tell" policy is ineffective and an invasion of privacy and that it prohibits gay and lesbian soldiers from having any kind of romantic relationships in their private lives. Critics also contend the policy violates one of America's most important values: that no person should be excluded from equal protection under the law because of the prejudice of others.[5] The controversy surrounding the military's policy on homosexuality as well as public opinion on alternative lifestyles leaves little doubt that gays remain a minority group in this country.

In this chapter we will focus on the ways in which homosexuality affects the criminal justice system. While homosexuals are sometimes victimized because of their lifestyle, also known as hate crimes, there are other dimensions of this phenomenon, such as the harassment and discrimination that many gay police officers face and homosexual behavior by inmates in prison.

✖ Defining Homosexuality

On one hand, defining homosexuality seems simple. Part of the difficulty in defining a topic like homosexuality, however, relates to the distinction between a person's behavior and the person's identity. Teenagers, for example, might vandalize an abandoned piece of property but are normally obedient and considerate to others. Or they might experiment with drugs but are not drug abusers. This distinction between behavior and identity is found in the discussion of homosexuality. While people may engage in homosexual behavior, this does not mean they have taken on a homosexual identity.

The word **homosexual** first appeared in German in an 1869 political pamphlet by Karl Kertbeny intended to protest the inclusion of Prussian sodomy statutes in the German constitution. The term coincided with the discovery of an extensive network of gay males in European and North American cities. While it is not clear which came first, the discovery of men with same-sex attractions or the term to identify them, by the mid-20th century, the term was frequently used to identify this segment of the population. The term also became compared to *heterosexuality,* which initially was understood to be connected to a desire for sexual contact with both sexes. Over time, however, *homosexuality* came to mean a desire for sexual contact exclusively with members of the same sex.[6]

The phrase **sexual orientation** is used to describe a sexual attraction toward people of the same sex, of the opposite sex, or of both sexes. The question of when someone is considered a heterosexual, homosexual, or bisexual is difficult to answer. Determining one's sexual orientation is not simply a matter of observing one's behavior because there is evidence that many heterosexuals have had homosexual encounters and vice versa. This runs counter to conventional wisdom: many people believe that if a person engages in homosexual activity, he or she must be a homosexual. However, there is substantial evidence to suggest this is not the case.[7] For example, Alfred Kinsey's controversial study in the late 1940s of American males and his study of American females in the 1950s found that 37% of the males and 13% of females in his sample had had at least one homosexual encounter. However, when does a man who has had a sexual encounter with another man become classified as a homosexual? Determining sexual orientation is further complicated by the fact that research shows many people engage in sexual experimentation before confining themselves to one type of sex partner.

An added complication relates to a person's thoughts as well as behaviors. What if a person is a heterosexual but has sexual fantasies about a homosexual encounter? How does one label that person? Sigmund Freud, for example, argued that a person's sexuality is determined by his or her thoughts and images when becoming sexually aroused. Thus, a man who has same-sex fantasies while having sex with his wife would be classified as a homosexual even though there is nothing in his behavior that would indicate homosexual tendencies.

In determining sexual orientation, there is also the consideration of what one might call **situational homosexuality:** instances in which homosexual behavior occurs between two persons who are otherwise heterosexuals. In this type of situation, homosexual behavior is contingent upon the environment in which people find themselves. Examples include prisons, ships at sea, monasteries and convents, and even boarding schools. Moreover, situational homosexuality consists of behavior that ranges from sexual experimentation, such as what might be found on a college campus, to prison rape. Even more complicated is the notion of **bisexuality,** in which the person is attracted to both sexes. Like homosexuality, this sexual orientation has been stigmatized, but by both heterosexuals *and* homosexuals, making bisexuals feel pressured to "choose" one sexual preference or the other.

The psychiatric literature on sexuality has several theories about why people become homosexuals. According to some experts, homosexuality is a regression to Freud's oral stage of development, meaning that most families of homosexuals are characterized by an overprotective mother and an absent father or that homosexuals fear a dominant mother in the pre-Oedipal stage.[8] Other experts have suggested that homosexuality may be an expression of nonsexual problems, such as a fear of adult responsibility, or it may be triggered by various sexual experiences, such as an enjoyable homosexual encounter at an early age. Theories to explain lesbianism include memories of abusive relationships with men or disappointing heterosexual relationships.[9]

There may also be cultural factors at work to explain homosexuality. The need to fit in may drive some people into a particular orientation when their preferences are for members of the same sex. Thus, it is not clear how one goes about choosing a sexual orientation. It may be that people choose heterosexuality because they are attracted to persons of the opposite sex, or it may be that they feel pressured to be "normal" even though their thoughts, fantasies, and attraction are toward people of the same sex. Others may choose a homosexual orientation because they feel the need to be honest with who they are and in what they believe. Still others may not be able to decide and choose bisexuality.

An added problem is that the research is not clear about whether sexual orientation is an actual choice. Some researchers have explored whether or not there is a biological connection to homosexuality. This is a very controversial topic, with biologists on one side and religious groups on the other. Some biological proponents argue that homosexuality might be related to hormonal imbalances in the mother during pregnancy. Others argue that homosexuality might be related to brain functioning. Some research suggests that the hypothalamus in homosexual men is between 25% and 50% smaller than in heterosexual men. Other studies have shown that homosexual men react differently to human pheromones than heterosexual men. Whatever the explanation, most theorists agree that homosexual orientation tends to arise at an early age.[10]

Differences Between Male and Female Homosexuality

The incidence of female homosexuality appears less than male homosexuality. Female homosexuality is much less visible. This is largely due to American social customs such as the greater tolerance for two females to hold hands in public, to dance, to kiss, or to share an apartment. Consequently, Americans are less likely to ascribe homosexuality to females than to males, making it much easier for females to conceal it if they choose to do so.

Lesbians tend to have fewer sexual partners than do male homosexuals. For example, while almost all males have "cruised" looking for sex with strangers, less than 20% of lesbians have done so. Lesbians tend to avoid the bar scene and tend to look for lasting relationships. This may explain in part why male homosexuals, who tend to have numerous partners, have a larger representation in the number of AIDS cases. This is not to say that homosexual men do not form lasting gay relationships; it simply means that male homosexuals are more likely than lesbians to "hook up" for casual sex.[11]

⚔ The History of Homosexuality in the United States

The general pattern of how American culture has perceived homosexuality over the sweep of history is best summarized by a transition from sinful conduct to a disease model to the development of gay identities.[12] Churches have been largely responsible for the overall condemnation of homosexuality. In early America, colonial ministers cited scripture that deplores homosexuality and spoke of an angry God who would rain fire and brimstone and destroy this segment of the population much in the same way he had destroyed Sodom and Gomorrah. The distaste for homosexuality was a very powerful element in holding people accountable for their actions. Bible scripture also justified the harsh punishment inflicted on homosexuals. In every colony, sodomy was a capital offense while other homosexual acts, such as lewdness between women, were punished with whippings and fines.[13]

After the American Revolution, although Enlightenment philosophy largely dictated how laws were created, there was resistance to removing sodomy statutes as "crimes against nature." As time went on, legislatures and courts included a wider range of activities, such as oral sex between men and sexual activity between women. In the late 19th century, the medical profession diagnosed homosexuality as a form of mental illness. The development of Freudian psychoanalysis led many physicians and psychiatrists to conclude that homosexuality was an acquired affliction that required medical treatment, some of which was barbaric and torturous. Examples included electroshock therapy, lobotomy, hysterectomy, and even castration.[14]

The development of psychiatry during this period also reinforced the medical model used to understand and treat homosexuality. Reflecting the attitudes, values, and beliefs about homosexuality at the time, many states enacted "sexual psychopath laws" to regulate consensual sex among same-sex partners. This medical model translated into criminal behavior for some adults. Not only were homosexuals determined to be in need of treatment more likely to spend time in mental institutions, district attorneys often used the sexual psychopath laws to criminally prosecute them.[15]

Despite these risks, in the late 19th century, some people began to organize their lives around a homosexual orientation. At first certain parks, streets, and bathhouses became meeting places for men. Bars and clubs also appeared in or near **red-light districts,** or centers for prostitution, of major cities. As a result, a hidden urban gay subculture began to be seen in the 1920s and 1930s.[16]

After World War II ended, many men returned to the cities rather than going home to small towns. In turn, many cities began to see the increase in the number of gay bars in the 1940s.[17] In the 1950s, during the time of the Cold War, not only were communists a threat to the American way of life, Senate investigations portrayed homosexuals in the same way. In fact, this perception was so pervasive that President Dwight D. Eisenhower issued an executive order barring gay men and lesbians from all federal jobs. In response, state and local governments followed suit as did many companies in the private sector. The FBI created a surveillance program against homosexuals, and local police departments conducted undercover operations in gay bars, making mass arrests on a regular basis. Wichita, Dallas, Memphis, and Seattle were among the cities that most intensely attacked the gay community, averaging 100 misdemeanor charges against gay men and lesbians per month.[18]

In the 1960s, influenced perhaps by the successes of the Civil Rights Movement and protests against the Vietnam War, the gay community began to organize politically. By 1969, nearly 50 gay rights organizations existed in the United States, with membership running in the thousands. However, on June 27, 1969, at the Stonewall Inn, a gay bar in New York City's Greenwich Village, the police conducted a raid. This time, members of the gay community resisted and violence broke out between citizens and the police. The angry response from patrons resulted in three nights of rioting and violence in New York City. The Stonewall incident also spawned the "Gay Power" movement. A massive grassroots gay liberation movement began, similar to the movements of Blacks, women, and college students in the 1960s.

Like their militant counterparts, gays challenged the public's perception of them, and the way they were treated by the larger society, with the proclamation that gays lived "alternative" rather than "deviant" lifestyles. The phrase "coming out of the closet" was born during this time to solidify their identity and value to the larger society. By 1973, there were almost 800 gay and lesbian organizations in the United States. By 1990, the number was several thousand.[19]

Much of the progress gays have achieved in the eyes of the law stem from their ability to change the public's perception of them through protests and demonstrations.

This politicalization of the homosexual community resulted in changes in legislation, public policy, and the way homosexuals were perceived by American society. Not only did half of the states decriminalize homosexual behavior over the next 20 years, public and political pressure reduced the incidence of police raids, harassment, and arrests as well. Many cities included sexual orientation in their civil rights statutes, and in 1974 the American Psychiatric Association removed homosexuality from its list of mental illnesses. In 1975 the Civil Service Commission eliminated the ban on the employment of homosexuals for federal jobs. In short, the gay and lesbian world was no longer hidden from public view. Homosexuals were very visible: There were gay businesses, political clubs, community centers, and gay candidates even ran for public office.[20]

However, the "coming out" of homosexuals was not universally welcomed. Mainstream society still had difficulty adjusting to the visible and militant presence of homosexuals. The late 1970s and 1980s were a turbulent time for the gay community. In 1977 singer Anita Bryant began an anti-gay campaign in Dade County, Florida. The basis of her efforts centered on her opposition of equal rights for homosexuals. Building on her efforts, by the 1980s, a conservative, Christian-based anti-gay movement had begun. Fundamentalist ministers such as Jerry Falwell, who formed the Moral Majority, Inc., worked with other groups to oppose equal rights for homosexuals.

The threat of the AIDS epidemic in the early 1980s intensified anti-gay groups' efforts against homosexuals, this time from a public health perspective. However, the threat of AIDS also galvanized the homosexual community. As a result, many gay organizations were created to address the practical consequences of infection with the disease as well as its treatment. While initially perceived as a catastrophic event in the pursuit of equality for gays, AIDS was actually instrumental in shaping and changing the gay rights movement.[21] AIDS has shaped the movement in terms of money for research on curing the disease, acclimating the public to the idea that it is not simply a gay disease; and fundraising campaigns have normalized the alternative lifestyle approach.

The current issue in the gay rights movement focuses primarily on same-sex marriage. Gay activists remain steadfast in their attempts to secure equal rights at a time when the public seems divided on the legal and social standing of homosexuality. The backlash against homosexuals can be seen not only in public opinion polls but also in the ways that homosexuals are victimized and discriminated against in the criminal justice system.

✂ Homosexuals and the Criminal Justice System

Hate Crimes and Victimization

On April 23, 1990, Congress passed the Hate Crime Statistics Act, which mandated that police departments collect data "about crimes that manifest evidence of prejudice based on race, religion, sexual orientation, or ethnicity." Management of these data was given to the FBI and the Uniform Crime Reporting program. The first report on hate crimes was issued in that same year, titled *Hate Crime Statistics 1990: A Resource*

Hate crimes are illegal acts motivated by prejudices of sexual orientation, religious beliefs, or race.

Book, which drew from data in 11 states. In 1994 Congress augmented the Hate Crime Statistics Act by passing the Violent Crime and Law Enforcement Act, which expanded the scope of the Hate Crime Statistics Act by including bias against persons with disabilities. In 1996 Congress further expanded its efforts to understand and prevent hate crimes by passing the Church Arson Prevention Act. It also mandated that hate crime data become a permanent part of the Uniform Crime Reporting program.[22]

Methods of Collecting Hate Crime Data

In an effort to provide comprehensive coverage of hate crime information, the Uniform Crime Reporting (UCR) program merged the usual information submitted to it by law enforcement agencies with hate crime data that include type of offense, location, bias motivation, type of hate crime, number of offenders, and the race of the offender.[23]

There are a number of challenges to collecting information on hate crimes. For instance, because motivation is subjective, it is difficult to know whether a crime resulted from an offender's bias or some other factor. Additionally, even if the offender was biased toward a particular group or individual, the person's action's do not necessarily qualify as a hate crime. The only way an act is considered a hate crime is if the investigation into the incident reveals sufficient evidence to conclude that the offender's actions were motivated in some way by his or her bias.

As mentioned, part of the collection of hate crime information consists of information on crimes that the police normally submit to the UCR program. This includes **crimes against persons,** or violent crimes, which include murder and non-negligent manslaughter, forcible rape, assaults, and intimidation. **Crimes against property,** or economic crimes, include burglary, larceny-theft, motor vehicle theft, vandalism, and arson. For those agencies that participate in the newest version of the

UCR, also known as the National Incident-Based Reporting System (NIB
is an additional category, **crimes against society,** which includes offens
gambling, prostitution, drugs, and weapons violations.

Incidents and Offenses

The UCR program collects data about single-bias and multiple-bias ha
For each offense reported, the police must indicate the motivation or
which it is based. A single-bias incident occurs when one or more offens
the same incident are motivated by the same bias. A multiple-bias incide
when more than one offense occurs in the incident and at least two offenses are
motivated by different biases. This means that there can be more incidents than
offenses because for each incident, multiple crimes may occur. For instance, let's
say that a gay man is in a bar and a homophobic male attacks him, steals his wallet,
and, as he leaves the bar, vandalizes the gay man's car. Three separate crimes
occurred: an assault, a robbery, and vandalism. However, because all three offenses
were based on the fact that the victim was gay, the UCR would consider that a
single-bias (sexual orientation) incident. Let's also say that in the same scenario,
the gay man is on a date with a Black man. During the course of the same events,
the offender shouts a racial slur at the Black man and threatens to kill both men.
Now there is an assault, a robbery, a threat, and vandalism. For the purposes of data
collection, that would be a multiple-bias incident since two different types of bias
are present: racial bias and sexual orientation bias.

Of the 12,400 agencies that participate in the hate crime program, 2,037
reported the occurrence of 7,160 hate crime incidents in 2005. These incidents
involved 8,380 offenses, 8,804 victims, and 6,804 offenders.[24]

What the Data Show

The UCR program's analysis of the 7,160 hate crime incidents in 2005 showed a
number of easily identifiable trends. That is, when hate crimes occur, they seem to
consistently occur against particular groups. For instance, overall, nearly 56% of
hate offenses were racially motivated, 17% were motivated by religious bias, and
14% occurred due to sexual orientation bias. The data also revealed that the majority
of hate crimes, 62%, were crimes against persons while 37% were crimes against
property (crimes against society accounted for only 1% of hate crime offenses).

Of the racially-based hate crime offenses in 2005, nearly 70% were the result
of anti-Black bias and 20% were motivated by anti-White bias. The remainder was
divided between multiple race groups, bias against Asian Americans and Pacific
Islanders (about 5% each) and bias against Native Americans (2%). Religious bias
represented about 17% of all hate crimes in 2005. Nearly 70% of these incidents
were motivated by anti-Jewish bias, about 11% by anti-Islamic bias, and another 8%
by bias against some unknown religion.

With regard to sexual-orientation hate crime offenses in 2005, almost 61% were
motivated by bias against male homosexuals. Another 20% were motivated by generic
anti-homosexual bias, and about 15% targeted female homosexuals. In terms of ethnicity, there appears to be a wave of anti-Hispanic sentiment in the United States. Of the
1,144 offenses based on the perceived ethnicity of the victim, almost 60% were
anti-Hispanic. And then there is disability bias. Recall that Congress included bias

against disabled people in the hate crime statistics in 1994. Only 53 offenses in 2005 were based on disability, with 32 of the 53 against mentally disabled victims.

In terms of the type of victimization, about 30% of the offenses in 2005 consisted of intimidation, 30% consisted of vandalism to property, and approximately 31% consisted of some type of assault, either a simple assault or one of a serious and aggravated nature. Further analysis of crimes against persons revealed that of the 5,190 hate crimes against persons in 2005, about half (48.9%) consisted of some form of intimidation, while 30% were simple assaults. The remaining 20% were serious assaults. Hate crimes against property consisted primarily of vandalism or destruction of property, which comprised 82% of the 3,109 bias crimes in that category.

Of the 6,804 known hate crime offenders in 2005, almost two-thirds (61%) were White and 20% were African American. The remaining percentages were primarily unknown race or multiple race categories. Finally, of the reported hate crime incidents in 2005, about 30% occurred in or near residences or homes. About 18% occurred on highways, roads, alleys, or streets, and about 14% happened at schools or colleges. Another 17% occurred in other locations, such as public buildings or restaurants. Of the 1,017 hate crime incidents motivated by a sexual orientation bias, about a third occurred in or near residences or homes and a quarter happened on highways, roads, alleys or streets. About 12% took place at schools or colleges, and 17% occurred in various locations.[25]

In sum, the picture of hate crimes consists primarily of anti-Black, anti-Jewish, anti-Hispanic, and anti-male-homosexual bias. The majority of events consisted of intimidation or assault and frequently occurred in or near the victim's home.

GAY BASHING

On October 7, 1998, Matthew Shepard, age 21, a student at the University of Wyoming, met Russell Henderson and Aaron McKinney in a bar in Laramie, Wyoming. Around midnight, Shepard asked the two men for a ride home. Subsequently, Shepard was robbed, severely beaten, and tied to a fence in a remote area, where he was left to die. About 18 hours later, a bicyclist discovered Shepard, barely alive. Shepard suffered a fractured skull and had severe brain damage. He never regained consciousness and died four days later. Police then arrested Henderson and McKinney.

There was an outcry of sympathy for Matthew Shepard. While he was in the hospital, candlelight vigils were held across the country. Moreover, people in the entertainment industry responded by making films about the case and writing songs in support of Shepard as a way of expressing their outrage over what happened.

Both defendants attempted to use the "gay panic defense" arguing that they were driven temporarily insane by Shepard's sexual advances toward them. Henderson subsequently pleaded guilty on April 5, 1999, and agreed to testify against McKinney to avoid the death penalty. In exchange, he received two consecutive life sentences. The jury found McKinney guilty of two counts of felony murder. As jury deliberations on whether to execute McKinney began, Shepard's parents intervened, which resulted in McKinney receiving two consecutive life terms without the possibility of parole.

The two defendants were not charged with a hate crime since Wyoming had no such statute. A year after the trial, the Wyoming Legislature introduced such a bill, but it was defeated on a 30-30 tie in the Wyoming House of Representatives.

Is Hate Crime Legislation Really Necessary?

Some researchers contend that hate crime legislation is not only unnecessary, it also sets in motion a double standard of accountability that can create a host of problems. These problems stem largely from the way hate crime legislation is interpreted. Critics also contend that many state legislatures have passed laws to expand the general categories of hate crimes. As one author noted, "ethnic intimidation" legislation, which was originally intended to protect homosexuals, transsexuals, and transvestites, has now expanded to include groups such as the elderly and the disabled. These "special status" crimes can include categories such as blindness, sensory handicap, involvement in human or civil rights activities, or even marital status and political affiliation.[26]

The main argument against hate crimes is that they are unnecessary. The logic behind the legislation in the first place, opponents argue, was that hate crimes are worse than other forms of violence against a particular group of people. However, critics contend that some advocacy groups exaggerate the extent of hate crimes, creating a climate of fear about persecution, exploitation, and victimization that requires greater protection by the law. As evidence of this claim, one social activist/commentator noted that

> a careful look at hate crimes data shows that such crimes are a tiny fraction of major violent crimes and that many "hate crimes" are non-violent personal conflicts. The federal Hate Crimes Reporting Act of 1990 requires that "intimidation" be included as a reported crime. This category, which consists of threats which are never carried out, accounts for 56% of the FBI's annually reported hate crimes against persons. In 2001, the FBI reported that there were 9,730 hate crime incidents, comprising 11,451 separate offenses. The fact that there were over 11,849,006 crimes reported to the police in 2001 suggests that less than one percent (0.09%) of personal or property crimes is a hate crime in the United States.[27]

In 2005 a similar trend showed that there were 8,380 hate crimes out of a total of 11,556,854 offenses known to the police. This, too, consists of less than 1% of all personal and property crimes (0.07%). In general, then, some experts contend a special category of hate crimes is not needed since existing criminal law adequately protects victims. As evidence, one opponent to hate crimes argues that

> Wyoming has no hate crime laws but the killers of Matthew Shepard were sentenced to life in prison without parole and would have been sentenced to death, but for the request of Shepard's parents. Likewise, when James Byrd was dragged to his death by three men in Texas, the Texas criminal justice system reacted with its characteristic severity; two of the killers are on death row and the third was sentenced to life imprisonment. A hate crimes law in Texas could not have increased their punishment by one iota, nor could it have deterred their acts any more than the existence of the death penalty did.[28]

As evidence of the problems in highlighting hate crimes, consider the case in which a man and his wife were camping at an Ohio campground. The couple played their radio too loudly, disturbing the family in the next campground. When the park ranger told the couple to turn the radio down, they did but fifteen minutes later they turned it up again. The husband who had been asked to lower his radio then yelled that he ought to shoot the campers at the next campsite. During his diatribe toward his fellow campers, the man used the word "nigger" and another racial epithet. He did not take any steps to carry out his threat nor did he act in a violent way. While the man should have been prosecuted for disturbing the peace and making a threat, he was convicted of a hate crime felony and sentenced to a year and a half in prison. If he had not said those words, his offense would have been a misdemeanor, subject to a sentence of perhaps no jail time or up to six months.[29]

Another potential problem with hate crimes, say critics, is that while ordinarily laws regarding harassment, disturbing the peace, and other forms of minor misbehavior require a fact finding about the offender's behavior, hate crime legislation often requires judges to determine a person's motives and opinions and whether he or she acted upon statements made, in either the present or past.

Critics of hate crime legislation also point out that once the government begins to identify some groups for special treatment, it is difficult to determine which groups should and should not be given the same consideration. For instance, the number of women with a divorced spouse who stalks them is greater than the number of homosexuals who are criminally attacked because of their sexual orientation; however, no such special crime is identified for the stalking of a woman by her ex-husband. Why does one group merit special consideration? If hate crime is based on extensive harm or violence, should women and other groups have similar protections?

Finally, critics of hate crime legislation argue that these statutes infringe upon freedom of thought. To punish people because of their bad thoughts or because of their inappropriate words expressed during a crime, is to punish them more for the beliefs they hold than for their actions.

Gay Police Officers

The idea of the police being a subculture is not new and has been well documented.[30] For our purposes, a **subculture** may be defined as the meanings, values, and behavior patterns unique to a particular group in a given society. Entry into the police subculture begins with a process of socialization whereby recruits learn the values and behavior patterns characteristic of experienced officers. The development and maintenance of attitudes and values by police officers have both positive and negative implications.

In addition to a certain **homogeneity,** or similarity in attitudes, values, and beliefs, in policing, many experts have argued that law enforcement embraces ideas of masculinity, strength, and bravery and that femininity is equated with weakness. It should not be surprising, then, to realize that there is also a tendency for police officers to be homophobic, particularly toward homosexual males. Essentially there are two issues relating to the relationship between homosexuals and police officers. The first relates to how heterosexual police officers treat gay suspects, victims, and citizens, while the second focuses on the way gay police officers are treated by their heterosexual law enforcement colleagues.

Homophobia and Policing

While **gay bashing,** or unprovoked attacks on homosexuals, remains a fundamental problem for homosexuals, another area of concern relates to the way police officers treat gay and lesbian victims. Many homosexuals argue that they are forced to remain in the closet in part because the police will not help them should they be victimized. While neglect by the police was clearly the case in the 1960s and even 20 or 30 years later, some evidence suggests these perceptions may be changing.

One study showed that officers believe a correlation exists between general attitudes toward gays and lesbians and actual discriminatory behavior. Between 30% and 40% of officers indicate that gays and lesbians will not be treated the same as heterosexuals, and that they will not be taken as seriously by the larger society. Although the study points out that this might be an improvement over how gays have been treated in the past, the implication is that problems will still be evident for gays and lesbians and they will remain relatively easy targets for harassment.[31]

Another study examined police officers' responses to incidents of domestic violence involving same-sex couples compared to such incidents involving opposite-sex couples. Although members of the gay and lesbian community believe that police officers respond differently to same-sex couples, this study offered four versions of a scenario depicting an incident of domestic violence to which two imaginary police officers responded. The study found that the sexual orientation of the couple did not play a role in how the officers handled the situation. While this study could not predict how officers would respond to an actual incident, the findings do raise a number of questions about the way in which officers are trained to handle same-sex domestic disputes and whether special attention is needed when interacting with this segment of the population.[32]

Homophobia Within Policing

Historically, homosexual police officers felt that they could not reveal their sexual orientation among colleagues since law enforcement is known to be male dominated and portrays a macho image. Gay officers feared embarrassment, harassment, or isolation if their sexual identities became known. In the past, one of the attractions to law enforcement as a career was the sense of brotherhood and camaraderie that exists in policing. To be excluded from that community, particularly since police officers often feel isolated from the larger society, would make it difficult for officers to function effectively. It also meant that, in emergency situations, officers might not receive assistance from their fellow officers. Thus, many homosexual officers felt they could not reveal their identities and had to hide behind a macho image.

Some of the early research on homosexuality in policing suggested there was a lot of truth to these perceptions. For instance, in perhaps one of the most thoughtful books on the subject of gay police officers, *Gay Cops* (1993), Steven Leinen, a former New York City Police Department (NYPD) supervisor, who went on to complete a Ph.D. from New York University, interviewed 41 gay NYPD officers. In the vast majority of cases, homosexual officers described the fear of being discovered by other officers as well as the struggles of passing themselves off as heterosexuals.[33]

More recently, in response to court cases, many police departments, which had previously refused to hire known homosexuals and did not offer any type of support for gay cops, began to develop programs to address their needs. There are mixed findings about how gay police officers are treated. On one hand, there is evidence that officers remain hostile toward gay officers. Being an openly gay officer once meant being subject to overt ridicule, including anti-gay graffiti painted on an officer's locker or having his uniform soaked in urine. Like much of the overt racism against Blacks, outright anti-gay behavior in law enforcement has been replaced with subtle forms of discriminatory treatment. One study of the San Diego Police Department found that while having openly gay and lesbian officers does not undermine the effectiveness of the department, some forms of discrimination and harassment do exist. This means that openly gay officers face a number of challenges.[34]

Two groundbreaking court decisions made it easier for gay officers to publicly proclaim their sexual orientation. In *Romer v. Evans* in 1996, the U.S. Supreme Court struck down a Colorado constitutional amendment that denied gay men and lesbians anti-discrimination protections. Some legal experts argued that this case cleared the way for other states to protect gay employees. In 2003 the U.S. Supreme Court struck down anti-sodomy laws, which essentially took away termination for cause options for police departments. Prior to 2003, departments could refuse to hire gays and could fire officers who came out because they were presumed to be engaging in illegal behavior.[35]

Some gay officers have successfully sued police departments for discriminating against them. For instance, a California Highway Patrol officer won $1.5 million in damages after other officers used derogatory names to describe him and urinated on his uniform and stuffed it in his locker. In 1993 a Los Angeles Police Department officer sued the department and settled once the department agreed to create anti-gay harassment policies. He sued the department again in 1996 for failure to implement those policies. In 2005 a New Jersey police officer sued his department for failing to protect him from taunts and harassment by his coworkers. These lawsuits were successful. Departments had to change policy or comply and/or were assessed damages.

Additionally, if the number of gay police officers is any indication of a willingness to reject traditional views of homosexuality in law enforcement, there may be reason for optimism. Gays and lesbians have become an increasingly larger part of policing over the past two decades. In fact, some departments have actively recruited homosexual officers, particularly in areas heavily populated by gays and lesbians.

The law has granted gays some protections, but there remains a considerable level of fear among gay officers. While some officers argue that being gay is less stigmatizing than ever before, pointing to the creation of liaison officers between departments and the gay community[36] as well as the creation of gay officers associations in many agencies across the country, other officers contend that problems occur even when departments seem to be attempting to minimize the effects of homophobia in their organizations. Gay officers argue they are still the target of harassment and jokes, and, perhaps most important, they say other officers will not provide them "backup" on calls for service.[37]

There is also the issue of the type of homosexuality when considering the treatment of gay officers by non-gay officers. Some male officers feel that lesbians in policing are more likely to be accepted than gay male officers, partly, they say, because of their common interest in women. As one gay female officer put it, "It's plain to me that it's much easier for women to be accepted. We work mainly with men and are treated like one of the guys. They'll joke around with you, like saying 'check out that hot chick over there.'"[38]

Some gay officers believe that their sexual orientation is actually an asset in the performance of their duties. One study in a midwestern police department found that gay officers viewed themselves as particularly qualified to work with marginal groups, largely because they understand the implications and consequences of being stigmatized by the larger society. Officers in this study described the double marginality they experience: As police officers they are prevented from being fully integrated into the larger community, and they are also homosexuals, which creates a host of problems in terms of their place in the larger culture.[39]

Other gay officers believe that sexual orientation matters less than people think in policing. Rather, these officers argue that acceptance by non-gay officers has more to do with professional competency. There may be some empirical support for this perception. One study found that gay officers balance the stigma of being homosexual with the value of being a "good cop." This study found that officers did not view themselves in terms of men, women, or even as homosexuals or heterosexuals. Rather, they believed that officers who worked hard and proved themselves to be competent were more likely to be accepted by other officers. This study also found that gay officers viewed their sexual orientation as a professional asset rather than as a liability in dealing with the public.[40]

To be designated a "good cop," police officers must have professional skills that are needed to survive the work environment. Among police officers, a good cop was characterized by the following general terms:

- an officer who backs up a partner and coworkers in emergency situations;
- an officer who covers up coworkers' indiscretions or misconduct at work or, at the very least, does not betray a fellow officer who is accused of having engaged in misconduct;
- an officer who is a risk-taker and not afraid to deviate from departmental rules to get the job done;
- an officer who shares in the workload, especially in the handling of routine or tedious jobs, and who does not look for others to do his or her work.[41]

A fascinating dimension of the study of homosexual police officers is the fact that the issues of stigmatization, discriminatory practices, and the lack of legal protections are rather unique to American policing. Other countries, particularly the United Kingdom, have dealt successfully with the issue of homosexuality in law enforcement for some time. One example of this acceptance is the popularity of the Gay Police Association (GPA) in England. Formed in 1990, it has grown into a formidable agency with members in all of the 52 police forces in England. Focusing on policy development, hate crimes, victim care, and training in cultural diversity, the GPA has been a leader not only on issues relating to homosexuality, but also on issues relating to persons with physical disabilities, minority groups, and women. Other studies in England point to the ways in which homosexual police officers are treated there as compared to those in the United States.[42]

The Courts and Homosexuality

Like police departments, the courts also appear to have some difficulty in dealing with the homosexual community. Some scholars argue that the status of homosexuals in society is reflected in the kind of treatment they get by the courts. This is particularly true with regard to jury bias. The jury is one of the most important parts of the legal system in this country, and juries are required to be composed of a fair cross section of the population. If a jury is biased against homosexuals, a gay defendant might be convicted for being a homosexual rather than for the crime he or she has committed. Further, jury bias against homosexuals can raise questions about the credibility of a gay witness despite the fact that the witness's homosexuality should have no bearing on whether she or he is telling the truth. Juror bias against gays can also result in reduced sentences against an offender who victimizes a homosexual since the jury might perceive the victim as deserving of what happened to him or her.[43] Thus, the composition of juries, jurors' perceptions of homosexuals, and how sexuality factors into jury decisions play a pivotal role in understanding the relationship between gays and the justice system.

Perhaps one of the most obvious instances of jury bias relates to the treatment of defendants who are accused of victimizing homosexuals. One controversial legal aspect of homophobia occurred in the 1990s, called the **homosexual advance theory,** in which courts allow a nonviolent homosexual advance to constitute sufficient provocation to incite a reasonable man to "lose his self-control and kill in the heat of passion, thus mitigating murder to manslaughter." The homosexual advance theory is different from self-defense in that it does not attempt to justify the behavior of the offender. Rather, the theory states that it is a mitigating factor that should reduce the severity of the crime. While not all courts allow this theory to be introduced in homicide cases, the fact that some do raises concerns that perhaps some juries and judges allow their individual preferences on sexuality to interfere with equality of justice.[44] For example, in *Schick v. State* (Indiana Court of Appeals, 1991), the defendant, Schick, claimed that after being propositioned by a man for sex, Schick attacked him, knocking him to the ground. When Schick stopped hitting and kicking the man, he heard "gurgling noises" coming from the man's chest. Schick took the man's wallet and left the scene. The man later died. At trial, Schick argued that he was so repulsed by being propositioned by another man that he lost control. The jury found Schick not guilty of murder while attempting to commit robbery, but he was convicted of voluntary manslaughter.

In other cases, however, the homosexual advance theory played no part in the decision at trial. For example, in *State v. Volk* (Minnesota Court of Appeals, 1988), the defendant, Volk, was convicted of second-degree murder after the trial court refused to give a manslaughter instruction to the jury. Volk allegedly was hitchhiking with his friend, who testified that they planned to pose as prostitutes, pick up a homosexual man, and rob him. They found the victim at a store, and he invited Volk and his friend to his apartment. Volk allegedly hit the victim over the head with a liquor bottle and tied him up. When Volk's friend left to search the victim's car for money, the victim freed himself, attacked Volk, and during the fight, Volk shot him twice. At trial Volk argued that, in part, he was revolted by the victim's homosexual advance and this should serve, like intoxication and exhaustion, as a mitigating factor in the crime. The court found that there "was no provocation sufficient to elicit a heat of passion response." The court further found that a reasonable person finding himself in such circumstances would have simply walked away from the scene.

These cases show how divided the courts are in deciding which sets of circumstances warrant the homosexual advance criterion as a mitigating factor. The most important point with regard to the homosexual advance theory is that if juries are allowed to use a homosexual advance as a mitigating factor in the commission of a crime, courts reinforce the idea that gay men do not have the same protections afforded to non-homosexuals in the criminal justice system.[45]

Whereas the homosexual advance theory remains controversial, there is greater agreement about the likelihood of jury bias against homosexuals in the jury selection process. This is not to say that all juries are biased against homosexuals; however, there is greater concern over how and in what ways jury bias can creep into the selection process, causing a host of problems in the administration of justice. The main question surrounding *voir dire,* or the jury selection process, concerns jurors' sexuality and how such information should be used.

In some cases, sexual orientation is one of the main issues presented to the jury, such as in hate crime or sexual discrimination cases. Thus, in those cases where sexual orientation is a central issue, prospective jurors' attitudes toward homosexuality may affect whether attorneys can select an impartial jury. What is less clear are those cases in which jurors should be questioned about homosexuality when sexual orientation is not an issue in the case, but when the defendant or the victim is a homosexual. Considering that jury bias against homosexuals plays a crucial role in the outcome of such cases, is it fair for a court to ask individual jurors about their sexual orientation or is it an invasion of privacy?

The courts have indicated that jurors have some privacy rights when asked to serve on juries. It appears that two conditions must be met if a prospective juror can legitimately be asked about his or her sexual orientation. First, it must be clear that sexual orientation–related bias might bear on deliberations. As was mentioned, in those cases involving hate crimes or sexual discrimination suits, clearly the jurors' sexual orientation is a significant factor in the case. However, in those cases where the victim or the defendant is a homosexual, and there is no legal question about sexual orientation, it is unlawful for attorneys to ask jurors about their own sexuality.

The second condition relates to the first in that it is an invasion of privacy for attorneys to ask prospective jurors about their own sexuality when any bias against homosexuals could be discovered simply by asking jurors about their attitudes toward homosexuality. In other words, the attorney cannot circumvent a juror's right to privacy under the guise of trying to determine juror bias by starting with a round of questions about how the juror feels about homosexuality and then asking about his or her own sexual orientation. The best way to avoid jury bias against homosexuals appears to be to allow the questioning of jurors about their attitudes toward homosexuality in general.

Some experts believe that an unbiased jury will not allow evidence of sexuality of the victim or the defendant to affect the outcome of the case—that they will not care if the defendant in a rape case is gay or if the murder victim made a homosexual advance.[46] Jury bias and homophobia by court personnel sometimes affects decision making. While the courts have never provided a constitutional protection of a jury of one's peers (meaning that a homosexual cannot ask for a jury made up of only other homosexuals), they have provided that a jury will come from a cross section of the population, and there are steps that can be taken to minimize the bias many jurors feel toward homosexual defendants and victims.

Men, Homosexuality, and Prison Life

Certain places, such as prisons, induce situational homosexual behavior, which includes acts of homosexuality by people who do not otherwise practice it. The first ethnographic study of sex by male inmates was conducted in 1934. Joseph Fishman, a former inspector for federal prisons, found that inmates engaging in homosexual activity were divided into different categories based on whether or not the behavior was coerced or consensual.[47]

In the late 1950s, Gresham Sykes, a famous criminologist, wrote a book on prison life entitled *The Society of Captives.* Sykes describes the process by which a person becomes socialized into prison life. He refers to it as **prisonization,** a social and physical transformation of the individual in an effort to compensate for the pains of imprisonment, one of which relates to sexual behavior. Sykes argues that being deprived of heterosexual outlets leads prisoners to find ways to alleviate the stress of being in prison and denied access to women.[48]

Building off of Sykes's and Fishman's work, research in the 1970s on prison life included homosexual behavior. The findings of several studies resulted in a number of typologies to describe participants who engage in homosexual activities. The first is the **Queen.** Inmates and staff use the term to refer to a male inmate who prefers male sexual partners. The Queen is not really engaged in situational homo-sexual behavior, for "she" would prefer male partners in prison or on the outside. To attract partners, the Queen exaggerates aspects of female sexuality. She may take on a feminine nickname and let her hair grow long, wear jewelry and makeup, and so on. The Queen is accorded some social status in the prison, but not much.

The second type of participant is called the **Punk.** This group of homosexual inmates is accorded one of the lowest statuses in the institution. Punks are despised by heterosexual inmates, who see their homosexual behavior as the result of either weakness in the face of pressure or a willingness to sacrifice their manhood to obtain goods and services. There are essentially two types of Punks: **Canteen Punks,** who perform oral or anal sex for candy, cigarettes, or other items purchased at the prison store or canteen; and **Pressure Punks,** who submit to homosexual behavior because they have been threatened or raped by other prisoners. There are generally two ways to become a Pressure Punk. The first way is for an inmate to offer help of some sort to a new inmate, or "fish." If the fish accepts the offer, he then becomes indebted to his benefactor. The second way is for an inmate to rig a gambling game so that the fish loses. In either case, when the debt is called, the fish cannot usually pay, so the inmate demands sex as payment. This leaves the fish with two choices: fight the inmate or submit to the sexual advances. Anyone who submits will likely be pressured to do so for the rest of his prison term.

The third type of participant in prison is called the **Wolf** or the **Jocker.** This type of inmate is viewed by his colleagues as a "man." To remain a "man" and still engage in homosexual acts, the Jocker has to present an image of exaggerated toughness. So the Jocker uses force: he rapes. The more violence that surrounds his sexual acts, the more he is seen as masculine. To maintain his status, he must also keep his sexual acts emotionless and impersonal. It is not uncommon for a Wolf to own a Punk and to prostitute him much in the same way a pimp uses a female prostitute on the street.[49]

Explanations for Homosexual Behavior in Prison

As was mentioned, the research on situational homosexual behavior indicates that men in single-sex environments such as the military, correctional institutions, boarding schools, or remote work sites have been known to engage in sexual activities with one another yet maintain a heterosexual identity. The behavior is simply defined as a response to the deprivation or lack of mixed-sex interactions. The general belief is that most men who engage in this type of activity will return to heterosexual sexual activities once they return to a mixed-sex environment.

The early explanations for homosexual behavior in prison focused on environmental influences. That is, the social structure of the prison produces and promotes homosexual behavior. First, the lack of female companionship may drive some men toward homosexual behavior, particularly if this type of behavior is tolerated by prison officials and understood as necessary by other inmates.

Another factor relating to prison homosexuality is idleness. Some research suggests that, without opportunities to work or engage in distracting activities, prisoners are more likely to engage in homosexual behavior. Another reason for homosexual behavior in prisons relates to overcrowding. Currently, many prisons exceed their maximum capacity for inmates, with some institutions at three times their normal population. Overcrowding means more inmates per cell, less privacy, and the greater likelihood of inmates acting upon their sexual urges. Finally, experts note that when prisons prohibit pornography or conjugal visits, which can act as release methods for prisoners to achieve some of their sexual desires, the incidence of homosexual behavior and prison rape increases. Currently, only five states allow conjugal visits in their correctional facilities.[50]

Another significant issue with regard to homosexual behavior in prisons relates to HIV/AIDS. Clearly the spread of sexually transmitted diseases is an important area of concern for all institutions, particularly those that house violent inmates, where prison rape is more common. While abstinence is clearly the most effective method to prevent the transmission of HIV/AIDS or other sexually transmitted diseases, this is less likely to occur in prison. The other primary method to prevent the spread of diseases is through safe sex practices. However, many prison officials are reluctant to promote safe sex since it suggests that they are supplying condoms to inmates for the purpose of engaging in prohibited behavior inside the institution. Currently, only five correctional systems allow the distribution of condoms within their facilities: Mississippi, New York City, San Francisco, Vermont, and Washington, D.C.[51]

While the subject of coerced sexual behavior in prison has been studied extensively, consensual homosexual behavior between inmates has been largely ignored in the literature. Most of the research on this subject focuses on the formation of surrogate families in female prisons. What appears to be missing from the literature is research on masturbation and consensual sex among males in prison. While these two practices appear to be vastly more common than prison rape or some type of coerced sex, only a few studies exist on consensual homosexual activity in U.S. male prisons, four of which were conducted in the 1980s or early 1990s. The general findings of these studies showed that the vast majority of inmates masturbated on a regular basis and that, if consensual homosexual behavior occurred, inmates who considered themselves heterosexuals almost always took on the masculine role (insertor) in the interaction, while the feminine role (insertee) was associated with being a homosexual or bisexual.[52]

A more recent study explored the dynamics of these activities in an attempt to understand how and in what ways the prison environment induced changes in one's sexual identity both inside the institution and once the inmate was released. The findings of this study showed that race significantly affected an inmate's decision to engage in homosexual behavior. Whites were more likely to engage in homosexual activity than non-Whites. Additionally, White inmates were more likely to be targeted for sexual approaches than non-White inmates. The explanation for this may be that non-White inmates perceive homosexual activity as a threat to their identity as both males and heterosexuals. In fact, there are some studies that show Black inmates are more likely than White inmates to rape White inmates while incarcerated.[53]

It is important to note that whether or not inmates remain involved in homosexual activity after their release is unclear. While the prison environment can explain why some inmates engage in homosexual activity, whether as consensual partners or due to the threat of violence, what is unclear is what happens after they are released.[54]

Women, Homosexuality, and Prison Life

The early research on same-sex behavior among female inmates suggested that, in an effort to replace lost family roles, "pseudo-families," or kinship networks, dominated life in women's prisons. The homosexual relationships formed in prison dominated social life for inmates, and the social structure they created simulated life outside prison walls. "Marriages," "divorces," "infidelity," and other evidence of family drama were found in prisons among women.[55] Although the relationships women form in prison continue to reflect early research trends discovered in the 1960s, 1970s, and even 1980s, there is some evidence that these types of prison relationships have diminished in recent years. One researcher noted that while female offenders still participate in pseudo-families and form homosexual relationships with other inmates, this is not considered acceptable nor is it practiced by all inmates.[56]

The dynamics of social interaction among female inmates suggests that the move away from rehabilitation as a philosophy of punishment, which has been replaced with a punitive orientation, has had an impact on the types of social relationships they form with each other. Rather than forming caring relationships, or extended networks of pseudo-families, female inmates are more reluctant than in previous decades to become involved with others. Preferring instead to "do time" alone, many female inmates are beginning to resemble their male counterparts in that they prefer to avoid common areas in the prison and rely only on a few trusted friends. This is done in an attempt to survive an increasingly violent and unstable environment in women's prisons.

Some of the changes in female inmates' relationships are structural: In the past, women's institutions were designed to be more conducive to social interaction. The cottage system of the 1960s was designed to facilitate a rehabilitative approach to women largely because it was felt that if the prison environment was more like a home than a cell, inmates would be more likely to be rehabilitated. With the change in orientation, from rehabilitation to an emphasis on punishment, many women's prisons now resemble male prisons. Additionally, prisons are less isolating than in the past. Inmates can continue to be influenced by the larger culture through television, movies, radio, visits with family members, and, in some cases, conjugal visits.

This makes the aforementioned "pains of imprisonment" different than what it was in the past. It also means that the need for a single unifying inmate subculture that provides surrogate roles for inmates to emulate the outside is unnecessary. Thus, inmates today simply do not need the same types of relationships inmates did in the past, and given the wider diversity of female offenders entering prisons, there is less cohesiveness and greater levels of violence. Consequently, while homosexual relationships still occur in women's prisons, the need for them and their pervasiveness have declined.[57]

Summary

There can be little doubt that the debate over homosexuality and same-sex marriage in this country remains controversial. While public opinion polls in past years showed a general tolerance for gay lifestyles, more recently they have found Americans to be less willing to grant homosexuals equal rights. It may appear that the United States is less homophobic than in the past, as evidenced by the public opinion polls, but the fact that about half of the respondents do not approve of homosexuals, their lifestyle, or gay marriage suggests that the discussion is far from over. Evidence of the intolerance of homosexuals is seen throughout American history. It was only in the 1960s, with the Stonewall incident, that the gay community began to assert themselves and organize politically in an effort to change people's understanding of their lifestyle. Despite the apparent progress, homosexuals remain a stigmatized and victimized group. Hate crime legislation, which was enacted in 1990 to provide additional protection against offenders motivated by a racial, religious, or sexual orientation bias, made it a federal crime to victimize homosexuals. Despite the small number of hate crimes, the symbolic importance of hate crime legislation is an important illustration of the position of gays in America.

The homosexual community has also experienced discrimination and other problems when homosexuals have entered certain professions such as law enforcement. Like society as a whole, while it appears progress is being made in terms of equal treatment, gay police officers still encounter problems, such as harassment, in their profession. Similarly, when homosexuals find themselves in court, as defendants, victims, or witnesses, a number of unique challenges are presented. Juror bias in particular is perhaps the greatest problem in the courts in the administration of justice for gays.

Finally, homosexual behavior in prison has been a long-standing problem. Prison rape as well as consensual sex has created numerous problems for prison officials, particularly as it relates to sexually transmitted diseases such as HIV/AIDS. Additionally, the changing nature of prison life for women, with a greater emphasis on punishment rather than rehabilitation, has also affected the nature of social interaction. The nature of homosexual relationships in women's prisons historically took on the characteristics of pseudo-families, with less violence and more cooperative roles. As the philosophy of punishment shifted to a model in prison with an emphasis on punishment, the prevalence of pseudo-families appears to have decreased. Female inmates now resemble their male counterparts in terms of their relationships with other inmates.

You Make the Call

Hate Crimes

Consider the following scenario. Debate the pros and cons of all options and decide what you would do.

You are a criminal defense attorney who has been asked to represent two youths who engaged in "gay bashing" against a homosexual male. The two defendants, both males, were propositioned by the victim in a bar near a college campus. In response to the solicitation by the victim, your clients brought the victim to a motel under the guise of a romantic encounter, but once the three arrived, the two youths attacked the victim, beating him with fists, feet, and clubs. The victim sustained serious injuries and was in a coma for ten days. The two suspects were arrested a few days after the assault and contacted you to represent them.

You have taken a strong and very public stance against homosexuals and same-sex marriage. You have also tried to influence Congress to repeal hate crime legislation, stating that it unfairly discriminates against some types of victims. This public stance was the main reason the two suspects contacted you to represent them.

Questions

1. Do you agree to represent the two suspects or turn them down? Why?
2. If you agree to represent the two suspects, could you separate your personal biases against homosexuals and adequately represent them?
3. Do you think your public (and personal) stance on homosexuality will adversely affect the jury? If so, in what ways?
4. Should there be a different standard of justice on the basis of race, religious beliefs, or sexual orientation? Why or why not?
5. Would you use the homosexual advance theory in this case? Why or why not?

Key Terms

bisexuality (p. 176)
Canteen Punk (p. 190)
crimes against persons (p. 180)
crimes against property (p. 180)
crimes against society (p. 181)
gay bashing (p. 184)
homogeneity (p. 184)
homosexual (p. 175)
homosexual advance theory (p. 188)
Jocker (p. 190)

Pressure Punk (p. 190)
prisonization (p. 190)
Punk (p. 190)
red-light districts (p. 177)
sexual orientation (p. 175)
situational homosexuality (p. 176)
subculture (p. 184)
Queen (p. 190)
voir dire (p. 184)
Wolf (p. 190)

Discussion Questions

1. Do you think the change in the structure of women's prisons so that they now resemble male institutions has affected the nature of social interaction and sexual behavior? Is this a good thing, or does it present more serious problems for prison officials?
2. As homosexual behavior continues to gain some level of acceptability in society, do you think the police subculture will become more tolerant of gay police officers? Why or why not?
3. Do you think that jurors are biased against homosexuals? What do you think about the homosexual advance theory—should offenders' responsibility be reduced for the crime they committed if the victim made a sexual advance toward them?
4. Why do you think many Americans are opposed to same-sex marriage? Is it simply based on religion, or are homosexuals perceived as a threat in some ways?
5. Should gay couples be allowed to adopt a child? Why or why not?
6. Some people argue that if a person engages in homosexual behavior, then that person must be a homosexual. Do you agree? Why or why not?

Endnotes

1. Gentile, G. 2007. "Disney Opens Weddings to Gay Couples. *The Associated Press,* April 6. www. newsvine.com/_news/2007/04/06/ 651488-disney-opens-weddings-to-gay-couples (accessed December 2007).
2. Page, S. 2005. "Poll Shows Backlash on Gay Issues." *USA Today,* May 20. www.usatoday.com/news/nation/2004-01-14-gay-civil-union_x.htm (accessed December 2007).
3. Ibid.
4. "General Regrets Remarks on Homosexuality." MSNBC.com, March 3, 2007.
5. Page 2005.
6. Summers, C. J. (ed.) 2004. *An Encyclopedia of Gay, Lesbian, Bisexual, Transgender, and Queer Culture.* Chicago: Glbtq, Inc.
7. Ibid.
8. Calhoun, C. 1994. "Separating Lesbian Theory from Feminist Theory." *Ethics* 104 (3) (April): 558–581.
9. Ibid.
10. Ibid.
11. Grov, C., Parsons, T. J., and Bimbi, D. S. 2006. "Cruising for Sex Among Gay and Bisexual Men: Different Venues, Different Risks." *Journal of Sex Research* 43 (1): 1–22.
12. D'Emilio, J. 1983. *Sexual Politics, Sexual Communities: The Making of a Homosexual Minority in the United States 1940–1970.* New York: Basic Books.
13. Ibid.
14. Ibid.
15. Katz, J. 1978. *Gay American History.* New York: Avon Books.
16. D'Emilio 1983.
17. Katz 1978.
18. D'Emilio 1983.
19. Ibid.
20. Katz 1978.
21. D'Emilio 1983.
22. Department of Justice, Uniform Crime Reports. 2005. *Hate Crimes in the United States, 2005.* Washington, DC: U.S. Government Printing Office.
23. Ibid.

24. Ibid.

25. Ibid.

26. Kopel, D. 2003. "Hate Crime Laws: Dangerous and Divisive." www.i2i.org/main/article.php?article_id=564 (accessed February 12, 2008).

27. Ibid.

28. Ibid.

29. Ibid.

30. See, for instance, Bittner, E. 1970. *The Functions of Police in Modern Society.* Chevy Chase, MD: National Clearinghouse for Mental Health; Kirkham, G. 1976. *Signal Zero.* New York: Ballantine; Rokeach, M., Martin, M., and Hohn, S. 1971. "The Value Gap Between Police and Policed." *Journal of Social Issues* 27: 155–171; Westley, W. 1970. *Violence and the Police: A Sociological Study of Law, Custom, and Morality.* Cambridge, MA: MIT Press.

31. Bernstein, M., and Kostelac, C. 2002. "Lavender and Blue: Attitudes About Homosexuality and Behavior Towards Lesbians and Gay Men Among Police Officers." *Journal of Contemporary Criminal Justice* 18 (3): 302–328.

32. Younglove, J., Kerr, M. G., and Vitello, C. J. 2002. "Law Enforcement Officers' Perceptions of Same Sex Domestic Violence: Reason for Cautious Optimism." *Journal of Interpersonal Violence* 17 (7): 760–772.

33. Leinen, S. 1993. *Gay Cops.* Brunswick, NJ: Rutgers University Press,

34. Belkin, A., and McNichol, J. 2002. "Pink and Blue: Outcomes Associated with the Integration of Openly Gay and Lesbian Personnel in the San Diego Police Department." *Police Quarterly* 5 (1): 63–95.

35. Henneman, T. 2006. "A Gun and Badge for Gays: Becoming an Openly Gay Police Officer Used to Mean Facing Harassment and Rejection. Now Departments Across the Country Are Actively Seeking Gay Recruits." *The Advocate: The National Gay and Lesbian News Magazine,* May 9, pp. 23–24.

36. Keegan, A. 2005. "Gay Police Officers Struggle for Acceptance in South." *Atlanta Journal Constitution,* August 19, pp. A1–A4.

37. Henneman 2006.

38. Keegan 2005.

39. Miller, S., Forest, K. B., and Jurik, N. C. 2003. "Diversity in Blue: Lesbian and Gay Police Officers in a Masculine Operation." *Men and Masculinities* 5 (4): 355–385.

40. Myers, K. A., Forest, K. B., and Miller, S. L. 2004. "Officer Friendly and the Tough Cop: Gays and Lesbians Navigate Homophobia and Policing." *Journal of Homosexuality* 47 (1): 17–37.

41. Leinen 1993, p. 79.

42. Burke, M. E. 1993. *Coming Out of the Blue: British Police Officers Talk About Their Lives in "The Job" as Lesbians, Gays and Bisexuals.* London: Cassell.

43. Brunelli, H. C. 2004. "The Double Bind: Unequal Treatment for Homosexuals Within the American Legal Framework." *Boston College Third World Law Journal* 20 (1): 201–230.

44. Minson, R. 1992. "Homophobia in Manslaughter: The Homosexual Advance As Insufficient Provocation." *California Law Review* 80: 133. See also Dressler, J. 1995. "When Heterosexual Men Kill Homosexual Men: Reflections on Provocation Law, Sexual Advance and the Reasonable Man Standard." *Journal of Criminal Law and Criminology* 85: 726.

45. Brunelli 2004.

46. Ibid.

47. Hensley, C., Wright, J., Tewksbury, R., and Castle, T. 2006. "The Evolving Nature of Prison Argot and Sexual Hierarchies." In R. Tewksbury (ed.), *Behind Bars: Readings in Prison Culture,* pp. 421–429. Upper Saddle River, NJ: Prentice Hall.

48. Sykes, G. 1958. *The Society of Captives: A Study of a Maximum Security Prison.* Princeton, NJ: Princeton University Press.

49. Ibrahaim, A. I. 1974. "Deviant Sexual Behavior in Men's Prisons." *Crime and Delinquency* 20 (1): 38–44. See also Bowker, L. 1980. *Prison Victimization.* New York: Elsevier North Holland.

50. Hopper, C. 1989. "The Evolution of Conjugal Visiting in Mississippi." *The Prison Journal* 69 (1): 103–109.

51. Saum, C., Surratt, H., Inciardi, J., and Bennett, R. 1995. "Sex in Prison: Exploring the Myths and Realities." *The Prison Journal* 75 (4): 413–430.

52. See, for instance, Naccis, P., and Kane, T. 1983. "Sex and Sexual Aggression in Federal Prisons." *Federal Probation* 47 (4): 31–36; Saum et al. 1995; Tewksbury, R. 1989. "Measures of Sexual Behavior in an Ohio Prison." *Sociology and Social Research* 74 (1): 34–39; Wooden, W., and Parker, J. 1982. *Men Behind Bars: Sexual Exploitation in Prison.* New York: Plenum.

53. Hensley, C., Tewksbury, R., and Wright, J. 2006. "Exploring the Dynamics of Masturbation and Consensual Same-Sex Activity Within a Male Maximum Security Prison." In R. Tewksbury (ed.), *Behind Bars: Readings in Prison Culture,* pp. 97–109. Upper Saddle River, NJ: Prentice Hall.

54. Ibid.

55. Pollock, J. 1998. *Counseling Women in Prison.* Thousand Oaks, CA: Sage.

56. Owens, B. 1989. *In the Mix: Struggle and Survival in a Women's Prison.* Albany: State University of New York at Albany Press.

57. Greer, K. 2006. "The Changing Nature of Interpersonal Relationships in a Women's Prison." In R. Tewksbury (ed.), *Behind Bars: Readings in Prison Culture,* pp. 110–128. Upper Saddle River, NJ: Prentice Hall.

The Elderly and the Criminal Justice System

Chapter Objectives

After reading this chapter, you should be able to

❖ Describe the characteristics of the elderly population in the United States.

❖ Understand victimization patterns for the elderly.

❖ Describe the types of activities elderly criminals engage in.

❖ Discuss the challenges elderly criminals and inmates pose for the criminal justice system.

There can be little doubt that the population in the United States is getting older. According to *Statistical Abstract of the United States,* in 2005 there were approximately 36,790,000 people aged 65 and over, which represented about 13% of the population. While there are various opinions about what constitutes "elderly," the generally accepted age category is 65 and older. As a result of improvements in health and medicine, people are living longer in this country. According to the Centers for Disease Control, the life expectancy of an American in 1960 was 69.7 years, in 1990 it was 75.4 years, and in 2003 it was 77.5 years.[1] Additionally, all of the age categories one might use to describe the elderly—55 and over, 65 and over, and 75 and over—have witnessed dramatic increases in size since 1980. The 55 and over category increased by 42%, the 65 and over category increased by 44%, while the 75 and over category had an 82% increase.

This explosive growth is expected to continue. According to the U.S. Census Bureau, by 2010, people aged 55 years and over will constitute 25% of the population. The Census Bureau has included a new category, 85 years and over, in making its projections for the next 50 years. In fact, by 2050, the Census Bureau expects that those aged 55 and over will constitute over 52% of the population. The corresponding median age of U.S. citizens will be 39.1 by 2050.[2] This means that half of the population will have reached middle age in less than 50 years.

The Census Bureau notes that in 2005 there were 35 million people in the 65 and over age group: 14.4 million men and 20.6 million women. The majority, 58%, of this group were married, while 30% were widowed and 8% were divorced. About a third in this age category were high school graduates and 19% had a college degree. Only about 10% of the 65 and over age group were living below the **poverty line,** the income level at which people are entitled to public assistance such as welfare. The low poverty rate among the elderly is primarily due to Social Security benefits. Without programs like Social Security, most experts believe that about half the elderly would be poor.[3]

When one examines the elderly with regard to gender, a somewhat different picture emerges. A little over half of the women in this age group live alone. Additionally, older women are less educated than their male counterparts—only 13.7% had a college degree compared to 25% of men. Census data also show that elderly women were more likely to be poor. In 2005, 12% of women, compared to 7% of men, were living below the poverty line.[4]

In regard to the racial composition of the elderly, in 2005 Whites comprised about 75% of the U.S. population, and Whites aged 65 and over represented about 12% of the population. Similarly, overall African Americans comprised about 13% of the U.S. population in 2005, and Blacks aged 65 and over represented approximately 8% of the African American population. Those who were identified as having Hispanic or Latino origin represented about 14% of the U.S. population in 2005—clearly the largest minority group—and Hispanics aged 65 and over consisted of only about 5% of the Hispanic population.

If expected trends continue as projected, California, the state with the largest number of elderly persons, will see a 21% increase in the number of those 65 years and over between 2010 and 2015. As a result, the elderly will represent about 13% of that state's population. Florida will witness a 24% increase of its elderly during that same period, representing about 20% of the population. Texas, with the country's third largest cluster of people in the 65 and over category, will see a 22% increase, representing about 12% of that state's population. New York will experience a smaller increase, only 15%, which will still constitute 15% of that state's population.[5] In general, then, the population as a whole is getting older, the number of people considered elderly is growing, and the social and economic issues that an aging population represent are considerable. One of those costs relates to health care, another relates to crime.[6]

✵ Baby Boomers, Generation X, and Generation Y

After World War II ended, the United States experienced an explosion of births, nearly 76 million from 1946 to 1964. Sociologists define persons born during those years as **Baby Boomers.** This group represents about 28% of the U.S. population and is responsible for some of the most dramatic changes in American history. From the Vietnam War protests to the Civil Rights Movement to the rise of feminism and the hippie movement, Baby Boomers have been at the center of the debate, discussion, and social change. This group, many of whom turned 60 years old in 2006, comprises some of the country's leading politicians, entertainers, and social activists. Baby Boomers have also been referred to as the "Me" generation for their emphasis on narcissism and individual pleasure. In fact, this group has fundamentally altered the way in which the elderly are understood in American society. Not content to simply age gracefully like their parents, this group has remained healthy, wealthy, and active into their retirement years. As a result, Baby Boomers have changed the way most Americans conceive of normal aging.[7]

Baby Boomers focused on their careers and leisure activities, and many delayed having children or remained childless. As a result, an anticipated second Baby Boom generation did not occur. The subsequent generation, clearly smaller in size, consisting of about 41 million, were born between roughly 1968 and 1979 and are often referred to as **Generation X (Gen Xers).** Many experts argue that this group has often been ignored and misunderstood and that it is a disheartened generation.[8] Gen Xers are generally marked by their lack of optimism for the future and an absence of trust in traditional values. During the early 1990s, the media portrayed Gen Xers as a group of overeducated, underachieving "slackers," who are more concerned with tattoos and body piercings and who spawned the grunge music movement.

Gen Xers grew up during the end of the Cold War and the Reagan administration, and they witnessed the economic depression of the 1990s. Many members of this generation watched as their parents coped with the loss of their careers and jobs due to outsourcing, deindustrialization, and corporate mergers. This had a profound impact on many Gen Xers, who realized that company loyalty and sacrifices to get ahead did not always pay off. As a result, many Gen Xers did not take advantage of their education or talents and ended up in **"McJobs,"** or jobs in the lowest-paying sectors of the market, including many minimum-wage jobs. This lack of stability in the job market has left many Gen Xers with a strong sense of cynicism about their lives, future, and the country as a whole. This group is also generally critical of the Baby Boomer generation, whom many Gen Xers look upon as self-centered and impractical.[9]

Generation Y (Gen Yers), those born between about 1977 and 1994, make up over 20% of the U.S. population, or 70 million people. Because this generation is a large one, its members are likely to have a significant impact on this country's social and economic landscape in the future. Generation Y is characterized by three main elements. First, members are comfortable with and tolerant of the racial and ethnic diversity around them and feel comfortable interacting with people outside their own ethnic group.

Second, one of the most noted trends in the Generation Y segment of the population is that the parents of Generation Y children are the focus of the family. Unlike Generation X, parents of Generation Y kids are very involved in the daily lives and decisions of their children. Parents often help Gen Yers plan their achievements, take part in their daily activities, and strongly encourage their children to succeed. This encouragement by parents makes members of the Y generation believe they can accomplish anything. Their relationship with their parents also makes it more likely for them to feel they can always return home to their parents for support and assistance.

Third, an important characteristic of this generation is that its members are technologically savvy—Gen Yers tend to be more sophisticated in their computer skills than Baby Boomers and Gen Xers. This is largely due to being exposed to and using technology at an early age. For instance, three out of four teenagers go online and 93% of those aged 15–17 are computer users. The time spent online consists of gaming, emailing, and instant messaging according to the National Center for Health Statistics.[10] In short, Gen Yers are educated and technologically adept and have been encouraged by their parents that they can achieve whatever goals they set for themselves. It is not surprising to learn, then, that there is a strong sense of entitlement felt by this group about wanting the best in life and thinking they deserve it.

Gen Yers are ambitious and have high expectations of themselves and those around them. They also are accustomed to instant gratification, tend to be overly confident, and are often characterized as those who are willing to cheat, if necessary, to achieve their goals. On the positive side, members of this group are very adaptable in a variety of settings, are efficient multi-taskers, and possess the technological skills and educational talents to achieve significant goals.[11]

✕ Elderly Crime

Since the early 1970s, some attention has been paid to the relationship between crime and the elderly.[12] The majority of this focus has been on fear of crime as well as elderly victimization. While conventional wisdom has been that the elderly are the age group at the greatest risk of becoming the victims of crime, research has consistently shown that they have the lowest rates of actual victimization.[13] However, fear itself can be seen as a form of victimization, and the elderly, along with females of all age groups, express the highest levels of fear. Moreover, the consequences of actual victimization can be more severe for the elderly than other age groups because of their physical limitations as well as their limited economic ability to recover from the financial losses sustained by crime.

Elderly Victims

As a general rule, as a person ages, rates of victimization tend to decline. According to the National Crime Victimization Survey (NCVS), the elderly, those over the age of 65, experienced less violence and fewer property crimes than younger persons between 1993 and 2002. Property crime provided the greatest threat to those age 65 and older. About 1 in 5 of personal crimes against the elderly were thefts compared to about 1 in 33 for younger persons.[14]

The NCVS for 2005 showed that between 1993 and 2002, more than nine in ten crimes against the elderly were property crimes. With regard to violent crime victimization, such as homicide, the rate of victimization of the elderly is quite low (see Figure 9.1). The data also reveal that older teens and young adults (18–24 years

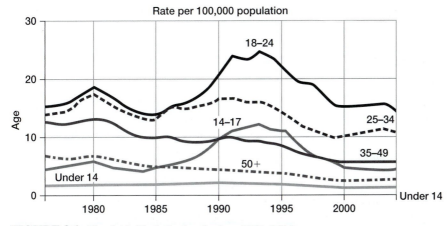

FIGURE 9.1 *Homicide Victimization by Age, 1976–2004*

SOURCE: National Crime Victimization Survey 2005.

old) experienced the highest homicide rate; however, this trend has shown a decline since its peak in the early 1990s. Similarly, the homicide victimization rates for adults aged 35–49 and 50 and older have also declined. Thus, for homicide, almost every category showed a decline between 1976 and 2004, and this trend continued in 2005, particularly for those over the age of 50.

There is also the concept of **eldercide,** which is the murder of a person 50 years or older. This particular type of homicide comprised about 15% of all homicides in 2005. As the NCVS shows, between 1976 and 2004, about half of the offenders of this type of homicide were in the 18–34 age group. Moreover, as Table 9.1 shows, workplace murder (39.1%) and felony murder (23.9%) claimed a relatively large percentage of older victims.

TABLE 9.1

Homicide Type by Age, 1976–2004

	Victims				Offenders			
	Under 18	18–34	35–49	50+	Under 18	18–34	35–49	50+
All homicides	9.8%	52.7%	22.8%	14.7%	10.9%	65.0%	17.3%	6.9%
Victim/offender relationship								
Intimate	1.7%	46.8%	34.1%	17.5%	1.1%	46.6%	34.7%	17.7%
Family	19.5	32.1	26.5	21.9	6.1	49.2	28.0	16.7
Infanticide	100.0				8.2	81.1	9.6	1.1
Eldercide				100.0	10.4	49.5	18.9	21.2
Circumstances								
Felony murder	7.6%	46.8%	21.7%	23.9%	14.9%	72.9%	10.2%	2.0%
Sex related	19.7	45.2	16.6	18.6	10.7	73.8	13.4	2.0
Drug related	5.4	71.5	19.8	3.2	10.6	76.8	11.3	1.2
Gang related	24.5	68.3	6.0	1.3	29.4	68.8	1.6	.3
Argument	5.4	56.2	26.2	12.1	6.9	60.2	23.1	9.8
Workplace	2.0	27.4	31.5	39.1	4.9	53.0	27.1	15.0
Weapon								
Gun homicide	7.4%	59.2%	22.4%	10.9%	11.9%	64.6%	15.9%	7.6%
Arson	28.2	27.1	19.2	25.5	11.6	57.8	23.5	7.1
Poison	26.7	23.9	16.6	32.7	4.5	50.9	26.2	18.4
Multiple victims or offenders								
Multiple victims	18.4%	46.2%	19.1%	16.4%	9.5%	66.1%	18.6%	5.8%
Multiple offenders	11.3	55.4	19.8	13.6	18.4	73.0	7.4	1.2

Source: *FBI Supplementary Homicide Reports 1976–2004, Crime in the United States.* (Washington, D.C.: U.S. Government Printing Office).

Elder Abuse

Another type of victimization concerns **elder abuse.** No one knows exactly how many older Americans are abused, neglected, or exploited each year; part of the reason for this has to do with the problems of defining elder abuse. Additionally, there is no uniform reporting system, rendering any type of comprehensive national database difficult to obtain. The research that exists on elder abuse has shown that between 1 and 2 million Americans 65 and older have been mistreated by someone on whom they depend for care or protection.[15]

Like many crimes, elder abuse often goes unreported. According to the National Center on Elder Abuse, for every case of elder abuse, neglect, exploitation, or self-neglect reported to authorities, about five more incidents go unreported.[16] Additionally, the types of abuse vary. One type involves financial exploitation. This is usually the result of some sort of confidence game or fraud committed against the

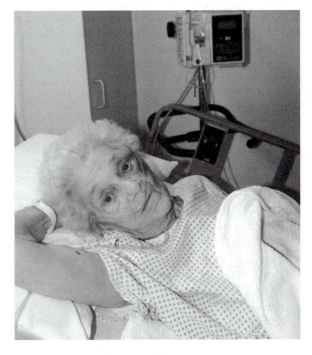

The elderly are often victimized in the form of abuse, often by family members.

elderly. According to one study, the overall reporting of financial exploitation is about 1 in 25 cases, which translates into about 5 million financial-abuse victims each year.[17]

Another type of elderly victimization is physical abuse. A 2003 study of nursing homes found that among seven types of abuse, physical abuse was the most common type reported.[18] In a 2004 survey of Adult Protective Services agencies, the National Center on Elder Abuse found that older women were far more likely than older men to suffer from physical abuse or neglect—almost two-thirds (65.7%) of elder abuse victims were women. This study also found that 43% of abuse victims were 80 and older. The abusers in this study were primarily females (52.7%), and three-fourths of offenders were under 60. About half of the perpetrators of elderly abuse were members of the victim's family—a third of the perpetrators were adult children and another 21% were other family members. Spouses or intimate partners accounted for only 11% of the total number of offenders. According to the study, caregiver neglect accounted for about 20% of all neglect cases.[19]

Elderly Offenders

While a great deal of attention has been given to elderly victims, relatively little has been given to elderly offenders. The image that the elderly offender conjures up is filled with stereotypes and misinformation. Because people think of the elderly as infirm or limited in mobility, it is relatively easy to conclude that these individuals commit relatively "harmless" crimes, such as shoplifting or other nonviolent acts. However, as was mentioned, there is no consensus in determining when someone is considered "elderly." Most people use 65 years old as the cutoff point. This is the usual retirement age, the point at which one is eligible for Social Security benefits, pensions, retirement income, Medicare, and so on. But the number is rather arbitrarily designated. Additionally, the agencies that collect data on crime vary considerably in their **operationalization** of age, or how they define it for the purpose of analysis. For example, the FBI, in its analysis of crime statistics, uses "65 and over" as the uppermost category in arrest data, but includes 55–59 and 60–64 age groups as well. Other agencies in the criminal justice system, such as the Federal Bureau of Prisons, use 45 as their cutoff point, while some state systems use 60. More recently, some states have taken to using the degree of disability, rather than chronological age, in their definition. An added problem with understanding elderly crime is that the elderly population tends to overlap with two other special needs categories: the chronically ill and the terminally ill.[20] In general, the criminal justice system often classifies those "55 and over" as elderly. Opinions vary as to why this is the case, but many researchers contend that the reason for the differences has to do with collapsing intervals in order to have enough people in the respective categories.[21] However, this variability makes it difficult to compare information about elderly criminals from one study to the next.

To complicate the problem further, some researchers relate age categories to the type of crime committed. For instance, "joyriding" tends to be committed by teenagers. If a person 35 years of age is arrested for joyriding, for the purpose of statistical analysis, he or she could be defined as an elderly offender, largely because people in this age group typically do not engage in this type of activity. As a result of these problems, most researchers rely on the chronological categorization of age, but even here, problems emerge.[22]

The classification based on age is only one part of the problem in determining the extent of the elderly population's involvement in crime. There is also the issue of defining a crime. When people typically talk about the "crime problem," they are referring to street crime. Using this definition, crime statistics reflect the image that crime tends to be a young, minority, male phenomenon. However, this is an overly simplistic definition of crime since it does not take into account white-collar or organized crime, nor does it include professional criminals, most of whom tend to be older. While crime is generally considered a "young man's game," it is important to account for when, and under what circumstances, the elderly become involved in criminal activity. According to the *Uniform Crime Reports,* which classifies arrests by age, there are three general categories to use in assessing elderly criminals: 55–59, 60–64, and 65 and older. Given the problems of operationalizing the term "elderly," for the purpose of this chapter, all three categories will be used.

Research on Elderly Criminals

While there are a few older studies and some current research on this population, the vast majority of attention on elderly offenders occurred in the 1980s. The most recent research generally focuses on older inmates. Offenders who have been in prison for a long period of time inevitably encounter physical problems. The problems stemming from an elderly inmate population are serious and costly, ranging from concerns about victimization to health care issues.[23]

AGING MOBSTER, 96, SENTENCED

In February 2007, in U.S. District Court in Fort Lauderdale, Florida, 96-year-old Albert "The Old Man" Facchiano, a "made member" of the Genovese crime family, the nation's largest and most powerful Mafia family for decades, pleaded guilty to charges of racketeering, conspiracy, and jury tampering. According to prosecutors, Facchiano supervised robberies, money laundering, bank fraud, and stolen merchandise from 1994 to 2006. He also pled guilty to trying to locate and intimidate a government witness in New York in 2005. Facchiano becomes one of the oldest criminals to plead guilty to federal crimes and one of the oldest to have committed crimes at such an advanced age. During the court hearing, Facchiano used a special headset to hear questions from the U.S. District Court judge. When asked by the judge "Is your mind okay?" Facchiano eventually responded, "Oh yes, I can't hear, but I can understand, your honor." Facchiano's attorney stated that his client sees a doctor four times a week and suffers from back pain and a host of other ailments. While the charges against Facchiano carried a prison sentence of up to 30 years and $500,000 in fines, because he pled guilty, prosecutors recommended Facchiano serve house arrest, citing that any form of incarceration would be a form of capital punishment.

What is interesting about the research on this population during the 1980s is that many experts were looking at elderly criminals as the onset of a social problem.[24] In their seminal text, *Constructing Social Problems* (1977), John Kitsuse and Malcolm Spector state that **claims making** is a fundamental aspect of how social problems are defined in a given society. When people, particularly experts, assert that an event or a phenomenon is problematic for a society, the process of making a claim occurs, and a social problem is created. This same process occurred in the literature on elderly criminals. Because it seemed logical at the time, and because many researchers were pointing to the inevitability of an increase in elderly offenders, many criminal justice researchers and sociologists were convinced of the validity of these claims. As an illustration, the authors of one of the most comprehensive texts on the subject of elderly criminals offered this prediction:

> It is a rare opportunity to see a social problem coming with enough lead time to do something about it. We are very sure that the demographic balance of our population will shift so that more people will be in the upper age ranges. As this occurs, the elderly crime problem can only assume a more important position on our list of domestic problems. It seems particularly appropriate to begin developing policies of control and prevention right now.[25]

However, just as the research in the 1980s intensified in anticipation of a significant social problem, the research nearly stopped in the 1990s. As was mentioned, while some assessment of this subject continues, it is usually much more focused on the effects of incarceration than on the incidence of elderly crime.[26] Few studies make reference to the expectations of a decade earlier. However, this is not to say what was discovered during this time period was flawed—a great deal was learned about the range of activities of many elderly offenders.

At first glance, the dramatic decrease in the number of studies suggests a wavering interest in the topic, which could be taken as evidence that the elderly crime wave failed to occur. However, a better indicator of the accuracy of this prediction would be an analysis of arrest statistics much in the same way that studies were conducted in the 1980s. One study, for example, analyzed arrest statistics from the *Uniform Crime Reports* between 1964 and 1979 and found a dramatic increase of arrests for serious crimes among those 55 and over. The findings of this study showed a significant increase in the percentage of elderly arrests for property crime, motor vehicle theft, and sex offenses, especially when compared to the rest of the offender population. The conclusion drawn from this study was that while the elderly constituted only a small part of the total arrests, there was every reason to expect the number of elderly arrests would increase dramatically as the entire population grew older.[27] An analysis of the *Uniform Crime Reports* arrest statistics from 1990 to 1994 was done in an effort to assess these predictions over time. The findings showed that the percentage of arrests for the population increased from 1990 to 1994, but the overall arrest rate for elderly offenders decreased by 5%.[28]

There was also a difference from the previous research with regard to violent crime, which increased almost as much for elderly offenders as it did for the rest of the population, while property crimes witnessed a dramatic decrease for elderly offenders. A comparison of arrest statistics for 2000 and 2005 showed an increase in property crime rates but significant reductions in violent crime. On average, elderly criminals represented about 1.2% of the total number of arrests in 2000 and about 1% in 2005. The real differences are found in comparing property crimes. Between 2000 and 2005, the proportion of property crime for the 55–59 age group increased about 5% and the proportion of property crime in the 60–64 age category increased only about 2%. The property crime rate for the oldest category remained about the same during this five-year span. (See Table 9.2.)

Thus, the current trends in crime committed by the elderly, as well as the types of crimes, vary considerably from what was known in the 1980s. In fact, while the research predicted the number of offenders would increase as the population got older, this has not occurred. However, while the early data suggested that older offenders were more likely to be involved in alcohol-related crimes, recent arrest data indicate a decrease has taken place. The incidence of elderly sex offenders increased in the 1990s; however, the evidence suggests the number has decreased substantially in recent years.

TABLE 9.2

Violent and Property Crime by Age Group, 2000 and 2005

	2000			2005		
	55–59	**60–64**	**65 and over**	**55–59**	**60–64**	**65 and over**
Violent Crime	4,824	2,427	2,983	2,369	1,101	1,133
Property Crime	8,637	4,262	5,699	14,513	6,192	5,444
Total Arrests		**9,116,967**			**10,369,819**	

Because of the unique problems stemming from prosecuting and sentencing elderly offenders, some experts advocate for a separate geriatric court.

⚔ Types of Elderly Offenders

Shoplifting

As was mentioned, the image of the elderly criminal strikes most people as incongruous with their understanding of crime in society. When Americans think of elderly criminals, it is not uncommon to envision a rather passive and benign type of offender: one who does not injure his or her victims and commits economic crimes rather than violent ones. Shoplifting is one type of crime that fits this image. It is passive, it does not usually lead to injuries to bystanders, and one does not need a great deal of dexterity or mobility to commit it.

Many people also attempt to deflect the culpability of the elderly offender by offering exculpatory reasons for committing this act, such as economic hardship or that the crime was committed without any intent. In other words, elderly shoplifters are simply those people who forget to pay for their purchases and then are apprehended when they attempt to leave the premises. Loneliness is also used as an explanation by some scholars: The elderly criminal is in need of contact with others and, like a young child, steals for the attention he or she receives.[29]

But what do we really know about elderly shoplifters? One of the few studies of this population examined 191 first-time offenders in Florida who agreed to participate in a court-ordered diversion program. In trying to answer the question of whether elderly shoplifters steal because they are poor, researchers in this study collected data on the offenders' income, occupation, and whether or not they owned a home. The median annual income of these offenders was approximately $7,500 and about half of them (45%) derived their incomes from three or more sources: interest from savings, stocks and bonds, and Social Security benefits. Most of them had been white-collar workers, professionals, and administrators in their former careers. Moreover, 83% of offenders owned their place of residence. Thus, the vast majority of elderly shoplifters in this study were homeowners and not without resources, which runs counter to the indigent argument.

Additionally, of the objects stolen by these elderly offenders, the most common were clothing items and cosmetics rather than subsistence or need-based items such as food or drugs. Researchers in this study also attempted to document the "lack of intent" explanation, whereby shoplifting cases by the elderly were due to forgetfulness rather than to intentionally stealing. While there are instances where people innocuously take items and forget to pay for them, this explanation loses much of its validity when multiple items are taken. That is, most people can understand forgetting one item, but the intent to shoplift becomes more credible as the number of items increases. In this study, about half (48%) of the cases involved two or three stolen items.[30]

Finally, as was mentioned, a popular explanation for elderly shoplifting involves loneliness. In these cases, the elderly offender is isolated from social interaction and craves attention. However, the findings of this particular study showed that approximately 70% of the offenders did not live alone and 65% were married. In addition, approximately 80% indicated that they had family members or close friends living in the area. Other tests of social isolation given to offenders supported the conclusion that the offenders were not stealing due to loneliness or feeling isolated from the larger community.

In sum, the research on the elderly shoplifter, while still scant, runs counter to popular understanding of why these individuals engage in this type of criminal activity. They are not indigent, are not without other resources, and appear to have adequate social and emotional support networks. Moreover, elderly shoplifters do not appear to be retaliating against businesses they patronized. In fact, many offenders rate the establishments from which they steal rather high in terms of the services they provided.

While no formal category of shoplifting exists in official statistics, according to the *Uniform Crime Reports,* there has been a dramatic increase in the number of arrests for crimes like shoplifting among older age groups (see Table 9.3). In 2000, there were 16,467 larceny-theft arrests. In 2005, there were 22,782 larceny-theft arrests, a 38% increase. For the 55–59 age group, the increase was 40%; for the 60–64 group, it was 30%; and there was a small increase of 4% for the over 65 group.[31]

TABLE 9.3

Larceny-Theft by Age Group, 2000 and 2005

	2000			2005		
	55–59	**60–64**	**65+**	**55–59**	**60–64**	**65+**
Larceny-Theft	7,506	3,824	5,137	12,451	5,421	4,910
Total Arrests		9,116,967			10,369,819	

Homicide

Relatively few homicides occur in the United States each year, and less than 2% are committed by the elderly in any given year, according to arrest statistics from the *Uniform Crime Reports.*[32]

While a great deal of attention is given to older victims of homicide, information is generally lacking on older homicide offenders. In the quest to demystify some of the notions about this topic, one study used the FBI's *Supplemental Homicide Reports* to profile elderly homicide offenders. The study showed that, like the fluctuation in the overall homicide rate, the rate for the elderly is not stable across jurisdictions. As a result, the elderly offender is affected by the same sociological factors that create different murder rates among younger adults from state to state.

Some experts argue that elderly offenders would be more likely than younger offenders to kill those of their own age. Some of the research on this topic shows that many young homicide offenders kill people older than they are as a result of robberies or the commission of other felonies.[33] Since the data show that the elderly are not as likely to be involved in these kinds of activities, one might conclude that older people *would* be more likely to kill within their own age group. However, the data suggest that the opposite is true. According to the *Uniform Crime Reports* for 2005, people in the 60–64 and 65–74 groups were actually less likely to kill someone of their own age and about 21% of those aged 50 and over killed victims of the same age.

Finally, it has been argued that elderly offenders would be more likely to use firearms than offenders in other age groups. The logic, of course, is that since the elderly are not as strong as younger people, they would be more likely to use a gun to commit the crime. Twenty years ago a study found that this was supported by the data: Elderly offenders were more likely to use firearms than the non-elderly. In the mid-1990s, another study of elderly homicide offenders was conducted in Detroit.[34] Many of the trends identified in the initial study of elderly homicide remained constant almost ten years later. This study found that older homicide offenders were more likely to use firearms in the commission of a crime than their younger counterparts. The author of this study also found that "proportionally fewer homicides perpetrated by older persons appear to be committed between 8:00 P.M. and 1:59 A.M. For some reason, the elderly are less inclined to kill late at night than are the non-elderly."[35]

An analysis of homicide statistics from 1976 to 2004 revealed that only about 8% of offenders aged 50 and older used a firearm to commit a homicide.[36] This suggests that elderly homicide offenders are not significantly different in many ways from murderers in younger age groups, although some of the practical aspects of committing the crime account for some differences in their rates. For instance, unlike younger offenders, older killers commit many of their crimes within their own residences. This may be due to a variety of reasons, but perhaps the most significant is that elderly people tend to spend more time at home than in public or commercial establishments. Finally, the low incidence of murders by the elderly may have something to do with the shorter life span of violent individuals. Some research suggests that people with predispositions toward violence are less likely to reach the age of 55 and thus are at lower risk to become an *elderly* offender. Thus, while it is true the

TABLE 9.4

Homicide by Age Group, 2000 and 2005

	2000			2005		
	55–59	**60–64**	**65+**	**55–59**	**60–64**	**65+**
Homicide	102	56	96	155	73	119
Total Arrests	**9,116,967**			**10,369,819**		

elderly commit fewer homicides, in general the patterns are similar to those of younger offenders.

The most recent data available on elderly homicide show some dramatic increases. This comes at a time when the number of homicides, particularly in large cities, has had a sudden increase. According to a report issued by the Police Executive Research Forum titled *Violent Crime in America: 24 Months of Alarming Trends*, the murder rate has increased more than 10% since 2004. In addition, the report showed that robberies, felony assaults with a gun, and other violent crimes have increased.

According to the *Uniform Crime Reports,* in 2000, there were approximately 254 elderly arrests for homicide (see Table 9.4). This number increased 27% in 2005 to a total of 347.[37]

Sex Offenses

As with other crimes, stereotypical images exist about elderly sex offenders that interfere with an accurate understanding of this phenomenon. Some people believe, for instance, that sexual offenses involving children are the sex crime most often committed by old men.[38] The media has also created a climate in which the image of a sexual predator is an elderly man, likely a Catholic priest, who preys upon innocent children. In fact, there is a great deal of distortion of sex offenses among the elderly and the pedophilia of priests in particular. Much of what has been called pedophilia is actually consensual sex among older boys, not child abuse or sexual assault as has been portrayed in the media. This trend does not suggest that pedophilia is acceptable or what some priests have done is appropriate. However, the media's distorted image does suggest that perhaps the elderly are not as involved in sex offenses as is commonly believed.[39]

One study attempted to synthesize the information on the subject by examining 86 elderly and young sex offenders (young was defined as 30 years old and younger, while elderly was defined as 60 years and older). The results were that elderly offenders had more stability in terms of their marital status, occupational income, and ties to the community. Younger sex offenders were more likely to have higher education levels, a history of drug and alcohol abuse, and to have had a sexual encounter with a child in a public place, such as a local park. Elderly sex offenders were more likely to have been a passive recipient in the exchange with a child and to have engaged in this activity in the privacy of their own home.[40] In virtually all of

TABLE 9.5

Sex Crimes by Age Group, 2000 and 2005

	2000			2005		
	55–59	60–64	65+	55–59	60–64	65+
Sex Crimes	1,618	999	1,346	2,022	1,214	1,439
Total Arrests	**9,116,967**			**10,369,819**		

the cases involving elderly sex offenders, there was some sort of relationship between the victim and the offender and the nature of the activity was usually non-violent. This study and others have found that mental disorders, organic brain dysfunctions such as dementia and delirium, as well as neurosis, personality disorders, and alcoholism, are much more common among elderly offenders than younger offenders.[41]

For the purposes of analysis, according to the *Uniform Crime Reports,* sex crimes include all activities except prostitution and forcible rape. While this covers a wide range of activities, the data suggest that the incidence of sex crimes increased considerably between 2000 and 2005 (see Table 9.5). According to *Uniform Crime Reports* data, the total number of older persons arrested for sex offenses in 2000 was 3,963. In 2005, this number was 4,675, an increase of approximately 18%. For the 55–59 age group, the increase was about 25%; for the 60–64 group, it was about 22%; and the increase was about 6% for the over 65 group.[42]

Alcohol-Related Crimes

Unlike other forms of crime committed by the elderly, the evidence on the relationship between alcohol use and criminal activity among the elderly has a larger empirical foundation. The questions and controversy surrounding this type of criminal behavior stem largely from whether or not elderly people drink more than young people. While some experts argue that older people drink to alleviate feelings of isolation and emotional loss, or to derive some sense of satisfaction in life, others contend that the incidence of crimes while under the influence of alcohol decreases with age.[43]

Alcohol-related arrests, such as driving while intoxicated and public drunkenness, account for the majority of criminal behavior of people 55 and older. Other research on alcohol-related crime by the elderly has shown that the majority of offenders are males with long-term, chronic drinking problems and equally long histories of crime while under the influence of alcohol.[44] However, there are also data that suggest older people generally drink less than their younger counterparts. In fact, in contrast to these prevailing theories, some studies suggest that the very old, those 75 and older, are more likely to abstain from alcohol.[45] While there remains a great deal of debate about this issue, the research suffers from methodological problems and often lacks comparability with other studies. However, the

TABLE 9.6

DUI by Age Group, 2000 and 2005

	2000			2005		
	55–59	**60–64**	**65+**	**55–59**	**60–64**	**65+**
DUI	22,260	11,704	1,216	29,014	14,013	11,663
Drunkenness	10,785	5,378	4,668	13,196	5,787	4,049
Total Arrests		9,116,967			10,369,819	

weight of the evidence suggests that the problem of alcohol-related crime by the elderly is not of epidemic proportions. The data do show that if older people are arrested for crimes, they are very likely to be alcohol-related ones. However, alcohol-related offenses, such as drunk driving and public drunkenness, account for only 0.2% of all reported arrests of older adults.

According to the *Uniform Crime Reports,* in 2000 there were 45,180 elderly arrests for driving under the influence (DUI) (see Table 9.6). In 2005, there were 54,690 such arrests, an increase of 21%. Public drunkenness also witnessed a slight increase between 2000 and 2005. There were 20,831 elderly arrests for public drunkenness in 2000 compared to 23,032 arrests for that crime in 2005, about an 11% increase.

✖ Formal Reactions to the Elderly Criminal

It should be clear at this point that the "problem" of elderly crime is really not a problem in terms of the actual numbers of offenders or offenses. It is unlikely, either now or perhaps even in the future, that an "elderly crime wave" will occur. Despite its limitations and flaws, the *Uniform Crime Reports* has consistently shown that elderly criminals do not represent a significant crime problem. However, perhaps the problem should not be understood in terms of its volume or magnitude but, rather, in terms of its uniqueness. The fact that elderly individuals commit various types of crime, including violent offenses, raises a number of questions about the pursuit of justice, the goals of punishment, and the purpose of the criminal justice system.

The problem of elderly crime is somewhat similar to the problem of juvenile crime in that society recognizes young people as being different from adults when they commit criminal acts. Consequently, this system has a different philosophy than the adult system: one that tempers the culpability of the offender while still holding youth accountable. Add to the fact that since most of the recent research focuses on the particular problems elderly criminals encounter when they are processed through the system,[46] many criminal justice experts have argued that perhaps one way to alleviate these problems is to establish a separate system for the elderly, or what is sometimes referred to as a **geriatric court.**[47]

Proponents of this type of change argue that elderly criminals are inherently different from younger criminals and merit special consideration in the justice process. Moreover, the pains of punishment are more taxing on elderly offenders. Advocates of the geriatric court also contend that there should be a more lax approach by law enforcement, a more lenient attitude by the courts in sentencing, and a sympathetic approach to punishment by correctional institutions. The logic, of course, is that neither society nor the individual benefits from the unilateral treatment of offenders. What good does it serve society, for example, if a 65-year-old man is given a 30-year prison sentence? The same punishment for a 15-year-old does not end his life; however, for an elderly criminal, this sentence may in fact be a form of capital punishment. Moreover, since the legal precedent for a separate system has already been established for juveniles, and the particular needs and problems of older offenders are similar to those of juveniles (in terms of vulnerability and risks, as well as the issue of rehabilitation), why not create a separate system?

It may very well be that a geriatric court can lead to improvements in meeting the needs of the elderly population. While the answer to this question cannot be found without additional and extensive research, the idea of a geriatric court requires an examination of many current policies and practices involving the administration of justice.

On the other hand, opponents of this approach argue that distinctions of crime cannot be based on chronological age. In other words, a person is ultimately responsible whether he or she is 18 years old or 80. In this model, one that clearly fits within the **just deserts** philosophy, which argues that all people are equally responsible for their actions and should be punished according to what they have done, the symbolic and practical consequences of taking a lenient attitude toward the elderly may encourage other potential offenders to commit crime.

Finally, as was mentioned, while there is much left to be done in terms of understanding elderly crime, the vast majority of the research has focused on how and in what ways offenders are forced to cope with the pains of imprisonment. This includes the organizational and logistical problems faced by correctional institutions that have an increasingly older inmate population. The problems are many and quite diversified, and they will likely increase with time. Thus, the handling of elderly inmates, in terms of both physical safety and health care, will likely remain a central feature in the study of elderly offenders.

Elderly Inmates

The research on elderly criminals shows that the number of offenders over the age of 55 going to prison is increasing and that the ones already in prison are getting older. Added to the aging of the inmate population is the fact that tougher sentencing laws mean that younger offenders who commit serious crimes will also likely spend longer periods of time in prison. In 2001, according to the National Institute of Corrections, the number of state and federal inmates aged 50 and older increased 173% from 1992 and comprised about 8% of the overall prison population. In 2005, elderly inmates 55 and over comprised 10% of the total inmate population in state and federal prisons. The day-to-day stressors and risks associated with institutional life are exceptionally hard on elderly offenders. Elderly inmates also require more correctional officer protection from younger predators.

The number of offenders over the age of 55 going to prison is increasing, and the ones already in prison are getting older.

The most common health-related problems elderly inmates experience include incontinence, respiratory illnesses, cardiovascular disease, and chronic problems such as arthritis, high blood pressure, prostate problems, and ulcers. Elderly inmates also suffer from typical age-related illnesses such as cognitive impairment, reduced vision and hearing, loss of physical strength, and emotional disorders.[48] Given the nature of these problems, it should not be surprising that the cost of incarcerating an elderly inmate averages $60,000–$70,000 per year, nearly three times the amount for incarcerating the average healthy and younger inmate.

The special circumstances surrounding the incarceration of elderly inmates also create a number of challenges for correctional institutions. For example, older inmates have greater health care needs, may require a number of structural changes in the facility to accommodate them, such as single beds instead of bunk beds and fewer inmates per cell, and even the creation of geriatric units within the prison. The special health care needs of elderly inmates also require correctional institutions to either establish or contract comprehensive health care services.[49]

Across the country, some states are attempting to address the escalating health care costs for elderly inmates. For example, at least 16 states have established separate facilities to house older inmates, and many are offering hospice care for dying prisoners. In Texas, for example, about 200 inmates over the age of 65 receive round-the-clock care. The state of Nebraska offers nursing-home living for some inmates, and Oklahoma is creating a separate unit for older inmates.[50]

In California, where there are 172,000 prisoners in the state system, the problem has become acute, with jails releasing convicted felons because of overcrowding. In the state prisons, inmates are stacked three high in cells and housed in hallways and converted gyms. Some California prisons are even 200–300% over capacity. In order to provide space for inmates, some facilities have had to rent cell space from other, less crowded prisons. As prison officials struggle to find solutions to the problems of overcrowding, they are faced with a 70% **recidivism rate,** also known as the reoffending rate. California's recidivism rate is currently the highest in the nation. This means that 70% of the inmates convicted of a crime will commit another one within three years of release**.**

In California, the number of prisoners 55 and older has doubled since 1997, with almost 20,000 prisoners over age 50 and almost 750 over 70 years old. As one expert on prisons noted, there is evidence that prisoners are physiologically ten years older than their chronological age. This means that inmate needs are increasing as are the costs of their incarceration.[51] Because of this, some experts have suggested that the best way to alleviate overcrowding in prison would be to release the inmates who pose the least risk to the community. Given that recidivism rates generally drop around the age of 30 and continue to fall after that, an argument can be made that releasing elderly criminals makes sense in that they are least likely of all age groups to commit another crime against the community.[52]

As the current research tries to show, there are a number of practical issues surrounding elderly inmates. These range from the pragmatic difficulties of maneuvering a wheelchair in a prison cell to improving health care facilities. For example, it seems obvious that planners did not, and perhaps could not, have foreseen these issues when prisons were being constructed ten, twenty, or even forty years ago. Prison cells were simply not designed for offenders who were limited in mobility. However, the realities of incarcerating older inmates, as well as caring for those who become ill, need to be incorporated into the design and construction of new facilities. While this will increase the costs, it may be one of the consequences of incarcerating older offenders and keeping them incarcerated for long periods of time.

Law Enforcement and Elderly Offenders

Related to the issues surrounding elderly inmates are several philosophical and pragmatic questions raised by many criminal justice scholars. David Newman, a noted expert on elderly crime, makes an interesting point about the practical problems for police officers who encounter elderly criminals. He questions whether handcuffing or shackling a 75-year-old is really in line with the goals of the criminal justice system. Newman also questions whether or not booking procedures, including fingerprinting, photographing, and lineups, are really necessary and appropriate for 70-year-old suspects. In addition, Newman argues against monetary bail as the only way elderly offenders can be released while awaiting trial. He asks, "Are they likely to flee? Do many or most elderly offenders really need to be jailed or imprisoned?"[53] In short, Newman calls into question the issue of whether or not the criminal justice system effectively addresses the problems of elderly offenders.

While Newman raises some interesting points, should chronological age play a factor with these issues? There are many instances in which exceptions are made for all types of offenders. If the person is violent, whether elderly or not, one would think that the safety of the arresting officers, the citizens of that community, and the well-being of the individual offender would override any embarrassment or humiliation the particular suspect might feel. In short, it is not clear whether older offenders should be given special considerations with regard to the early stages of the justice process. Where there is stronger support in Newman's argument concerns the pragmatic problems of being imprisoned. Prison cells are not designed for the elderly, which presents a number of problems for the correctional institution as well as the inmate.

The subject of elderly criminals presents one of the most interesting juxtapositions of the disciplines of criminology, criminal justice, and gerontology. Despite the fact that crime committed by the elderly has not grown in the way the research had predicted, the issues and problems surrounding this phenomenon will continue to have an impact on the understanding and perceptions of aging in American society as well as how and in what ways crime influences social life.

Summary

This chapter explored the phenomenon of elderly crime. There can be little doubt that as the population gets older, the number of people involved in crime, whether as victims or as offenders, will likely increase. Baby Boomers, those born between 1946 and 1964, represent the newest group of elderly in this country. As a generation, they have redefined the face of America with the Civil Rights Movement and protests against the Vietnam War, and represent some of the leading figures in politics, economics, and social activism. As this generation becomes older, it is likely that they will also redefine the criteria used to evaluate the concept of aging. Generation X, or Gen Xers, are those individuals born between about 1968 and 1979. This group is generally considered an underachieving generation, critical of the self-indulgence of Baby Boomers, and who grew up amid a host of social problems in the 1980s and 1990s. Generation Y is the latest group of young people in this country, born between about 1977 and 1994. Gen Yers are characterized by their willingness to embrace cultural diversity, are educationally and technologically sophisticated, and have a strong sense of self including feelings of entitlement, self-confidence, and impatience in climbing the ladder of success.

Conventional wisdom concerning elderly crime typically focuses on elderly victimization. As this chapter has shown, the elderly are the least likely to be victimized of any age group, but this should not be interpreted to mean the elderly are not victimized. There is a great deal of empirical evidence on elderly abuse as well as research on elderly offenders.

Early predictions of an elderly crime wave, based largely on population and demographic shifts, have failed to emerge. However, the research on elderly criminals, found primarily in the official crime statistics, shows that elderly crime is not as frequent as crime committed by younger offenders; however, it is sufficient to warrant more attention. Generally speaking, most of the elderly crime noted in the data relates to minor forms of crime, usually alcohol related or some type of larceny. Despite noted cases of elderly criminals commiting violent acts, these instances are relatively rare.

Most of the research interest on elderly criminals has focused on the area of incarceration and prison life in general. As inmates are sentenced to longer prison terms, issues relating to health care and the overall quality of life for inmates become a topic of keen interest to researchers.

 # You Make the Call

Elderly Criminals

Consider the following scenario. Debate the pros and cons of all options and decide what you would do.

You are an appellate court judge who has received an appeal from a 65-year-old inmate who was serving a sentence for having murdered his terminally ill wife. Knowing that she was going to endure extraordinarily painful treatments, the man, overcome with emotion, decided to throw his wife off of the balcony of their ten-story apartment. Upon conviction, he received a 30-year sentence for his crime, but is appealing on the basis that this constituted cruel and unusual punishment. The reason for this, obviously, is that such punishment is, effectively, a death sentence given his age. The public is supportive of a merciful approach, particularly given the fact that the offender's crimes, while heinous, merit some consideration.

Questions

1. What is your decision on his appeal?
2. Should there be a different standard of justice on the basis of the man's age?
3. Should the way the man killed his wife factor into the sentencing decision?
4. Does the public's sentiment toward the man merit consideration? Why or why not?

Key Terms

Baby Boomers (p. 199)

claims making (p. 205)

elder abuse (p. 203)

eldercide (p. 202)

Generation X (Gen Xers) (p. 200)

Generation Y (Gen Yers) (p. 200)

geriatric court (p. 212)

just deserts (p. 213)

McJobs (p. 200)

operationalization (p. 204)

poverty line (p. 198)

recidivism rate (p. 214)

Discussion Questions

1. Do you think a geriatrics court would be helpful in the processing of elderly offenders? Could it be used in a similar fashion as the juvenile justice system? Why or why not?
2. What responsibility does the government have to provide comprehensive health care to elderly inmates? Should correctional agencies be forced to meet serious and chronic health care needs of elderly inmates, or should they be responsible only for routine care and emergencies?
3. In what ways do you think the Baby Boomer generation will change the way the elderly are perceived? Is this characterization of Baby Boomers seen in a positive or negative light?
4. How is elderly abuse different from child abuse? Should elderly abusers be given the same punishments as child abusers? How do you think elderly abusers would be perceived in prison compared to child abusers?
5. Given the role that alcohol plays in elderly crime, do you think society should be able to restrict its use among the elderly in the same way it limits access for minors? Why or why not?
6. Given the public's perception of elderly criminals, what steps can you think of to help merchants prevent elderly shoplifting?

Endnotes

1. U.S. Department of Health and Human Services, Centers for Disease Control and Prevention. 2004. *Trends in Health and Aging: Life Expectancy*. Atlanta, GA.
2. Department of Commerce, Census Bureau. *Statistical Abstract of the United States, 2007*. Washington, DC: U.S. Government Printing Office.
3. Renzetti C., and Curran, D. 2004. *Social Problems*. Boston: Allyn & Bacon.
4. *Statistical Abstract of the United States, 2007*.
5. Ibid.
6. Ibid.
7. Department of Commerce, U.S. Census Bureau. 2006. Facts for Features. *Oldest Baby Boomers Turn 60*. Washington, DC: U.S. Government Printing Office.
8. IT Management. 2006. "Generation X for Dummies." www.eweek.com/article (accessed November 1, 2007).
9. Zemke, R., Raines, C., and Filipczak, B. 2000. *Generations at Work: Managing the Clash of Veterans, Boomers and Xers and Nexters in Your Workplace*. New York: American Management Association.
10. NAS Recruitment Communication. 2006. *Generation Y: The Millennias, Ready or Not, Here They Come.* www.nasrecruitment.com/TalentTips/NAS insights/GenerationY.pdf (accessed November 1, 2007).
11. Ibid.
12. See, for instance, Seigel, L. J. 2005. *Criminology*. New York: West Publishing; Sykes, G. M., and Cullen, F. T. 2005. *Criminology*. New York: Harcourt Brace and Jovanovich.
13. Livingston, J. 1992. *Crime and Criminology.* Clifton Hill, NJ: Prentice Hall; Adler, F., Mueller, G. O. W., and Laufer, W. S. 1995. *Criminology*. New York: McGraw-Hill.
14. Department of Justice, Bureau of Justice Statistics. *Criminal Victimization 2005*. Washington, DC: U.S. Government Printing Office.
15. National Research Council. 2003. *Mistreatment: Abuse, Neglect, and Exploitation in an Aging America.* Washington, DC: U.S. Government Printing Office.
16. National Center on Elder Abuse. 2005. *National Elder Abuse Incidence Study*. Washington, DC: U.S. Government Printing Office.
17. Wasik, J. 2000. "The Fleecing of America's Elderly." *Consumer's Digest,* March/April.
18. National Ombudsman Reporting System Data Tables. 2003. Washington, DC: U.S. Administration on Aging.
19. National Center on Elder Abuse. 2004. *Abuse of Adults Age 60+: 2004 Survey of State Adult Protective Services.* Washington, DC.
20. Shimkus, J. 2007. *The Graying of America's Prisons: Corrections Copes with Care for the Aged.* Washington, DC: National Commission on Correctional Healthcare.
21. See, for instance, Newman, D. J. 1984. "Elderly Offenders and American Crime Patterns." In E. S. Newman, D. J. Newman, and M. L. Gerwitz, *Elderly Criminals,* pp. 3–16. Cambridge, MA: Oelgeschlager, Gunn and Hain.
22. Ibid.
23. Shimkus 2007; Deluca, H. 1997. "Managing Elderly Inmates: It's More Than Just Time." In R. P. McNamara and D. E. Redburn (eds.), *Social Gerontology*, pp. 209–220. Westport, CT: Auburn House.
24. Newman, E. S., Newman, D. J., and Gerwitz, M. L. 1984. *Elderly Criminals*. Cambridge, MA: Oelgeschlager, Gunn and Hain.
25. Ibid, p. 209.
26. See, for instance, Jones, G., Connelly, M., and Wagner, K. 2001. *Aging Offenders and the Criminal Justice System.* Maryland State Commission on Criminal Sentencing; Harrison, M. T.

2006. "True Grit: An Innovative Program for Elderly Inmates." *Corrections Today Magazine,* 68 (7): 46–49; Wallace, S. 1992. "Health Status of Federal Inmates: A Comparison of Admission and Release Medical Records." *Journal of Prison and Jail Health* 10 (2):133–151; Long, L. 1992. "A Study of Arrests of Older Offenders: Trends and Patterns." *Journal of Crime and Justice* 15 (2): 157–175.

27. Shichor, D. 1984. "The Extent and Nature of Lawbreaking by the Elderly: A Review of Arrest Statistics." In E. S. Newman, D. J. Newman, and M. L. Gerwitz, *Elderly Criminals,* pp. 17–32. Cambridge, MA: Oelgeschlager, Gunn and Hain.

28. Ames, M. A., and Houston, D. A. 1990. "Legal, Social, and Biological Definitions of Pedophilia." *Archives of Sexual Behavior* 19 (4): 333–342.

29. Curran, D. 1984. "Characteristics of the Elderly Shoplifter and the Effect of Sanctions on Recidivism." In W. Wilbanks and P. K. Kim (eds.), *Elderly Criminals,* pp. 123–142. New York: University Press of America.

30. Feinberg, G. 1984. "Profile of the Elderly Shoplifter." In E. S. Newman, D. J. Newman, and M. L. Gerwitz, *Elderly Criminals,* pp. 35–50. Cambridge, MA: Oelgeschlager, Gunn and Hain.

31. *Uniform Crime Reports, Crime in the United States,* 2000 and 2005.

32. Ibid.

33. See, for instance, Blum, A., and Fisher, G. 1979. "Women Who Kill." In I. L. Kutash, S. B. Kutash, L. B. Schlesinger, and Associates (eds.), *Violence: Perspectives on Murder and Aggression,* pp. 102–155. San Francisco: Jossey-Bass; Goetting, A. 1992. "Patterns of Homicide Among the Elderly." *Violence and Victims* 7 (3): 203–215; Hucker, S. J., and Ben-Aron, M. H. 1984. "Violent Elderly Offenders: A Comparative Study." In W. Wilbanks and P. K. Kim (eds.), *Elderly Criminals,* pp. 69–82. New

York: University Press of America; Silverman, R. A., and Kennedy, L. W. 1987. "Relational Distance and Homicide: The Role of the Stranger." *Journal of Criminal Law and Criminology* 78: 272–308; Wilbanks, W., and Murphy, D. D. 1984. "The Elderly Homicide Offender." In E. S. Newman, D. J. Newman, and M. L. Gerwitz, *Elderly Criminals,* pp. 79–92. Cambridge, MA: Oelgeschlager, Gunn and Hain; Wolfgang, M. 1958. *Patterns of Criminal Homicide.* Philadelphia: University of Pennsylvania Press; Zahn, M. A., and Sagi, P. C. 1987. "Stranger Homicides in Nine American Cities." *Journal of Criminal Law and Criminology,* 78: 377–397.

34. Goetting, A. 1992. "Patterns of Homicide Among the Elderly." *Violence and Victims* 7 (3): 203–215.

35. Ibid., p. 212.

36. Department of Justice, Federal Bureau of Investigation. 2005. *FBI Supplementary Homicide Reports 1976–2004.* Washington, DC: U.S. Government Printing Office.

37. *Uniform Crime Reports, Crime in the United States,* 2000 and 2005.

38. Hucker, S. J. 1984. "Psychiatric Aspects of Crime in Old Age." In E. S. Newman, D. J. Newman, and M. L. Gerwitz, *Elderly Criminals,* pp. 67–78. Cambridge, MA: Oelgeschlager, Gunn and Hain.

39. See, for instance, Ames, M. A., and Houston, D. A. 1990. "Legal, Social, and Biological Definitions of Pedophilia." *Archives of Sexual Behavior* 19 (4): 333–342; Briere, J., and Runtz, M. 1989. "University Males' Sexual Interest in Children: Predicting Potential Indices of 'Pedophilia' in a Nonforensic Sample." *Child Abuse and Neglect* 13 (1): 65–75.

40. Hucker, F., and Ben-Aron, M. H. 1984. "Violent Elderly Offenders: A Comparative Study." In W. Wilbanks and P. K. Kim (eds.), *Elderly Criminals,* pp. 69–82. New York: University Press of America.

41. See, for instance, Revitch, E., and Weiss, R. 1962. "The Pedophiliac Offender." *Diseases of the Nervous System* 23 (2): 1–6; Mohr, J., Turner, R. E., and Jerry, M. B. 1964. *Pedophilia and Exhibitionism.* Toronto: University of Toronto Press.

42. *Uniform Crime Reports, Crime in the United States,* 2000 and 2005.

43. See, for instance, Burnett, C., and Ortega, S. T. 1984. "Elderly Offenders: A Descriptive Analysis." In W. Wilbanks and P. K. Kim (eds.), *Elderly Criminals,* pp. 17–40. New York: University Press of America.

44. See, for instance, United States Department of Justice. 1984. *Jailing Drunk Drivers: Impact on the Criminal Justice System.* Washington, DC: U.S. Government Printing Office; Cahalan, D. 1970. *Problem Drinkers.* San Francisco: Jossey-Bass.

45. See, for instance, U.S. Department of Justice 1984; Atkinson, J. H. 1981. "Alcoholism and Geriatric Problems, I and II." *Advances in Alcoholism* 11 (8–9): 1–3; Gomberg, E. 1980. *Drinking and Problem Drinking Among the Elderly.* Ann Arbor, MI: Institute for Gerontology, University of Michigan.

46. See, for instance, Kratcoski, P. C., and Babb, S. 1990. "Adjustment of Older Inmates: An Analysis by Institutional Structure and Gender." *Journal of Contemporary Criminal Justice* 6 (4): 264–281; Aday, R. H. 1990. "Golden Years Behind Bars: Special Programs and Facilities for Elderly Inmates." *Federal Probation* 58 (21): 47–54; Long, L. 1992. "A Study of Arrests of Older Offenders: Trends and Patterns." *Journal of Crime and Justice* 15 (2): 157–175; Wallace, S. 1992. "Health Status of Federal Inmates: A Comparison of Admission and Release Medical Records." *Journal of Prison and Jail Health* 10 (2): 133–151.

47. See, for instance, Abrams, A. J. 1984. "Foreword" In E. S. Newman, D. J. Newman, and M. L. Gerwitz, *Elderly Criminals.* Cambridge, MA: Oelgeschlager, Gunn and Hain.

48. Shimkus 2001.

49. Lemieux, C. M., Dyeson, T. B., and Castiglione, B. 2002."Revisiting the Literature on Prisoners Who Are Older: Are We Wiser?" *Prison Journal* 82 (4): 440–458.

50. Johnston, C. W., and Alozie, N. O. 2001. "Effect of Age on Criminal Processing: Is There an Advantage to Being Older?" *Journal of Gerontological Social Work* 34 (4): 65–82.

51. Turley, J. 2006. "Release Elderly Inmates." *Los Angeles Times*, October 7. www.latimes.com/news/opinion/ commentary.

52. Ibid.

53. Newman, D. J., and Gerwitz, M. L. 1984. *Elderly Criminals.* Cambridge, MA: Oelgeschlager, Gunn and Hain.

Internal Issues in the Criminal Justice System and Multiculturalism

Policing and Multiculturalism

Chapter Objectives

After reading this chapter, you should be able to

❖ Understand how the historical development of policing relates to current concerns regarding multiculturalism.

❖ Understand the extent, nature, and need for multiculturalism among police personnel.

❖ Recognize how police practices exist with regard to multiculturalism, and how those actions affect police–community relations and perceptions of the police.

❖ Understand the significance of training as it relates to policing in a multicultural society.

The nature of police work, including the constant human interaction with varied groups, sometimes results in officer misbehavior or unsubstantiated claims of officer misconduct. Put simply, police practices are sometimes controversial, and failure to recognize cultural diversity is occasionally a primary contributing factor. In their book *Contemporary Municipal Policing,* Justice Administration Professor William McCamey and colleagues write, "Some of the most problematic encounters involving the police occur between white police officers and minority citizens. Encounters between the police and Blacks, Hispanics, Native Americans, and, increasingly, Asians indicate that a good deal of hostility remains as a result of racist attitudes, historical distrust, and past discrimination."[1] The diverse culture in which policing is practiced requires officers to maintain, at minimum, a base-level recognition and understanding of cultural differences in order to ensure justice, personal safety, and the safety of others.

The police are the primary agents of social control in our society. Charged with the dubious and vague tasks of "serving and protecting," officers must find a balance between controlling and preventing crime and preserving individual rights. It could be argued that at times the police too often sacrifice individual rights for the sake of crime control and vice versa. Finding an approach that suits everyone is much easier said than done.

Modern police practices largely reflect the roots of historical policing. In their insightful and thorough work, *Police in a Multicultural Society,* David Barlow and Melissa Hickman Barlow discuss the historical evolution of policing and relate it to modern police practices.[2] They comment on police practices such as **underpolicing,** which involves the police denying "equal protection to racial and ethnic minorities in the United States by failing to protect them from violent racist actions by Whites, by declining to ensure their basic human rights, and by inadequately responding to problems of crime and neglect in minority neighborhoods."[3] Barlow and Barlow also discuss **overpolicing,** which involves "the oppressive and often brutal treatment of marginalized groups by police."[4] These styles of policing highlight the historical conflict between police and underrepresented groups in society.

Throughout this book you've read numerous accounts of how multiculturalism affects policing. This chapter focuses specifically on how policing came to be, why it exists, and how concerns for diversity and multiculturalism have shaped modern policing. Included is discussion of policing and multiculturalism as it pertains to critical issues in policing. Of particular interest is the history of policing, police personnel issues, police practices and behavior, and police training. As demonstrated throughout this book, police officers, as the primary gatekeepers to the criminal justice system, should be well versed in recognizing and understanding cultural diversity.

✖ The History of Policing

Much of what police do today is similar to what was done when formal policing began. In other words, policing has not changed much in the roughly 180 years of its existence. There have been alterations and developments in the manner in which policing exists and occurs. However, there have been few major changes to policing in general. With regard to policing in the United States, the activities and practices of the earliest periods of policing largely reflect those found in England. The following discussion of the history of policing maintains a primary focus on diversity and multiculturalism.

The Roots of U.S. Policing

The history of formal policing dates back to the development of the Police of the Metropolis, the name for the police department established in London in 1829 and organized by Sir Robert Peel.[5] Prior to formal policing, social control was primarily the responsibility of the citizens. Citizens lived communally for several reasons, including the need for enhanced farming practices and for safety and security. With regard to the latter, it became evident to citizens that there was strength in numbers. Under what was known as the **Frankpledge System,** or the practice of informal social control in which community members protected one another, citizens raised the **hue and cry,** or call to arms, upon being victimized.[6] Raising the hue and cry generated a response from every able-bodied male in attempts to bring the offenders(s) to justice; failure to respond could result in punitive sanctions. Citizens also protected one another through night watch and day ward systems in which constables and/or citizens were expected to watch out for danger—whether it be in the form of weather, fires, or individuals. Such informal social control was initially effective given the small population sizes and the homogeneity of groups living communally.

The need for formal social control became evident as small towns became large cities and England began transitioning from an agrarian society to one focused on industrialism. Numerous individuals migrated to cities in hopes of great success, only to find a great deal of social disorganization, poverty, and difficulty in attaining success. Many individuals abandoned their lifestyles and belongings in their attempt to find success in the big city only to find limited opportunities and great difficulties upon their arrival. The increased cultural diversity during this transitional period also contributed to the difficulties. No longer could informal social control (e.g., fellow citizens) serve the purposes of law enforcement. The need for formal social control (e.g., policing) became increasingly evident as rioting occurred and populations significantly increased in the cities as industrialization took hold.

London Magistrate Sir Henry Fielding is credited with creating the **Bow Street Runners,** a precursor to the first formal police department.[7] Fielding noticed the frequency with which particular individuals were brought into his court and decided something needed to be done. Mind you, bringing someone to justice during this time (circa 1750) was not as easy as it is today. Citizens had to hire private security to bring the accused before the court, or do it themselves. Fielding decided to hire individuals to seek law violators in the Bow Street region of London, and paid a sum of money to those who brought suspects before the court. The limitations of this approach are clearly evident (e.g., unethically bringing forth suspects in efforts to make money); however, the Bow Street Runners helped cleanse the area of much crime and inspired the **London Metropolitan Police Act,** which was passed in 1829. This act led to the first formal police department, the London Metropolitan Police, led by Sir Robert Peel. Peel's approach centered on serving the public. Much of what Peel proposed is evident in the community policing approaches found in many of today's police departments. Peel's principles generally emphasized crime prevention, police cooperation with the public, and police professionalism.

The London Police initially were not well accepted by Londoners, who believed that their rights were being violated. To proactively seek law violators and monitor societal behavior was a new practice at the time, and not all citizens appreciated the perceived intrusion. Such public disapproval of policing would eventually subside as citizens recognized that the police provided citizens with protection. Such frustration in public approval of the police was a sign of things to come, as throughout the history of policing we've seen peaks and valleys regarding public approval of police and police actions. The development of policing in England would mirror the development of policing in the United States, and the London Metropolitan Police would provide a blueprint for all police practices.

Historical U.S. Policing

Policing in the United States developed in much the same manner as policing in England. Informal social control in which citizens protected one another, and relied on the hue and cry and the watch and ward system, was used prior to the development of large cities. Formal policing would emerge in areas where small towns grew into larger ones. Cities along the eastern seaboard were among the first to have formal police departments, as settlers recognized the need for formal law enforcement. Formal policing would soon extend across the entire country, as settlers moved west and small towns grew into large ones.

Slave Patrols and Black Codes

Policing in Southern states, however, took a notably distinct approach compared to elsewhere in the United States. The roots of policing in the South are found in the **slave patrols** used in the Southern states and colonies prior to and following the

Revolutionary War to prevent slave revolts and apprehend runaway slaves. Slave patrols are considered by some experts as the first American police departments[8] and were established as early as the 1740s. By 1750, every Southern colony maintained a slave patrol.[9] The large population of slaves in the South prompted plantation owners to create special codes of laws and, subsequently, special forces to ensure that slaves abided by the laws. These laws, for instance, prevented slaves from having weapons, leaving plantations without permission, gathering in groups, and resisting punishment.[10] Southern states also made it legal for any White freeman to stop, search, and apprehend any Black person, regardless of whether or not he or she was a slave.[11] Most states and colonies permitted slave patrols to enter the dwelling of any slave, punish slaves who were away from their owner's plantation, and search, punish, and perhaps even kill slaves found to be in violation of the slave code.[12]

The emancipation of the slaves did not provide an end to the enhanced levels of social control faced by African Americans in the South. Southern states circumvented the emancipation by creating **Black Codes,** laws designed to nullify the rights granted to the newly freed slaves. Among the restrictions found in Black Codes were the prohibition of interracial marriage, renting land in urban areas, preaching the gospel without a license, and assuming any occupation other than servant or farmer unless the newly freed slave paid a tax. The mission of Southern police departments was to protect the White population from the violent threats of slaves and, later, freed slaves.[13] The **Civil Rights Act of 1866,** passed by Congress despite President Andrew Johnson's veto, was targeted to address the Black Codes by defining all persons born in the United States, with the exception of Native Americans, as national citizens who were to enjoy specific rights. These rights included permission to make contracts, bring lawsuits, and enjoy the full and equal benefit of the law.[14]

Three Eras of Policing

The history of policing in the United States has been divided into three eras: the Political Era, the Reform Era, and the Community Era.[15] While the history of a complex profession such as policing can be difficult to categorize into three periods, there are several identifiable characteristics of these eras, particularly as they relate to multiculturalism. While such a categorization provides for interesting discussion of the historical intervals of policing, it is argued that the categorization fails to consider the development of policing with regard to segregation, slavery, discrimination, and racism,[16] factors that have undoubtedly influenced modern U.S. policing. To understand our police requires understanding the barriers they've overcome, the obstacles they've provided, and their relationship with the communities they serve.

The Political Era

The **political era of policing** (1840–1930) was characterized by police officers seeking an intimate relationship with the community and politics heavily influencing police departments and police practices. The police had limited technology during this time, so they walked beats, which encouraged police–community interaction. In addition to crime control, officers provided a number of services to the public, such as operating soup kitchens, securing medical care for citizens, and helping the unemployed find work.[17] They relied heavily on their problem-solving skills to control crime, as there was no radio to call for backup and no police car to provide rapid assistance.

Police practices during this period were also influenced by politics, with political leaders rewarding law enforcement personnel who supported them during their candidacy and when in office. The spoils system was evident during this period and certainly influenced who worked for the police department and in what capacity they served. **Patronage,** or the practice of politicians rewarding friends, created police departments that often reflected the communities they served.[18] For instance, the Irish Americans began appointing their friends as police officers once the Irish Americans began to win political power.[19]

Police officers during the political era were not exempt from the lack of cultural sensitivity existent at the time, and minority police officers were treated differently from White officers. For instance, Black officers were prohibited from patrolling in predominantly White areas, were required to call a White officer to arrest a White suspect, and were given assignments in high-crime, predominantly minority neighborhoods.[20] The virtual absence of Black police officers resulted in less police attention and protection in areas heavily populated by minorities.[21] Other racial and ethnic groups, as well as women, were also underrepresented in, if not absent from, early police departments. Society in general at this time was largely unaware of the impending social unrest that would result from cultural insensitivity.

Police corruption was problematic during the political era, especially during the years of **Prohibition** (1919–1933), which criminalized the sale, transport, and manufacturing of alcohol. It was during Prohibition that police officers sometimes took advantage of "favors" offered in exchange for them looking the other way while alcohol was served. Prohibition had a significant impact on the history of policing, particularly with regard to police corruption and public perceptions of the police because officers were charged with enforcing an unpopular law.

Race riots and racial unrest, especially in New York City, Boston, and Philadelphia, significantly shaped policing during the political era, as departments developed and assumed the responsibility of quelling the disturbances. Unfortunately, little professional training existed for addressing civil disorders. The level of violence accompanying the unrest was sometimes agitated by officers too quickly resorting to violence. Civil disorder would not end with the political era.

The Reform Era

The **reform era of policing** (1930–1980), also known as the progressive era, was a time when police–community relations suffered and police became increasingly reliant upon technology and overly concerned with efficiency. It was during the reform era that police departments began heavily using police cars to enhance overall police practices. Although the automobile and other technological advances (e.g., the two-way radio) enhanced policing, police–community relations suffered as officers became distant from the public. Officers were no longer walking beats and interacting with the public. Police officers during the reform era generally focused on crime fighting. The "just the facts ma'am" approach to policing may initially enhance the efficiency of crime control, but it does very little for police–community relations, which became problematic during this period. Several turbulent incidents (discussed below) occurred during the reform era, which in turn impacted policing. Many of these events had direct relationships with policing a multicultural society. Among the happenings was the Civil Rights Movement, which began in the late 1950s and set in motion a series of actions that would change policing and, more generally, society.

The Civil Rights Movement initially began as a grassroots effort to highlight economic, political, and social inequality in the United States. Blacks who chose to protest were confronted by police officers, who were typically White males with limited training in how to confront such collective action. The officers' actions in handling protest marches and general civil disobedience often aggravated the situation.[22] The assassinations of several prominent figures such as Martin Luther King Jr., Malcolm X, President John Kennedy, and Medgar Evers contributed to the unrest during this period, as did the protest of those opposed to the war in Vietnam. Police were charged with handling, among other responsibilities, a series of race and anti-war demonstrations. The underrepresentation of African Americans and other minorities in policing contributed to clashes between the groups and certainly played a role in the hundreds of riots that occurred between 1966 and 1971. The unrest further separated the police from the public and created danger for officers, as police practices such as providing public protection sometimes were met with collective violence in the form of rioting.

A wave of riots occurred between 1964 and 1968 due in part to tensions between the police and the Black community. Almost all of the riots followed a situation involving police.[23] For instance, the New York City riot in 1964 began following the shooting death of a Black teenager by an off-duty police officer. The Watts (Los Angeles) riot in 1965 was initiated by a traffic stop.[24] Rioting during this time was largely perpetuated by negative public attitudes toward the police, the lack of preparedness of police to address civil unrest, and racial tensions between Blacks and Whites.[25] Racially selective policing exacerbated protest demonstration most significantly in areas with strained police–minority community relations.[26] The potential harm and costs of such unrest were alarming. For instance, the weeklong rioting in Detroit in 1967 resulted in 43 deaths and roughly $40 million in property damage. In 1966, 43 riots were identified in major urban areas across the United States.[27] These numbers say little about the damage done to police–community relations.

The lack of police training, particularly with regard to addressing cultural diversity, contributed to the police being seen by many civilians as the enemy. A confusing array of social movements, including the emerging drug culture, contributed to the problems faced by police.[28] Officers were commonly referred to as "pigs," and the isolation that was emerging between police and society was enhanced by the overall social unrest of the times. The White male police officers whose task was to maintain the peace in the predominantly minority urban ghetto faced numerous challenges, especially in light of the officer's symbolic representation of power and control. Many angry and frustrated Blacks viewed the police as symbolic of a criminal justice system that had been largely unresponsive to their needs.[29] To compound the situation, people across the United States could watch the events in the comforts of their own home as televisions were becoming increasingly common in households.

The tension and conflict between police and minority groups led to intense focus on the problems underlying the social unrest. Prominent among the national commissions formed to examine the situation and to offer recommendations for change was the 1965 **President's Commission on Law Enforcement and Administration of Justice** (also known as the President's Crime Commission).[30] The Commission focused on enhancing professionalization of policing and police officers by hiring more members of minority groups and encouraging departments to become more community-oriented. Another commission, the **National Advisory Commission on Civil Disorders** (also known as the Kerner Commission), was created to study the causes behind the rioting. The Commission identified a series of issues that contributed to the collective violence, including unequal justice, institutional racism, unemployment, and discrimination. With regard to policing, the Kerner Commission noted the lack of Black police officers, inadequate training and supervision, brutal and abrasive police conduct, and poor police–community relations.[31] The police during this period faced criticism from every direction.

Police practices were also the target of several landmark Supreme Court decisions made during this period. The decisions restricted police powers and provided greater citizen rights. Beginning in the 1950s, several Court decisions under the direction of Supreme Court Justice Earl Warren influenced police–community relations and the lives of many individuals from underrepresented groups. The Supreme Court ruled in cases such as *Mapp v. Ohio,*[32] which extended the **exclusionary rule,** or the prohibition of introducing illegally seized materials in court proceedings, to apply in all courts and jurisdictions in the United States; and in *Gideon v. Wainwright,*[33] which mandated that all defendants are entitled to representation. In *Miranda v. Arizona,*[34] the Court ruled that any evidence obtained by police during a custodial interrogation cannot be used in court unless the suspect is informed of his or her basic rights. In *Terry v. Ohio,*[35] the Court clarified the law surrounding when a police officer can stop and question a person. These cases restricted police discretion and provided numerous protections to individuals.

The reform era was influential in the history of U.S. policing. Police officers initially shifted their focus away from interacting with the public, yet, at the end of the era they were forced to confront violent reactions. Many of these reactions resulted from police practices. It was also a time when police departments were forced to reassess their relationship with the community. In turn, many departments recognized the need to get back in touch with the roots of policing and have more positive interactions with citizens.

The Community Era

The current **community era of policing,** which began around 1980, involves efforts by the police to re-connect with the public primarily through the adoption of the **community policing** philosophy. Clearly defining community policing, however, is not easily done. Criminal Justice Professor Willard Oliver is among those who have addressed the problems associated with defining community policing, primarily due to the different approaches to community policing taken by various departments and the difficulties departments face when implementing the community policing philosophy. In his book *Community-Oriented Policing: A Systemic Approach to Policing,* Oliver states that community policing is "a systemic approach to policing with the paradigm of instilling and fostering a sense of community, within a geographical neighborhood, to improve the quality of life."[36] He adds that community

Community policing encourages positive police–community relations.

policing accomplishes this through decentralizing the organization of the police and implementing three primary components: (1) strategic-oriented policing, (2) neighborhood-oriented policing, and (3) problem-oriented policing.[37] Strategic-oriented policing refers to the use of various strategically-designed patrol practices such as seatbelt checks. Neighborhood-oriented policing involves programs that are often associated with community-oriented policing. Communications programs (e.g., crime prevention newsletters), social control programs (e.g., juvenile curfews), and various public relations activities, such as participation in community fairs, are examples of neighborhood-oriented policing. Problem-oriented policing involves addressing particular problems in the community, such as automobile thefts. To be sure, community policing seeks to address many of the difficulties associated with policing a multicultural society.

Researchers have identified four dimensions of community policing: the philosophical, the strategic, the tactical, and the organizational dimensions.[38] The philosophical dimension requires officers and departments to adopt the underpinnings of community policing, particularly with regard to citizen input, the broad function of policing, and personalized service. Strategically, community policing focuses on reorienting police operations primarily through greater face-to-face interactions, officers focusing on smaller geographical regions, and crime prevention efforts. The tactical aspect of community policing largely involves positive interactions between the public and the police, enhanced use of partnerships between the police and society, and problem solving. Organizationally, community policing relies on targeting a department's organizational design to facilitate meeting the department's mission. It could also include changing managerial style and focusing more on information collection (e.g., program assessment and evaluations) and sharing information with the public.[39]

Community policing is by no means solely focused on public relations at the expense of crime fighting. One can easily recognize how the community era of policing combines the positive elements of the political era with the strengths of the reform era. Getting back in touch with citizens and doing so in an effective manner, for instance, through problem-oriented policing, highlights one of the strengths of community policing. **Problem-oriented policing** involves a four-step approach to addressing specific crimes in the community. These steps include scanning communities to identify problems, analyzing the nature and extent of the problem, responding to the problem, and assessing whether or not the problem is properly addressed. Without a doubt, police getting back in touch with the public while maintaining a concern for crime control was needed in light of events occurring during the latter part of the reform era.

Regardless of its strength and good intentions, community policing has not solved society's problems and not all departments have adopted a community-oriented approach. Because community policing is still a rather new concept, and some departments have adopted the philosophy on a piecemeal basis, it remains unclear whether or not community policing meets all of its goals. We do know that the approach improves police–community relations, which certainly provides optimism for police as they continuously engage in an increasingly multicultural society. In 2003, 58% of U.S. police departments, which employed 82% of all officers, had full-time sworn officers designated as community policing officers.[40] These officers are often referred to as community relations officers or community resources officers.

Despite the progress made with regard to police–community relations, many of the issues that contributed to the rioting in the 1960s remain.[41] The 1992 riots in Los Angeles following the acquittal by a mostly White jury of the Los Angeles Police Department (LAPD) officers seen beating Black motorist Rodney King sent a message that racial tensions had not disappeared. The riot, which led to 43 deaths, was perpetuated by economic tensions of residents in South Los Angeles and historical strains in police–community relations, especially with regard to claims of officers engaging in racial profiling and excessive force against minorities. The **Christopher Commission,** assembled in the wake of the Rodney King incident in response to claims of LAPD officer misbehavior, stated in its report that "there is a significant number of officers in the LAPD who repetitively use excessive force against the public and persistently ignore the written guidelines of the Department regarding force."[42] It added that "the problem of excessive force is aggravated by racism and bias" and noted that "failure to control [problem] officers is a management issue that is at the heart of the problem."[43]

More recently, rioting in Cincinnati began in April 2001 following the fatal shooting of 19-year-old Timothy Thomas by a White Cincinnati police officer. Similar to other riots, the riot stemmed from tension among the minority community and police. Fifteen Black males under the age of 40 were killed by Cincinnati police officers between 1995 and 2001, compared to no males from other races killed during the same period. Claims of officers engaging in racial profiling with regard to traffic stops also contributed to the violence. The Cincinnati Police Department was being investigated by the FBI in relation to officers shooting Black males at the time of Thomas's death.[44] The police argued that they were doing their job and had reacted in an appropriate manner, yet protesters claimed the police were biased and

Unethical police practices often contribute to social invest.

unjust. The rioting, which lasted three days, resulted in hundreds of thousands of dollars in property damage and over 800 arrests.

The short history of policing in the United States is rife with conflict between police and society. Much of the conflict involves members of underrepresented groups who feel the police overstep the boundaries of procedural law, which dictates how the police are to use their powers. To be sure, negative police–citizen interactions are often brought to the public's attention. It is rare that society hears how an officer successfully overcame cultural barriers and quelled a situation. Perhaps public opinion of police–minority contacts would improve if we heard more about the successes. Arguably, many of the previously discussed problems with regard to police–community relations were intensified and/or perpetuated by the lack of minority representation in policing.

✂ Police Personnel Issues

Police departments are actively and aggressively hiring new officers. Among other factors, the war in Iraq has reduced the size of police forces and limited the applicant pool. With the recent concern for homeland security, some local-level police officers have assumed positions in federal law enforcement agencies. The expansion of local-level policing duties to address homeland security issues has also led to the increased need for officers. The challenge of recruiting and selecting officers who maintain awareness of cultural diversity also poses difficulties for local law enforcement agencies.

White males have been overrepresented on police forces across the United States, meaning that non-Whites and females have been largely underrepresented. Part of the problematic relationship that departments and officers have with the public stems from the limited representation of minority groups. Further, the relationship is hampered by the influences of the **police subculture,** which promotes a distinct working personality that encourages solidarity, authoritarianism, and sometimes the exclusion of females and minority officers. The causes of the underrepresentation of minority people in policing include:

- Minority individuals were not aggressively sought by police departments until the 1980s.
- Police work has not been attractive to many minorities.
- Minority individuals have reason to doubt they will be accepted in policing.
- For social rather than racial reasons, numerous young African Americans have a criminal record, limiting their options for a career in policing.
- Many educationally better-qualified Blacks have sought and taken more attractive employment opportunities.[45]

Much has been done to increase the diversity of police departments. Addressing issues pertaining to the demographic makeup of officers is necessary for effective policing in a multicultural society. Increased diversity in policing promotes tolerance of different groups and helps defuse historical concerns regarding the underrepresentation of particular cultures in policing. Legislation and affirmative action programs influenced police departments to increase diversity and proactively seek and hire candidates from underrepresented groups.

Legislating Diversity in Policing

Title VII of the **Civil Rights Act of 1964** prevents governments, unions, employment agencies, and private employers with 15 or more employees from discrimination based on color, race, sex, religion, or national origin. The 1972 Equal Employment Opportunity Act extended the 1964 Act to state and local governments and placed further restrictions on hiring practices. Table 10.1 depicts other influential acts that

TABLE 10.1

Promoting Equal Employment Opportunities

Equal Pay Act, 1963   Prohibits unequal pay for men and women who perform the same work.

Age Discrimination in Employment Act of 1967   Prohibits employment discrimination against those over age 40.

Executive Order, 1969   Prevents the federal government from using gender as a qualification for hiring.

Crime Control Act, 1973   Ensures that police departments don't discriminate against women in hiring practices by threatening to withhold funding should departments do so.

Americans with Disabilities Act, 1990   Prevents agencies from discriminating against any person otherwise qualified for a job because of a disability.

Family and Medical Leave Act of 1993   Requires employers with 50 or more employees to grant eligible employees with up to 12 weeks of unpaid, job-secured leave for medical and family reasons.

promote equal employment opportunities for women and minorities. A series of **affirmative action** programs designed to promote the hiring of minority applicants accompanied these and related pieces of legislation.

In the 1960s, police departments were certainly in need of greater female and minority representation. Recall that the National Advisory Commission on Civil Disorders reported in 1968 that poor police–minority relations were prominent among the causes underlying the rioting. There's been notable success in this area as the number of females and racial minorities working in police departments steadily increased following passage of the Equal Employment Opportunity Act in 1972.[46]

Government agencies that receive public funds and all private employers must have affirmative action plans. Affirmative action plans require employers to (1) conduct a census of current employees, (2) identify underutilization or concentration of minorities and women, and (3) develop a recruiting plan to correct any underutilization. Further, there should be a demonstrated timetable for any corrections or adjustments.[47] Affirmative action plans have undoubtedly shaped the look of today's police departments and will likely continue to do so.

Failure to comply with affirmative action policies could result in an agency facing civil suits from the parties excluded and a loss of funding from major grant bodies. Affirmative action policies are controversial in that they generate charges of **reverse discrimination,** or claims that minorities are being hired at the expense of those in the majority. Further, some individuals from underrepresented groups are being hired as **"tokens,"** or officers who received their position solely because of affirmative action policies,[48] regardless of their ability to perform the job. In policing, tokens have often been treated differently by those in the majority race and gender, which has led to discrimination in assignments and evaluations, exclusion from the police culture, and harassment.[49]

Integrating Policing

In the mid-1990s, researcher Robin Harr used field observations and in-depth interviews to study patterns of interpersonal interaction in a police bureau. He found that "gender and racial integration failed despite various organizational structural devices to 'level the playing field' and carry out integration."[50] The results suggested that it wasn't a particular characteristic or condition that prevented integration. Instead, integration was prevented by organizational features such as tensions, conflicts, controversy surrounding affirmative action, dual promotion lists, and related factors such as the presence of females on patrol.[51]

Many police agencies seek to establish a department that reflects, from a race and ethnicity standpoint, the community in which they operate. Unfortunately, historical efforts have failed in many cases for several reasons. Prominent among the reasons for failure are (1) police departments failing to make their job searches extensive enough to attract the most qualified individuals to the job, (2) many African Americans failing to possess the minimum qualifications for the position, and (3) many African Americans possessing a negative impression of police officers and police work.[52] One could claim outright discrimination against underrepresented groups in hiring practices as a significant part of the failure. These difficulties are not restricted to African Americans, as individuals from

many minority groups have experienced difficulty obtaining and retaining positions in
policing.

Despite the problems noted above, both
females and minorities have become increasingly represented in policing. Recent research
found that racial and ethnic minorities comprised 23.6% of all full-time sworn personnel
in 2003, an increase from 2000 and 1987 when
the percentages were 22.6% and 14.6%,
respectively. Within minority groups, Hispanic
and Latino officers grew by the greatest percentage in local policing between 2000 and
2003, up 13% compared to African American
officers (+3%) and officers from other minority
groups (+7%). Females comprised 11.3% of
sworn personnel in 2003, compared to 10.6%
in 2000 and 7.6% in 1987.[53] Figure 10.1 highlights recent changes in the makeup of police
departments.

*Females are becoming
increasingly involved in all
aspects of police work.*

Steps to Diversify Policing

Departments actively recruit in minority communities to address the limited diversity in policing. Accordingly, departments should offer incentive pay to bilingual
officers with the intent to address existing and potential cultural and communication problems. Qualified individuals are available, but departments sometimes

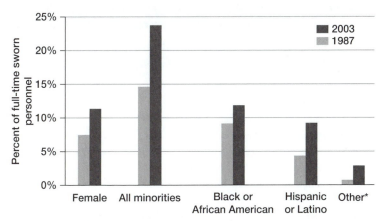

FIGURE 10.1   *Female and Minority Local Police Officers, 1987 and 2003*

SOURCE: Matthew J. Hickman and Brian A. Reaves, *Local Police Departments, 2003,* Bureau of Justice Statistics,
NCJ 210118. (Washington, D.C.: U.S. Government Printing Office, 2006).

face difficulty finding suitable candidates. In this situation, departments should not lower their standards to find suitable minority candidates. Instead, they should suspend hiring practices to do more recruiting.[54] The onus is on departments to enhance their search practices when faced with obstacles in hiring. Advertising in minority-specific media outlets, utilizing religious and community groups, and employing the services of bilingual recruiters can help departments become more diverse.[55]

Retaining and promoting underrepresented groups in policing are critical for diversifying a department. Too often women and minorities in policing, and many other occupations, experience the glass ceiling, or an abstract barrier preventing certain groups and/or individuals from moving beyond entry-level positions. The lack of minority promotion in policing is well documented in the research literature, although recent improvements suggest hope for a more positive future.

One cannot overlook the problems within police departments stemming from historical failures to diversify. Affirmative action policies, the Civil Rights Movement, and the demand for increased diversity in policing following the 1960s riots contributed to greater multiculturalism in our police departments. Evidence of the progress is noted in minority officers achieving representation in policing commensurate with their representation in society. Beverly Harvard became the first African American female to head a large municipal police department when she was appointed police chief of the Atlanta Police Department in 1994. Police departments are to be commended for their actions with regard to more culturally sensitive hiring practices. Table 10.2 highlights several organizations and associations that promote the interests of women and cultural/racial/ethnic groups in policing.

TABLE 10.2

Examples of Organizations and Associations Promoting Interests of Women and Cultural/Racial/Ethnic Groups in Policing

Federal Hispanic Law Enforcement Officers Association
Gay Officers Action League
Hispanic National Law Enforcement Association
International Association of Women Police
Irish American Police Officers Association
National Asian Peace Officers Association
National Association of Black Law Enforcement Officers
National Center for Women & Policing
National Coalition of Italian American Law Enforcement Organizations
National Latino Peace Officers Association
National Native American Law Enforcement Association
Polish American Police Association

⚔ Police Practices

Recent incidents involving controversial police practices in Cincinnati, Los Angeles, and New York City once again directed societal attention toward police practices. It's been more than 15 years since Rodney King was beaten by LAPD officers; however, questionable and unethical police practices throughout the country are continuously brought to public attention. For instance, in November 2006, four detectives and one police officer in New York City fired nearly 50 shots at three unarmed young men. One of the men, who was to be married later in the day, died as a result of the shooting. On March 16, 2007, three of the officers involved in the shooting were indicted by a grand jury. The incident sparked claims of racist police in New York City, as minority leaders and others claimed police brutality.

New York City police officers also faced criticism in 2000 following the shooting of Amadou Diallo, an unarmed immigrant who was shot at 41 times (and hit 19 times, ultimately resulting in his death) by members of a New York City Police Department (NYPD) "Street Crime Unit." The four officers involved in the shooting were acquitted of all charges, generating societal concerns in New York City and beyond. Charges of police abuse of power have not been restricted to the NYPD, as departments across the country have faced accusations of misbehavior and unethical practices. These and related incidents suggest the country is not far beyond the days of Rodney King.

Questionable Police Field Practices

Having special powers to actively enforce social control puts police in a notably difficult position. The profession has progressed with regard to the methods, strategies, and overall practices employed by departments and officers, yet controversy remains. Police field practices pose the greatest sources of tension between minorities and police.[56] Among the most important types of police practices that contribute to the tension are

- delays in responding to calls for service;
- verbal abuse, such as the use of racially offensive epithets or other forms of disrespect;
- excessive stopping, questioning, and frisking of African American citizens;
- discriminatory patterns of arrest and traffic citations;
- excessive use of physical force;
- excessive use of deadly force; and
- systematic underenforcement of the law and the failure to protect law-abiding citizens.[57]

This list is by all means significant and identifiable in modern policing. To what extent each practice exists is unknown. Research on policing has advanced in leaps and bounds following the research revolution of the 1960s when substantial government funding was allocated toward police sciences, yet it remains unclear to what extent police behave differently toward various groups in society.

Accordingly, there is ongoing debate regarding whether police treat groups differently. For instance, consider this scenario: A young man steals a clock radio from a department store. The police catch the suspect as he enters the parking lot of the store and arrest him. Seems pretty straightforward for sure. The police did their job. Now, let's alter the variables a bit. Suppose the young man is 10 years old and admitted stealing the radio so that he could buy food for his younger sister. His mother is always away from home and his father is in prison. His sister was painfully hungry. What should the police do in this case? What would you do? Arrest him? Give him a stern lecture? Hold his mother accountable? Let's say the young man is Latino. Does this change how officers would treat him? The answer is not so easy. The young man obviously had good intentions, but went about his business in an inappropriate manner. Police officers are often required to use their discretion and are criticized when they use it poorly or not in accord with community standards.

Q & A WITH FORT WORTH POLICE CHIEF RALPH MENDOZA

Ralph Mendoza was named the 22nd Chief of Police of Fort Worth, Texas, on February 1, 2000. Mendoza, a native of the city, was born in August 1953. He entered the Fort Worth Police Department in September 1972 as a police cadet and advanced through the ranks. After appointment to deputy chief in 1990, Mendoza served in every bureau of community policing and remains a staunch adherent. In 1998, he received the designation of executive deputy chief. While serving as acting chief of police in 1999, Mendoza received national attention for the decisive and sensitive manner in which he handled a mass shooting at the Wedgewood Baptist Church. Mendoza graduated from the University of Texas at Arlington with a degree in Criminal Justice in 1993, and he is a graduate of the FBI National Academy and the Southern Police Institute.

What type of pre-service and in-service training do your officers receive with regard to multiculturalism?

"The Texas Commission on Law Enforcement Officer Standards and Education (TCLEOSE) requires 12 hours of cultural diversity training during Basic Peace Officer licensing academies for police candidate recruits. Additionally, commissioned officers are required to attend 8 hours of cultural diversity training every 24 months as a part of their continued education program to retain their peace officer license. Our department has added additional hours to both of these minimum state requirements and expanded the curriculum to include multiculturalism and human relations training in this regard."

What primary obstacles do you face in encouraging officers to effectively deal with diverse cultures?

"From my perspective, our officers do a good job of effectively dealing with diverse cultures. The additional training this department provides certainly benefits these officers in their day-to-day dealing with the various cultures and other diversities that make up the unique tapestry that is Fort Worth. The obvious barriers encountered are primarily due to language and effective communication. However, about three years ago we began providing our officers with various levels of Spanish communication abilities to assist in bridging this gap."

What significant changes, if any, have you recognized with regard to multiculturalism in policing since you began your career?

"My career began before very many minorities or females were hired. At that time, there were height barriers in place, which no longer exist in hiring standards. We aggressively recruit diverse persons into our occupation. We have courses that teach our officers about diverse cultures. Most importantly, we represent diversity in all of our ranks."

What do you believe could be done to promote multiculturalism in policing?

"For some cultures that have language barriers, agencies could consider additional compensation for those officers who speak additional languages. This could also be a side benefit to hiring a more diverse workforce. In addition, such a program could be expanded to include a stipend or tuition reimbursement for those officers educating themselves in other languages or immersing themselves into other cultures to broaden their experience. Some of the international exchange programs have proven beneficial in this regard and others could certainly be started."

Any foreseeable changes or obstacles with regard to multiculturalism in policing and/or criminal justice in general?

"Criminal justice will continue to change rapidly, primarily due to technologies and increased information sharing. Cameras and the ability to exchange information as it occurs will become even more a reality in the near future. One obstacle to multiculturalism in policing is the anti-immigration challenges our country currently faces. There is a divide between expectations and the purpose of police, in my opinion. It gives people an opportunity to exhibit their racist attitudes and ignorance toward others and difference."

Source: Fort Worth Police Chief Ralph Mendoza, personal correspondence, February 19, 2007.

Police Discretion

Police discretion, which involves officer decision-making, is evident in all aspects of police practices and at times is recognized as a necessary evil. Discretion is necessary in policing as officers face difficult situations, involving multiple variables, as a regular part of their job. While police training provides the nuts and bolts for doing the job, no amount of formal training can ever fully prepare officers to properly handle all situations they encounter. Much of what is learned in policing comes from on-the-job practices or street experience.

It is hoped that an officer's formal training and street experience encourage him or her to properly exercise discretion. Researchers categorized the factors that influence an officer's use of discretion with the goal of better understanding police

Police officers maintain a great deal of discretion.

practices. These factors include (1) organizational influences (e.g., guidance from the department), (2) situational characteristics (e.g., time of day, presence of witnesses, race of suspect), (3) officer characteristics (e.g., male or female, minority or nonminority), and (4) neighborhood or community influences (e.g., poor or wealthy community). The research literature contains many accounts of how each of these factors influences police practices, yet policing does not occur in a vacuum; many variables influence policing.

Organizational Variables

Several organizational factors influence police discretion, including the professionalism or bureaucratic nature of the department, the size of the department, supervision levels, and the rotation of officers.[58] There is evidence that how closely a department adopts a militaristic style influences how officers police. Researchers found that officers in bureaucratic departments tend to focus more on law and order rather than providing general services.[59] Another study found that an officer's continued presence in a neighborhood promoted community relations and an understanding of community problems.[60]

Situational Factors

Situational factors are closely related to police violence. Factors such as suspect characteristics and behaviors, and the characteristics of the settings in which police and citizens interact, provide the most powerful explanations of police violence.[61] Of particular interest with regard to policing in a multicultural society are findings that African Americans are overrepresented in arrests, use of force, and police shootings, including the use of lethal force. Currently there exist two explanations for the disproportionality: (1) African Americans commit a disproportionate amount of crime, and (2) police treat African Americans more punitively than they treat other groups. Both explanations address the disproportionate level of interactions between African Americans and police, and both have been used for explanations and/or justifications for racial profiling. To what extent each contributes to the disproportionality is open for debate.

Officer Characteristics

Officer characteristics, in general, are not strong predictors of officer discretion and behavior. With regard to police violence, a National Institute of Justice report stated with modest confidence that "use of force appears to be unrelated to an officer's personal characteristics, such as age, gender, and ethnicity."[62] Some research suggests that officer race is related to arrest practices,[63] but other studies found no relation.[64] Other findings suggest African American officers are overrepresented in police shootings, but the notable level of deployment of African American officers in predominantly minority neighborhoods likely accounts for the differences.[65]

Earlier research suggested that Black officers were less lenient to Black suspects than were White officers.[66] More recent work in this area, however, found no strong evidence that African American or Hispanic officers police differently than White officers.[67] Minority officers may find interacting with minority suspects more difficult in that the officers may be viewed as representing a biased criminal justice system that imposes its will upon minority groups. Some research shows that Black officers suffer from double marginality, meaning that they are viewed as traitors by some in the Black community, while White officers may distrust them as colleagues.[68] Nevertheless, Black officers report that their on-duty relationships with White officers are satisfactory and are confident that their White partners would back them up if needed.[69]

There is scant information regarding Hispanic police officers and officers from other cultural backgrounds simply because it is only recently that policing has become more diversified. We do know that the Hispanic population in the United States is increasing, and their presence in police departments is beginning to keep pace. Hispanics bring diverse cultural backgrounds to policing. Of particular importance is the ability of Hispanic officers to speak Spanish and to better understand different cultures.

Hispanics have faced many of the same limitations as other underrepresented groups in policing, including difficulties in gaining employment with police departments. The historical underrepresentation of Hispanics in policing can be attributed to the language barrier, the height and weight requirements of police departments, the belief that many Hispanics may not wish to become police officers, and the fact that Hispanics have not been actively recruited by police departments.[70] The strengths and contributions of other underrepresented groups in policing are discussed throughout this book.

Neighborhood and Community Influences

There is a significant need to consider neighborhood-related variables when discussing policing and multiculturalism. For example, the research literature covering police use of deadly force highlights the impact of neighborhood or community variables on police discretion. Further, the literature highlighting inequities in wealth distribution suggests that income inequalities among groups promote instability in the social order. Responses to the instability in social order sometimes involve the use of force or coercion by the dominant class.[71] Some researchers argue that the economic power maintained by some individuals and groups provides the basis for formal social control, for instance, as income inequality appears to be the strongest explanation for police killings.[72]

Population variation also appears to influence police use of deadly force. It is well established in the criminology literature that population stability typically results in greater intimacy among members of society. Conversely, social disorganization prompts instability. Accordingly, the presence of particular minority groups appears to influence police practices. The percentage of African Americans in the population is unrelated to total police killings; however, it has a positive relationship with the extent to which officers use deadly force against African Americans. This relationship can be explained, in part, by the fact that municipalities with greater numbers of African Americans tend to have stronger policing agencies that act in a more punitive manner.[73]

Police practices range from simple police–citizen verbal exchanges to police use of deadly force. Police use of deadly force is obviously the most scrutinized aspect of policing and generates much concern with regard to policing in a multicultural society. Two explanations are offered for police killings: (1) political threat explanations suggest that such acts are more likely to occur where racial or economic differences are greater, because of the threat resultant from the divisions between the groups, and (2) reactive explanations suggest that police killings are more likely to occur in areas experiencing high rates of violent crime, or where officers must respond to urban conditions such as enhanced levels of poverty, thus making their job more difficult.[74] States with high rates of violence are more likely to experience more police killings.[75] These explanations facilitate understanding the influences of neighborhood and community variables with regard to police practices in a multicultural society.

The rate of African Americans shot or killed by police far exceeds the rate for Whites. However, as noted, there remains debate as to why this is the case. Several researchers subscribe to the belief that police discretion, or "differential policing," largely explains the disproportionality. Others hold that racial imbalance is a reflection of the struggles associated with being a member of a disadvantaged class, including social inequality and economic deprivation. Such a situation is evidenced in the earlier-referenced study, which found that lower-class suspects receive harsher treatment from the police.[76] Looking to the future of policing, author David Bayley argued in his article "Policing in America: Social Science and Public Policy in America" that the possibility of group violence in the United States is real, largely as a result of inequities in race, class, and ethnicity.[77] The 2001 riot in Cincinnati provides evidence for his claim.

Many examples throughout this book highlight the complexities and controversial practices involved with policing a multicultural society. This chapter highlights but a few of the many facets of police practices. It is perhaps with more efficient and effective training that police can overcome the many obstacles and challenges they face on a daily basis.

⚔ Police Training and Multiculturalism

One could argue that solid police training could solve many of the problems associated with the intersection of multiculturalism and policing. One could also argue that solid training wouldn't solve the problems. Such is the nature of police work and training. Consider a college-level criminal justice class, for example. Some students will comprehend all of the material and earn an "A" in the course. Others will get much (70–79%) of the information and earn a "C." Other students will get very little out of the course, and some will fail to receive credit. Both the students who earned a "C" and those who earned an "A" passed the class. They've demonstrated their ability to grasp much or perhaps all of the material. However, does comprehending "much" of the material mean that a student is trained in this area? And does a student's ability to pass exams and/or write papers necessarily demonstrate overall comprehension of the material? Many of the challenges found in training college students are evident in training police officers.

The Police Academy

The police academy serves several general purposes. It teaches officers the technical skills required for the job, indoctrinates cadets into the social world of policing, and identifies those unfit for a career in policing. Recent research on law enforcement agencies employing 100 or more officers sheds light on the amount and nature of training provided to officers. According to the research, in 2000 the median number of basic recruit training hours for officers in municipal departments was 720 hours across all police academies. The median number of training hours for state law enforcement agencies was 960, followed by county police departments with 896 hours. Sheriffs' offices required fewer training hours than municipal departments, the latter of which constitute the bulk of departments and employ most of the officers in law enforcement.[78] Many police academies provide recruits with more training than is required by state requirements. For instance, in 2002 the median number of hours provided to recruits above state requirements was 100.[79]

Aside from pre-service training, law enforcement officers receive in-service training to keep them abreast of recent developments in the field and to promote overall officer professionalism. Local, county, and state law enforcement officers generally receive 480 hours of field training, with municipal police departments requiring the greatest number of hours. Officers also receive roughly 40 hours of in-service training annually.[80] Table 10.3 depicts these findings. With regard to instruction time provided in the various components of policing, firearm skills (60 hours) involved the longest training, followed by health and fitness (50 hours), investigations (45 hours), self-defense (44 hours), criminal law (40 hours), emergency vehicle operations (36 hours), and basic first aid/CPR (24 hours).[81] The median number of training hours officers are required to take with regard to cultural sensitivity is 8, with 95% of all departments requiring such training. Basic foreign language training (e.g., Survival Spanish) was offered in only 35% of the academies with 16 as the median number of training hours.[82]

A Bureau of Justice Statistics report stated that 14% of U.S. police departments, which employed 23% of officers in 2003, assessed police recruits' understanding of

TABLE 10.3

Median Number of Training Hours Required for Officers in Law Enforcement Agencies with 100 or More Officers, 2000

	County Police	Municipal Police	Sheriff	Primary State Law Enforcement Agencies
Academy Training Hours for New Officers	896	720	640	960
Field Training Hours for New Officers	480	520	476	480
Annual In-Service Training Hours for Field/Patrol Officers	40	40	37	24

Source: Brian A. Reaves and Matthew U. Hickman, *Law Enforcement Management and Administrative Statistics, 2000: Data for Individual State and Local Agencies with 100 or More Officers,* Bureau of Justice Statistics, NCJ 203350 (Washington, D.C.: U. S. Department of Justice, 2004).

TABLE 10.4

Ability Assessment Used by Local Police for Selecting New Officers, 2003

Population Served	Percent of Agencies Considering Whether New Officers Have an Understanding of Culturally Diverse Populations
All Sizes	14%
1,000,000 or more	31
500,000–999,999	19
250,000–499,999	24
100,000–249,999	16
50,000–99,999	21
25,000–49,999	16
10,000–24,999	16
2,500–9,999	14
Under 2,500	13

Source: Matthew J. Hickman and Brian A. Reaves, *Local Police Departments, 2003,* Bureau of Justice Statistics, NCJ 210118 (Washington, D.C.: U.S. Department of Justice, 2006).

culturally diverse populations. Table 10.4 depicts the breakdown of departments, by size, with regard to their assessment of recruits' understanding of culturally diverse populations.[83] These numbers suggest departments serving larger populations are more concerned than those serving smaller populations with ensuring that new officers maintain an understanding of culturally diverse populations.

Cultural Diversity and Sensitivity Training

In discussing his many years of teaching a cultural diversity and ethics course to law enforcement groups, Daniel Carlson, former police captain and author of the book *When Cultures Clash,* suggested that training on topics such as ethics or cultural diversity is not popular among police officers. He states, "Very often in the heat of these classes, officers bemoan the fact that while they are 'forced' to endure training designed to improve police–citizen interactions, no such training exists for citizens." The officers argue that the public needs to better understand policing and police officers.[84] There is certainly merit to this argument, as policing arguably has a distinctive culture of its own. The dilemma exists in that it is a give-and-take situation that requires efforts from both sides.

Cultural sensitivity training for police officers largely emerged in the 1980s. The increased focus on cultural sensitivity training was designed to improve police–community relations and address citizen complaints of police officers misusing their powers against underrepresented persons in the community.[85] The need for greater cultural sensitivity training in policing has existed for some time. For example, the

1967 Kerner Report suggested that poor police–community relations were at the root of much civil unrest.

The Importance of Cultural Sensitivity Training

Cultural sensitivity training is imperative for today's police officers. Ideally, training should alter officer behavior, generate alternative solutions to problematic or confrontational situations, and encourage officers to adopt the values and ideals of the department.[86] The recent shift in policing toward greater interaction with the public necessitates greater emphasis on personal communication skills and on tolerating and appreciating diversity. Accordingly, many departments and police academies have enhanced their focus on cultural sensitivity training. Among the issues surrounding sensitivity training are gaining an understanding, recognition, and respect for the various groups and cultures in society. Training must consist of more than a briefing or cursory examination at the academy or generic comments offered at roll call. Such training must be ongoing and reinforced by fellow officers and superiors who should also have notable appreciation of cultural diversity. Further, cultural sensitivity training is more effective when various groups outside of policing—for example, civic leaders—offer input regarding their expectations and an overview of their cultural beliefs and practices.

It would be difficult for police officers, especially those in large cities where diversity is most prominent, to have a thorough understanding of all cultural beliefs and practices. Fortunately, community policing strategies emphasize police–citizen interaction, in part, by having officers consistently work in specific jurisdictions. In other words, maintaining an officer's presence in a particular neighborhood or community becomes important for officers to grasp the local culture as they become better able to understand those in the community. Learning how to grasp the local culture and how to respect cultural diversity are among the many topics addressed at the police academy.

What Cultural Sensitivity Training Includes

So, what exactly is cultural sensitivity training? Should coverage of hate or bias crime be included in such training? Departments have responded to concerns surrounding hate crimes, in part by training officers and administrators to understand how to identify hate crimes. Should cultural sensitivity training also include teaching officers to recognize the differences between persons with physical ailments and those who are intoxicated? Cultural sensitivity is a complex phenomenon that is created and shaped in individuals during their upbringing. What is taught in the academy and supplemented on the streets also contributes to how officers react to multiculturalism.

In general, cultural diversity training should include four primary components: awareness of one's own cultural influences; understanding of other cultures; comprehension of the emotional challenges faced in recognizing and understanding diversity; and the basic skills needed to appropriately address cultural differences.[87] A weakness in any of these components could hamper understanding cultural diversity. Self-reflection through examination of one's own cultural influences and understanding the emotional challenges with regard to diversity helps officers to overcome personal biases they may have toward other groups.

Researchers Myrna Cornett-DeVito and Edward McGlone propose two basic approaches—culture-specific training and culture-general training—with respect to multicultural skills development. Culture-specific training addresses the practices, beliefs, and traits of particular cultural groups. Culture-general training emphasizes the flexibility, skills, and understanding that would apply to understanding an array of cultures.[88] Their research with regard to these approaches found that the culture-general model and interactive training methods and trainer qualifications hold viable potential for positive training impacts.[89] These findings provide guidance for future training efforts.

Cultural diversity and awareness training should, at minimum, address

- police communication skills,
- understanding and recognizing bias,
- racism, bigotry, discrimination, and the like,
- understanding and appreciating various (or, if possible, most or all) cultures,
- understanding the benefits and challenges of diversity and its relationship to policing, and
- action steps to confront multicultural challenges.

Departments faced with limited resources should tailor their training to focus primarily on the groups within their jurisdiction. For example, there would be a need for officers working in an area with Native Americans to familiarize themselves with Native American culture.

Cultural sensitivity and diversity training are generally imposed on officers, but it also takes efforts by police administrators and supervisors to ensure that all personnel in the department are culturally sensitive, and to take remedial actions with those who are not. Diversity is a substantial issue in the workplace, yet many employers are ill-prepared to address it. The problem appears in part because many managers grew up isolated from other cultures.[90] Accordingly, it is imperative that cultural sensitivity training be provided not only to officers but to police administrators and supervisors as well. Fellow police officers, particularly the more experienced ones, provide the greatest source of influence on officer behavior.[91]

As an educational process, training begins at the police academy and is followed by field training with qualified officers. Such training is complemented by officers continuously taking in-service courses. Put simply, training is an ongoing process. As such, the significance of field-training officer programs, which pair new officers with experienced ones, cannot be overstated. It is at this point that new officers gain a foundation of skills, knowledge, and expectations that shape their future. Pairing new officers with culturally sensitive officers enhances policing in many ways. Continued in-service training reinforces earlier training and exposes officers to developments in policing. Unfortunately, the limitations of training in general make it difficult to expect that cultural sensitivity training will substantially impact all officers.

The Limitations of Training

The limitations of police officer training are highlighted by Samuel Walker and Charles Katz, who note that although training would seemingly improve an officer's performance, little evidence suggests that it does.[92] They argue in their book *The Police in America* that the culture of the department in general largely influences officer behavior, adding that a viable citizen complaint process and a system in which problematic officers are disciplined are essential to maintaining effective relations with all groups.[93]

The following common limitations appear inherent in police training:

- Programs may not cover significant areas (e.g., rape, human relations).
- There may be a lack of adequate facilities in which to train.
- Training instructors and directors are only part-time (full-time personnel with no other job duties should be provided).
- Officers who work *and* attend the academy face many difficulties.
- Training prior to exercising power prevents untrained officers from working the streets.
- Training does not occur often enough (it should occur at two-year intervals following initial pre-service training).
- High-quality field training officers are scarce in some departments.
- Instructors may not be effective teachers.[94]

The significant role played by police trainers cannot be ignored. White course facilitators discussing racial profiling are often easily dismissed by trainees, who generally believe the facilitator is unaware of life as an officer on the streets. Yet a racial minority police officer who shares personal experiences of being harassed by the police generates notable attention.[95]

Despite the limitations, one cannot overstate the significance of training. It could be argued, however, that we expect too much out of police training. This dilemma presents a challenge for policing and will continue to do so until the aforementioned limitations are addressed. In sum, much progress has been made to address the limitations involved in police training, although much work remains.

Training, similar to formal education, seeks to impart knowledge and skills on an individual in preparation for future endeavors. At the police academy, officers spend time on law; practical skills; human relations; criminal investigations; patrol procedures; the structure and practices of policing; and, more generally, the criminal justice system. Officers will later be provided in-service and field training to help them apply what they learned at the academy and keep them abreast of changes throughout their careers. Yet, at the most basic level, police officers are first and foremost human beings who were molded and shaped by various forces beyond policing prior to entering the field. Various types of police officer training may be expected to reduce internal limitations or conflicts among individual officers. Part of cultural sensitivity training involves "undoing" damage from the past and promoting tolerance. It is hoped that proper recruitment, selection, and training can provide police academies and police departments with individuals who won't let personal conflicts affect their ability to properly perform their job.

Perhaps the progress made with regard to multicultural policing is best summed up by authors Hubert Williams and Patrick Murphy in their government report "The Evolving Strategy of Police: A Minority View," when they state that "significant progress has been made, however. Large numbers of blacks and other minorities have joined—and in many cases have become leaders of—our major departments." They add that the use of violence against minorities has decreased, efforts have been made to make officers more sensitive to minority issues, and better-educated police officers and leaders have enhanced the profession.[96] Many signs point to a more positive future with regard to policing in a multicultural society.

Summary

Policing originated with informal social control efforts that evolved into formal social control in the form of the criminal justice system. Citizens in early societies provided protection for one another. Later, policing became institutionalized. Modern American policing has its roots in the British system of policing. Upon arriving in America, colonists adopted both the formal and informal approaches to social control.

The history of U.S. policing has been categorized into three eras: the political era, the reform era, and the community era. Several significant events in U.S. history helped shape the police. For instance, Prohibition, the Civil Rights Movement, and protests against the Vietnam War have largely impacted police practices. The current community era of policing provides an attractive alternative to earlier periods when police were heavily influenced by politicians or too focused on the crimefighting aspect of policing.

Great strides have been made in diversifying police forces. Legislation and the emergence of a more tolerant society with regard to racial and ethnic diversity have contributed to greater numbers of minorities in policing. The number and percentage of females in policing have also increased.

Officer and departmental practices do not occur in a vacuum, as officers and administrators maintain a great deal of discretion. Policing is shaped by many factors. Prominent among the categories of influences upon officer behaviors are organizational influences, situational characteristics, officer characteristics, and neighborhood or community influences. Effective police recruitment, selection, and training efforts help create more diverse, tolerant, and overall more professional police departments.

 You Make the Call

Ethical Policing?

Consider the following scenario. Debate the pros and cons of all options and decide what you would do.

You're a White rookie police officer patrolling a community heavily populated by Latinos and Latinas. The extensive ethnic tensions in the area are the result of alleged police abuse of young Latino males. You stop a car that made an illegal U-turn in the street. The car pulls over. You notice three young Hispanic males in the car as you approach the vehicle. The driver rolls down the window and you smell marijuana. The driver seems agitated that you pulled him over and begins making claims of racial profiling. You're somewhat sympathetic to his claims as you've personally seen officers profile Latino drivers. The others in the car chime in. You ask the driver to step out of the car and he refuses, claiming he wants a lawyer. You call for backup. As you're making the call, the three individuals step out of the car in what you perceive to be an aggressive manner. They're angry and not listening to your commands. Your backup is three minutes away. You reach for your baton and command the individuals to get on the ground. They refuse and move toward you. Their aggressive demeanor prompts you to use your baton on them. Your backup arrives as you wrestle with the suspects. You and the other officers successfully place the suspects in custody. The suspects claim you: (1) targeted them based on their ethnicity, (2) used excessive force by using a baton, and (3) said derogatory terms during the tussle. You don't recall saying anything of that nature.

Questions

1. How should your supervisor respond to the claims that you used derogatory terms?
2. How could you have prevented this incident from escalating into violence?
3. Do you believe the tensions in the community contributed to the unfortunate outcome of this incident?
4. What steps, if any, should the police chief take to ensure that an incident such as this does not occur again?

Key Terms

affirmative action (p. 234)
Black Codes (p. 226)
Bow Street Runners (p. 225)
Christopher Commission (p. 231)
Civil Rights Act of 1866 (p. 226)
Civil Rights Act of 1964 (p. 233)
community era of policing (p. 229)
community policing (p. 229)
exclusionary rule (p. 229)
Frankpledge System (p. 224)
hue and cry (p. 224)
London Metropolitan Police Act (p. 225)
National Advisory Commission on Civil Disorders (p. 229)

overpolicing (p. 223)
patronage (p. 227)
police discretion (p. 239)
police subculture (p. 232)
political era of policing (p. 226)
President's Commission on Law Enforcement and Administration of Justice (p. 229)
problem-oriented policing (p. 231)
Prohibition (p. 227)
reform era of policing (p. 227)
reverse discrimination (p. 234)
slave patrols (p. 225)
tokens (p. 234)
underpolicing (p. 223)

Discussion Questions

1. Discuss significant events in the history of policing that contributed to current problematic relations between underrepresented groups and the police.
2. Identify the three eras of policing and discuss the impact of each on public perceptions of the police.
3. What significant events have helped diversify police forces?
4. Identify and discuss the four categories of variables that influence police discretion. How do these factors affect policing a multicultural society?
5. Design a 40-hour training program to enhance policing in a multicultural society. What categories would you cover and how many hours would you devote to each?

Endnotes

1. McCamey, W. P., Scaramella, G. L., and Cox, S. M. 2003. *Contemporary Municipal Policing.* Boston: Allyn & Bacon. P. 150.
2. Barlow, D., and Hickman Barlow, M. 2000. *Police in a Multicultural Society: An American Story.* Prospect Heights, IL: Waveland Press.
3. Ibid., p. 53.
4. Ibid, p. xii.
5. Smith, P. 1985. *Policing Victorian London.* London: Greenwood Press.
6. Uchida, C. 1993. "The Development of the American Police: An Historical Overview." In R. Dunham and G. Alpert (eds.), *Critical Issues in Policing: Contemporary Readings,* 2nd ed., pp. 16–32. Prospect Heights, IL: Waveland Press.
7. Stead, P. 1985. *The Police of Britain.* New York: Macmillan.
8. Dulaney, W. M. 1996. *Black Police in America.* Bloomington: Indiana University Press.
9. Ibid.
10. Miller, L. S., and Hess, K. M. 2005. *Community Policing: Partnerships for Problem Solving,* 4th ed. Belmont, CA: Wadsworth.
11. Fagin, J. A. 2007. *Criminal Justice,* 2nd ed. Boston: Allyn & Bacon.
12. Miller and Hess 2005, p. 9.
13. Fagin 2007.
14. Williams, H., and Murphy, P. V. 1990, January. "The Evolving Strategy of Police: A Minority View." U.S. Department of Justice, National Institute of Justice.
15. Kelling, G. L., and Moore, M. H. 1991. "From Political to Reform to Community: The Evolving Strategy of Police." In J. R. Greene and S. D. Mastrofski (eds.), *Community Policing: Rhetoric or Reality,* pp. 3–25. New York: Praeger.
16. Williams and Murphy 1990.
17. Langworthy, R. H., and Travis III, L. P. 1999. *Policing in America: A Balance of Forces,* 2nd ed. Upper Saddle River, NJ: Prentice Hall.
18. Walker, S., and Katz, C. M. 2005. *The Police in America,* 5th ed. New York: McGraw-Hill. P. 31.
19. Ibid.
20. Alpert, G. P., Dunham, R. G., and Stroshine, M. S. 2006. *Policing: Continuity and Change.* Long Grove, IL: Waveland. Also, Kuykendall, J. L., and Burns, D. E. 1980. "The Black Police Officer: An Historical Perspective." *Journal of Contemporary Criminal Justice,* vol. 1, No. 4, 4–12 (1980).
21. Williams and Murphy 1990.
22. Miller and Hess 2005.
23. Walker and Katz 2005, p. 43.
24. Ibid.
25. Perez, A. D., Berg, K. M., and Myers, D. J. 2003. "Police and Riots, 1967–1969." *Journal of Black Studies* 34 (2): 153–182.
26. Ibid, p. 177.
27. White, M. D. 2007. *Current Issues and Controversies in Policing.* Boston: Allyn & Bacon.
28. Miller and Hess 2005, p. 12.
29. Williams and Murphy 1990, p. 11.
30. Miller and Hess 2005, p. 13.
31. National Advisory Commission on Civil Disorders. 1967. *Report of the National Advisory Commission on Civil Disorders.* New York: Bantam Books.
32. *Mapp v. Ohio,* 367 U.S. 643 (1961).
33. *Gideon v. Wainwright,* 372 U.S. 335 (1963).
34. *Miranda v. Arizona,* 384 U.S. 436 (1966).
35. *Terry v. Ohio,* 392 U.S. 1 (1968).
36. Oliver, W. M. 2004. *Community-Oriented Policing: A Systemic Approach to Policing,* 3rd ed. Upper Saddle River, NJ: Prentice Hall. P. 46.
37. Ibid.
38. Cordner, G. W. 2005. "Community Policing: Elements and Effects." In R. G. Dunham and G. P. Alpert (eds.), *Critical Issues in Policing: Contemporary Readings,* 5th ed., pp. 401–418. Long Grove, IL: Waveland Press.

39. Ibid.
40. Hickman, M. J., and Reaves, B. A. 2006. *Local Police Departments, 2003.* Bureau of Justice Statistics. NCJ 210118. Washington, DC: U.S. Department of Justice.
41. Perez, Berg, and Myers 2003, p. 179.
42. *Report of the Independent Commission on the Los Angeles Police Department.* 1991. July 9, p. iii.
43. Ibid., p. iv.
44. Perez, Berg, and Myers 2003.
45. Carter, D. L., and Radelet, L. A. 1999. *The Police and the Community,* 6th ed. Upper Saddle River, NJ: Prentice Hall. Pp. 298–299.
46. Longworthy and Travis 1999, p. 244.
47. Walker and Katz 2005.
48. Grant, H., and Terry, K. J. 2005. *Law Enforcement in the 21st Century.* Boston: Allyn & Bacon.
49. Ibid.
50. Harr, R. N. 1997. "Patterns of Interaction in a Police Patrol Bureau: Race and Gender Barriers to Integration." *Justice Quarterly* 14 (1): 53–85. P. 53.
51. Ibid.
52. Lyman, M. D. 1999. *The Police: An Introduction.* Upper Saddle River, NJ: Prentice Hall.
53. Hickman and Reaves 2006.
54. White 2007.
55. Alpert, Dunham, and Stroshine 2006.
56. Peak, K. J., and Glensor, R. W. 1999. *Community Policing & Problem Solving: Strategies and Practices,* 2nd ed. Upper Saddle River, NJ: Prentice Hall. Pp. 218–220.
57. Ibid.
58. Brooks, L. W. 2005. "Police Discretionary Behavior: A Study of Style." In R.G. Dunham and G. P. Alpert (eds.), *Critical Issues in Policing: Contemporary Readings,* pp. 89–105. Long Grove, IL: Waveland Press.
59. Skolnick, J. 1966. *Justice Without Trial: Law Enforcement in a Democratic Society.* New York: John Wiley & Sons.
60. Mastrofski, S. 1981. "Policing the Beat: The Impact of Organizational Scale on Patrol Officer Behavior in Urban Residential Neighborhoods." *Journal of Criminal Justice* 9: 343–358.
61. Burns, R., and Crawford, C. 2002. "Situational Determinants of Police Violence." In R. Burns and C. Crawford (eds.), *Policing and Violence,* pp. 73–100. Upper Saddle River, NJ: Prentice Hall. P. 76.
62. National Institute of Justice. 1999. Executive Summary. *Use of Force by Police: Overview of National and Local Data.* NCJ 176330. Washington, DC: U.S. Department of Justice. P. viii.
63. Sherman, L. 1980. "Causes of Police Behavior: The Current State of Quantitative Research." *Journal of Research in Crime and Delinquency* 17: 69–100.
64. Worden, R. E. 1989. "Situational and Attitudinal Explanations of Police Behavior: A Theoretical Reappraisal and Empirical Assessment." *Law and Society Review* 23: 667–711.
65. Geller, R., and Karales, K. 1981. *Split Second Decisions: Shootings of and by the Chicago Police.* Chicago Law Enforcement Study Group.
66. Alex, N. 1976. *Black in Blue: A Study of the Negro Policeman.* New York: Appleton-Century-Crofts.
67. Walker and Katz 2005, p. 162.
68. Alex 1976.
69. McCamey, Scaramella, and Cox 2003.
70. Ibid.
71. Jacobs, D., and O' Brien, R. 1998. "The Determinants of Deadly Force: A Structural Analysis of Police Violence." *American Journal of Sociology* 103: 837–862.
72. Jacobs, D., and Britt, D. 1979. "Inequality and the Police Use of Deadly Force." *Social Problems* 26: 403–412.
73. Jacobs and O'Brien 1998.
74. Ibid.
75. Jacobs and Britt 1979.
76. Banton, M. 1964. *The Policeman in the Community.* New York: Basic Books.
77. Bayley, D. 1998. "Policing in America: Social Science and Public Policy in

America." *Society,* November/
December, pp. 16–19.

78. Reaves, B. A., and Hickman, M. J. 2004, March. *Law Enforcement Management and Administrative Statistics, 2000: Data for Individual State and Local Agencies with 100 or More Officers.* Bureau of Justice Statistics. NCJ 203350. Washington, DC: U.S. Department of Justice.

79. Hickman, M. J. 2005. *State and Local Law Enforcement Training Academies, 2002.* Bureau of Justice Statistics. NCJ 204030. Washington, DC: U.S. Department of Justice.

80. Reaves and Hickman 2004, p. xiii.

81. Ibid.

82. Ibid.

83. Hickman and Reaves 2006, p. 21.

84. Carlson, D. P. 2002. *When Cultures Clash: The Divisive Nature of Police–Community Relations and Suggestions for Improvement.* Upper Saddle River, NJ: Prentice Hall.

85. Thibault, E. A., Lynch, L. M., and McBride, R. B. 1998. *Proactive Police Management,* 4th ed. Upper Saddle River, NJ: Prentice Hall.

86. Flynn, K. W. 2002. "Training and Police Violence." In R. G. Burns and C. E. Crawford (eds.), *Policing and Violence,* pp. 127–146. Upper Saddle River, NJ: Prentice Hall.

87. Brislin, R., and Yoshida, T. 1994. *Intercultural Communication Training: An Introduction.* Thousand Oaks, CA: Sage.

88. Cornett-DeVito, M. M., and McGlone, E. L. 2000. "Multicultural Communication Training for Law Enforcement Officers: A Case Study." *Criminal Justice Policy Review* 11(3): 234–253.

89. Ibid., p. 234.

90. Shusta, R. M., Levine, D. R., Harris, P. R., and Wong, H. Z. 2002. *Multicultural Law Enforcement,* 2nd ed. Upper Saddle River, NJ: Prentice Hall.

91. Flynn 2002, p. 129.

92. Walker and Katz 2005, pp. 164–165.

93. Ibid., p. 165.

94. Thibault, Lynch, and McBride 1998.

95. Carlson 2002, p. 61.

96. Williams and Murphy 1990, p. 13.

Courts and Multiculturalism

Chapter Objectives

After reading this chapter, you should be able to

❖ Discuss how pretrial processes maintain potential biases against underrepresented groups.

❖ Identify potential biases working against minorities with regard to the manner in which prospective jurors are identified and the manner in which jurors are ultimately selected.

❖ Discuss the steps of a trial, including areas where the prosecution may have an unfair advantage.

❖ Identify how sentencing practices and sentencing structures have contributed to the overrepresentation of minorities in prison.

❖ Explain why we need diversity among the courtroom personnel and identify whether race influences judicial practices.

The U.S. criminal court system consists of state and federal courts. State courts process those charged with state violations. Federal courts process those accused of committing federal offenses. The U.S. Supreme Court, the highest court in the land, hears cases from both state and federal courts. Most criminal case processing occurs in state courts. In 2002, an estimated 1,051,000 adults charged with a felony were processed in state courts (94% of all felony cases during the year), compared to only 63,217 felony defendants in federal court.[1] Multiculturalism plays a significant role in our court systems given the large number of defendants processed each year.

In their book *American Cultural Pluralism and Law,* Jill Norgren, a professor emeritus of government, and Serena Nanda, a cultural anthropologist, note that as the United States increasingly diversifies, "It faces a fundamental tension: on one hand there is the need to create national institutions, including law, which unify culturally different groups, and on the other, the need to protect human rights by allowing some degree of religious, personal, cultural and local political autonomy."[2] They add that "law ... is one of the most important mechanisms for addressing this inevitable tension between the needs of the nation-state for some growing consensus around a dominant set of cultural values and institutions, and the needs of groups to enact and increase their autonomy."[3] U.S. courts interpret, create, and apply criminal and civil law, and are particularly vulnerable to the previously described tensions.

Increased diversity in the courtroom perpetuates interpersonal misunderstandings. For example, the verbal and body language of non–English speaking defendants and witnesses are sometimes misinterpreted by English-speaking courtroom personnel. In response, courts have become increasingly sensitive to the needs of those unable to speak English.[4] Some suggest holding trials in Spanish should a defendant choose to do so.[5]

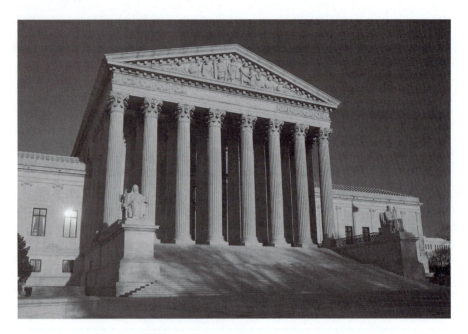

The U.S. Supreme Court is the highest court in the United States. As an appellate court, it hears cases that originate in both state and federal courtrooms.

In a newspaper article titled "Courts Asked to Consider Culture," journalist Richard Willing commented on the role of culture in U.S. courts, suggesting that "immigrants with roots in Africa, Asia and other non-Western cultures are winding up in America's courts after being charged with crimes for acts that would not be offenses in their home countries."[6] Incidents involving animal sacrifices, ritual mutilations and other customs of foreign cultures are increasingly showing up in U.S. courts, leading to the suggestion that the courts permit defendants from non-Western backgrounds to offer a "cultural defense" in response to being charged with a crime.[7] Cultural defenses have been reluctantly allowed in court, although, as Willing notes, "Exceptions have come when groups have been able to argue that their religious as well as cultural rights have been violated."[8]

Research addressing felony defendants in large urban counties found an overrepresentation of Blacks and an underrepresentation of Whites entering criminal court.[9] Black defendants comprised 15% of the populations included in the counties under study, yet they accounted for 43% of those entering courts on felony charges. Whites constituted 53% of the population yet 31% of those charged with felony offenses. The percentage of Hispanics entering the courts (24%) was representative of the larger population (23%). This pattern held true across all types of offenses. Of particular interest is the finding that 55% of those under age 18 and entering felony court were Black, compared to 18% for Whites. Males were far more likely than females to end up in felony court (82% compared to 18%).

The following discussion of multiculturalism in the courts is organized according to the stages of case processing in criminal courts. The discussion

Increased diversity in the courtroom requires greater levels of tolerance for multiculturalism by all parties.

begins with a look at multiculturalism in the events occurring at the initial appearance, followed by discussion of preliminary/grand jury hearings, arraignments, trials, sentencing, and appeals. This chapter concludes with discussion of the diversity of those working in our courts. Due to their overrepresentation in the courts, African Americans are the focus of much discussion regarding multiculturalism and the courts.

⚔ Initial Appearance

At the **initial appearance,** also referred to as the first appearance, defendants are

- brought before the court,
- informed of the formal charges against them,
- advised of their rights, including the right to retain a lawyer or have one appointed to them,
- possibly granted pretrial release, and
- made aware of the upcoming steps in their case.

In general, felony criminal case processing is more complicated than misdemeanor processing. The difference stems from the more severe or harmful circumstances typically involved in felonies than in misdemeanors. The more severe penalties associated with felonies also contribute to the differences in the resources devoted to each type of case. Misdemeanor processing often begins and ends with the initial appearance. Felony processing is more drawn out and more likely to involve the steps occurring after the initial appearance.

Notice of Charges

Decisions to charge a defendant and the nature of the charges are sometimes controversial. Prosecutors typically examine the evidence provided to them following an arrest and preliminary investigation and use their discretion to determine whether or not to file charges. If they choose to file charges, they must then determine what charge(s) to file. Prosecutors depend heavily on police reports and input from those involved with the incident to make their assessment. The power to make several key decisions, especially as they relate to filing charges, offers avenues for prosecutorial abuse of discretion.

Researchers Samuel Walker, Cassia Spohn, and Mariam Delone suggest prosecutors primarily rely on the strength of the evidence in their decisions to file charges against a defendant.[10] They found conflicting evidence that race influenced prosecutorial decision-making with regard to charging. Race played either a marginal role or no role at all. They note that despite the limited research on the effect of race on prosecutorial charging and plea bargaining decisions, several studies found that African American and Hispanic suspects were more likely than White suspects to face criminal charges. Further, African American and Hispanic suspects were more likely than White suspects to continue to be prosecuted at all stages of case processing. The researchers note the evidence pointing to the selective prosecution of racial minorities, especially for drug offenses.[11]

Counsel and the Initial Appearance

Defendants entering court are commonly represented by counsel. Very few defendants choose to represent themselves. Counsel comes in two forms: private counsel secured by the defendant and state-provided counsel. In *Gideon v. Wainwright* (1963), the U.S. Supreme Court ruled that all who enter our courts have the right to counsel at all critical stages of the criminal justice process.[12] Prior to *Gideon,* only defendants in federal courts had the right to counsel, as decided in *Johnson v. Zerbst.*[13]

State-issued counsel is provided by assigned counsel and public defenders. Both forms of counsel provide legal representation to **indigent defendants,** those who cannot afford representation. **Assigned counsel** involves the court appointing indigent cases to practicing attorneys. Attorneys are assigned indigent cases in return for a statutorily-determined fee. In many cases, these attorneys have a caseload in their private practice that generates more income than the indigent cases. The statutorily-prescribed fee for indigent representation is far below what attorneys earn in their private practice. Such a situation may result in attorneys devoting greater attention to their private practice than to the assigned cases, given the need for private entities to generate profit for their financial survival.[14]

Although most U.S. counties use the assigned counsel system, most defendants are represented by **public defenders** who work in offices that exist solely to provide indigent representation. Public defenders face many challenges, including responsibility for large caseloads and limited resources. Their offices are primarily located in large urban cities where large volumes of criminal cases require their services.

Minorities are more likely than Whites to receive state-issued counsel upon entering court. For instance, one report noted that 76.6% of Blacks and 73.1% of

Hispanic defendants received state-appointed counsel compared to 69% of Whites.[15] The economic differences between minorities and nonminorities significantly contribute to this finding.

It is important to take the limitations of indigent representation very seriously as public defenders and appointed counsel face several challenges in providing a quality defense. Those representing the poor are threatened by a lack of financial support, large caseloads, and questionable training and supervision.[16] Indigent defendants are often represented by overworked, underpaid, and unqualified attorneys.[17] Prosecutors typically have more resources than defense attorneys who represent the indigent, thus putting defendants with fewer means at a clear disadvantage.

The Supreme Court requires that indigent defendants receive "effective assistance," but the standard for "effectiveness" is subjective. The subjectivity of the term is evident in cases in which lawyers representing the indigent showed up in court drunk or fell asleep during the proceeding yet were deemed effective.[18] Those purchasing the services of private attorneys can shop around and determine for themselves who they wish to represent them, but indigent defendants are provided attorneys by the state. Such a situation has resulted in inexperienced lawyers with limited knowledge of the complex law pertaining to capital punishment trials representing some indigent defendants facing the death penalty.[19] Nevertheless, the research literature has not consistently demonstrated that those represented by public defenders receive harsher sentences than those who use private counsel. Overall, those providing representation for the indigent appear to do an effective job.[20]

Pretrial Release

Arrestees are sometimes detained following arrest and prior to trial. The severity of the offense for which they've been arrested largely determines whether or not they are detained. Those arrested for the more serious offenses and posing the greatest threat to society are most likely to be detained. While detained, most arrestees will be granted **pretrial release** at their initial appearance. Pretrial release can be secured monetarily, as in the case of bail, or nonfinancially, such as release on recognizance. Judges typically determine whether or not the accused will be released prior to trial and the nature of the release. Among the considerations related to the nature of one's pretrial release are ensuring that the defendant will stay out of trouble while released and that he or she will return to court for further processing.

Judicial discretion in setting or denying bail and the circumstances surrounding release generate controversy. Judges typically consider a variety of factors in the release decision, such as the seriousness of the offense, the defendant's criminal record, the likelihood of the defendant returning to court, and the anticipated behavior should he or she be released. Part of the controversy involves the uncertainty of how variables such as race, gender, and ethnicity influence judicial discretion.[21] Studies observing the effect of race on bail-setting decisions provide contradictory results. Much has improved with regard to the unfair treatment of racial minorities who are arrested and detained; however, evidence suggests that some judges still consider race and other extralegal variables with regard to decisions concerning bail.[22]

Research suggests that Black and Hispanic detainees are more likely than Whites to be detained in jail while awaiting trial.[23] Other research found that

Hispanics received significantly higher bail amounts than African American and White defendants who were charged with the same crimes.[24] Financial bail poses more of a challenge to the poor than it does to those with means. The inability to secure release provides many challenges for defendants, including the increased likelihood of being found guilty.[25]

⚔ Preliminary and Grand Jury Hearings

A preliminary hearing or grand jury hearing is required in felony cases due to the more severe circumstances associated with felonies than with misdemeanors. Preliminary hearings differ from grand jury hearings in several ways, although their primary goal remains the same: to determine if the accused should remain in the system. **Preliminary hearings** involve a prosecutor demonstrating to a judge why charges have been filed and giving justification for continued processing. The prosecutor must bear the burden of demonstrating guilt.

Grand jury hearings are also used to determine if continued case processing may be necessary. Grand jurors are laypersons selected to serve on the jury. In **grand jury hearings,** jurors basically replace the judge used in a preliminary hearing. The grand jury's task is to determine if the prosecutor's case is strong enough to warrant an indictment. An **indictment** is the charging document used by grand juries to suggest enough evidence exists to continue with case processing. Grand juries are also permitted to engage in evidence collection of their own, should they choose to do so. Some states rely on preliminary hearings; others use grand juries or both types of hearings.

Preliminary hearings and grand jury hearings are somewhat insignificant in criminal case processing due to the unfair advantage maintained by prosecutors. While there are no implications of racism or cultural bias with regard to grand jury and preliminary hearings, defendants are arguably at a disadvantage in both types of hearings.

Let's consider grand jury hearings as a potential setting for bias or discrimination. They are the only legal officers permitted in the room when grand jury members consider evidence.[26] Prosecutors assess what types of evidence will be presented to grand juries, which undoubtedly influences grand jury decisions to indict. The absence of defendants during grand jury hearings typically works to their disadvantage, as does the low level of proof required (probable cause) for an indictment. Other factors influencing the outcomes of grand jury hearings include the need for only a half to two-thirds of grand juror votes to find probable cause in most states; the permissible use of hearsay evidence in grand jury deliberations; and the effective screening practices on behalf of prosecutors who drop cases they perceive as unworthy of grand jury consideration. In light of these variables, it is understandable why a grand jury indictment is referred to as little more than a rubber stamp.[27] While the advantages provided to the prosecution by no means exemplify overt racism, the disproportionate number of minority defendants, particularly African Americans, entering our courts is most directly affected.

✌ Arraignment

An **arraignment** is the step in criminal case processing when defendants are formally notified of the charges against them and they enter a plea. At an arraignment, after the defendant enters a plea, pretrial motions are offered and "discovery" may occur. **Discovery** is the sharing of information among the attorneys with the goal of helping attorneys adequately prepare their cases.[28] None of these steps has proven challenging with regard to multiculturalism. There are critiques of certain steps that disproportionately affect the large number of minorities who enter our courts. One must remember the use of discretion inherent during the arraignment and throughout all stages of case processing that could pose problems for underrepresented groups entering our courts.

It is not until the arraignment that felony defendants enter a plea. As noted earlier, misdemeanor processing is more informal than felony processing. Thus, defendants charged with a misdemeanor often have their cases disposed of more quickly. Many individuals charged with a misdemeanor enter a plea upon first entering the court. Felony cases are typically more formal; a defendant's case may come up in court several times prior to the individual entering a plea.

Defendants typically enter one of three pleas during the arraignment: guilty, not guilty, or *nolo contendere*. Most who enter our courts enter a guilty plea after having engaged in **plea bargaining,** or an exchange between the prosecution and the defense that would encourage a guilty plea in exchange for a benefit for the defendant. Defendants sometimes enter a plea of ***nolo contendere,*** or "no contest," which has the legal effect of a guilty plea. Defendants may choose to enter a plea of *nolo contendere* instead of admitting guilt in an attempt to cooperate with the court (through essentially pleading guilty), but they do not wish to directly admit guilt. Pleading "no contest" is sometimes done in cases in which a forthcoming civil trial may occur between the defendant and the victim and/or the victim's family. The civil trial would be brief and perhaps unnecessary if a defendant earlier admitted guilt in criminal court, as evidence used in the criminal court case (e.g., the admission of guilt) could be introduced in the civil case. Defendants sometimes enter a *nolo contendere* plea out of principle; they do not believe they are guilty, yet they are attracted to the benefits of the plea bargaining negotiations. Defendants may stand mute or refuse to recognize the court, which is typically done when one is protesting the actions of the criminal justice system. The court recognizes standing mute as a "not guilty" plea.

Plea bargaining has replaced the criminal trial in most cases. Pleading guilty facilitates case processing and rewards defendants. By eliminating the need for a trial through pleading guilty, defendants generally receive reduced sentences or other beneficial treatment by the court (e.g., lowering the charge to a less-stigmatized type of crime). Roughly 95% of felony defendants plead guilty, many of whom are minorities.[29]

The level of justice inherent in plea bargaining is a topic of scholarly debate. To be sure, our court system would collapse if all defendants who entered a courtroom requested a jury trial or even a **bench trial,** in which the judge serves as both judge and jury. Our court system simply does not have the resources to provide everyone a trial. One negative aspect of plea bargaining is that it encourages certain individuals to admit guilt when they are innocent. Further, there's evidence of discriminatory practices with regard to the deals offered and the opportunities to engage in plea bargaining.[30] Defendants have no right to plea bargaining; it occurs only when both the prosecuting attorney and the defense attorney agree to an arrangement and a judge approves the deal.

Pleading not guilty means one is willing to go to trial. In preparation for the trial, attorneys may begin, at the arraignment, offering **pretrial motions.** These motions help ensure that each side's interests are recognized by the court. Among the more popular motions are the following:

- *Motion to dismiss*—typically filed by the defense in hopes that the case will be dismissed, for example, based on due process violations or insufficient evidence.
- *Motion to determine the competency of the accused to stand trial*—designed to protect mentally ill persons from improperly being held responsible for their acts.
- *Motion to suppress evidence obtained through an unlawful search or seizure*—designed to protect a defendant's Fourth Amendment rights.
- *Motion to suppress confession, admissions, or other statements made to the police*—protects against violation of the suspect's legal rights.
- *Motion to require the prosecution to disclose the identity of a confidential informant*—enables the defense to better understand the sources of information and evidence to be used against the defendant.
- *Motion for a change of venue*—offered in an attempt to relocate the setting for a trial with the goal of ensuring that a fair verdict can be rendered. This motion is sometimes offered in response to pretrial publicity.
- *Motion for a continuance*—provides attorneys more time to prepare their case.

These motions are presented to a judge and can be a determining factor in the outcome of a case. For example, should a judge deny a defendant's motion to suppress illegally obtained evidence, a defense attorney may wish to initiate plea negotiations since his or her likelihood of winning a case may be severely diminished. The discretion inherent in judicial decisions to grant or deny particular motions provides further evidence of the need for cultural awareness in the criminal justice system in order to ensure that extralegal factors, such as characteristics of one's cultural background, don't interfere with justice.

⚔ Trials

The events involved with criminal trials largely reflect our society's quest for justice. The formality associated with the criminal trial, including much of the symbolism found in the courtroom (e.g., the judge's robe and gavel), suggests that justice will be served. History suggests, however, that our courts suffer from several limitations, not the least of which is the desire of attorneys to "win" cases as opposed to finding justice. Further, there's evidence of the differential treatment of certain groups that enter our courts. While the modern-day criminal trial is certainly more civil than earlier forms of seeking justice, there is great room for improvement. For example, the substantial levels of prosecutorial and judicial discretion inherent in trials have, on occasion, generated ethical concerns and questions of misbehavior.

TABLE 11.1

Steps in a Criminal Trial

Jury selection → Opening statements → Presentation of evidence → Closing arguments
→ Judge's charge to jury → Jury deliberations → Verdict → Sentencing if verdict is "guilty"

Judges and prosecutors play significant roles in the **adjudicatory process,** or the act of settling a case judicially in a courtroom. Judicial discretion is evident in many areas, especially in bench trials, where judges serve as both judge and jury. Judges are also influential with regard to the decision to allow or disallow evidence to be introduced or objections to be acknowledged, their directions to jurors, certain sentencing decisions, and many other areas. Prosecutorial discretion at trial includes decisions such as whether or not to introduce particular pieces of evidence and whether continued case processing is warranted. Among the key decisions made by the defense at trial are whether or not to put the suspect on the stand and what type of defense, if any, he or she should offer. Defense attorneys typically don't have to prove much of anything; their clients enter court innocent until proven guilty.

Trials involve a series of events (see Table 11.1). They begin with the selection of jurors, followed by opening statements, the presentation of evidence, closing arguments, the judge's charge to the jury, jury deliberations, the jury offering a verdict, and sentencing if the defendant has been found guilty. Although some level of controversy exists at each of these steps, several steps are more controversial than others in regard to multiculturalism, as we will discuss in the sections that follow.

Jury Selection

Jury selection has an influence on the outcome of many criminal trials. The biased selection of jurors and unethical jury behavior have unfortunately hampered the effectiveness of jury trials. For instance, we sometimes hear statements such as "he was convicted by an all-White jury," suggesting that race may have impacted the jury's decision. Controversy with regard to jury selection and multiculturalism exists primarily in the manner in which potential jurors are identified and the process of questioning prospective jurors known as *voir dire*. A series of changes in jury selection practices attempted to overcome the historical underrepresentation of minorities and other groups; however, racial discrimination in the selection of jurors remains problematic.[31]

Constructing the Venire

States use various means to assemble a jury pool, or **venire,** from which prospective jurors will be selected and questioned. Voter registration lists are most commonly used and are often supplemented with driver's license lists, automobile registration lists, and property tax rolls. The **Federal Jury Selection and Service Act of 1968** prohibited the exclusion of individuals based on religion, race, gender, national origin, or economic

Judges, prosecutors, and defense attorneys assume significant roles and perform various functions throughout the trial process.

status. Nevertheless, the ability of currently used lists to adequately provide a cross section of society has been questioned by scholars. Minorities and low-income individuals are less likely than nonminorities and those with higher incomes to be identified for jury selection, as they are less likely to own property and cars, be registered voters, or have a driver's license. Further, minorities and the poor are more likely to change residence;[32] thus, they are less likely to receive a **summons,** a document informing individuals of their call to jury duty. Using multiple lists of potential jurors, which is done in certain jurisdictions, widens the pool of potential jurors and increases the likelihood of adequate representation of all groups.

Those targeted for potentially serving on a jury are required to report to a particular location on a specified date for jury duty. At this point, names will be randomly selected and prospective jurors will be instructed to report to a specific courtroom for questioning regarding their suitability to serve. Accordingly, not all who are included in the venire will be selected for participation on a jury. Potential jurors may not even make it to *voir dire*, and others will be excused following *voir dire*. Some will be excluded due to legal stipulations surrounding participation on a jury. Virtually all states have provisions requiring jurors to be U.S. citizens, residents of the locality, at least a certain age, and able to understand English.[33] Most states do not permit convicted felons or insane persons to serve. Certain states maintain statutory exemptions for select individuals (e.g., government officials, lawyers), who are excused.[34] These restrictions have implications for creating culturally diverse juries. Excluding those unable to understand English, non-U.S. citizens, and convicted felons (who are disproportionately of minority groups) all pose problems in a multicultural society.

Voir Dire

During *voir dire,* the final step in jury selection, prospective jurors are questioned by a judge and/or attorneys to determine their suitability for serving on a jury. The questioning seeks to identify whether jurors have any familiarity with the primary actors in the case, the individual's beliefs or attitudes regarding specific issues that may arise in the trial, and any other matters that may influence the prospective juror's ability to render a fair decision in the case.[35] Unsuitable jurors are dismissed by the defense attorney or the prosecution during *voir dire* via one of two manners: challenges for cause and peremptory challenges. These options are designed to promote the assemblage of an unbiased jury.

Attorneys who wish to eliminate a juror because of an identifiable bias, or a juror's apparent inability to judge a case fairly, file a **challenge for cause** motion. The judge rules on the motion and, if it is sustained, the prospective juror is dismissed. The fact that judges assess the appropriateness of a challenge for cause demonstrates the presence of judicial discretion in jury selection. In practice, few challenges for cause are offered and not all are sustained.[36] Peremptory challenges, on the other hand, generate much greater controversy with regard to multiculturalism in U.S. courts.

Peremptory challenges, similar to challenges for cause, enable attorneys to eliminate seemingly unfit or inappropriate members of the jury pool. However, unlike with challenges for cause, attorneys typically do not need to justify using a peremptory challenge. They are provided an unlimited number of challenges for cause, although they are limited in the number of peremptory challenges they can use. Controversy surrounds the use of peremptory challenges, leading University of New Orleans Professor David Neubauer to state that "based on hunch, prejudice, or pseudoscience, a lawyer may peremptorily exclude a juror without giving a reason."[37]

In 1986, the U.S. Supreme Court ruled in *Batson v. Kentucky* that a prosecutor's use of peremptory challenges may not include the dismissal of members of the jury pool based solely on their race.[38] The Court ruled that doing so was in violation of the equal protection clause of the Fourteenth Amendment. Despite the positive intentions of the *Batson* decision to enhance jury selection practices, the decision hasn't eliminated the use of race-based peremptory strikes.[39] In *Batson* the Court sought to retain a great deal of the freedom inherent in peremptory challenges, while excluding challenges based strictly on race. In turn, attorneys have much freedom in their use of peremptory challenges as courts must accept any explanation for exclusion that is not race-based.[40] Accordingly, minorities continue to be excluded from juries, as lawyers offer spurious reasons for the dismissal of minority individuals.[41] The result is that racial and ethnic minorities are often tried by all-White juries.[42] Recent reform in the pretrial stages of adjudication, such as reconsideration of the sources via which potential jurors are identified, has reduced discrimination, making it less likely that minority defendants will be tried by an all-White jury.[43]

Attorneys seek to assemble a jury that will view a case according to the attorney's interest. Put simply, jury selection is sometimes more about winning a case than seeking justice. To be sure, discrimination exists with regard to both prosecutors and defense attorneys as the practices of using peremptory challenges to eliminate minorities from a jury pool could just as easily be used to eliminate Whites from a jury. The bottom line is that racial, ethnic, and cultural considerations are prevalent in jury selection. Such is the nature of seeking justice in a multicultural society.

The Body of the Trial

Scarce scholarly attention has addressed multiculturalism as it pertains to particular steps of a trial. Limited attention has focused on the impact of various cultural groups with regard to opening statements, the presentation of the evidence, closing arguments, and the judge's charge to the jury. These important stages often impact the outcome of criminal cases.

Once the trial stage is set, attorneys offer opening statements. The prosecution typically offers the initial opening statement to the jury (or the judge, depending on whether it's a jury or bench trial), followed by the defense. It could be argued that being permitted to make the "first impression" with the jury is an unfair advantage for the prosecution. However, someone has to go first, and the prosecution seems suitable given their task of having to prove guilt. Opening statements permit attorneys to outline their case for the jury.

During opening statements, attorneys must consider the background of the jury and be able to speak in comprehensible terms. They are encouraged to avoid "legal speak" and to recognize that the jury may not have a large vocabulary. These suggestions hold true throughout all stages of a trial.

Both the prosecution and defense present evidence following opening statements. The presentation of evidence can be controversial in several ways. Some public defenders don't have the resources to thoroughly investigate their cases. As mentioned earlier, public defenders are often overworked and have limited resources. The impact of their situation may be evident during the presentation of the evidence. For instance, those with greater resources can sway juries with impressive technology-based presentations. Limited resources also hamper a public defender's ability to locate witnesses or to obtain other helpful information.

Notable judicial and attorney discretion exists with regard to the presentation of evidence. For example, attorneys make key decisions regarding what pieces of evidence are introduced at trial, and judges may allow or disallow particular pieces of evidence to be introduced. Legal guidelines certainly assist with judicial discretion, as judges must abide by a code of conduct. The failure of judges to properly use their discretion regarding the introduction of key evidence can be grounds for a case to undergo appeal. Cases are sometimes won or lost depending on a judge's decision regarding the introduction of key pieces of evidence.

Among the many decisions they face at trial, defense attorneys must decide whether or not to put the defendant on the stand. Juries would seemingly like to hear from the defendant,[44] but it may not be strategically effective for the defense if the defendant is not an effective communicator. Defense attorneys should assess both at trial and during *voir dire* whether or not a jury will be receptive to their client. Cultural differences could certainly influence whether or not a defendant takes the stand. For example, a minority defendant might not want to take the stand if the jury is predominantly White.

At trial, defendants offer one of two defenses. They may offer an **alibi** that suggests that they did not commit the crime (e.g., they were in another location at the time of the crime). Defendants may also offer an **affirmative defense,** in which they admit committing the action in question, although they have legal justification for doing so. Entering an affirmative defense requires defendants to demonstrate that their action was justified. Self-defense, insanity, coercion, and entrapment are affirmative defenses. Although not widely used, the defense **"Black rage"** attempts to provide legal justification for criminal behavior by some African Americans frustrated by oppression resulting from living in a White-dominated society.

Closing arguments are offered once the defense and prosecution present their evidence and cross-examination of that evidence is completed. Closing arguments allow attorneys to make a final impression on the jury by recapping their arguments. The prosecution closes first.

Following closing arguments, the judge prepares the **charge to the jury,** a written document that explains how the law applies to the case.[45] Charges to the jury are typically assembled in an informal conference involving the judge and trial attorneys. The charge generally

- reminds the jury of the prosecution's responsibility to prove guilt beyond a reasonable doubt,
- provides procedural directions for deliberations,
- identifies evidence that may or may not be considered during deliberations, and
- lists the options of verdicts for jury consideration.

Cultural differences and general familiarity with trial procedure and the law are relevant factors at this point. It is important for judges to provide clearly defined and readable instructions for jury members. Scholars have questioned the ability of jurors to clearly understand the directions provided by judges.[46] In turn, there have been calls for improving jury instructions. Providing visual aids to jury members[47] and offering instructions in multiple languages are among the suggestions for improvement.

Juries leave the courtroom and begin deliberating upon receiving the judge's instructions. A foreperson is elected by the jury, or one is appointed by the court prior to deliberations. This individual presides over jury deliberations and ultimately reads the verdict in the courtroom. One stronghold of jury deliberations is the secrecy involved. No outsiders are permitted in deliberations. The secrecy prohibits much understanding of the dynamics involved in deliberations. What we know about jury deliberations comes mostly from mock juries (research endeavors in which outside of the courtroom lawyers assemble jurors and evaluate juror reactions to the evidence and arguments prior to a case going to trial), interviews of jurors following their dismissal, and the questions the jurors asked the judge during deliberations.[48]

A unanimous verdict is always necessary in a capital (death penalty) case but is not necessary in noncapital cases although most jurisdictions require it. Federal cases must be unanimous. It can be challenging to have a group of strangers from various cultural backgrounds come to agreement. Juries may be requested to further deliberate if not enough members concur with the verdict, or a judge may rule the case a mistrial, which means there will be a new trial with new jurors.

Jury Nullification

Jury members are charged with assessing the facts of the case and rendering a verdict. **Jury nullification** permits juries to acquit even when the facts of the case suggest they convict, and thus enables citizens to play a more active role in determining justice and what/whom should be punished.[49] It is rooted in English common law[50] and is sometimes used in cases where the jury believes a prosecutor enforced an unpopular law or a jury sympathizes with the defendant.[51] Jury nullification has become controversial as several prominent African American scholars encouraged Blacks to acquit other Blacks due to perceived mistreatment of African Americans by the courts and, more generally, by the criminal justice system.

Former U.S. Attorney Paul Butler commented on the power involved with jury nullification. He suggested that African American jurors should consider jury nullification in cases involving victimless, nonviolent offenses (e.g., drug possession). He argues that White jurors have historically engaged in jury nullification and that Black jurors should follow suit. He adds that jury nullification would generate controversy and call into question the existing problems in the use of juries. Such attention could lead to methods of correcting the injustices faced by African Americans and other minorities.[52] Butler's comments are controversial to be sure and have generated critical responses. It is argued that race-based jury nullification further damages race relations, has moral implications, and generates greater racial discrimination.[53]

Enhancing Jury Trials

The limitations inherent in the selection of juries have led to suggestions of alternatives, or enhancements of current practices. Professional juries, involving full-time, trained, salaried professional jurors, would address many of the problems associated with the use of laypersons serving as jurors. Professional jurors would provide the benefits of dependability, knowledge, and equity.[54] Allowing jury members to have a notebook during the trial and participate in trials by posing questions to witnesses are also feasible options for enhancing jury trials. Some California courts present jurors with notebooks containing trial exhibits and legal papers to help them render a fair verdict.[55] Other courts provide legal instructions to jurors before the trial begins, instead of at the conclusion of the trial, to enable them to better understand their role in assessing the evidence and reaching a verdict.

The need for effective verbal and nonverbal communication is evident throughout the trial. Attorneys must be clear and concise when addressing the court, especially in communication with jurors who have limited experience in legal terminology or courtroom procedures. As noted earlier, communication is largely conveyed nonverbally. Accordingly, the ability to speak clearly and "visually appeal" to those in the courtroom is important. This point should be noted by defense attorneys, who should prepare their clients for trial, for instance, by telling them how they should dress for and act in the courtroom. Jury members are often unfamiliar with legal terminology and the overall legal culture of the courtroom. Enhanced use of interpreters would help, as would an overall assessment/evaluation of the jury process to determine what would improve it.

Much of the needed change with regard to trials and, more generally, our criminal justice system, stems from the misuse of individual discretion. As evidenced throughout this book, discretion is inherent in the criminal justice system. Although most criminal justice professionals use their discretion in a very professional manner, there remains controversy when one makes decisions that appear to, or are intended to, negatively impact certain groups.

⚔ Sentencing

What purposes are to be served through criminal sentences? The primary purposes of criminal sanctions include offender rehabilitation, retribution, deterrence, and incapacitation. **Rehabilitation** involves attempts to "cure" or "fix" the ills leading to the offender's behavior. **Retribution,** or punishment, adopts the "eye for an eye" approach. **Deterrence** seeks to dissuade the offender (specific deterrence) or society in general (general deterrence) from engaging in acts for which the offender is being punished. **Incapacitation** involves physically preventing one from committing similar criminal acts in the future. Incarceration is the most widely used form of incapacitation. Each sentence has a purpose or perhaps several purposes. For instance, a judge who orders an offender to life in prison without the possibility of parole is intent on incapacitation and/or retribution. The drug offender who receives treatment is targeted for rehabilitation. Multiple goals may be evident in a criminal sentence. For example, the offender who receives house arrest has likely been targeted for punishment and rehabilitation.

Do the courts deal too harshly or not harshly enough with regard to crime? A recent survey of U.S. citizens asked subjects about the severity of treatment in our courts. Several significant findings emerged, including minorities being twice as likely as Whites to believe our courts treat those in our courts "too harshly." Males, younger respondents, those with a low level of education, and those with low annual incomes concurred, suggesting our courts are too punitive toward those who are processed in the system.[56] Of note, it seems those most affected by the courts are the ones most likely to be critical of courtroom practices.

Discriminatory Sentencing?

Males and minorities have been largely overrepresented in the criminal justice system. A report from the Bureau of Justice Statistics noted that although males comprised 48% of the United States' population in 2002, they constituted 83% of those convicted of a felony and 89% of those convicted of a violent crime. Blacks constituted about 13% of the U.S. population, yet 37% of those convicted of a felony. Whites comprised about 82% of the population, yet only 60% of those convicted of a felony. A greater percentage of Blacks than Whites were convicted of felonious murder (51% of Blacks compared to 45% of Whites), robbery (59% compared to 39%), and weapon offenses (50% compared to 47%).[57] These numbers do not directly indicate discrimination in criminal courts or, more generally, criminal justice practices. They do, however, generate discussion regarding the possibility of differential treatment of groups and at the very least highlight the overrepresentation of males and Blacks in the criminal justice system.

Early research on the sentencing of minorities suggested discrimination in the types of sentences and sentence severity, but recent research has produced conflicting findings. For example, the research literature provides conflicting results regarding the possibility of discrimination against Native Americans sentenced in court.[58] Several studies find that Blacks receive harsher sentences than Whites, while other findings suggest the opposite is true. Still, some findings suggest no differences in sentencing practices with regard to race.

If sentencing practices are unbiased, why are a disproportionate number of minorities entering our prisons? An obvious response concerns socioeconomic status. While race may not be evident in sentencing decisions, one's socioeconomic status certainly influences the likelihood of being incarcerated. The disparity with which minorities are incarcerated is explained, in large part, by unfavorable social conditions faced by many minorities. Further, the sentencing structures appear to unfavorably influence poor minorities. Thus, discrimination may not be evident in the actions of those imposing sentences; instead, it may be located within the structural components of criminal sentencing.

Sentencing Structures

Sentencing is perhaps the most controversial aspect of courtroom practices, primarily because it is the most obvious. We can easily view the penalties received by various individuals in relation to their demographics, the crime(s) they committed, and their criminal history. Historically, judges maintained wide latitude in sentencing practices. But beginning in the late 1960s and early 1970s, conservatives and liberals, albeit for different reasons, agreed that sentencing reform was needed. The indeterminate sentencing structure that existed provided too much discretion. Both liberals and conservatives agreed that consistency was needed; conservatives pointed to judges giving sentences that were too lenient, while liberals believed punishments were too harsh. It was agreed that determinate sentencing would reduce disparity and alleviate discrimination.[59]

A number of states have adopted **determinate sentencing** practices that involve offenders receiving a specific amount of time to be served based on the crime for which they were convicted. Determinate sentencing differs from indeterminate sentencing, which relies on parole board determinations regarding an offender's readiness for reentry to society. The move to determinate sentencing is typically accompanied by the elimination of parole.[60] Instead of relying on discretionary release from a parole board, offenders processed in jurisdictions using mandatory release are free to leave prison upon expiration of their sentence minus "good time." Good time is time taken off of a prison sentence for good behavior. Determinate sentencing was designed to reduce discretion in the courts and help ensure equal treatment for all.

Early efforts toward determinate sentencing suffered because legislative bodies lacked the resources to enact detailed sentencing rules.[61] Since the 1980s, legislatures have created commissions to look into sentencing practices. Among the developments are sentencing guidelines, which are used by courts in about half of the states and by all federal courts. The guidelines provide a risk assessment of the offender based on current offense and past history. The ultimate goal is to ensure justice with limited discretion. However, sentencing guidelines prompt enhanced sentencing severity, and federal sentencing guidelines are highly controversial.[62] The controversy stems from the belief that sentencing guidelines are harsh, haven't reduced sentencing disparities between minorities and nonminorities, and are too rigid and complex.[63] State guidelines are less controversial than the federal provisions, as state courts make adjustments to accommodate particular cases and provide judges a sense of discretion as needed.

Sentencing guidelines appear to shift discretion from judges to prosecutors. The guidelines have increased the proportion of minority defendants adjudicated in federal courts, as prosecutors increasingly choose to adjudicate cases at the federal level where penalties are harsher than in state courts. Prosecutors are also more frequently filing charges in federal court with marginal cases that wouldn't have been worth the effort in state court.[64] Consideration of prior criminal record in sentencing guidelines leaves minorities at a disadvantage compared to nonminorities, who are less likely to have a criminal history.[65]

In the 1970s, legislators responded to public sentiment that prison sentences are too lenient by imposing **mandatory minimum sentencing.**[66] Mandatory minimums require offenders convicted of certain offenses to be sentenced to prison for no less than a specified term of years, and nonprison sentences (e.g., probation) are not an option. Mandatory minimum sentences are typically imposed on violent offenders. Similar to sentencing guidelines, mandatory minimum sentencing has generated criticism. African Americans are disproportionately impacted by these laws primarily due to their overrepresentation in drug offenses and the disparity in sentences given to offenses involving crack cocaine.[67]

Between 1993 and 1995, many states imposed varied versions of **"three strikes and you're out"** sentences targeted toward repeat offenders. The legislation demonstrates the public's disdain for crime and an attempt to target those who seem undeterred by criminal law and punishment. Three strikes laws vary among the states that use them, with offenders in certain jurisdictions facing life sentences following conviction for a third felony. The idea behind the legislation and its application are popular, yet implementation of the legislation has posed several problems, especially for minorities, who are overrepresented as second and third strike offenders.[68] One researcher commented on the "draconian results" associated with the penalties, in which some offenders, especially minorities, have received notably stringent penalties for minor offenses.[69] Further, one cannot ignore the influence of the legislation on many offenders who don't commit a third offense until late in their criminal careers. The costs associated with the laws are also problematic as offenders serve longer sentences. Further, three strikes laws arguably increase the risks for police officers as "two strike" defendants being pursued by officers may be willing to attempt escape at all costs.[70]

In his article "The Impact of Federal Sentencing Reforms on African Americans," Marvin D. Free Jr., an associate professor of sociology at the University of Wisconsin–Whitewater, commented on the influences of sentencing practices in stating that "neither mandatory minimum sentences nor the guidelines have been effective in eliminating racial disparity in sentencing in federal court."[71] The disparity is affected by drug laws, especially with regard to the harsher penalties for crack cocaine than for powder cocaine. Selective law enforcement on the streets also impacts the disparity.[72] Recent sentencing reform involving determinate sentencing and sentencing guidelines has reduced the likelihood of overt discrimination in the courts, yet discriminatory sentencing practices have not disappeared.[73]

Scholar Samuel Walker and colleagues identified four reasons why African American and Hispanic defendants receive harsher penalties than their White counterparts.[74] First, differences in sentence severity could be explained by African Americans and Hispanics committing more serious crimes, and having more serious criminal histories, than Whites. Second, the differences could be explained through economic discrimination, with poor defendants (typically minorities) receiving differential treatment in the courts, for instance, in that they are typically unable to secure private counsel or pretrial release. Third, blatant racial or ethnic discrimination on behalf of those involved in sentencing could explain the disparity. Finally, contextual discrimination could exist, in the sense that minorities are treated differently upon being sentenced for certain crimes (e.g., violent crimes). Each explanation has merit and combined they largely explain the disparity in sentencing. The first argument, that minorities commit more serious crimes and are thus punished more severely than Whites, is the only one of the four explanations that doesn't involve some form of discrimination.

As suggested in Chapter 3 of this book, evidence suggests that racial minorities have disproportionately received the death penalty. Accordingly, in his book *No Equal Justice,* Georgetown University Law Professor David Cole stated, "Virtually every study of race and the death penalty has concluded that, all other things being equal, defendants who kill white victims are much more likely to receive the death penalty than those who kill black victims."[75] Recent efforts to reform the application of the death penalty, beginning with the 1972 Supreme Court case *Furman v. Georgia,*[76] provide perhaps the best evidence of the discrepancies found in its application.

The preceding discussion of multiculturalism and sentencing, and more generally our court system, has focused primarily on African American and Hispanics. This is not to disregard the plight of many other underrepresented groups who enter our courts. The research in this area, especially with regard to sentencing, focuses primarily on Blacks, with less information on Hispanics and even less information on other groups.

Appellate Courts

Defendants have the right to appeal following their conviction. Accordingly, U.S. courts can be categorized based on their trial or appellate jurisdiction. Among other functions, appellate courts help protect defendants' rights according to state or federal constitutions, criminal court procedural law, and substantive law.

Most criminal cases do not involve an appeal given the large percentage of cases settled by plea bargaining. Defendants forfeit their right to appeal following the admission of guilt, although they can appeal the sentence unless it was part of the plea bargain. Appeals involve the legal issues surrounding the trial, often focusing on issues such as the introduction of illegally seized evidence, improper jury instructions, and denial of competent counsel or a fair trial.[77]

Although defendants have the right to counsel during the appellate stage, many of the same limitations faced by underrepresented groups in the trial court jurisdiction appear in the appellate court system. Discretion is inherent in the appellate process, and historical evidence suggests that groups have received differential treatment. For example, researchers found that a defendant's race significantly influenced an appellate court's decision to uphold a trial court's decision in which a judge departed from the sentence recommended by guidelines.[78]

High levels of judicial and attorney discretion exist in the appellate courts. For instance, discretion is involved with appellate court judges' determining the significance of alleged errors at trial. The **harmless error doctrine** holds that a trial court decision will not be overturned based on small, insignificant errors that appear to have little or no impact on the outcome of the trial. The term "harmless" is certainly subjective and open to interpretation by appellate judges. In practice, technical errors recognized as worthy of appeal by defendants are often treated by appellate courts as harmless and not worthy of reversing trial court decisions.[79]

⚔ Multiculturalism and Courtroom Personnel

Thus far this chapter has focused predominantly on the role of underrepresented groups who enter our courts. What about members of the various cultural groups working in our courts? Have minorities assimilated into the courtroom workgroup? Are they treated differently than nonminorities? Do they act differently? Progress has been made toward increasing the diversity of those working in our court system. Affirmative action programs have increased the presence of historically underrepresented groups, and it is anticipated that greater representation is forthcoming.

The lack of diversity working in the courts is well documented in the research literature. Systematic discrimination targeting females and minorities in the legal arena has been endemic in the United States.[80] Such discrimination has occurred formally, for instance, via the choices and actions of courts, legislatures, law schools, and bar associations to disallow or discourage minorities from entering the legal profession and informally through mistreating minorities in the legal field.[81]

A report by the American Bar Association found that minority judges made up only 10.1% of those presiding over state supreme courts, intermediate appellate courts, and trial courts of general jurisdiction. African Americans (5.9%) constituted the largest percentage of minority judges across the three levels of courts, followed by Latino/a (2.8%) and Asian/Pacific Islander (1.1%) judges.[82] These percentages suggest that greater diversity is needed on the bench. Further disparity exists with regard to the percentages of lawyers and others working in the courts, such as paralegals and legal assistants. In 2007, only 4.9% of lawyers were African American, followed by Hispanic or Latino/a (4.3%) and Asian (2.6%) attorneys. Females

Greater levels of ethnic and racial diversity are needed in our courts. Minority groups are notably underrepresented as judges.

(32.6%) were also underrepresented. Hispanic or Latino/as were more likely than other minority groups to work as paralegals or legal assistants in 2007, although other groups appear underrepresented, including African Americans (9.7%) and Asians (3.4%).[83] Minorities are severely underrepresented in private law firms, particularly as associates and partners.[84]

Why are minorities underrepresented as professionals in the courts? Edward Chen, the first Asian American judge appointed to the federal bench for the Northern District of California—despite the significant number of Asian Americans in the area—noted that the lack of diversity in the judiciary is attributable to several factors. Prominent among the factors are the lack of diversity in the pool of experienced attorneys, the influences of political ties negatively affecting minorities, and the limited access of networking for minorities.[85]

Why do we need greater diversity in the courts? To begin, greater diversity promotes greater cultural sensitivity and comprehension of the varied issues addressed in the courts. Courtroom personnel may be able to recognize differences within their objective context, as opposed to at face value. Further, greater diversity promotes respect for the courts from underrepresented groups. Minorities are more likely than Whites to view the courts with apprehension. Past discriminatory practices could be mended, in part, if it appeared that our court system wasn't primarily staffed with nonminorities. Used in this context, the term **symbolic representation** refers to making our courts more representative of all groups.[87] In other words, the

MULTICULTURALISM IN THE WORKFORCE

Failing to promote a multicultural workforce is costly in many aspects. Popular shoe manufacturer Nike recently found out how financially costly it can be. Roughly 400 former and current employees of Niketown Chicago won a class action suit against Nike, and will share an estimated $5 million after attorney fees, or about $12,500 each. The suit, settled in July 2007, was filed after workers claimed that African American employees were treated unfairly by Nike supervisors. The suit claimed that African American workers were treated more harshly than other employees, were refused benefits even though they worked 20 or 30 hours weekly, and were less often promoted from the stockroom to the sales floor than other employees.

The case was generated by two Nike workers who complained to managers that they weren't being treated fairly. One of the workers, Keith Smith, was fired shortly after he complained about the treatment to his managers. In 2002 Smith filed a report with the Illinois Department of Human Rights and the Equal Employment Opportunity Commission (EEOC). In late 2003 the EEOC granted Smith permission to proceed with the litigation. Smith decided to file a class action suit with the goal of protecting a larger pattern of bias against African Americans working for Nike.

In reaching a settlement agreement, Nike denied the allegations and admitted no wrongdoing but settled the case to avoid continued and prolonged litigation. The company agreed, however, to provide diversity training for supervisors and managers at Niketown Chicago, review and revise the store's human resources and other policies, and permit an independent monitor to report on compliance. Nike also agreed to name a compliance officer and establish a mentoring program for African American employees.[86]

perceived legitimacy of the courts would be enhanced through greater diversity among courtroom personnel.

Recent efforts to promote diversity on the bench have resulted in greater representation of minority judges and an opportunity to better understand the behaviors of minority judges in the courtroom. There are conflicting research results regarding the practices of minority and nonminority judges. One study found that African American and White judges considered case and offender information similarly when imposing punishment decisions. Black judges were more likely than White judges to impose a prison sentence on both Black and White offenders. The more punitive approach taken by Black judges may be attributable to their perceptions of themselves as "tokens," or it may be that they maintain greater sensitivity to the harms associated with crime.[88]

Researchers found conflicting results when comparing the sentencing and incarceration practices of Black and White judges. White judges were more likely than Black judges to treat White defendants leniently. Little discrimination was found with regard to sentence severity. However, White judges treated Black and White defendants equally severely. Black judges treated Black defendants more leniently than they treated White defendants.[89] With regard to gender, early research found that female judges were more likely than male judges to treat men and women defendants equally.[90]

Research on judicial practices in Detroit identified few differences with regard to race and judicial behavior. There were notable similarities in the sentencing practices of both Black and White judges, with race offering limited significant predictive powers with regard to judicial sentencing practices. It was found that both Black and White judges sentenced Black defendants more severely than their White counterparts.[91] The similarities in sentencing practices could be attributed to the judicial recruitment process, which produces a somewhat homogeneous judiciary with regard to judicial practices. The socialization practices of judges certainly influence the behaviors of all who sit on the bench.[92]

Defendants should, and do, consider cultural factors in choosing a bench or jury trial. For instance, given public sentiment, an Arab American charged with robbery shortly after the September 11, 2001, terrorist attacks may have had a better chance of receiving a fair trial absent a jury. However, one cannot discard the accelerated level of judicial discretion inherent in bench trials. It is hoped that judges are better able than jurors to put aside biases and/or personal beliefs in favor of professionalism.

✂ A Time for Change

While this discussion of the U.S. court system and multiculturalism centers on criminal courts, one cannot overlook the accomplishments of federal civil courts in shaping state and local criminal justice practices with regard to diversity. Several areas of federal civil legislation have important consequences for criminal justice officials. The more significant legislation relates to

- civil rights violations, which enable individuals to sue civilly city or state employees who deprive them of their constitutional rights;
- equal employment opportunities, which prohibit discrimination based on race, color, religion, sex, age, or national origin;

- sex discrimination; and
- discrimination against the disabled, which protects Americans with disabilities from discrimination in employment in the use of public facilities and services.[93]

Steven Vago, author of the book *Law and Society,* stated that "racism is embedded in the system and proponents recognize that its elimination is impossible but at the same time they insist that an ongoing struggle to countervail racism must be carried out."[94] To be sure, disparity and discrimination in the courtroom are not restricted to one's race, as gender, ethnicity, cultural, and socioeconomic factors influence discretionary practices at all stages of the system. As an example, minority women face special concerns upon entering the criminal justice system, particularly given their high rates of poverty and unemployment, and the increased likelihood of them being a single parent. Unfortunately, the plight of minority women who enter our courts has been the subject of scant research efforts. What we do know about this group suggests differential treatment of minority women in the courts and throughout the criminal justice system.[95]

Much has changed in our courts, as numerous reforms directed at leveling the playing field for minorities and all groups have influenced courtroom practices and personnel. Nevertheless, much work remains. It is hoped that recognizing and highlighting the problems and accomplishments provides an impetus for continued progress.

Summary

The American court system is symbolic of many things: justice, freedoms, individual rights, and so on. Too often, however, our courtrooms are places where injustices restrict freedoms and violate individual rights. As noted throughout this chapter, such unfortunate situations disproportionately involve members from minority groups and occur throughout criminal case processing.

Criminal case processing consists of an initial appearance, preliminary/grand jury hearings, arraignments, trials, sentencing, and appeals. Much evidence suggests that cultural, racial, and ethnic diversity impacts decisions made throughout case processing. To what extent and why diversity impacts courtroom decisions remains in question. However, it is certain that compared to Whites, minority groups often face particular challenges when charged with a crime. Prominent among these challenges are biases in decisions by judges to grant pretrial release and the conditions under which individuals are to be released; jury selection practices; and sentencing practices, particularly the manner in which many states structure their sentencing practices.

Historically, our courts were staffed with White males. While White males remain the most common demographic group in our courts, women and other minorities are becoming increasingly represented among those working in courtrooms. Nevertheless, greater diversity is needed in the courtroom. Given demographic changes in society, it is expected that the personnel staffing future courtrooms will look different from those currently working in the courts. Such change holds the potential to reduce any biases against minorities.

You Make the Call

Courtroom Controversy

Consider the following scenario. Debate the pros and cons of all options and decide what you would do.

You're a public defender assigned to represent a defendant who is charged with 15 counts of animal cruelty involving the sacrificing of cats. The defendant claims the sacrifices were part of his religious practices and that he has not done anything illegal. He cites his constitutional right to freedom of religion. Professionally, you have an obligation to provide appropriate representation for your client. Personally, you're an animal lover. Particularly, you love cats and have four of them. You're familiar with the judge presiding over this case. She also loves animals. The prosecuting attorney in this case is a member of the People for the Ethical Treatment of Animals (PETA).

Questions

1. Does your client enter court at a disadvantage?
2. Will you be able to put aside your personal feelings and provide effective counsel for the accused?
3. Should you decline to defend the client (if possible) and/or request a new judge?
4. Do you encourage your client to plea bargain, request a bench trial, or take a chance with a jury trial?

Key Terms

adjudicatory process (p. 261)
affirmative defense (p. 264)
alibi (p. 264)
arraignment (p. 259)
assigned counsel (p. 256)
bench trial (p. 259)
Black rage (p. 264)
challenge for cause (p. 262)
determinate sentencing (p. 268)
deterrence (p. 266)
discovery (p. 259)
Federal Jury Selection and Service
    Act of 1968 (p. 261)
grand jury hearing (p. 258)
harmless error doctrine (p. 270)
incapacitation (p. 267)
indictment (p. 258)
indigent defendants (p. 256)

initial appearance (p. 255)
judge's charge to the jury (p. 264)
jury nullification (p. 265)
mandatory minimum sentencing (p. 269)
nolo contendere (p. 259)
peremptory challenge (p. 263)
plea bargaining (p. 259)
preliminary hearing (p. 258)
pretrial motions (p. 260)
pretrial release (p. 257)
public defenders (p. 256)
rehabilitation (p. 266)
retribution (p. 266)
summons (p. 262)
symbolic representation (p. 272)
"three strikes and you're out"
    sentencing (p. 269)
venire (p. 261)

Discussion Questions

1. Identify and discuss the steps of the trial. Which step do you believe involves the greatest area of controversy with regard to discrimination? Why?
2. Identify how judicial, prosecutorial, and defense attorney discretion influences the outcome of court cases.
3. How are jurors selected? Does this process seem fair to you? Discuss why or why not.
4. How have recent sentencing reform efforts failed to eliminate disparity in sentencing? What steps would you take to improve sentencing practices?
5. Are racial and ethnic minorities adequately represented among the courtroom personnel? If not, what steps could be taken to diversify the courts?

Endnotes

1. Durose, M. R., and Langan, P. A. 2004, December. *Felony Sentences in State Courts, 2002.* Bureau of Justice Statistics. NCJ 206916. Washington, DC: U.S. Department of Justice.
2. Norgren, J., and Nanda, S. 1988. *American Cultural Pluralism and Law.* New York: Praeger. P. 1.
3. Ibid.
4. Norgren and Nanda 1988.
5. Tuchman, G. 1979. "Let's Hold Trials Here in Spanish." *New York Times,* August 28, p. A17.
6. Willing, R. 2004. "Courts Asked to Consider Culture." *USA Today,* May 25, p. 3A.
7. Ibid.
8. Ibid.
9. Cohen, T. H., and Reaves, B. A. 2006, February. *Felony Defendants in Large Urban Counties, 2002.* Bureau of Justice Statistics. NCJ 210818. Washington, DC: U.S. Department of Justice.
10. Walker, S., Spohn, C., and DeLone, M. 2004. *The Color of Justice,* 3rd ed. Belmont, CA: Wadsworth.
11. Ibid., p. 172.
12. *Gideon v. Wainwright,* 372 U.S. 335 (1963).
13. *Johnson v. Zerbst,* 304 U.S. 458 (1938).
14. Schmalleger, F. 2005. *Criminal Justice Today: An Introductory Text for the 21st Century.* Upper Saddle River, NJ: Prentice Hall. Pp. 392–393.
15. Harlow, C. W. 2000, November. *Defense Counsel in Criminal Cases.* Bureau of Justice Statistics. NCJ 179023. Washington, DC: U.S. Department of Justice.
16. Gershman, B. L. 1999. "Themes of Injustice: Wrongful Convictions, Racial Prejudice, and Lawyer Incompetence." In L. Stolzenberg and S. J. D'Alessio (eds.), *Criminal Courts for the 21st Century,* pp. 354–363. Upper Saddle River, NJ: Prentice Hall. P. 360.
17. Cole, D. 1999. *No Equal Justice: Race and Class in the American Criminal Justice System.* New York: The New Press. P. 89.
18. Ibid., p. 64.
19. Ibid., p. 76.
20. Walker, Spohn, and DeLone 2004.
21. Ibid., p. 157.
22. Ibid., p. 162.
23. Kappeler, V. E., and Potter, G. W. 2005. *The Mythology of Crime and Criminal Justice,* 4th ed. Long Grove, IL: Waveland. P. 274.
24. Turner, K. B., and Johnson, J. B. 2005. "A Comparison of Bail Amounts for Hispanics, Whites, and African Americans: A Single County Analysis." *American Journal of Criminal Justice* 30 (1): 35–53.

25. Neubauer, D. W. 2005. *America's Courts and the Criminal Justice System,* 8th ed. Belmont, CA: Wadsworth.
26. Burns, R. G. 2007. *The Criminal Justice System.* Upper Saddle River, NJ: Prentice Hall. P. 41.
27. Neubauer 2005 p. 229.
28. Barkan, S. E., and Bryjak, G. J. 2004. *Fundamentals of Criminal Justice.* Boston: Allyn & Bacon. P. 301.
29. Cohen and Reaves 2006.
30. Walker, Spohn, and DeLone 2004. See Pp. 170–172 for discussion of race and plea bargaining decisions.
31. Cole 1999, p. 101.
32. Ibid.
33. Neubauer 2005.
34. Ibid.
35. Ibid.
36. Ibid., p. 312.
37. Ibid.
38. *Batson v. Kentucky,* 476 U.S. 79 (1986).
39. Cole 1999, p. 120.
40. Ibid.
41. Gershman 1999, p. 359.
42. Walker, Spohn, and DeLone 2004, p. 185.
43. Ibid., p. 197.
44. Burns 2007, p. 56.
45. Fagin, J. A. 2003. *Criminal Justice.* Boston: Allyn & Bacon. P. 328.
46. For example, Dattu, F. 1998. "Illustrated Jury Instructions." *Judicature* 82 (2): 79. See also Foglia, W. D. 2003. "They Know Not What They Do: Unguided and Misguided Discretion in Pennsylvania Capital Cases." *Justice Quarterly* 20 (1): 187–211.
47. Dattu 1998.
48. Burns 2007.
49. Samaha, J. 2005. *Criminal Procedure,* 6th ed. Belmont, CA: Wadsworth. P. 490.
50. Walker, Spohn, and DeLone 2004.
51. Samaha 2005.
52. Butler, P. 1995. "Racially Based Jury Nullification: Black Power in the Criminal Justice System." *Yale Law Journal* 105 (3): 677–725.
53. Kennedy, R. 1997. *Race, Crime, and the Law.* New York: Vintage.
54. Schmalleger, F. 2005. *Criminal Justice Today,* 8th ed. Upper Saddle River, NJ: Prentice Hall.
55. Willing, R. 2005. "Courts Try to Make Jury Duty Less of a Chore." *USA Today,* March 17, pp. 17A–18A.
56. *Sourcebook of Criminal Justice Statistics, 2003.* 2005. Bureau of Justice Statistics, U.S. Department of Justice. Washington, DC: U.S. Government Printing Office.
57. Durose and Langan 2004.
58. Walker, Spohn, and DeLone 2004.
59. Neubauer 2005.
60. Ibid.
61. Ibid.
62. Ibid.
63. Tonry, M. 1993. "The Failure of U.S. Sentencing Commission's Guidelines." *Crime & Delinquency,* 39: 131–149.
64. Free, M. D., Jr. 1997. "The Impact of Federal Sentencing Reforms on African Americans." *Journal of Black Studies* 28 (2): 268–286.
65. Ibid.
66. Neubauer 2005.
67. Free 1997.
68. Cole 1999.
69. Ibid., p. 147.
70. Ibid.
71. Free 1997, pp. 283–284.
72. Ibid.
73. Walker, Spohn, and DeLone 2004, p. 243.
74. Ibid., pp. 205–207.
75. Cole 1999, p. 132.
76. *Furman v. Georgia,* 408 U.S. 238, 245 (1972).
77. Burns 2007.
78. Williams, J. J. 1991. "Predicting Decisions Rendered in Criminal Appeals." *Journal of Criminal Justice* 19: 463–469.
79. Scheb, J. M., and Scheb, J. M., II. 2003. *Criminal Procedure,* 3rd ed. Belmont, CA: Wadsworth.
80. Hurwitz, M. S., and Lanier, D. N. 2003. "Explaining Judicial Diversity: The Differential Ability of Women and Minorities to Attain Seats on State Supreme and Appellate Courts." *State Politics and Policy Quarterly* 3 (4): 329–352. P. 329.

81. Ibid.
82. American Bar Association. "National Database on Diversity in State Courts: A National Report." www.abanet.org/judind/diversity/national.html (accessed February 16, 2008).
83. Bureau of Labor Statistics. 2007. "Household Data Annual Averages." www.bls.gov/cps/cpsaat11.pdf.
84. Johnson, A. M., Jr. 1997. "The Underrepresentation of Minorities in the Legal Profession: A Critical Race Theorist's Perspective." *Michigan Law Review* 95 (4): 1005–1062.
85. Chen, E. M. 2003. "The Judiciary, Diversity, and Justice For All." *California Law Review* 91: 1109–1124.
86. Rose, B. 2007, August 13. "Workers Took on Nike and Won." *Chicagotribune.com*. www.chicagotribune.com/business/chi-mon_spae1aug13,0,3309021.column (accessed August 21, 2007).
87. Welch, S., Combs, M., and Gruhl, J. 1988. "Do Black Judges Make a Difference?" *American Journal of Political Science* 32 (1): 126–136.
88. Steffensmeier, D., and Britt, C., L. 2001. "Judges' Race and Judicial Decision Making: Do Black Judges Sentence Differently?" *Social Science Quarterly* 82 (4): 749–764.
89. Welch, Combs, and Gruhl 1988, p. 126.
90. Gruhl, J., Welch, S., and Spohn, C. 1981. "Women as Policy Makers: The Case of Trial Judges." *American Journal of Political Science* 25: 308–322.
91. Spohn, C. 1990. "The Sentencing Decisions of Black and White Judges: Expected and Unexpected Similarities." *Law & Society Review* 24 (5): 1197–1216.
92. Ibid.
93. Neubauer 2005, p. 62.
94. Vago, S. 2003. *Law and Society,* 7th ed. Upper Saddle River, NJ: Prentice Hall. P. 71.
95. Mann 1989.

Corrections and Multiculturalism

Chapter Objectives

After reading this chapter, you should be able to

❖ Recognize the significance of multiculturalism with regard to institutional corrections.

❖ Identify and discuss the significance of cultural diversity as it relates to prison life.

❖ Understand the challenges associated with incarceration.

❖ Recognize the importance of cultural diversity as it pertains to community corrections.

❖ Understand the significance of ensuring that correctional staff is aware of and tolerant of cultural diversity.

Enforcing formal social control over those convicted of crimes is no easy task, and current correctional practices in the United States generate controversy. The controversy largely stems from the lack of directed goals with regard to many correctional practices, the limited capacity of correctional practices to "correct" human behavior, and the problems stemming from the multicultural makeup of our correctional system. With regard to multicultural makeup, it is well documented that the demographics of those under correctional supervision are unlike the demographics of society in general. The diversity within our correctional system coupled with controversial correctional practices makes for interesting study and is the focus of this chapter.

It is argued that heterogeneous countries, in which citizens differ based on race, ethnicity, religion, and other traits, are more punitive in nature than are homogeneous countries. Support for this argument is found in imprisonment rates in the 1990s during which the United States, Russia, and South Africa led all other nations in the rate of incarceration. All three countries faced difficulties related to multiculturalism, compounded in the case of Russia and South Africa by changing government regimes. Law and punishment were increasingly used to formally control the disorder and conflict found in these countries.[1]

In recent years the United States has increasingly relied on incarceration and punishment as means to address crime. These approaches have disproportionately impacted many lower-class minority communities, which have suffered in numerous ways, such as the loss of husbands and fathers to prison. While it is argued that imprisonment and overall correctional practices help protect society, we must remember that most offenders eventually return to the same communities and environments in which they committed their offense. Some may have been "corrected"; however, there are many who return to society to face the same difficulties they faced prior to correctional intervention. Their problems are often amplified in various means, not the least of which involves being labeled a "criminal" or an "ex-con."

The status change from accused to offender leads to those under correctional supervision being viewed as criminals. In other words, upon being convicted they lose their status as "innocent until proven guilty." Offenders are often recognized by society as law violators who must be punished. Accordingly, our correctional system deals with individuals who maintain the lowest status of all who enter the criminal justice system. Upon release these same individuals will continue to be looked down upon by society. This is but one of the many challenges faced by those entering corrections.

The complexities of more frequently interacting with diverse groups and individuals are another difficulty faced by those under correctional supervision. Prison inmates face many struggles associated with being incarcerated, including contending with cultural biases. The situation is enhanced in jails, where the classification of inmates is less of a concern than in prisons. To increase the likelihood of success in community corrections, probationers, parolees, and the officers who supervise offenders in the community must overcome cultural differences. Discussion of multiculturalism and corrections becomes more important as the number of individuals under correctional supervision increases and subsequently diversifies.

This chapter addresses multiculturalism and corrections by focusing on the main components of corrections: institutionalization in the forms of prisons and jails and community corrections in the forms of probation and parole. This discussion is preceded by an observation of the organization and structure of corrections and characteristics of those under correctional supervision. The chapter concludes with a look at how cultural diversity impacts correctional staff.

✕ The Organization of Corrections

The organization of correctional agencies is complex, due to the varied approaches comprising corrections and the different practices adopted by the 50 states and the federal government. Perhaps the best way to summarize the organization of corrections is to begin with observation of corrections at the federal level and follow with examination of how states organize their correctional practices.

The **Federal Bureau of Prisons,** which is within the Department of Justice, operates 114 institutions and 28 community corrections offices. It oversees roughly 193,000 offenders convicted of federal offenses. Included in these facilities are detention centers, which, similar to jails, hold those awaiting trial. The approximately 35,000 employees responsible for the day-to-day functioning of the Bureau are spread throughout the United States.[2] The **U.S. Probation and Pretrial Services System** is responsible for several tasks, not the least of which is assisting the federal courts with pretrial practices and supervising federal probationers. The **Federal Parole Commission** oversees federal parolees.

The organization of state correctional facilities is more complex, as each state designs its organizational structure. **Prisons** are state-run correctional facilities administered by the executive branch of each state government. They hold inmates serving sentences of one year or more. **Jails** hold detainees awaiting trial and those sentenced to incarceration for less than a year. In most states, jails are operated by county-level officials, mostly sheriff's departments. The organization of **probation** and **parole,** both forms of **community corrections** in which offenders are supervised in the community, is quite elaborate. Among the issues of concern with regard to probation is whether it should be organized in a centralized or decentralized manner; administered by the executive branch or the judiciary; or combined with parole services.[3] States vary in their approach to these issues, as they consider what works best with regard to their resources and culture. Parole is administered by state parole boards, which may or may not work in conjunction with probation services. State correctional systems oversee far more offenders than the federal system as most crimes are prosecuted at the state level.

⚔ The Correctional Population

Corrections in the United States took an interesting turn beginning in the early 1980s. Crime control became a primary focus and greater use of incarceration was a significant part of the approach. Enhanced focus on incarceration increased the number of individuals who have ever been incarcerated by nearly 3.8 million between 1974 and 2001. Much of the impact was felt by minority groups, as Blacks (39%) and Hispanics (18%) constituted the majority of those who had ever served time in prison as of 2001. Whites accounted for only 39% of those ever incarcerated as of 2001, down from 51% in 1974. Projections based on this trend data suggest that 6.6% of all persons born in 2001 will go to prison should current rates of first incarceration remain unchanged.[4]

At year-end 2001, about 1 in every 37 U.S. adults had served time in prison. This rate is not equally distributed among all groups. Gender and minority status are certainly related to incarceration rates. As an example, the rate of ever having gone to prison was much higher for adult Black males (16.6%) than for Hispanic (7.7%) and White (2.6%) males. This pattern held true for adult female inmates, as adult Black females (1.7%) were far more likely than Hispanic (0.7%) and White (0.3%) females to have served time in prison.[5]

The U.S. Bureau of Justice Statistics (BJS) provides the most accurate demographic account of prison and jail inmates. Recent reports suggest that over 2.1 million persons are incarcerated in U.S. prisons and jails, with prisons holding roughly two-thirds of the population. State prisons saw their population increase 1.2% from June 2004 to June 2005, while the federal prison population increased 2.9%. Admission to state prison rose 11.5% from 2000 to 2004, while admission to federal prisons rose 21.2%.[6] Such a large increase in the number of inmates suggests that incarceration plays a significant role in formal social control. The annual rate of growth for female inmates between 1995 and 2005 was 4.7%, higher than the 3.0% increase for males.[7]

Concerns for multiculturalism in corrections arise when one considers that as of June 2005, there were 91,117 noncitizens under the supervision of state or federal correctional authorities. Noncitizens constituted 6.4% of state and federal inmates. Further, although females are far less likely than males to end up in prison (they account for only 7.0% of all prisoners), their presence in prison is growing.

Perhaps the most significant issue with regard to multiculturalism and incar-
tion involves the overrepresentation of African Americans. As of June 2005,
inmates in local jails were ethnic or racial minorities, with Blacks comprising
% and Hispanics accounting for 15.0%. White inmates constituted 44.3% of jail
es. Overall, about 12% of all Black males, 3.7% of all Hispanic males, and
of all White males in their late twenties were incarcerated. Perhaps the most
notable finding is that there were 4,682 Black male inmates in state/federal prisons
and local jails per 100,000 Black residents, compared to rates of 709 for Whites and
1,856 for Hispanics.[8]

Probation is widely used in corrections. Probationers have accounted for over
half of the total growth in the correctional population since 1990. A BJS report noted
that over 4.1 million probationers were supervised in the community in 2005, an
increase of 2.5% since 1995. Most of those on probation were male (77%), although
the rate of female probationers is increasing. Most probationers were White (55%),
followed by Black (30%) and Hispanic (13%) probationers.[9]

The parole population experienced a 15.4% increase between 1995 and 2005.
Over 784,000 adult men and women were on parole or mandatory release at the end
of 2005. Women are increasingly represented among parole cases, comprising 12% of
those on parole in 2005 compared to 10% in 1995. Of particular interest with regard
to multicultural issues is that the percentage of Blacks on parole decreased during the
same period, dropping from 45% of all parolees in 1995 to 40% in 2005. The percentage of Whites on parole increased during this period, up from 34% in 1995 to 41% in
2005. Hispanics constituted 18% of those on parole at the end of 2005.[10]

These numbers provide an overview of those incarcerated and those on probation and parole. They say little of why these individuals ended up under correctional
supervision and the difficulties they face. Nonetheless, the numbers provide a foundation for examination of multiculturalism as it relates to corrections. Knowing who
is incarcerated or being supervised in the community facilitates discussion of the
multicultural issues that exist within corrections.

⚔ Incarceration

Incarceration, or the physical detention of an inmate, exists primarily in two forms:
prison and jail. These institutions have much in common, yet they differ in several
ways. Prominent among the differences is the length of sentence served by those
incarcerated. Jails typically hold those serving a sentence of less than one year, while
prisons hold those serving a sentence of a year or more. Another significant difference is the clientele. Jails hold those unconvicted awaiting trial and those convicted
of crimes. Prisons do not hold unconvicted individuals. The demographics of jail and
prison inmates are somewhat similar in the sense that one typically does not get to
prison without having first entered jail. Accordingly, many of the issues associated
with prisons are found in jails and vice versa.

Inmates face numerous difficulties upon being incarcerated. The challenges
are so severe that several guidebooks for surviving prison life are available.[11] The
loss of liberty, goods and services, autonomy, heterosexual relationships, and security are prominent among the deprivations faced by the incarcerated.[12] In his book

The Warehouse Prison, John Irwin, professor emeritus at San Francisco State University, identifies some of the main sources of harm in the modern warehouse prison, where inmates are stockpiled much like merchandise in a department store warehouse. Particularly, Irwin cites the troubles associated with health and disease, psychological damages, and prisonization,[13] or an inmate's adaptation to the prison culture. Each of these issues makes prison life profoundly different from life outside of prison.

Female inmates face additional challenges, including concerns related to lack of privacy, separation from their children, pregnancy, inadequate clothing and hygiene, a loss of dignity, ineffective programming to meet the needs of female inmates, damage to mental and physical health, strict enforcement of prison rules, and difficulty in maintaining psychological and physical safety.[14] Needless to say, institutionalization generates significant changes and demands, including forced daily interaction with individuals from diverse cultures.

Inmates from different ethnic and religious groups often have a dislike for each other, which sometimes leads to violent encounters and promotes greater separation among the groups.[15] Inmates will further gravitate to those of a similar culture as dividing lines are drawn.[16] Accordingly, jail and prison administrators need to strategically house inmates within facilities and recognize that cultural factors influence staff and inmate safety and well-being.

Violence among inmates is of utmost concern for correctional officials. Prison rape is often mentioned with regard to prison violence, as the nature of institutionalization seems ripe for such attacks. Same-sex, regimented institutions such as prison tend to precipitate deviant sexual behavior.[17] It appears that inmate race is related to sexual violence in prison. It was found that Whites comprised 73% of victims of inmate-on-inmate prison and jail sexual violence, yet they were the perpetrators in only 43% of such incidents. Blacks constituted 12% of the victims and 39% of the perpetrators of such attacks.[18] Violence in prisons and jails extends beyond sexual attacks, and factors such as overcrowding, improper classification, and race relations certainly underlie much of the violence in prison. These and related issues, as they relate to prison and jail, are discussed below.

Prison

You're driving along the highway after having a few too many drinks. The next thing you know you wake up in a jail cell inhaling an odor you've never smelled, nor do you care to ever again. With a heavy head, you listen to the rumblings of the other jail inmates, none of whom seem to be like you, and none seems friendly. Eventually, a jailer approaches your cell, only to tell you that last night you crossed the highway dividing line and killed a passing driver. Your heart drops into your stomach as you realize what you've done. Then you realize the potential consequences of your actions, not the least of which involves taking an innocent victim's life and the fact that you're not, nor perhaps will you ever be, prepared for prison life.

You initially think and hope you'll receive a sentence of probation, as you've never been in trouble before. But, killing someone? That's pretty serious. Perhaps you can plea bargain for only a few years in prison. Still, you're not "prison material." What will you do upon entering prison, and how will you protect yourself?

What about your family? How will they get along without you? What will you do upon exiting prison?

Prison life poses many difficulties for those who enter. Consider the scenario described above. Picture the offender as a middle-class, White male enrolled in college. How do you perceive this individual faring in prison? How do you envision this individual will be upon exiting prison? Would you perceive the situation differently if the offending drunk driver were an African American male with a criminal history? Do you believe that person would have an easier time adjusting to prison life and life after prison? How would you fare in prison?

The detrimental effects of going to prison extend beyond the incarcerated individual. Families may struggle in response to the absence of a parent, and society, in general, may experience the effects of prisonization once the individual returns to the community following incarceration. It is reasonable to expect that inmates will bring some effects of prison life back into society upon their release.

The impacts of incarceration are many. Of particular interest is the absence of a parent. This concern notably influences Black inmates, who are far more likely than their White and Hispanic counterparts to have young children. Research on incarcerated parents found that roughly half of state prisoners who were parents were Black, followed by White (29%) and Hispanic inmates (19%). A similar pattern emerged in federal prison, although Hispanic inmates (30%) were more likely than White inmates (22%) to be parents. Forty-four percent of Black inmates in federal prisons were parents.[19] The absence of a parent poses numerous challenges for young children, particularly in relation to accountability, financial support, and overall family well-being.

Prisons maintain very diverse populations that provide challenges for all who work or stay in them.

Have you ever visited a prison? If so, did you consider racial, ethnic, and cultural issues as they pertain to social control? If you haven't visited a prison and are interested in criminal justice, you are encouraged to do so. Among the many interesting things you'll notice in prison is the diverse population under formal social control. Further, you'll notice a prisoner lifestyle that is likely much different from the one you live.

Prison Life

The prison life observed in most institutions differs from life on the outside in many facets. Prominent among the differences are the presence of a particular inmate subculture, recognition of the need to balance constitutional rights with concerns for safety and security, the enhanced influences of gang members, and the notable concerns surrounding the spread of communicable diseases. These and related issues continuously challenge prison officials, and the impact of those issues will increase as we rely on imprisonment as a primary form of social control.

Researchers have identified a subculture among prisoners that maintains characteristics different from those of society in general. For instance, **ultramasculinity,** or an emphasis on being strong, is a priority.[20] The **inmate code,** which involves the norms and values developed and stressed in prison, encourages toughness, insensitivity, and disdain and manipulation of fellow inmates and the prison staff. The inmate code generally varies among institutions, as does inmate commitment to the code. Nevertheless, a notable trend among institutions is the social organization of inmates along racial and ethnic lines.[21] White inmates, with few exceptions, associate with White inmates, Blacks with Blacks, and Hispanics with Hispanics.[22]

Prison staff trainees often ask why prisons accommodate a large number of religions.[23] The simple answer to the question involves respect for inmates' First Amendment right to religious freedom. Federal and state legislation may further define the religious freedom of inmates, and prison systems have policies and procedures designed to ensure that constitutional and statutory religious rights are recognized. The American Correctional Association's standards for accreditation require that inmates be provided the right to practice religion. Such practices should be considered with concern for institutional order and safety.

Religion offers an avenue of solidarity among inmates, provides a mechanism of adjustment to incarceration for some individuals,[24] and encourages rehabilitation and overall self-improvement. Religion also provides avenues of differences among inmates and staff and sometimes generates struggles in regard to multiculturalism. The Black Muslim movement and concerns from Native Americans with regard to their religious freedom in prisons were among the factors influencing how correctional officials recognize religious practices in prison. Over the years we've seen religion play an integral role in prison organization and overall prison practices.

Researchers have commented on the changing nature of gangs in prisons as a new generation of inmates is incarcerated. The more-established gangs remain active in prison, although several new groups have emerged largely in response to older gang members dropping out of gang life or being segregated from the other inmates.[25] These newer gangs, much like their predecessors, are heavily influenced by race and ethnicity. On the West coast, among the new Chicano and Latino gangs are the Norteños and the Sureños, which hail from northern and southern California. The Bloods and their traditional rival, the Crips, are still prominent among the Black prison gangs and are complemented by the 415s, a Black prison gang consisting of members hailing from the San Francisco Bay Area (415 is the telephone code for the area).[26]

To be sure, street and prison gangs are largely intertwined; involvement in gang life doesn't necessarily cease upon incarceration. Pressures emanating from gang involvement on the inside or outside of prison provide numerous difficulties for any attempts to correct criminal behavior. With regard to multiculturalism, the organization and practices of prison gangs certainly highlight the significance of race and ethnicity.

CULTURAL SOLIDARITY AMONG PRISON GANGS

Prison gangs increase the likelihood of violence in prison and strongly define the social structure of prison life. Gangs in prison are organized along hierarchical lines and typically have a creed or motto, symbols signifying membership, and a constitution that guides member behavior. Further, prison gangs are divisive, adversarial factions that are largely based along racial and ethnic lines.

The organization of prison gangs along racial and ethnic lines demonstrates the solidarity and commitment associated with various cultural groups. Examples of the divisive nature of prison gangs are found in Hispanic inmates assembling into gangs such as the Mexican Mafia and the Nuestra Familia, Black inmates belonging to the Black Guerilla Family, and White inmates being actively involved in the Aryan Brotherhood. The organization of gang-involved inmates according to race and ethnicity suggests that multiculturalism is not well accepted among inmates.[27]

The exclusivity and seclusion associated with prison gangs prohibits in-depth understanding of prison gangs in general. At face value, however, there is little doubt that prison gang members typically associate with those from a similar racial or ethnic background. While it is admirable that prison gang members remain committed to their ancestral heritage, aligning oneself with others simply based on race or ethnicity does little toward the advancement of multiculturalism. Almost all inmates who enter prison will return to society. Unfortunately for some former inmates, their time in prison will have been spent festering dislike and even hatred of others simply based on race or ethnicity. These feelings will likely remain within the individual as he or she readjusts to life outside prison, making it less likely that society will adopt a true appreciation of multiculturalism.

Prison life provides an excellent opportunity to test the effectiveness of pro-multicultural programs. For instance, the divisive nature of inmates among racial and ethnic lines and the captive audiences found in prisons provide ample opportunities for prison officials to "test" or "experiment" with programs that promote diversity. Promoting multiculturalism in prison has many benefits, not the least of which involves the decreased likelihood of violent behavior.

Prison life is challenging to say the least. Protecting oneself from exploitation or attack is a round-the-clock job. Protection from disease and illness is also of concern. Consider the "cold and flu" season that occurs each winter. Both colds and the flu seem to spread quite easily, affecting large numbers of persons. Now, consider a communicable disease in prison, where individuals are confined and aren't always able to purchase over-the-counter drugs to address the ill effects of the disease.

Now, let's up the ante a bit. Let's change the communicable disease from colds and the flu to the human immunodeficiency virus (HIV), which causes AIDS. We most certainly need to alter our scenario in response, particularly with regard to the methods of transmitting this harmful virus. Sharing colds and the flu is much more easily done than is transmitting HIV. Nevertheless, inmates are at a much greater risk of being infected by HIV and transmitting the virus given their increased involvement in particular activities associated with transmission, including sharing hypodermic needles and engaging in unprotected sex. Absent from this discussion is the effects of other communicable diseases such as various types of hepatitis and the more easily transmitted tuberculosis.

In 2004 the overall rate of confirmed AIDS cases among the prison population (.50%) was over three times the rate in the U.S. general population (.15%).

Fortunately, the situation seems to be improving. At the end of 2004, 1.8% of the prison population tested HIV positive, a decrease from 1998 when 2.2% of the total U.S. population tested positive. Nevertheless, African American inmates seem to be more affected by these deadly diseases than their counterparts. In 2004, Black, non-Hispanic inmates accounted for over 68% of AIDS-related deaths among inmates, and were nearly 2.5 times more likely than Whites and almost 5 times more likely than Hispanics to die from AIDS.[28] This situation provides guidance for corrections officials charged with the safety and well-being of inmates.

These health and safety concerns as they relate to prison most certainly also apply to all other aspects of corrections. Those on probation and parole, and those incarcerated in jail, have many of the same concerns. Jail inmates face particular challenges due to the limited testing, treatment, and classification of inmates. Individuals who supervise offenders with communicable diseases face specific challenges, particularly as they relate to the need for face-to-face contact and confidentiality, for offenders who are on probation or parole to maintain employment, and to prevent inmates from engaging in sexual contact with others.

Multiculturalism and Challenges in Prison

Prisons are full of demands, not the least of which involves the need to control a diverse group of seemingly dangerous individuals. The increasingly diverse nature of corrections poses particular difficulties, several of which are identified and discussed below. Critical issues with regard to multiculturalism and prisons involve specific needs of select groups, counseling methods that must consider cultural diversity, and overall correctional approaches designed to address cultural needs.

Labeling

Many of the challenges stemming from living in a multicultural society result from society often categorizing individuals based on a particular label, trait, or characteristic. Consider, for instance, the term "inmate." Many in the general population assume that most inmates are similar simply because they broke the law and were convicted of a crime. Yet there are notable differences among inmates that need to be recognized before we can expect significantly positive results from incarceration or any other type of correctional intervention.

Individuals maintain several roles, belong to specific groups, and are categorized and/or stereotyped accordingly. Of particular interest in prisons and, more generally, corrections, is categorizing individuals as Hispanic. Consideration of the differences among inmates deemed "Hispanic" in prison is needed given the differences among those who constitute the group (Chapter 4 elaborates on those differences). The classification of all Hispanics into one group blurs a great deal of cultural diversity.[29] Groups classified under the label "Hispanic," including Mexicans, Puerto Ricans, and Cubans, show notable differences with regard to offense characteristics, criminal records, family background, and personal characteristics.[30] Prison officers and others throughout the criminal justice system should recognize the distinct characteristics of those comprising the term "Hispanic."

Coexistence

Perhaps one of the most effective means of observing how multiculturalism impacts corrections requires observation of how particular groups exist, coexist, and function while incarcerated. Researchers suggest that there are differences between Black and White prison inmates, perhaps due to Blacks facing discrimination from those involved in all steps of the criminal justice system.[31] Particularly, researchers have identified differences among inmates, with Black inmates more likely than White inmates to engage in conflicts with other inmates and the staff.[32] Blacks are also more likely than Whites to engage in conduct that attracts the attention of prison administrators. Racial biases on behalf of prison staff and administrators may contribute to the differential.[33]

Research on racial differences among inmates further suggests White inmates experience higher levels of fear and stress than Black inmates, and it appears that White inmates have more positive perceptions of prison officers than do their minority counterparts. One study found that Black **exmates,** those released from prison, were significantly more likely than White exmates to perceive that prison officers use too much force on inmates. Further, Whites were more likely than Blacks to believe they were treated "pretty good" in prison and were almost twice as likely as Black and Hispanic exmates to disagree with the suggestion that prison officers treated them as if they were less than human.[34]

Gender Identity

Race, however, is not the only variable of concern with regard to multiculturalism in corrections. Consider the prison experience of a transgender individual. Given the emphasis on masculinity in male prisons, what obstacles does the transgender male inmate face? Further, what challenges does this inmate pose for prison officials? At the very least, determination of what prison the inmate is sent to and the classification of the inmate is of notable significance. The inmate's right to treatment must also be considered. Should this treatment include hormones used to maintain one's transgender appearance?

In 1993 Robert Kosilek was sentenced to a life sentence for the murder of his wife, Cheryl. Kosilek had strangled his wife with the wire from a planter, then concealed her body in the backseat of a car and left the car in a parking lot at a Massachusetts mall. While in prison, Robert changed his name to Michelle and has received hormone shots, laser hair removal, female undergarments, and some makeup. He has since filed two lawsuits claiming the state Department of Corrections should pay for sex-change surgery, which could cost between $10,000 and $20,000. Several inmates have filed similar lawsuits, although none was successful.

Kosilek claims that his gender-identity disorder is a medical necessity and that denying him treatment would be in violation of the Eighth Amendment right to protection from cruel and unusual punishment. He, like other inmates who filed similar lawsuits, argues that gender-identity disorder is a serious illness that can lead to depression, severe anxiety, self-castration, and suicide attempts. Should Kosilek and other inmates be granted sex-change surgery, paid for by the Department of Corrections? Needless to say, there is much debate surrounding the issue, as both advocates and attorneys are keeping a close watch on such cases.

Transsexual people who haven't had genital surgery are typically classified according to their birth sex, regardless of how long they've lived as the opposite sex. Those who have had genital surgery are typically classified and housed based on their reassigned sex.[35] Some transsexual inmates are permitted to maintain their hormone treatment while in prison. The Bureau of Prisons provides transsexual inmates with hormones at the level that was maintained prior to incarceration.[36]

Homosexuality in prison poses particular difficulties for correctional officials. The extent of homosexual activity varies by prison and by the methods used to assess such behavior. Inmates report higher levels of homosexual activity than are recognized in official accounts.[37] Nevertheless, the most commonly used policy option in response to homosexual activity in prison is to do nothing or pretend it doesn't exist. This approach is limited in the sense that it may neglect nonconsensual acts of homosexuality, and it may lead to sexual discrimination claims by heterosexual inmates who may argue for conjugal visits.[38] In other words, it could be argued that heterosexual inmates are subject to sexual discrimination when they're prevented from having sexual relations while homosexual inmates are not. Other policy approaches to homosexuality in prison include providing condoms to promote safe sex, permitting conjugal visits with same-sex partners, and the more radical approach of permitting homosexual activity.[39]

Special Needs for Counseling and Treatment

Native Americans face particular problems upon entering the correctional system. As an example, Native American culture differs from the dominant culture in that maintaining eye contact conveys disrespect.[40] As noted elsewhere in this book, failure to maintain eye contact when communicating can play an integral role in miscommunication. Further, some Native Americans view being under correctional control as an extension of their ancestral experiences.[41] Many institutions limit participation in Native American healing ceremonies to individuals who are enrolled in federally recognized tribes. This policy neglects Native Americans' First Amendment right to freedom of religion and the fact that not all tribes are recognized by the federal government. The possession of items considered sacred by Native Americans is also problematic for the incarcerated and prison officials. Eagle feathers, bear claws, pipes, and other artifacts may be viewed by correctional officers as potential safety and health risks.[42] Further, Native Americans reared in traditional manners are prompted to learn through experience, which isn't always possible while incarcerated. In turn, some of the Native American culture is lost when young adults are incarcerated.[43] Gayl Edmunds, program director for the Indian Alcoholism Treatment Service in Wichita, Kansas, commented on the problems faced by Native Americans in the correctional system in stating that a "total lack of understanding and often respect for American Indians' spiritual beliefs and practices has created fertile ground for an ethnic community that feels misunderstood, disenfranchised, and powerless."[44]

The organization and practices found at the Kainai Community Correctional Center in Alberta, Canada, provide evidence of how criminal justice efforts can directly address concerns for multiculturalism. The minimum security facility, complete with community corrections programs, is staffed entirely by natives of the Blood Indian Reserve and is a cooperative effort on behalf of the Alberta Solicitor General's Department and the Blood Tribe Band. Most of the offenders within the institution hail from the Reserve. The staff's native heritage contributes to recognition of the cultural background of much of the inmate population, which facilitates understanding the troubles inmates face. Elders from the tribe play a significant role in group counseling by providing cultural leadership and offer support for native offenders who appear in court.[45]

Traditional counseling methods in prison are targeted toward the White middle class, which poses challenges for those from diverse backgrounds. Such counseling may neglect diverse beliefs, values, experiences, and behaviors maintained by the varied groups that enter prison.[46] The concentration is often focused on helping inmates adapt to the dominant culture, while neglecting multiculturalism.

The term "corrections" suggests that some form of correcting is being done. Treatment is not the primary concern of many prisons these days as punishment and deterrence have become increasingly popular. Nevertheless, counseling and therapeutic approaches are found in most, if not all prisons. Selecting a treatment approach that suits all offenders is challenging to prison officials, particularly since inmates come from diverse backgrounds. A single approach to treating the ills of all inmates will not work. Accordingly, prison officials must identify and adopt the most effective approach for each individual.

Puerto Rican inmates, as an example, face particular challenges with regard to counseling. Puerto Rican cultural issues as they pertain to time, relationships and friends, morality, responsibility, and decision making require recognition on behalf of counselors to consider how to shape their counseling efforts. For instance, cultural influences prompt Puerto Rican inmates to believe moral issues are discussed only with family members, while in the dominant culture morality is often a public issue.[47] Recognition of these and related issues can only serve to enhance counseling inmates.

Research on the educational attainment levels of inmates suggests a significant need for educational opportunities in corrections. Particularly, minority state prison inmates are substantially less likely than Whites to have graduated from high school. In one study, 44% of Black state inmates and 53% of Hispanic inmates had not graduated from high school, compared to only 27% of Whites. Correctional agencies have responded to this need for education among minority groups, as Black and Hispanic inmates were more likely than Whites to engage in vocational training and educational classes while in prison.[48]

The formal and social organization of inmates highlights the significance of the classification and day-to-day functions of inmates. Multiculturalism is certainly on the minds of prison administrators who must determine, among other things, who should share a cell with whom and what groups should eat or recreate at the same time. Failure to consider inmate hostility toward particular groups contributes to a disruptive prison. However, it could be argued that isolating inmates of different backgrounds for the sake of safety discourages tolerance and acceptance of different groups and perpetuates the associated problems.

Jail

Jails have been described by some experts as "poorhouses of the twentieth century,"[49] "festering sores," "cesspools of crime," "teeming houses of horror," and "the ultimate ghetto."[50] In contrast to prisons, jails are the least understood and least frequently studied component of the criminal justice system.[51] Yet the significance of jails to the criminal justice system cannot be overstated, particularly because

- more people pass through jail than through prison,
- critical decisions are often made while inmates remain in jail or are released on bond,
- jail-related experiences often influence inmates' minds, and
- jail arguably imposes the cruelest means of punishment in the United States.[52]

Jails have a constantly changing population and much potential for cultural misunderstanding and conflict. Jail officials can eliminate their need to engage in physical forms of social control through greater understanding of cultural differences. Entering jail can be a traumatic experience for some who may soon realize that they face an unpleasant environment. Their reaction can be violence directed toward themselves (e.g., suicide) or others, including jail officials and/or other inmates. Effective assessment of an individual's dangerousness is facilitated through better understanding of those who enter jail.

Effectively assessing individuals requires recognition of cultural backgrounds. Behaviors or responses that seem dangerous may be attributable to cultural practices. Cultural practices seemingly influence assessment practices regarding the suicidal risks of American Indians placed in jail. Particularly, researchers found that American Indians were discomforted by the interview process involved in screening practices concerning jail inmate suicide. Many American Indians considered the screening intrusive and feared the repercussions

Jails have a consistently changing population and maintain much potential for cultural misunderstanding and conflict.

of admitting a propensity to harm themselves. These and related reactions were not found among non-Indian counterparts. Part of the American Indian reactions and responses to the suicide-risk screening is attributed to the American Indian concept of respect, which discourages prying into the innermost thoughts and feelings of others as is done in this type of screening.[53]

Jails differ from prisons in several ways. Among the differences are the higher turnover rate of inmates, the enhanced control over inmates, and the limited influence of an inmate subculture found in jails.[54] Much of the research literature on incarceration focuses on life in prison, in contrast to the scant study of life in jails.[55] One area of neglect is research on violence in jails.[56] What is known, however, suggests that many of the same factors influencing prison violence affect violence in jails. Overcrowding, poorly trained correctional staffs, acts of social injustice, and the aggressive personalities of some inmates are among the factors influencing jail violence.[57] Inmate age also influences behavior, as younger inmates are generally more unruly than older inmates. Researchers have found mixed results with regard to inmate misconduct and race,[58] although it appears that Black inmates are more often written up for misconduct than are other groups. The disproportionality is possibly the result of reactions to perceived mistreatment, including closer scrutinization of Black inmates by correctional officials.[59]

Time spent in jail may influence offender behavior. As mentioned earlier, for some, entering jail is a traumatic experience. The inmates most influenced by jail placement may be most vulnerable to treatment. Accordingly, jails sometimes have chaplains, clergy, and related individuals who interact with inmates in attempts to make the best of a difficult situation. These groups are also present in prisons; however, their influence on jail inmates is of importance given the vulnerability of some inmates. Among the benefits of providing religious faith and spirituality in jails (and prisons for that matter) are positive influences on character development, recovery from various types of addiction, and overall transformation and rehabilitation.[60] The need to provide jail chaplains or clergy who recognize different faiths provides for a more effective jail experience[61] and demonstrates the significance of concerns for multiculturalism in the criminal justice system.

⚔ Community Corrections

Community corrections involves correctional supervision provided outside an institution. Community corrections personnel are expected to change, punish, control, and manage offenders.[62] The practice is traced back to the pre-revolutionary colonial period, although at that time the community was not viewed as either a cause of crime or an avenue to correct criminal behavior.[63] Today, community corrections is used largely to reduce prison overcrowding. Correctional practices in the community include probation, parole, halfway houses, residential centers, and work furloughs.

Correctional supervision in the community is preferable to most inmates and is often used by courts and correctional personnel as an incentive toward good behavior. Offenders typically view community supervision as preferable to incarceration, yet they remain aware that misbehavior could result in (re)commitment to prison or jail. Determining who receives community corrections involves discretion and opens opportunities for differential treatment of various groups. The situation is perhaps best summed up by researchers Todd Clear and Harry Dammer, who note:

> Where there is discretion, there is the possibility of abuse of decision-making authority. Judges, parole boards, and program administrators are human. When they consider an offender for a community program in place of incarceration, they are looking for attributes that give reason to believe the offender will succeed in that program. It is not difficult to imagine that some of those attributes might be correlated with social statuses we think are not permissible for them to use. The most significant problems have to do with race and ethnicity.[64]

Clear and Dammer comment on the difficulties faced by Black Americans in the criminal justice system, who are more likely than their White counterparts to be unemployed, less educated, younger, and less skilled and to have a more serious criminal record. These characteristics could result in a partiality that involves biases in selecting clients for community corrections.[65]

Gender discrimination is also apparent with regard to community corrections programs. Females, aside from having some different needs or concerns than males undergoing community corrections (e.g., females are more likely to be single parents), also face difficulties stemming from community corrections programs that often structure their strategies toward males.[66] This could result in an emphasis on surveillance and control at the expense of support, the latter being of greater importance to females than males.[67]

Probation and parole are the most frequently used forms of community corrections. The terms *probation* and *parole* are often used to refer to the same thing: supervision in the community. However, they differ in several ways. Probation is a front-end strategy in which judicial bodies place conditions on offenders in lieu of incarceration. Parole is a back-end strategy that is imposed following a period of incarceration.[68] Many of the challenges of dealing with multiculturalism and probationers are evident with regard to parolees, as both require supervision in the community. Recognizing cultural differences in the manner in which supervision is conducted benefits both the supervising agents and the individuals under supervision.

Offenders typically view community supervision as preferable to incarceration.

Probation

Probation practices in the United States are traced back to 1841 when shoemaker John Augustus supervised minor offenders in his community. Probation is conditional freedom offered by a judicial officer to an alleged or adjudged offender, provided the individual abides by certain conditions of behavior.[69]

Conditions of probation may require offenders to submit to random drug tests, obey curfews, report to a probation officer on a regular basis, and/or avoid particular individuals or locations. Judges may impose a prison sentence upon an offender following a guilty verdict and subsequently suspend the sentence in lieu of probation. These offenders would be accountable for their actions and subject to additional penalties should they commit another crime. If they violate the terms of their probation, or commit what is referred to as a **technical violation,** they would serve the suspended sentence of incarceration. Commission of a technical violation may be grounds for probation revocation, in which the offender may lose the privilege of being on probation and is incarcerated. Technical violations involve infractions committed by those on probation or parole that are not necessarily illegal; however, they violate the terms of the probation or parole agreement. Failing a drug test, staying out past curfew, or moving out of the community without permission are three of the more recognizable types of technical violations.

Investigation and supervision are at the heart of probation. Investigation involves preparing and presenting a presentence investigation report to judges involved in sentencing hearings. Supervision involves what most people associate with probation: supervising offenders in the community. The difficulties associated with the supervisory component of probation is perhaps best summed by researchers Clear and Cole, who identify the informal nature of the supervisory aspect of probation "as a complex interaction between officers (who vary in style, knowledge, and philosophy) and offenders (who vary in responsiveness and need for supervision) in a bureaucratic organization that imposes significant formal and informal constraints on the work."[70]

Supervising probationers consists of three primary components: the written conditions of probation, probationer reporting, and enforcing the orders of the court.[71] Perhaps the most significant aspect of probation involves enforcing the terms of probation. Enforcement of probationer behavior requires probation officers to properly process cases in which probationers commit new offenses or technical violations. The discretion inherent in this aspect of the job provides probation officers the power to involve or avoid judicial intervention when dealing with minor infractions. In other words, probation officers use their discretion to formally or informally confront problematic situations. They may also choose to ignore the problem. An officer's level of discretion decreases as the severity of the violation increases.

Is it possible for probation officers to use their discretion in an unfair and biased manner through bringing minor infractions of particular groups to the attention of the courts, yet not doing so for other groups? Absolutely. How often this happens is unknown, although it could be argued that one time is too many. Discretion to involve or avoid contact with judges provides an avenue for the differential treatment of probationers. Probation officers who work in a jurisdiction where judges closely follow the probation revocation recommendations of the probation officer maintain notable influence on the outcome of the revocation hearing. Officers who possess a solid understanding and appreciation of different cultures reduce the likelihood that probationers will be treated unfairly.

Research on probation revocation practices found that young Black male individuals received the harshest penalties, while their Hispanic and White counterparts were generally treated the same. Further, employment status at the time of probation violation seemed to offer no support for young Black males since employed young

Black males received harsher treatment than their unemployed White counterparts. The lack of statutory or administrative guidelines permits wide judicial discretion with regard to probation revocation.[72]

Offenders' responses to the supervision they're provided influence the effectiveness of their probation sentence.[73] Put simply, how probationers respond to a probation officer's supervisory powers greatly affects the probationer's behavior. How the roles of probationer and probation officer are initially established influences supervision practices, and differences among cultures dictate that different approaches to establish and enforce "supervisor–supervised relationships" are needed.

The diverse nature of the individuals entering our correctional agencies dictates that corrections personnel maintain a keen awareness of cultural differences, for instance, as they relate to transgender and transsexual persons. Many probation officers will at some point encounter a transgender person. Those who lack knowledge about transgenderism feel less confident than those with more knowledge in dealing with specific issues that pertain to transgenderism.[74] Privacy and confidentiality are primary among the issues raised when dealing with transgender probationers. The need to understand one's transgender status becomes important for presentence investigation reports, particularly if the punishment may involve incarceration.[75] Probation officers must appropriately confront their own perceptions of transgenderism when dealing with these individuals, and recognize that transgender individuals have higher rates of psychological and substance abuse problems than their counterparts.[76] The difficulties associated with the social isolation of many transgender individuals are compounded by probation officers not overly familiar with support networks for transgender persons.[77]

The vast number of individuals entering probation come from diverse cultures. The extensive and diverse caseloads maintained by probation officers require staff recognition of multicultural issues. Cross-cultural barriers provide a primary impediment to constructing an effective officer–client relationship.[78] Diversifying probation officer staffs is a step in the right direction, as these individuals provide many contributions to offender supervision in the community. However, there remains a significant need to ensure that field officers recognize, consider, and appreciate cultural differences. Sincerity, the energy to provide high levels of service to clients, knowledge of diverse cultures, resourcefulness, and a nonjudgmental attitude are characteristic of a culturally competent probation officer.[79] Having a solid grasp of the innuendos of multiculturalism and actively questioning one's assumptions regarding particular groups undoubtedly contribute to the effectiveness of probation officer supervision.

Release from Prison and Parole

Inmates are released from prison conditionally or unconditionally. Those released "under conditions" face community supervision for a specified time upon exiting prison. **Conditional release** can involve **discretionary release**—for instance, when a parole board grants an inmate parole—or inmates can receive **mandatory release** in states that have abandoned traditional parole practices in favor of "good time" practices. States that use mandatory release eliminate parole board discretion through a policy in which inmates earn time off of their prison sentence through various incentives, such as behaving appropriately in prison and taking advantage of self-improvement programs. Individuals released unconditionally have "maxed out," or served their entire sentence, and are released from prison without conditions or supervision in the community.

The manner in which inmates are released from prison is currently changing. Most inmates on parole were traditionally sanctioned in jurisdictions utilizing **indeterminate sentencing** practices in which inmates were released via discretionary decisions after a period of incarceration. However, changes in policy resulted in most inmates being granted mandatory release. Roughly half of all inmates faced a parole board in 1995, and 45% received mandatory parole. Following the elimination of discretionary parole in some states, only 37% received discretionary release in 2000 compared to 54% receiving mandatory parole.[80]

Unlike probationers, parolees have spent time in prison and face particular obstacles. Prominent among the difficulties faced by those released from prison are the influences of prisonization; being labeled a "former prisoner;" losing the right to vote, hold public office, or sign contracts in some states; and having to survive without much state support. The need to find employment and reestablish ties with family and community members poses particular problems for some parolees. The financial cutbacks in many prisons have contributed to some inmates failing to address the factors leading to their incarceration. Financial concerns have led some prisons to reduce the number of counseling and treatment opportunities for inmates.

While the challenges of parole apply to all groups, cultures, and individuals, the disproportionate number of African American prisoners in the United States results in enhanced struggles for this group. One could argue that failing to address the initial causes underlying the incarceration and the difficulties of adjusting to parole perpetuates the overrepresentation of Blacks in prison and the criminal justice system in general.

Parole board members in most states are politically appointed and serve terms of six years or less.[81] Members primarily assess inmate suitability for parole and assist with parole policy development. Participation on a parole board requires thorough knowledge of crime, the justice system, and human behavior, and recognition and appreciation of cultural diversity. A preparole investigation report, similar to a presentence investigation report, contains vital information regarding the potential parolee and assists parole board members with their decision. The discretion of parole board members in determining whether or not to grant an inmate parole is notable for any discussion of multiculturalism in corrections.

Those currently released on parole are being supervised by parole officers emphasizing *surveillance* over *assistance* even though both components are essential to parole. It is argued that inmates are receiving longer prison sentences coupled with limited pre-release or rehabilitation programs. This problem is compounded by the increased level of disorganization in the communities to which inmates are returning, inmates' families being less likely to support them upon their release, and fewer available social services for parolees.[82]

Parole officers supervise parolees and are influential in determining who is brought to the attention of the court following parole violations. Their duties are quite similar to those provided by probation officers. Parole officers provide law enforcement and social services primarily through ensuring that parolees abide by the terms of their parole agreement and referring parolees to social services as needed.

Recent research found that just less than half (47%) of parolees successfully met the terms of their parole agreement. One's parole can be revoked following the commission of a new offense or a technical violation of the parole agreement. As noted, parole officers use their discretion to decide whether or not to pursue revocation of parole, an issue of particular significance with concern for multiculturalism.

Aside from parole or maxing out, inmates are released from prison via other means. Inmates may be granted **clemency,** which permits legislative action to reduce the severity of one's punishment, waive the punishment associated with a crime, or exclude certain individuals from prosecution of a specific crime.[83] Clemency comes in the form of pardons, amnesty, commutations, and reprieves. **Pardons** involve the restoration of a former inmate's rights and privileges, such as the right to vote or sit on a jury. **Amnesty** is similar to pardons, although it involves groups of people instead of individuals. Granting rights and privileges to illegal aliens is an example of amnesty. **Commutations** involve shortening or changing an inmate's prison sentence, for instance, when an inmate becomes terminally ill or when death sentences are switched to sentences of life in prison. **Reprieves** involve the postponement of a sentence and are typically associated with delaying an execution. The decision to grant clemency is often influenced by several individuals, such as the president and, in 35 states, the governor. The extent to which cultural diversity influences such decisions remains unknown. Given historical use of discretion in the criminal justice system, it can be stated with modest confidence that multicultural issues play a role in the decision making.

✂ Correctional Staff and Training

Commenting on the difficulties of working with a correctional staff, Deputy Secretary Mary Leftridge Byrd of the Pennsylvania Department of Corrections stated, "The convergence of public expectation, responsibilities of correctional professionals, and demands of the correctional environment, coupled with the cultural influence of the large world, creates incredible dynamics."[84] The hands-on approach of correctional professionals evident throughout corrections requires directed attention toward multiculturalism. Given the day-to-day interaction between those under correctional supervision and those supervising, it is important to recognize the training and preparation of correctional officials with regard to multiculturalism.

Diversity and Correctional Staff

Several trends impacted the correctional workforce. Prominent among the trends are the increased number of privately operated prisons, the continued introduction of technology, the imposition of standards on correctional facilities by outside agencies, and changes in the workforce demographics.[85] With regard to the latter, the demographic changes involve increases in the number of female and minority correctional staff.

Diversity among correctional staff was limited until about 30 to 40 years ago. The infamous rioting at the Attica Correctional Facility in New York in 1971 was largely encouraged by inmate perceptions of the correctional staff's inability and failure to recognize and respect varying cultures, ethnic backgrounds, and religious practices and rights.[86] The lack of multicultural awareness contributing to the rioting was evidenced by the staff's seeming lack of concern for religious beliefs. As noted by Howard Abadinsky, a professor of criminal justice and legal studies at St. John's University,

> Attica had a large number of Black Muslims (members of the Nation of Islam) who had difficulty with a prison diet that was heavy with pork. Muslims also objected to the lack of ministers. Correctional officials would not allow the ministers, many of whom had prison records, into Attica. Black Muslims spent their recreation time in the yard engaging in worship and highly disciplined physical exercise. The correctional staff, which never understood the Black Muslims, was quite fearful of this group, who exhibited military-type discipline and remained aloof from both staff and other inmates.[87]

Accordingly, Black Muslims played a significant role in the rioting that ensued.

Since the time of the Attica prison riot, there has been increased representation of various ethnic and racial minority groups among correctional staffs and the benefits have become obvious to corrections professionals.[88] The opportunities of diverse groups to work together in correctional settings facilitate staff interaction and sharing multicultural perspectives.[89] Creating a diverse correctional staff also encourages inmates to recognize that the criminal justice system does not solely consist of middle-class White men who don't understand cultural diversity.

Prisons were historically built in rural locations, often in areas with homogeneous populations from which staff members were drawn. The inmates placed in these institutions, however, often hailed from urban, heterogeneous areas.[90] Such a situation clearly encourages culture-based conflict. Conflicts between the traditional rural–White prison officer and the urban–minority prisoner still exist in some states, although they have largely diminished in large, urban states.[91] Creating a diverse staff provides several challenges, such as encouraging minority workers to move to rural locations; the ability of minorities to find employment in more attractive public service and private industry positions; and the unwillingness of some minorities to work in a system they view as racist.[92] Equal opportunity programs have assisted in diversifying correctional staff; however, working in prisons where racial and ethnic tensions contribute to an already challenging situation discourages some minorities from seeking such work.

The close contact between inmates and correctional staff mandates the need for all to maintain an understanding and appreciation of multiculturalism.

Non-Whites, particularly African Americans, have increasingly assumed prison staff positions. Unfortunately, they've faced many obstacles working in prison. Early resentment from White officers, many of whom hailed from rural backgrounds, was complemented by the perception that Black prison officers would be more sympathetic to inmates, particularly Black inmates.[93] However, Black and Latino officers have generally been accepted into the prison officer culture. Inmates currently recognize little difference among White and non-White officers.[94] It is projected that females and minorities will increasingly join correctional staffs and bring their cultural beliefs and backgrounds into an arena that has long been secluded from such input.

There is sometimes an assumption among inmates that cultural similarities will outweigh prison officer responsibilities and commitment to the job.[95] In other words, some inmates feel that prison officers will provide favoritism to inmates from the officers' cultures. Determining the extent to which prison officers let cultural influences dictate their actions is difficult, if not impossible. However, we would be foolish to believe that cultural influences are completely unrelated to officer discretion.

Research has produced mixed results with regard to the differences among correctional officer attitudes and practices. Some studies suggest minority officers assume more punitive attitudes toward inmates than do White officers.[96] Others suggest the opposite[97] or argue there's no difference between the groups.[98] Some suggest African American correctional officers are more likely than their White counterparts to support rehabilitative practices and are more likely to perceive the current court system as too harsh.[99] Nevertheless, there is not enough research support to confidently state that minority correctional officers use their discretion differently than nonminority officers.

Multiculturalism and Correctional Staff Training

Correctional officers maintain a great deal of discretion in their day-to-day functions. Determining whether to confront troubling situations with formal or informal methods is one example of this discretion. Improper use of discretion could explain why inexperienced prison officers are more likely than their experienced counterparts to be assaulted by inmates.[100] Violent inmate reactions may be spurred by perceptions of injustice. Sensitivities to race, age, and crime-related factors of individual inmates undoubtedly factor into how corrections officers use their discretion.[101] Training officers to properly consider such extralegal factors and continuous reinforcement of that training should be of primary concern to correctional administrators.

Correctional agencies typically do not have the resources to train all staff regarding the cultural differences of the incarcerated. Accordingly, training resources must be used wisely. Employees working with special populations, such as the elderly or mentally impaired, receive specific sensitivity training. Those assuming leadership roles in the institution receive more advanced training in diversity.[102] In the end, exposing all staff members to as many cultural differences as feasible contributes to a smoother running institution. Correctional leadership needs to promote tolerance and cultural diversity among the officers and encourage officers to develop the interpersonal skills necessary to operate in a multicultural institution. Effective communication skills are necessary for working in corrections since poor communication is a major source of problems.[103] The ability to speak a second language can largely contribute to a correctional or any other criminal justice officer's effectiveness. Bi- or multilingual prison officers provide much needed safety and security in institutions with great diversity.[104] Considering cultural context in the course of communicating promotes a more effective work environment.

The use of community resources to assist correctional staff is important in many ways, particularly in cases in which there is a notable lack of familiarity with a particular culture. Incorporating input from volunteers, guest speakers, professional associations, and specific interest groups demonstrates to correctional staff and the individuals they supervise that the agency respects cultural diversity. The onus is on correctional agencies to proactively identify means by which they can send a message of tolerance to all individuals with whom they associate.

One difficulty associated with multicultural awareness training involves a method or technique of assessing awareness or knowledge with regard to cultural diversity.[105] In other words, how do we know if someone (e.g., a probation officer) is prepared to supervise individuals from diverse cultures? Part of correctional officer training involves role play, in which cadets act as unruly inmates demonstrating cultural idiosyncrasies that test the correctional officials' ability to properly respond. The actor's cadet colleagues learn methods of responding appropriately to the challenges. Communication skills, including interpreting and using nonverbal communication, are stressed, as is the need to recognize and appreciate culture-related symbolism. While these and related training skills will not end culture conflict throughout correctional systems, they certainly will help alleviate tensions among correctional officials and those under correctional supervision.

Institutional administrators play a significant role in promoting cultural diversity. Proper recruitment, selection, and continuous training contribute to recognizing and promoting multiculturalism in corrections. The organizational culture of the institution should be one in which cultural diversity is among the primary concerns. Failure to recognize diversity results in a much greater likelihood of violence and related negative consequences. Promoting cultural tolerance among staff members is significantly important for administrators, as failure to properly resolve situational conflicts and misunderstandings is related to

- lost productivity,
- increased isolation of staff members,
- enhanced suspicion and distrust among staff members,
- increased staff turnover,
- disgruntled employees, and
- overall negative changes in the climate of the correctional institution.[106]

The organizational culture found in any correctional agency should be tolerant of cultural diversity. Anything less would be unprofessional and pose multiple demands for all parties.

Summary

None of the many facets of corrections is exempt from multicultural concerns. The diversity within our correctional system warrants significant societal attention. What type of attention is needed and what can society do? Being tolerant of diversity would break down many barriers between cultural groups. Trying to understand the many cultural lifestyles found in society may help us better understand why people commit crime and how we can correct their behavior.

Cultural intolerance has existed for some time. So has the inability of correctional practices to fully correct. These statements, taken together, do not infer that becoming tolerant of other cultures will substantially change corrections. There are far too many variables involved with correctional practices to suggest that enhanced tolerance is the solution to solving crime. However, understanding the uniqueness of individuals and groups certainly plays a significant role in correcting human behavior.

This chapter addressed multiculturalism as it relates to corrections. To be sure, our correctional agencies supervise a disproportionate percentage of minorities, particularly African Americans. Accordingly, it is important that correctional officials maintain appreciation for multiculturalism. Those under correctional supervision should also recognize and respect diversity, as our correctional system has largely become demographically diverse.

Multiculturalism is of notable concern with regard to both institutional and community corrections. Community correctional officials must be aware and appreciative of cultural differences among those being supervised. For instance, probation and parole officers often visit inmates in inner-city locales heavily predominated by minorities. The officers should be aware of the expectations of the people in that community; if they aren't, they may find difficulties during their visits (e.g., they may wish to avoid investigating anything unrelated to their client as prying into the affairs of others is shunned in these areas). Prison and jail officials also face concerns related to multiculturalism, for instance, in controlling prison gangs, which typically assemble according to racial and ethnic lines. Further, proper treatment and rehabilitation as provided both within institutions and while on community corrections requires due consideration of cultural backgrounds.

What can we expect with regard to multiculturalism and corrections in the near future? The increased presence of females and minorities on correctional staffs suggests a more diverse correctional workforce. Such diversity will seemingly coincide with an increasingly diverse correctional population. Demographic trends suggest increased minority representation in the larger society, and statistical trends suggest greater representation of minorities under correctional supervision. It is hoped that the continuous search for alternatives to crime can someday eliminate the need for correctional intervention.

You Make the Call

Probation Officer Challenges

Consider the following scenario. Debate the pros and cons of all options and decide what you would do.

You became a probation officer because you like to help people and you appreciate the spontaneity associated with the job. As an African American male, you face particular challenges when visiting your clients, especially those who live in predominantly nonminority neighborhoods. On one occasion you were (wrongfully) stopped by police who claimed you failed to come to a complete stop at a stop sign as you approached the client's home. Personally, you believe the officers were engaging in racial profiling. You decide not to let it bother you. However, three weeks later, officers (again wrongfully) stopped you in the same neighborhood claiming that you failed to signal during a lane change. Again, you believe the officers were targeting you because you're a Black man in a predominantly White neighborhood. To make matters worse, you receive suspicious looks from the citizens in the community, and have had the police slowly drive by you and monitor your actions as you walked toward your client's home. Your probation client is a blatant racist who has no respect for you and on several occasions has filed claims of impropriety against you. You like the job, but begin to wonder whether the hassles are worth it.

Questions

1. Should you simply explain to the police officers why you're in the neighborhood, ignore the unjustified stops, or report the wrongful actions of the police to the police department or some other official agency?
2. Should you request to be removed from this client's case, in light of the disturbance your presence causes in the neighborhood?
3. Should you attempt to enlighten the probationer regarding his racist attitude, adopt a more punitive approach toward him, or ignore his shortsighted racist behavior?
4. Do you believe your continuous presence in the neighborhood helps or hinders efforts toward multiculturalism? In other words, do you believe it is a positive or negative experience for citizens to have diversity in their surroundings?

Key Terms

amnesty (p. 297)
clemency (p. 297)
community corrections (p. 281)
commutations (p. 297)
conditional release (p. 295)
discretionary release (p. 295)
exmates (p. 288)
Federal Bureau of Prisons (p. 280)
Federal Parole Commission (p. 280)
incarceration (p. 282)
indeterminate sentencing (p. 296)
inmate code (p. 285)

jail (p. 280)
mandatory release (p. 295)
pardons (p. 297)
parole (p. 281)
prison (p. 280)
probation (p. 281)
reprieves (p. 297)
technical violation (p. 294)
ultramasculinity (p. 285)
U.S. Probation and Pretrial Services
    System (p. 280)

Discussion Questions

1. How are correctional agencies organized? Do you believe that a centralized approach to corrections (e.g., in the form of one unified correctional system) would be more effective than our fragmented approach?
2. Discuss the difficulties of being incarcerated.
3. What particular challenges do Native Americans face upon incarceration?
4. Why is concern for multiculturalism of significance to probation and parole officers? What steps can be taken to address this concern?
5. Discuss the evolution of diversity in corrections. Why is it important for correctional agencies to incorporate cultural diversity into their staffs?

Endnotes

1. Foster, B. 2006. *Corrections: The Fundamentals*. Upper Saddle River, NJ: Prentice Hall.
2. "About the Bureau of Prisons." www.bop.gov/about/index.jsp (accessed February 18, 2008).
3. Clear, T. R., Cole, G. F., and Reisig, M. D. 2006. *American Corrections,* 7th ed. Belmont, CA: Wadsworth.
4. Bonczar, T. P. 2003, August. *Prevalence of Imprisonment in the U.S. Population, 1974–2001.* NCJ 197976. Bureau of Justice Statistics. Washington, DC: U.S. Department of Justice.
5. Ibid.
6. Harrison, P. M., and Beck, A. J. 2006, May. *Prison and Jail Inmates at Midyear 2005.* NCJ 213133. Bureau of Justice Statistics. Washington, DC: U.S. Department of Justice.
7. Ibid.
8. Ibid.
9. Glaze, L. E., and Bonczar, T. P. 2006, November. *Probation and Parole in the United States, 2005.* NCJ 215091. Bureau of Justice Statistics. Washington, DC: U.S. Department of Justice.
10. Ibid.
11. For example, Ross, J. I., and Richards, S. C. 2002. *Behind Bars: Surviving Prison.* Indianapolis, IN: Alpha; and Hogshire, J. 1994. *You Are Going to Prison.* Port Townsend, WA: Loompanics Unlimited.
12. Sykes, G. M. 1958. *The Society of Captives.* Princeton, NJ: Princeton University Press.
13. Irwin, J. 2005. *The Warehouse Prison: Disposal of the New Dangerous Class.* Los Angeles: Roxbury.
14. Owen, B. 2005. "The Case of Women: Gendered Harm in the Contemporary Prison." In J. Irwin, *The Warehouse Prison: Disposal of the New Dangerous Class,* pp. 261–289. Los Angeles: Roxbury.
15. Moriarty, D. 1991. "Training Detention Officers to Understand Inmate Behavior." *Corrections Today,* December pp. 72, 74–75.
16. Ibid.
17. Awofeso, N. 2005. "Managing Homosexuality in Prison: A Brief Review of Policy Options." *American Jails,* January/February, pp. 79–81.
18. Beck, A. J., and Harrison, P. M. 2006, July. *Sexual Violence Reported by Correctional Authorities, 2005.* NCJ 214646. Bureau of Justice Statistics. Washington, DC: U.S. Department of Justice.
19. Mumola, C. 2000, August. *Incarcerated Parents and Their Children.* NCJ 182335. Bureau of Justice Statistics. Washington, DC: U.S. Department of Justice.
20. Sabo, D. Kupers, T. A., and London, W. 2001. "Gender and the Politics of Punishment." In D. Sabo, T. A. Kupers, and W. London (eds.), *Prison Masculinities,* p. 3. Philadelphia: Temple University Press.
21. For example, Sabo, Kupers, and London 2001; Ross and Richards 2002.
22. Ross and Richards 2002.
23. Woodruff-Filbey, D. 2004. "Religious Diversity: A Kaleidoscope of Faiths." In C. Smalls (ed.), *The Full Spectrum: Essays on Staff Diversity in Corrections,* pp. 53–64. Lanham, MD: American Correctional Association.
24. Walker, S. Spohn, C., and DeLone, M. 2004. *The Color of Justice,* 3rd ed. Belmont, CA: Wadsworth.
25. Hunt, G., Riegel, S., Morales, T., and Waldorf, D. 1993. "Changes in Prison Culture: Prison Gangs and the Case of the 'Pepsi Generation.'" *Social Problems* 40 (3): 398–409.
26. Ibid.
27. Foster, B. 2006. *Corrections: The Fundamentals.* Upper Saddle River, NJ: Prentice Hall.
28. Maruschak, L. M. 2006, November. *HIV in Prisons, 2004.* NCJ 312897. Bureau of Justice Statistics. Washington, DC: U.S Department of Justice.

29. Martinez, D. J. 2004. "Hispanics Incarcerated in State Correctional Facilities: Variations in Inmate Characteristics Across Hispanic Subgroups." *Journal of Ethnicity in Criminal Justice* 2 (1/2): 119–131.

30. Ibid.

31. Hemmens, C., and Marquart, J. W. 2000. "Friend or Foe? Race, Age, and Inmate Perceptions of Inmate-Staff Relations." *Journal of Criminal Justice* 28: 297–312.

32. Ibid.

33. Flanagan, T. J. 1983. "Correlates of Institutional Misconduct Among State Prisoners." *Criminology* 21: 29–39.

34. Hemmens and Marquart 2000.

35. See *Farmer v. Brennan,* 511 U.S. 825, 829 (1994); *Farmer v. Haas,* 990 F.2d 319, 320 (7th Cir. 1993).

36. U.S. Dept. of Justice, Federal Bureau of Prisons Program Statement 6031.01, *Patient Care,* January 15, 2005, www.bop.gov/policy/progstat/6031_001.pdf (accessed February 18, 2008).

37. Awofeso 2005.

38. Ibid.

39. Ibid.

40. Cesarz, G., and Madrid-Bustos, J. 1991. "Taking a Multicultural World View in Today's Corrections Facilities." *Corrections Today,* December, pp. 68, 70–71.

41. Archambeault, W. G. 2003. "The Web of Steel and the Heart of the Eagle: The Contextual Interface of American Corrections and Native Americans." *The Prison Journal* 83 (1): 3–25.

42. Ibid.

43. Ibid.

44. Edmunds, G. R. 2004. "American Indians." In C. Smalls (ed.), *The Full Spectrum: Essays on Staff Diversity in Corrections,* pp. 81–85. Lanham, MD: American Correctional Association. P. 82.

45. Hepher, I. L. 1991. "Correctional Center on Reserve Gives Natives Control of Their Community." *Corrections Today,* December, pp. 86–89.

46. Rivera, E. T., Wilbur, M. P., and Roberts-Wilbur, J. 1998. "The Puerto Rican Prison Experience: A Multicultural Understanding of Values, Beliefs, and Attitudes." *Journal of Addictions & Offender Counseling* 18 (2): 63–78.

47. Ibid.

48. Harlow, C. W. 2003, January. *Education and Correctional Populations.* NCJ 195670. Bureau of Justice Statistics. Washington, DC: U.S. Department of Justice.

49. Goldfarb, R. 1975. *Jails: The Ultimate Ghetto.* Garden City, NY: Doubleday. P. 29.

50. Thompson, J. 1986. "The American Jail: Problems, Politics, and Prospects." *American Journal of Criminal Justice* 10: 205–221. P. 205.

51. Kiekbusch, R. 1999. "Misinformation About the American Jail and Our Duty to Inform." *American Jails,* March/April, pp. 119–120. P. 119.

52. Irwin, J. 1985. *The Jail: Managing the Underclass in American Society.* Berkeley: University of California Press. P. xi.

53. "American Indian Suicides in Jail: Can Risk Screening Be Culturally Sensitive?" 2005. NCJ 207326. Office of Justice Programs. Washington, DC: U.S. Department of Justice.

54. Senese, J. D., and Kalinich, D. B. 1993. "A Study of Jail Inmate Misconduct: An Analysis of Rule Violations and Official Processing." *Journal of Crime & Justice* 15 (1): 131–147.

55. Burns, R. 2002. "Assessing Jail Coverage in Introductory Criminal Justice Textbooks." *Journal of Criminal Justice Education* 13 (1): 87–100.

56. McManimon, P. F., Jr. 2004. "Correlates of Jail Violence." *American Jails*, May/June, pp. 41–43, 45–47.

57. Braswell, M., Dillingham, S., and Montgomery, R., Jr. 1985. *Prison Violence in America.* New York: Anderson.

58. McManimon 2004.

59. Poole, E. D., and Regoli, R. M. 1980. "Race, Institutional Rule Breaking, and Disciplinary Decision Making in Prison." *Law and Society Review* 14 (4): 931–946.

60. Toll, R. (2004). "How a Multifaith Chaplaincy Program Operates in a County Detention Facility." *American Jails*, January/February, pp.19–24.

61. Kerle, K. 2004. "Religion and Jails." *American Jails,* May/June, p. 5. See also Toll 2004.

62. Clear, T. R., and Dammer, H. R. 2000. *The Offender in the Community.* Belmont, CA: Wadsworth.

63. Dean-Myrda, M. C., and Cullen, F. T. 1998. "The Panacea Pendulum: An Account of Community Response to Crime." In J. Petersilia (ed.), *Community Corrections: Probation, Parole, and Intermediate Sanctions,* pp. 3–18. New York: Oxford University Press.

64. Clear and Dammer 2000, p. 40.

65. Ibid.

66. Ibid.

67. Ibid.

68. For elaboration of the ways in which probation and parole differ, see Champion, D. J. 1999. *Probation, Parole, and Community Corrections,* 3rd ed. Upper Saddle River, NJ: Prentice Hall.

69. Rush, G. E. 2003. *The Dictionary of Criminal Justice,* 6th ed. Guilford, CT: Dushkin/McGraw-Hill.

70. Clear, T. R., and Cole, G. F. 2003. *American Corrections,* 6th ed. Belmont, CA: Wadsworth. P. 200.

71. Clear and Dammer 2000.

72. Tapia, M., and Harris, P. M. 2006. "Race and Revocation: Is There a Penalty for Young, Minority Males?" *Journal of Ethnicity in Criminal Justice* 4 (3): 1–25.

73. Clear and Cole 2003.

74. Poole, L., Whittle, S., and Stephens, P. 2002. "Working with Transgendered and Transsexual People As Offenders in the Probation Service." *Probation Journal* 49 (3): 227–232.

75. Ibid.

76. Ibid.

77. Ibid.

78. Shearer, R. A., and King, P. A. 2004. "Multicultural Competencies in Probation—Issues and Challenges." *Federal Probation* 68 (1): 3–9.

79. Sanders, M. 2003. "Building Bridges Instead of Walls: Effective Cross-Cultural Counseling." *Corrections Today*, February, pp. 58–59.

80. Hughes, T. A., Wilson, D. J., and Beck, A. J. 2001, October. *Trends in State Parole, 1990–2000.* NCJ 184735. Bureau of Justice Statistics. Washington, DC: National Institute of Justice.

81. McCarthy, B. R., McCarthy, B. J., Jr., and Leone, M. C. 2001. *Community-Based Corrections,* 4th ed. Belmont, CA: Wadsworth.

82. Seiter, R. P., and Kadela, K. R. 2003. "Prisoner Reentry: What Works, What Does Not, and What Is Promising." *Crime & Delinquency* 49 (3): 360–388.

83. Clear and Dammer 2000, pp. 193–194.

84. Leftridge Byrd, M. V. 2004. "African-American Women in Corrections." In C. Smalls (ed.), *The Full Spectrum: Essays on Staff Diversity in Corrections,* pp. 105–116. Lanham, MD: American Correctional Association. P. 115.

85. Hunt, P. 2004. "Correctional Officers Need Cultural Diversity Training." In C. Smalls (ed.), *The Full Spectrum: Essays on Staff Diversity in Corrections,* pp. 127–155. Lanham, MD: American Correctional Association.

86. Booker, J. W., Jr. 1999. "Staff Equality: A Welcomed Addition to the Correctional Workplace." *Corrections Today,* June, pp. 94–95. P. 95.

87. Abadinsky, H. 1997. *Probation & Parole: Theory & Practice,* 6th ed. Upper Saddle River, NJ: Prentice Hall. P. 193.

88. Ibid.

89. Ibid.

90. Booker 1999.

91. Irwin 2005.

92. Camp, S., Saylor, W. G., and Wright, K. N. 2001. "Racial Diversity of Correctional Workers and Inmates: Organizational Commitment, Teamwork, and Workers' Efficacy in Prisons." *Justice Quarterly* 18 (2): 411–427.
93. Byrd 2004.
94. Ibid.
95. Aguire, A. T. 2004 "Latinos in Corrections: One View." In C. Smalls (ed.), *The Full Spectrum: Essays on Staff Diversity in Corrections,* pp. 65–74 Lanham, MD: American Correctional Association.
96. Jacobs, J. B., and Kraft, L. 1978. "Integrating the Keepers: A Comparison of Black and White Prison Guards in Illinois." *Social Problems* 25: 304–318.
97. Jurik, N. 1985. "Individual and Organizational Determinants of Correctional Officer Attitudes Towards Inmates." *Criminology* 23: 523–539.
98. Crouch, B. M., and Alpert, G. P. 1982. "Prison Guards' Attitudes Towards Components of the Criminal Justice System." *Criminology* 18: 227–236.

99. Author, J. A. 1994. "Correctional Ideology of Black Correctional Officers." *Federal Probation* 58: 57–65.
100. Kratcoski, P. C. 1988 "The Implications of Research Explaining Prison Violence and Disruption." *Federal Probation* 52 (1): 27–32.
101. McManimon 2004.
102. Wilkinson, R. A. 2004. "Diversity in Correctional Management: An Essential Tool." In C. Smalls (ed.), *The Full Spectrum: Essays on Staff Diversity in Corrections,* pp. 117–125. Lanham, MD: American Correctional Association.
103. Hunt 2004.
104. Aguire 2004.
105. Shearer and King 2004.
106. Dillon, L. 2004. "Effective Communication Embraces Diversity." In C. Smalls (ed.), *The Full Spectrum: Essays on Staff Diversity in Corrections*, pp. 1–9. Lanham, MD: American Correctional Association.

The Future of Multiculturalism: Strategies for Success

Chapter Objectives

After reading this chapter, you should be able to

- ❖ Understand the methods by which the future is forecasted.
- ❖ Recognize the drivers that influence the future of multiculturalism and criminal justice.
- ❖ Identify and discuss the critical issues challenging the future of multiculturalism and criminal justice.

- ❖ Understand the significance of teaching multiculturalism to criminal justice students and identify the means of doing so.
- ❖ Discuss the extent to which progress has been made with regard to multiculturalism and criminal justice.

The future of multiculturalism, particularly as it relates to criminal justice, can be viewed in many lights. For instance, one could observe the positive changes, such as the increased presence of minority groups working within the system, and have hope for a brighter future. Conversely, differential treatment of groups still exists in the criminal justice system, contributing to the perception that multiculturalism is simply a buzzword for something not likely to occur in criminal justice or in society in general. How, exactly, will we know what the future holds for multiculturalism?

The answer to this question can only be answered with time as the future plays out and we see what becomes of our increasingly diverse society. Yet sitting back and waiting to see what happens (i.e., taking a reactive approach) is likely detrimental. Tomorrow's criminal justice professionals are tasked with making society a better place, and doing so requires proactive efforts. Recognizing the nature and extent of the problems faced by our current justice system is the most appropriate place to begin. Accordingly, the preceding chapters have examined the obstacles faced by different groups within the criminal justice system. The chapters have also examined how the criminal justice system has responded to an increasingly diverse society. Thus, the foundation for progress has been set. Now comes the tricky part: understanding what can be done.

❖ Forecasting the Future

Futurists are scientists who forecast future developments in society. Notice the term "forecast" is used in place of the term "prediction." **Forecasting** involves the use of scientific techniques regarding future developments. These developments can be topic- or discipline-specific (e.g., pertain solely to criminal justice) or general in nature. **Predictions,** on the other hand, involve instinctual feelings (aka "gut feelings") that lack scientific validity. The difference between the terms is evidenced in your local news programming when meteorologists forecast the weather through the use of various models. Meteorologists offer weather forecasts based on scientific evidence as opposed to gut feelings. As we all know, however, the forecast is not always correct. While forecasting provides a scientific-based assessment of future developments, there is certainly an element of error involved.

Forecasting the weather and forecasting what will become of multiculturalism and the criminal justice system seem quite different, and in many respects they are. Nevertheless, the incorporation of scientific methods makes both types of forecasting similar. Weather patterns are distinct from human behavior, yet science enables us to anticipate changes in the weather much like we anticipate changes in human behavior. As a social science, criminal justice is vulnerable to changes in human behavior. It differs from the hard sciences such as chemistry where it is certain that the combination of particular substances will have a certain effect. Errors are more likely to occur in the social sciences given the varied nature of society in general.

Consider the changes that occurred following the terrorist attacks against the United States on September 11, 2001. Many forecasts made as late as September 10, 2001, were largely, and unexpectedly, impacted by the changes that ensued. The resulting reorganization of federal law enforcement agencies in the United States and an overriding concern for homeland security changed daily lives and significantly impacted the criminal justice system. For example, local law enforcement agencies now must maintain an intensified concern for homeland security and are competing for scarce personnel resources as the war in Iraq has required the services of qualified applicants.

Futurists use several techniques to forecast the future. Prominent among them are **quantitative analyses,** which involve the use of statistics and trends to anticipate changes in society. Demographers, for instance, observe population trends and offer input regarding the demographic nature of society in the forthcoming years. Forecasters and futurists also consider **qualitative approaches,** which largely involve examination of non-numerical trends and patterns in an attempt to anticipate future developments and changes. Among the qualitative approaches to forecasting the future is the **Delphi Method,** which allows experts to offer input regarding anticipated developments in their area of expertise. For instance, a forecaster intent on using the Delphi Method to anticipate the future of criminal behavior may seek input from experts in the fields of sociology, biology, demography, economics, and criminal justice. The collaborative efforts of the professionals result in anticipated changes in the future. Futurist Gene Stephens used the Delphi Method when he surveyed police experts regarding the role of the police in the future. Briefly, the group agreed that better-educated police officers with enhanced interpersonal skills and an understanding of technology are needed for the future success of policing.[1] The use of **scenarios,** in which a narrative is used to describe anticipated future events, is another method utilized by forecasters. Advanced statistical analyses and the increased incorporation of technology in forecasting, specifically computers, have improved the accuracy of future expectations.

There is debate regarding which forecasting method is most effective; however, analyses of multiple forecasts of the future may show consistencies and offer substantial confidence. In addition to selecting a forecasting method, futurist researchers must select appropriate variables for their analyses. Of particular concern when forecasting are **drivers of the future,** or particular issues that have significant impacts on the future. Among the drivers of forecasting, particularly with regard to criminal justice, are economics, crime factors (e.g., the increasing amount of international and computer crime), demographics, technology, and politics. Time frame is also of significance to forecasting, as researchers must consider how far out into the future they're projecting. There are no restrictions on how far into the future one can forecast; however, the accuracy of the forecast generally decreases as one looks further into the future.[2]

Forecasting Multiculturalism in the Criminal Justice System

So, what's expected with regard to multiculturalism and criminal justice? In this section we offer our analyses, using various forecasting methods, regarding what can be expected regarding the future of criminal justice with concern for multiculturalism. There are many limitations to our analyses, as we provide a simplified, broad forecast of the future. For instance, we provide general overviews of trend data and forgo advanced statistical analyses of the many significant factors that drive changes in the criminal justice system. We leave the hard-core forecasting to futurist researchers. Our analyses, nevertheless, offer a general overview of expected changes and demonstrate how forecasting the future is conducted.

To begin, we must first consider a time frame. Let's look at anticipated changes in ten years. Next, we have to identify our method of forecasting the future. As mentioned, comparing the outcomes of multiple forecasting methods generally provides a greater level of confidence; thus, let's conduct both a qualitative and quantitative approach. We also must consider what exactly we're trying to forecast. For instance, are we forecasting the anticipated increase or decrease in the number of minorities working in the criminal justice system? Or are we interested in the projected number of minority offenders? Let's consider diversity and the anticipated number of prisoners.

In 1995 the incarceration rate in the United States was 411 inmates in state and federal prisons per 100,000 population. By 2005 that number had steadily increased to 491 inmates. The rate of incarceration has steadily increased from a rate of 139 inmates per 100,000 population in 1980 to 491 in 2005.[3] Based on this trend, it's relatively safe to suggest that the incarceration rate will continue to rise in the next ten years. Still, we must address issues pertaining to diversity.

Demographics are a primary driver of change in the criminal justice system with regard to diversity and multiculturalism. Data from the U.S. Census Bureau suggests that Hispanics will constitute nearly one-quarter of the U.S. population by the year 2050. It is anticipated that by 2010 Hispanics will represent 15.5% of the U.S. population, up from 12.6% in 2000. The percentage of African Americans in the United States will also increase, although not as steeply. African Americans are expected to constitute 13.1% of the population in 2010 and 14.6% by 2050; both percentages are higher than the 12.7% of African Americans measured in 2000.[4] Overall, roughly 30% of the U.S. population are individuals of color. That percentage is expected to increase to 45% by 2050. Increased diversity is also expected with regard to sexual orientation and religious background.[5] Given that Hispanics and African Americans are overrepresented in U.S. prisons and the percentages of African

Americans and Hispanics in society are expected to increase, one can anticipate continued minority overrepresentation in our prisons. Thus, the importance of studying diversity within the criminal justice system is even more important and necessary.

To be sure, this is a *very* simplistic quantitative forecast. Many factors besides historical practices influence incarceration trends. True forecasting methods take much more into account and involve more advanced analyses. This example, however, is offered to broadly demonstrate how forecasting is conducted. Below we offer an equally simplistic qualitative forecast regarding multiculturalism and incarceration. Again, hard-core qualitative forecasting involves much more analysis, consideration, and depth than the cursory examination we provide. Our analyses are based on recent developments in several areas that appear to have implications for the future of incarceration.

Below we discuss three significant societal trends that will likely impact the future of incarceration as it pertains to diversity and culture. Many other qualitative factors will certainly impact the nature and extent of U.S. incarceration. We've identified factors that we believe are among the most significant drivers of incarceration in the future, with particular concern for multiculturalism.

First, issues pertaining to homeland security will continue to result in the expansion of law enforcement. For better or for worse, ours is a time of enhanced social control primarily due to terrorist threats. Accordingly, enhanced law enforcement and other social control efforts will mean continued increasing incarceration rates and the continued overrepresentation of minorities in the criminal justice system, as these groups are continuously closely monitored by law enforcement.

Second, females and other minorities will continue to be more visible in the criminal justice system. For instance, Chapter 7 of this book highlighted the changing nature of the criminal justice system as females become more actively involved as arrestees/offenders and practitioners. As females become increasingly involved in the workforce, it is expected that their presence in the criminal justice system will continue to increase.

Additionally, no signs point to decreased involvement of racial and ethnic minorities in the criminal justice system. The continued overrepresentation of minorities, particularly African Americans, as suspects and offenders in the criminal justice system does not seem to be waning. The social factors that contribute to the increased incarceration among minority groups persist and are perhaps becoming even more pronounced than during the past 20 to 30 years when incarceration rates notably impacted minority communities. Increased levels of poverty and single-parent families are prominent among the factors contributing to increased minority representation in the criminal justice system.

Another qualitative factor likely to influence the nature of U.S. incarceration in the coming years concerns the increasing frequency with which international crimes occur. Thomas L. Friedman's best-selling book *The World Is Flat: A Brief History of the Twenty-First Century* documents how increased globalization has and will continue to impact the world.[6] Along these lines, it is anticipated that an increased amount of crime will have an international flavor as more opportunities for criminal behavior appear. In turn, the criminal justice system in the United States will have to continue working with the criminal justice systems in other countries and promoting cooperative and collaborative efforts to ensure justice. Such efforts will result in the continued diversification of the U.S. criminal justice system. For the purposes of our forecasting efforts, increased international crime will result in a greater need for multiculturalism in corrections. The need to recognize and react to various cultural backgrounds will increase as more offenders from around the globe enter our prisons.

Our forecasting efforts have targeted the future of incarceration with concern for multiculturalism. We could also observe the future of criminal behavior with concern for multiculturalism, the future of minority involvement as practitioners in the criminal justice system, and a variety of other, related issues. Regardless of our approach, the future of the criminal justice system and multiculturalism will be shaped by a variety of factors. Below we turn our attention to several critical issues that affect and are expected to continue impacting the criminal justice system. The mere existence of these issues provides discouraging commentary on the current state of multiculturalism as it exists in society in general.

Critical Issues Affecting Multiculturalism and Criminal Justice

Several critical issues hamper and will continue to impact efforts toward a multicultural society in the United States. These issues are not restricted to the United States, as other countries face the same obstacles. Prominent among the issues hampering a completely multicultural society are racial profiling, hate crimes, and immigration.

Racial Profiling

Racial profiling is discussed in several chapters of this book, particularly in our focus on policing and multiculturalism in Chapter 10. Police officers are often criticized for disproportionately targeting minority drivers in an attempt to uncover drug

Racial profiling is prominent among the obstacles hampering police–minority group relations.

trafficking. However, racial profiling is not restricted to our roadways, as minorities have been unlawfully approached in their homes, while walking on public streets, at airports, in shopping areas, and in other places. An estimated 32 million Americans believe they have been subject to racial profiling in their lifetime.[7]

The practice of racial profiling provides a gauge to determine society's concern for due process and crime control. Scholar Herbert Packer commented on these two competing models of criminal justice. The **crime control model of criminal justice** maintains an emphasis on expediency and reducing crime, yet such practices often occur at the expense of individual rights. The **due process model of criminal justice** is primarily concerned with respecting individual rights, yet doing so often comes at the expense of controlling crime.[8] In the United States, concern for homeland security and drug crimes has resulted in a criminal justice system focused on crime control that too often comes at the expense of individual rights. The notable concern about racial profiling among minority communities provides evidence of this claim. Finding the proper balance between crime control and individual rights is often difficult in a multicultural, heterogeneous society such as the U.S. A criminal justice system that recognizes and responds to multiculturalism is one that includes no racial profiling. Future criminal justice practices will hopefully be void of race-based and culture-based crime fighting efforts.

FLYING WHILE BLACK

In 2007, 62-year-old Benita Rhodes Berg settled a lawsuit with the U.S. Drug Enforcement Agency (DEA) following her claims that DEA agents engaged in racial profiling. The incident occurred in 2001 when Berg, an African American, was returning to the Minneapolis-St. Paul International Airport after visiting her son in Los Angeles. She had a carry-on bag that contained Bible studies materials and diet and cosmetics items. Berg was stopped by DEA Agent Tammy Key and an airport police officer assigned to the DEA, who asked if they could search Berg's bag. Berg asked the law enforcement agents why they wished to look in the bag. The agents noted that the bag looked heavy. Berg, who agreed to the search, believed she was being targeted because she is an African American woman.

Support for the claims that Agent Key's actions were racially motivated was found in records documenting the number and nature of "cold" stops made by Key at the airport. A "cold" stop is when an agent

stops a traveler based solely on the individual's appearance, in contrast to a "hot" stop, which is based on evidence. Minorities constituted 88% of the cold stops made by Agent Key during the first year of data collection. No White males were stopped by Key during this time, and none of the minority individuals stopped by Key were found to be carrying drugs. Key commented that the criteria she used to conduct cold stops involved travelers who were carrying little or no baggage upon their return from cities where drugs were prominent.

As part of the settlement, Berg received $20,000, and both she and the American Civil Liberties Union of Minnesota secured the public release of data collected by the DEA and information pertaining to the DEA's efforts to correct efforts that appear to involve racial profiling. The DEA data and information to remedy racial profiling will hopefully address future misunderstandings and/or misbehavior. The settlement involving racial profiling is believed to be the first of its kind for the DEA.[9]

Hate Crimes

Hate crimes involve illegal actions that are motivated by hate and taken against particular groups. The term "hate crime" didn't exist prior to the 1980s and is sometimes used interchangeably with **bias crime,** which involves illegal acts taken against a group based on bias. While the motivation, hate, is consistent in all hate crimes, the target and offender characteristics of hate crimes are not. The hatred, or bias, can be based on one's race, gender, religion, ethnicity, sexual orientation, disability, age, or political affiliation. Hate crimes are not, however, solely committed against minority groups, as White males have also been the target of hate-motivated incidents. That an individual would be motivated to break the law based on hatred of a particular group suggests that not everyone is tolerant of diversity. The mere existence of hate crimes in society demonstrates that much work remains with regard to creating a society that embraces multiculturalism.

Hate crime statistics, albeit controversial, speak loudly of the need for acceptance of multiculturalism. There was an annual average of 210,000 hate crimes from July 2000 through December 2003. Most of these incidents involved violent crimes. In most cases, race was the motivating factor for the hate crime, followed by association with persons who have particular characteristics (e.g., a multiracial couple) and ethnicity. Negative comments, harmful words, or abusive language was present in roughly 99% of the hate crime incidents. Discouragingly, less than half (44%) of hate crime victimizations were reported to the police.[10]

As discussed in Chapter 8, determining what, specifically, constitutes a hate crime is difficult. Similar to the difficulties found in courtrooms when attorneys attempt to determine whether or not the accused had the intent to commit a crime, determining one's motivation for committing a crime is not always easily done. Is the White supremacist who robs an African American female guilty of a hate crime? Yes, if he admits his motivation was hatred or his actions (e.g., verbal comments) toward the victim suggest hatred prompted the robbery. Otherwise, attorneys, judges, and jurors have to speculate or assume the crime wasn't hate-motivated. Perhaps the African American female provided the most opportune target for the offender.

Accordingly, one must consider hate crime statistics with caution, as there are several limitations to measuring hate crime. Particularly, the varied definitions of hate crime, the difficulty in determining one's motivation, and the sometimes unreliable data-gathering methods of researchers, the government, and advocacy groups can distort the prevalence of hate crime in society. Law professor James Jacobs and attorney Kimberly Potter argue that there is no reliable evidence pointing to an increase in hate crimes. They suggest the current hate-crime movement is motivated by increased sensitivity to prejudice and bigotry.[11]

Hate crime laws provide enhanced penalties for offenders charged with crimes motivated by hatred. The ultimate goal is to promote tolerance and to recognize the benefits of diversity. The argument is that offenders who commit crime out of hatred or bias are morally worse, and thus more culpable, than those who engage in crime for other reasons. Hate crime laws are also justified on the grounds that hate crimes disproportionately impose injuries and harms to victims, have more substantial negative impacts on the community than do typical crimes, and facilitate the potential for retaliation and intergroup conflict. Hate crime legislation is intended to send a message that society is concerned about diversity and tolerance and to ultimately deter criminal behavior. Whether or not the goals of hate crime legislation are being reached is the subject of debate.[12]

Hate crimes would not exist in a society that embraces multiculturalism. What current and future efforts are needed to eliminate or at the very least reduce hate crime incidents? This and related questions are addressed later in this chapter.

Immigration

The multicultural makeup of the United States is one of the many strengths of the country. Accordingly, the United States takes pride in its diversity. The excerpt from Emma Lazarus' poem "The New Colossus" engraved at the bottom of the Statue of Liberty speaks loudly:

> Give me your tired, your poor,
> Your huddled masses yearning to breathe free,
> The wretched refuse of your teeming shore.
> Send these, the homeless, tempest-tossed, to me:
> I lift my lamp beside the golden door.[13]

Despite these words, there is current debate regarding immigration into the United States. When discussing immigration, a distinction must be made between legal and illegal immigration. Legal immigration can be controlled by the government, in turn providing a monitor to protect overpopulation and the economic well-being of the country, among

Immigrants who come to this country legally are often treated as though they have entered the U.S. illegally. Consequently they are sometimes discriminated against and denied constitutional protections

other things. Illegal immigration is a different matter. The government attempts to prevent illegal immigrants from entering the country; however, doing so has been difficult and controversial. Too often, discussions of immigration intermix references to both groups and the discussion becomes clouded. Currently, there is a particular concern with illegal immigration, which is making life more difficult for legal immigrants.

Illegal immigration attracts substantial attention given the illegal status of those who enter the country without permission. In the fight against illegal immigration, those opposed to immigration are joined by those opposed to lawbreakers. The fight against illegal immigration extends from the federal government to local communities. In 2006 the U.S. Congress introduced legislation to make illegal immigration a felony and build a 700-mile fence along the Mexican border. Immigration and Customs Enforcement, under direction of the Department of Homeland Security, announced in 2006 that it would triple the number of fugitive-hunting teams, with the goal of doubling the number in 2007.[14]

Critics of illegal immigration argue that the federal government hasn't done enough in response to the number of immigrants illegally entering the United States. Accordingly, state legislatures and local municipalities have taken action by considering and adopting an unprecedented number of measures to address the issue. From January through June 2007, 171 immigration bills became law in 41 states, which is twice as many as the 84 laws passed in all of 2006.[15] Tennessee made it a criminal offense, rather than a civil offense, to "recklessly employ" illegal immigrants. Fines for doing so can be up to $50,000. Other states have made it more difficult or impossible for illegal immigrants to obtain a driver's license.[16] These are just a few of the many steps taken by state legislatures to control illegal immigration.

City governments around the country are also responding to complaints about illegal immigrants. In 2006 the city of Hazleton, Pennsylvania, passed the Illegal Immigration Relief Act, which included fines for landlords who rent to illegal immigrants and outlawed business permits to companies that employ them. Hazleton Mayor Lou Barletta cited drug, crime, and gang problems involving illegal immigrants as the impetus behind the act. Critics of the act stated that the law usurps the federal government's power to regulate immigration, deprives residents of their constitutional rights to due process, and violates federal housing laws.[17] A federal judge voided the Illegal Immigration Relief Act. Hazleton, however, is not the only city to react to illegal immigration, as cities around the United States have responded in a similar and sometimes more punitive manner. These actions will also be considered in courts around the country.

While much of the debate concerning immigration centers on illegal immigration, legal immigrants face particular challenges. For instance, from a criminal justice perspective, immigrants are victimized at rates similar to the general population, yet their rate of reporting victimization is much lower. The underreporting of criminal victimization of immigrants stems largely from the hardships associated with appearing in court, including language barriers, uncertainty regarding the U.S. criminal justice system, and general cultural differences.[18]

Among other effects, the failure to report crime fails to ensure the protection of all citizens and undermines the effectiveness of the criminal justice system. At the very least, it increases the likelihood of the offender committing further crime. Efforts have been made to address the underreporting by providing interpreters during court hearings and various victim outreach programs in communities heavily populated by immigrants.[19] Certainly, the future of criminal justice and multiculturalism will be heavily impacted by immigration issues.

Racial profiling, hate crimes, and immigration concerns are not the only critical issues challenging efforts toward multiculturalism. These issues were discussed based on their relevance to the criminal justice system. Several other issues are affecting multiculturalism in the larger society. For instance, there has been and continues to be debate regarding whether or not students should be permitted to express their religious beliefs (e.g., pray) in a school setting.

Bigotry, prejudice, and bias are evident in many issues and at minimum hamper efforts toward tolerance. So, what can be done? Are the immigration laws and reactions to our diverse society appropriate? The criminal justice system has, in the past, responded to discrimination and diversity-related issues. Recent efforts to eliminate or at least reduce discrimination in the criminal justice system are evident in actions such as sentencing guidelines, the 1970s decision to nullify existing capital punishment statutes, and an increased focus on diversity training among all criminal justice practitioners. However, attempts to limit or remove the impacts of discretionary actions by criminal justice professionals do not always reduce discriminatory practices. For instance, the manner in which capital punishment is used continues to be controversial in that poor minorities convicted of murder are more likely than their nonminority counterparts to face execution.[20]

Is there an "American culture" to which all groups in the United States must subscribe? Given the historical development of the United States (in which waves of immigrants landed on U.S. soil and helped build the country into what it is today) and failed efforts to change cultural beliefs, one could make a strong argument that tolerance of diverse cultures is needed. To be sure, culture conflict will continue. The goal is to eliminate, or at least minimize, the harmful effects of such conflict. Perhaps the best way to promote tolerance and accept diversity is to enlighten individuals to the benefits of multiculturalism.

✕ Teaching Multiculturalism

One of the more notable shifts in the focus of higher education involves greater consideration for diversity and multiculturalism.[21] There exist many ways to cover these topics in the classroom, and the issues covered by general university-level training regarding diversity and multiculturalism range from understanding basic concepts to interpretation of advanced statistical analyses regarding race and gender. Unfortunately, most university students will get only one course on multiculturalism.[22] Similar to those who have taken only one semester of a foreign language, students taking only one course on multiculturalism will have a broad overview but lack substantial comprehension of the many-faceted aspects of the topic. It is not uncommon for instructors who teach a sensitive topic such as diversity or multiculturalism to sacrifice complexity for morality.[23]

Teaching about diversity, multiculturalism, and tolerance should not be restricted to university settings. Changing stereotypical images and discriminatory practices requires teaching at an early age. The onus is on both public and private educational institutions from kindergarten through college to address tolerance and diversity, as today's students are tomorrow's professionals.[24] Recognizing and incorporating the many significant accomplishments of individuals from various cultures encourages young, impressionable students to embrace multiculturalism. Pointing out accomplishments of diverse groups of individuals offers significant contributions toward promoting tolerance, but that alone is not enough.

The goal in teaching multiculturalism is to structure one's mind toward tolerance and acceptance of a diverse society. To do so, it is important to observe historical events that shaped current thought. Throughout this book we've commented on the historical treatment of various cultures both within and outside of the criminal justice system. Teaching multiculturalism, particularly to students of criminal justice, requires a holistic approach that encompasses, in addition to historical events, various social, political, economic, demographic, and related considerations. In other words, we can't simply consider the role of various cultures in the criminal justice system without recognizing the significance of political influences, the effects of poverty, the impact of racist attitudes, and the changing nature of our society's population.

In discussing an approach to incorporating multiculturalism into the criminal justice curriculum, researcher and professor of criminal justice William Calathes argues that cultural pluralism, intergroup relations, demography, and involvement constitute the theoretical component of multiculturalism. He adds that such topics are often neglected in traditional criminal justice textbooks, which neglect the complexities of the criminal justice system as it pertains to various cultures.[25] At the very least, concepts that highlight the contextual nature of diversity within the system should be emphasized in any discussion of multiculturalism within the criminal justice system.

Calathes argues that a multicultural approach to criminal justice would help students recognize the "present and future eventualities" and obtain the critical thinking skills and ability to work, teach, and engage in research from that perspective.[26] Calathes offers a series of steps that would promote teaching multiculturalism in the criminal justice curriculum. Included among his suggestions are

- informing students of the experiences of different cultures as they relate to life both within and outside of the criminal justice system;
- teaching from the perspective of the subjects;
- emphasizing the relationship between law and politics, including examination of the power differentials in society;
- teaching students to recognize various cultures, with particular concern for racism and oppression; and
- preparing students to understand the problems of different groups and conflicts between groups.[27]

> A multicultural approach to criminal justice education would help all who work, or will work, within the system to better address many of the problems inherent in the system.

Teaching tolerance for diversity should not be restricted to schools. Parents, coaches, mentors, and other role models need to stress the importance of recognizing and appreciating other groups. For instance, athletic coaches are often in ideal situations to stress teamwork among individuals from different backgrounds. The lesson that individuals need to work as a team could be generalized to society with the goal of encouraging athletes (and others) to recognize the beneficial contributions from diverse individuals. The same idea holds true for band leaders, church group facilitators, and others. There are many avenues where progress can be made with regard to accepting and appreciating diverse individuals and groups.

⚔ Progress?

Arguably, criminal justice education has promoted assimilation, in contrast to multiculturalism, through adopting the idea that the U.S. is a melting pot.[28] Is the United States a melting pot that welcomes individuals from different backgrounds and promotes assimilation? Or is the term "salad bowl" better suited to describe the integration and interaction of different groups in society? Earlier interpretations of ethnic relations in the United States used the term "melting pot," but more recently, "salad bowl" is used. Why? The melting pot metaphor conjures images of individuals molding together or assimilating in society. The salad bowl metaphor suggests that each individual retains her or his cultural characteristics and integrity and contributes to the final product. References to cultural relations in terms of a salad bowl are another way of promoting multiculturalism.

Some sociologists actually use a "stew" metaphor instead of a salad since there are distinct differences between the groups; inevitably the groups affect each other in profound ways and the groups shape the overall culture. The melting pot illustration was popular among the public but never really given any credence by the academic community, largely because of the racial and ethnic conflicts that have always existed.

The power differentials in a capitalistic society are such that individuals without means are more often brought to the attention of the criminal justice system. Whether or not the differential power structure encourages the less-powerful to commit crime, or the criminal justice system disproportionately focuses on crimes of the lower class, it remains that the less-powerful constitute the vast majority of our prison population. How do we change this unfavorable situation? The answer to this question involves radical changes in the sociocultural, socioeconomic, and sociopolitical makeup of the United States. Radical changes, however, are not beyond the capacity of any society. Consider the fact that at the time of this writing the leading Democratic presidential candidates are Hillary Clinton (a female) and Barack Obama, who is part African American. The election of either as president would denote a significant step for diversity in the United States.

If indeed we haven't seen progress with regard to diversity, multiculturalism, and tolerance in the criminal justice system, then what should we do? What changes are needed to improve the system? The answer to these questions is twofold, as we must consider increasing equity, diversity, and tolerance with regard to the accused and the offenders entering and within the system, in addition to those working within the system. Several authors have commented on the changes necessary for a

Diversity is increasingly influencing politics.

more equitable system of criminal justice. For instance, scholars Coramae Richey Mann and Marjorie Zatz suggest that significant changes are needed in the major social institutions in the United States to erase the stereotype of people of color. Particularly, they cite changes needed in relation to housing, health, education, family, religion, political, and economic issues. Mann and Zatz argue that changes in these institutions will eradicate the negative stereotypical images of minorities as they pertain to crime.[29]

Author David Cole offers three promising and challenging solutions to address the inequities in today's criminal justice system. First, he argues that we must acknowledge that all are not equal before the law. The privileged still maintain a distinct advantage in many aspects of the criminal justice system. Second, Cole argues that we must restore the legitimacy of criminal law to eliminate or reduce the existing double standards for minorities and nonminorities. He cites the differential treatment of groups in many stages of the criminal justice system (as noted throughout this text) as evidence. Further legitimizing the criminal justice system would help address the existing disparities and bring to light charges of discrimination and differential treatment. Third, Cole argues that effective community-based responses to crime are needed at both the preventive and punitive stages.[30] His call for the further integration of the community in preventing and responding to crime is supported by many others, including those supporting community policing efforts, community courts, and community corrections.[31]

With regard to increasing the diversity of the criminal justice workforce, scholar Becky Tatum offers several suggestions to achieve and maintain diversity within the criminal justice system. Particularly, she encourages criminal justice organizations to

- understand that diversity enhances organizational effectiveness and success;
- continue practicing and promoting affirmative action policies;
- be committed to diversity;
- establish effective recruitment, selection, training, and promotion practices;
- create effective complaint policies and procedures to ensure that employees are not treated differently; and
- evaluate progress and the results of policies and procedures.[32]

To be sure, progress has been made with regard to multiculturalism in the criminal justice system. Despite existing problems, our system is fairer than it's been in the past and the criminal justice workforce is more diverse than ever before. However, the continued disintegration of affirmative action policies warrants mention. Affirmative action has played an integral part in diversifying the criminal justice workforce, although recent court rulings have limited its effectiveness. Further, affirmative action programs have not corrected the underlying causes of inequality and prejudice in many arenas, such as the lack of minority attorneys.[33] Accordingly, the reduced impact of affirmative action and the general climate of intolerance in the United States may contribute to increased discriminatory practices.[34]

If progress has been made with regard to multiculturalism in criminal justice, why the concern? The obvious answer is because there's room for improvement. Progress refers to advancement and does not necessarily mean that success has been achieved. The concern regarding diversity and criminal justice relates to the work that remains, including greater sensitivity to diversity issues. Society is quite sensitive to culture-based issues. That we are more sensitive to such issues suggests progress has been made and provides an ample opportunity for change. Nevertheless, the efforts pertaining to cultural sensitivity continue to highlight the existing challenges.

Each time we hear that a homosexual candidate was denied an employment position in criminal justice based on his or her sexual orientation, we believe we're taking a step backward. In many ways, such claims and actions are a step backward. One could equally look at such claims as progress, as in years past we may not have heard of the situation. The candidate may have simply accepted the discriminatory practice and moved on. Or, perhaps even worse, the candidate wouldn't have applied for the position out of a belief that he or she would be denied a position based on his or her sexual orientation. Hearing about discrimination can make the problem appear more prominent than it truly is; simultaneously, it sends a message that such practices are unacceptable.

Efforts toward multiculturalism are enhanced when individuals who have faced discrimination speak out about the mistreatment. Bringing the issue to light, in a nonconfrontational manner, draws attention. Such individuals must use caution, however, as exaggerated or elaborated stories often hamper efforts toward progress. The media can play a vital role in helping victims of discrimination or of other kinds of mistreatment share their stories.

Summary

One cannot consider the future without recognizing the impact of technology, although technological changes appear to have little impact on cultural relations. Nevertheless, the future of multiculturalism and the criminal justice system will be influenced by several changes in the larger society. Demographic trends will impact the system, as will the increased international nature of crime. The increasing separation of socioeconomic classes will continue to negatively impact multiculturalism and the criminal justice system, as will the ever-prominent crime control approach we've adopted.

All is not lost, however, as positive changes may be on the horizon. The changing demographics of society will dictate greater minority involvement as criminal justice practitioners, which should promote positive changes to the system. Individuals from diverse backgrounds are increasingly assuming more powerful roles in public service, politics, and private business. While there may be current tensions between cultural groups (as evidenced in the anti–illegal immigration legislation), signs point toward greater recognition of diversity and increased acceptance of multiculturalism.

Changes in the criminal justice system begin with changes in people. The system is composed of and influenced by individuals from various backgrounds. The system, as designed on paper, is not biased, racist, or anti-multicultural. What's needed for acceptance of multiculturalism is tolerance among individuals in society. The problems and challenges faced by different cultures in the criminal justice system were created by people—including biased and unbiased people. The problems posed by the unbiased can be addressed through greater professionalism in criminal justice. Fortunately, many signs point to greater professionalism in the discipline. The problems posed by biased individuals are fixed through identifying and correcting the problems, while removing such individuals from their influential positions.

 ## You Make the Call

Teaching Diversity

Consider the following scenario. Debate the pros and cons of all options and decide what you would do.

You're a new college faculty member at a historically African American university. As part of your teaching assignment, you've been asked to teach the upper-level undergraduate "Minorities and Crime" course. As a White male, however, you're a bit apprehensive. Sure, you know all about crime and took courses and researched minority issues, but you never anticipated such a challenge this early in your teaching career. Aside from having to be current on your knowledge of crime, you also have to discuss minority issues in a class that has a large group of minorities. On the first day of class, a student asks how you can comment on minority issues, when you have absolutely no life experience being a minority. You hoped this wouldn't be an issue, but you are prepared to answer the question.

Questions

1. How will you build credibility with this large group of minority students?
2. How will you structure the course? In other words, would you approach the course from the views of minority groups or the views of the majority? Or would you attempt to provide an adequate balance between both?
3. How would you answer the student's question?
4. Discuss how the following teaching tools could assist with your situation:

   - class discussion
   - videos (what movies would you include?)
   - guest speakers
   - lecture

Key Terms

bias crime (p. 313)

crime control model of criminal justice (p. 312)

Delphi Method (p. 308)

drivers of the future (p. 309)

due process model of criminal justice (p. 312)

forecasting (p. 307)

futurists (p. 307)

hate crimes (p. 313)

predictions (p. 308)

qualitative approaches (p. 308)

quantitative analyses (p. 308)

scenarios (p. 308)

Discussion Questions

1. Provide a scenario of the criminal justice system in the year 2075. Be sure to focus on issues pertaining to diversity, tolerance, and multiculturalism.
2. Compare and contrast the various methods of forecasting the future. Which do you believe offer the greatest accuracy? Why?
3. Discuss how racial profiling, immigration, and hate crimes will impact the future of multiculturalism and criminal justice.
4. Create an outline for an undergraduate-level course on multiculturalism and criminal justice. What topics would you include? How would you structure the course?
5. Identify and discuss three changes you believe are necessary for the criminal justice system to welcome diversity among the ranks of practitioners. Further, identify and discuss three changes you feel are needed to facilitate tolerance among criminal justice practitioners with consideration of the diverse criminal population.

Endnotes

1. Stephens, G. 2005. "Policing the Future: Law Enforcement's New Challenges." *The Futurist*, March/April, pp. 51–57.

2. Burns, R. 2007. "The Future of Delinquency Prevention and Treatment." In M. D. McShane and F. P. Williams III

(eds.), *Youth Violence & Delinquency*, Volume 3. Westport, CT: Praeger.

3. U.S. Department of Justice. Bureau of Justice Statistics. 2007. "Key Facts at a Glance: Incarceration Rate, 1980–2005." www.ojp.usdoj.gov/bjs/glance/tables/incrttab.htm (accessed August 2, 2007).

4. U.S. Census Bureau. 2004. "U.S. Interim Projections by Age, Sex, Race, and Hispanic Origin." www.census.gov/ipc.www/usinterimproj (accessed August 2, 2007).

5. U.S. Census Bureau. 2001. *Population Profile of the United States: America at the Close of the 20th Century*. Washington, DC: U.S. Department of Commerce.

6. Friedman, T. L. 2005. *The World Is Flat: A Brief History of the Twenty-First Century*. New York: Farrar, Straus and Giroux.

7. Amnesty International. 2004. "Threat and Humiliation: Racial Profiling, Domestic Security, and Human Rights in the United States." www.amnestyusa.org/racial_profiling/report/rp_report.pdf (accessed August 6, 2007).

8. Packer, H. L. 1968. *The Limits of the Criminal Sanction*. Stanford, CA: Stanford University Press.

9. American Civil Liberties Union of Minnesota. 2007, August 9. "Unprecedented Settlement in Racial Profiling Case." www.aclu-mn.org/home/news/unprecedentedsettlementinr.htm (accessed August 23, 2007).

10. Harlow, C. W. 2005, November. *Hate Crime Reported by Victims and Police*. NCJ 209911. Bureau of Justice Statistics. Washington, DC: U.S. Department of Justice.

11. Jacobs, J. B., and Potter, K. 1998. *Hate Crimes: Criminal Law & Identity Politics*. New York: Oxford University Press.

12. Ibid.

13. Lazarus, E. 1883."The New Colossus."

14. Cullen, L. T. 2006, March 27. "Mission: Search and Send Back." *Time*. www.time.com/time/magazine/article/0,9171,1176999,99.html (accessed August 6, 2007).

15. LeBlanc, S. 2007, August 5. "States Enter Void Left by Immigration Bill." Associated Press. www.chron.com/disp/story.mpl/ap/nation/5029404.html (accessed August 8, 2007).

16. Preston, J. 2007, August 6. "Surge in Immigration Laws Around the U.S." *New York Times*. www.nytimes.com/2007/08/06/washington/06immig.html?ex=1187064000&en=9269b383a0d29231&ei=5123&partner=BREITBART (accessed August 7, 2007).

17. Associated Press. 2007, July 26. "Judge Voids Pa. City's Illegal Immigration Law." www.msnbc.msn.com/id/19978003 (accessed February 18, 2008).

18. Davis, R. C., and Erez, E. 1998. *Immigrant Populations as Victims: Toward a Multicultural Criminal Justice System*. Bureau of Justice Statistics. Washington, DC: U.S. Department of Justice.

19. Ibid.

20. Welch, M. 1999. *Punishment in America: Social Control and the Ironies of Imprisonment*. Thousand Oaks, CA: Sage.

21. Magner, D. K. 1996. "Fewer Professors Believe Western Culture Should Be the Cornerstone of the College Curriculum." *Chronicle of Higher Education,* September 13, pp. 12–13.

22. Platt, T. 2002. "Desegregating Multiculturalism: Problems in the Theory and Pedagogy of Diversity Education." *Social Justice* 29 (4): 41–46.

23. Ibid.

24. See Mann, C. M., and Zatz, M. S. 2006. "A Fragile Future: Pitfalls and Possibilities." In C. R. Mann, M. S. Zatz, and N. Rodriguez (eds.), *Images of Color, Images of Crime*, 3rd ed., pp. 252–264. Los Angeles, CA: Roxbury.

25. Calathes, W. 1994. "The Case for a Multicultural Approach to Teaching Criminal Justice." *Journal of Criminal Justice Education* 5 (1): 1–14.

26. Ibid., p. 4.

27. Ibid., pp. 9–11.

28. Ibid.

29. Mann and Zatz 2006.

30. Cole, D. 1999. *No Equal Justice: Race and Class in the American Criminal*

Justice System. New York: The New Press.

31. Among the many resources addressing community-based criminal justice are Clear, T., and Cadora, E. 2003. *Community Justice*. Belmont, CA: Wadsworth; Kappeler, V. E., and Gaines L. K. 2005. *Community Policing: A Contemporary Perspective*, 4th ed. Cincinnati, OH: Anderson; and Lee, E. 2000, October. *Community Courts: An Evolving Model*. NCJ 183452. Office of Justice Programs. Washington, DC: U.S. Department of Justice.

32. Tatum, B. 2005. "Criminal Justice Personnel in the Twenty-First Century." In R. Muraskin and A. R. Roberts (eds.), *Visions for Change: Crime and Justice in the Twenty-First Century*, pp. 670–683. Upper Saddle River, NJ: Prentice Hall.

33. Thomas, R. 1990. "From Affirmative Action to Affirming Diversity." *Harvard Business Review*, March/April, pp. 107–117.

34. Morgan, E. F. 2005. "The Administration of Justice Based on Gender and Race." In R. Muraskin and A. R. Roberts (eds.), *Visions for Change: Crime and Justice in the Twenty-First Century,* pp. 652–669. Upper Saddle River, NJ: Prentice Hall.

Glossary

A

acquaintance rape   An act of rape involving individuals familiar with one another.

adjudicatory process   The act of settling a case judicially in a courtroom.

affirmative action   Programs designed to promote the hiring of minority applicants.

affirmative defense   A defense in which the defendant admits committing the action in question, although they have legal justification for doing so. Entering an affirmative defense requires defendants to demonstrate that their action was justified. Self-defense, insanity, coercion, and entrapment are affirmative defenses.

alibi   One of two types of defenses that may be offered at trial (affirmative defenses being the other). It states that the defendant did not commit they crime (e.g., they were in another location at the time of the crime).

Alien Land Act   Prohibited anyone who was ineligible for citizenship to own land and limited leases to three years. The land laws drove many first-generation Japanese into cities.

American Indian Movement   A movement which began in 1968 and became the most visible reminder of the Red Power Movement. Its original purpose was to monitor the police and to document evidence of police brutality. Eventually, the movement turned its attention to solving problems within the Native American community by initiating various programs to reduce alcoholism among Native Americans and improve educational programs.

amnesty   A type of clemency that restores rights and privileges of groups of people.

appearance   Items that signify a performer's social status.

arraignment   The step in criminal case processing when the accused is formally notified of the charges against them, and he or she enters a plea. At an arraignment, defendants enter a plea, pretrial motions are offered, and discovery may occur.

Asian Indian   A term that represents a wide range of populations. India itself is a diverse nation with dozens of languages and ethnic enclaves.

assigned counsel   Court appointed representation for indigent cases. Attorneys are assigned indigent cases in return for a statutorily-determined fee

B

Baby Boomers   A term to describe a segment of the population. This group represents about 28% of the U.S. population and is responsible for some of the most dramatic changes in American history.

barrios   Concentrations of segregated areas or ghettos in the Southwestern portion of the U.S.

Battle at Little Big Horn   A battle fought in 1876 in which Custer and his men were defeated.

Battle of Wounded Knee   The battle heralded by historians as significant because it extinguished the hope of the Sioux Nation of ever returning to a life of freedom.

bench trial   Trials in which judges serve as both judge and jury.

bias crime   Illegal acts taken against a group based on bias.

bisexuality   A term used to describe an individual's attraction to both sexes.

Black Codes   Laws designed to nullify the rights granted to the newly freed slaves. Among the restrictions found in Black Codes were the prohibition of interracial marriage, renting land in urban areas, preaching the gospel without a license, and assuming any occupation other than servant or farmer unless the newly freed slave paid a tax.

Black middle-class   A term used to describe relatively affluent African Americans.

Black Nationalism   The philosophy that encourages Blacks to see themselves as Blacks first rather than as Americans.

Black Power   A political movement that encouraged Blacks to create new institutions and emulate the political path followed by many European immigrant groups.

Black rage   A defense offered in court which attempts to provide legal justification for criminal behavior by some African Americans frustrated by oppression resulting from living in a White-dominated society.

Bow Street Runners   A precursor to formal policing, this group consisted of individuals who sought law violators in the Bow Street region of London. The Runners were paid a sum of money for bringing suspects before the court.

Bureau of Indian Affairs   The primary regulatory arm of the federal government as it relates to Native Americans.

C

Canteen Punk   An inmate who performs oral or anal sex for candy, cigarettes, or other items purchased at the prison store or canteen.

challenge for cause   A motion through which attorneys may eliminate a potential juror because of an identifiable bias and/or an apparent inability to assess a case fairly.

Chicanos   Americans of Mexican origin.

Chinese Exclusion Act   An act, passed in 1882, which outlawed Chinese immigration for ten years. It lasted in various forms for over sixty years.

Christopher Commission   A commission assembled in the wake of the Rodney King incident in response to claims of LAPD officer misbehavior. The Commission identified several areas and instances of unethical behavior by LAPD officers.

Civil Rights Act of 1866   This Act was targeted to address the Black Codes by defining all persons born in the United States, with the exception of Native Americans, as national citizens who were to enjoy specific rights. These rights included permission to make contracts, bring lawsuits, and enjoy the full and equal benefit of the law.

Civil Rights Act of 1964   Prohibited discrimination in hiring on the basis of color, race, sex, religion, or national origin.

Civil Rights Movement   A movement designed to provide equal rights to minorities.

claims making   A fundamental aspect of how social problems are defined in a given society.

clemency   Legislative actions which reduce the severity of one's punishment, waive the punishment associated with a crime, or exclude certain individuals from prosecution of a specific crime.

collective conscience   Shared beliefs and moral attitudes which contribute to unifying society.

color gradient   Distinctions in terms of group membership based on a light-to-dark skin continuum.

community corrections   Correctional supervision in a community setting.

community era of policing   This era of policing began around 1980 and continues today. It involves efforts by the police to re-connect with the public primarily through the adoption of the community policing philosophy.

community policing   A philosophical approach to policing that stresses creating and perpetuating a sense of community. It promotes positive police-citizen interaction and focuses on quality of life issues.

commutations   A type of clemency which involves shortening or changing an inmate's prison sentence.

concealing errors   Nondisclosure of errors that have been made in the preparation of a performance as well as steps that have been taken to correct these errors.

concealing secret pleasures   Nondisclosure of activities engaged in prior to a performance or in past lives that are incompatible with a performance.

conditional release   Release from prison accompanied by community supervision.

continuum of force   A concept that guides officer behavior with respect to use of force.

courtroom workgroup   Individuals who work on a regular basis in a courtroom setting.

crime control model of criminal justice   A perspective on the administration of justice, as described by Herbert Packer, which maintains an emphasis on expediency and reducing crime.

crimes against persons   Violent crimes. Examples include murder and non-negligent manslaughter, forcible rape, assaults, and intimidation.

crimes against property   Economic crimes. Examples include burglary, larceny-theft, motor vehicle theft, vandalism, and arson.

crimes against society   Often referred to as victimless crimes, they are a series of crimes in which there is no easily discernable victim. It includes offenses such as gambling, prostitution, drugs, or weapons violations.

culture   Beliefs, values, behaviors, and material goods that collectively constitute a people's manner of life. Culture shapes what we do and our personalities.

D

Delphi Method   A qualitative approach to forecasting the future in which experts offer input regarding anticipated developments in their area of expertise.

de-policing   A tactic employed by some officers who answer only high-priority calls instead of engaging in routine patrol.

determinate sentencing   Sentencing practices in which offenders receive a specific amount of time to be served based on the crime for which they were convicted.

deterrence   Efforts to dissuade the offender (specific deterrence) or society in general (general deterrence) from engaging in acts for which the offender is being punished.

discovery   The sharing of information among attorneys with the goal of helping them adequately prepare their case.

discreditable stigma   A stigma in which the differences are neither known by audience members nor perceivable by them. An example might be a homosexual trying to hide his sexual orientation in a heterosexual environment.

discredited stigma   A type of stigma in which the actor assumes that the differences contributing to the stigma are known by the audience members or are evident to them.

discretionary release   Involves the use of discretion in the decision to release an inmate from prison. It most commonly refers to parole board decision-making.

discrimination   The unequal treatment of people based on their membership in a particular group.

double bind   Refers to the challenges specifically faced in the criminal justice system by females from other minority groups.

double jeopardy   A term sometimes used to describe the challenges faced specifically by female officers from minority groups.

downward social mobility   A change in a person's social status resulting in the individual receiving a lower position in their status system.

dramaturgical circumspection   The logistical planning involved in carrying out a performance. Examples include planning for emergencies, making only brief appearances, and preventing audiences access to private information.

dramaturgical discipline   Concise preparation of a performance. It includes such things as having the presence of mind to avoid slips, maintaining self-control, and managing facial expressions and the tone of voice of one's performance.

dramaturgy   A view of social life as a series of dramatic performances like those performed on stage.

drivers of the future   Particular issues which have significant impacts on the future.

due process model of criminal justice   A perspective on the administration of justice, as described by Herbert Packer, that is primarily concerned with respecting individual rights.

E

elder abuse   The abuse, neglect, or exploitation of the elderly.

eldercide   The murder of a person 50 years or older.

Emancipation Proclamation   The document that freed slaves in the Confederacy.

Equal Employment Opportunity Act of 1972   This act extended the protections of women and other minorities to local governments.

ethnicism   Emphases on ethnic identity. Preference for a particular ethnicity.

ethnocentrism   Believing that one's culture or group is superior to others.

exclusionary rule   Prohibits illegally seized materials from being introduced in court.

exmates   Former prison inmates.

F

Federal Bureau of Prisons   A bureau within the federal government that operates 114 institutions and 28 community corrections offices across the United States. The Bureau oversees roughly 193,000 offenders convicted of federal offenses.

Federal Jury Selection and Service Act of 1968   This Act provided greater equity in jury selection practices in that it prohibited the exclusion of individuals based on religion, race, gender, national origin, or economic status.

Federal Parole Commission   A federal-level group that oversees federal parolees.

feminist movements   Social movements which generally promote the idea that males and females should be politically, socially, and economically equal.

forecasting   The use of scientific techniques to anticipate future developments.

Frankpledge System   The early English practice of informal social control in which community members protected one another.

freedom schools   Private all-White schools that enrolled an estimated 300,000 White children by 1970. Their development occurred with the intent of evading the *Brown* decision.

fugitive slave acts   Legislation which required slaves who had escaped, even to a free state, to be returned to their owners.

futurists   Scientists who forecast future developments in society.

G

gay bashing   Unprovoked attacks on homosexuals.

gender   It is a social characteristic that varies from one social group to another and refers to femininity or masculinity. It is a master status as it cuts across all walks of life.

Generation X (Gen Xers)   The period of time including individuals born between 1968 and 1979. This group is generally considered an underachieving generation and critical of the self-indulgence of Baby Boomers. Gen Xers grew up amid a host of social problems in the 1980s and 1990s.

Generation Y (Gen Yers)   The period of time including individuals born between approximately 1977 and 1994. Gen Yers are characterized by their willingness to embrace cultural diversity, are educationally and technologically sophisticated, and have a strong sense of self including feelings of entitlement, self-confidence, and impatience in climbing the ladder of success.

genocide   The deliberate, systematic killing of an entire people or nation. While it has been associated with Nazi Germany, other forms of ethnic cleansing have occurred in other parts of the world.

geriatric court   A distinct system of justice for the elderly.

Ghost Dance religion   A religion that included dances and songs proclaiming the return of the buffalo and the resurrection of dead ancestors in a land free of White people.

glass ceiling   An abstract barrier preventing certain groups and/or individuals from moving beyond entry-level occupational positions.

going rate   The penalties associated with particular criminal offenses.

grand jury hearing   Hearings used to determine if continued case processing is necessary. In grand jury hearings jurors basically replace the judge used in a preliminary hearing. The grand jury's task is to determine if the prosecutor's case is strong enough to warrant an indictment.

group goals   Agreed-upon tasks or activities that a group seeks to complete or accomplish.

group structure   The characteristics of a group. A group's structure is largely determined by group roles, and typically evolves in accord with, or from, group norms and rules. The structure is vulnerable to change as norms, goals, and other factors impacting the group change.

H

harmless error doctrine   A doctrine which holds that a trial court decision will not be overturned in an appellate court based on small, insignificant errors that appear to have limited or no impact on the trial outcome.

hate crimes   Illegal actions that are motivated by hate and taken against particular groups.

heterogeneous   Something diverse in nature. Societies in which people come from a wide range of backgrounds and experiences.

homogeneity   Similarity in attitudes, values, and beliefs.

homogeneous societies   Societies in which individuals share similar attitudes, values, and beliefs.

homosexual   An individual attracted to those of the same sex.

homosexual advance theory   The justification for courts to allow a non-violent homosexual advance to constitute sufficient provocation.

hue and cry   An early form of informal social control in which a call to arms generated a response from every able bodied male in attempts to bring offenders(s) to justice.

human snakes   Individuals who leave China illegally.

I

incapacitation   Physically preventing one from committing similar criminal acts in the future. Incarceration is the most widely used form of incapacitation.

incarceration   The physical detention of an inmate; it consists primarily of prison and jail.

indeterminate sentencing   A type of sentence in which inmates are released via discretionary decisions after a period of incarceration. Inmates are released after being deemed fit to return to society.

Indian Claims Commission   Although not an official U.S. court, the Commission operates somewhat like one in that lawyers present evidence for both sides. If the commission agrees with the tribe, it then determines the value of the land at the time it was illegally seized.

Indian Removal Act of 1830   An act which called for the relocation of all Eastern tribes to west of the Mississippi River.

indictment   The charging document used by grand juries to suggest enough evidence exists to proceed with case processing.

indigent defendants   Defendants who cannot afford privately-secured representation.

initial appearance   The stage of criminal case processing in which defendants are brought before the court, informed of the formal charges against them, advised of their rights, possibly granted pretrial release, and made aware of the upcoming steps in their case.

inmate code   The norms and values developed and stressed in prison; it encourages toughness, insensitivity, disdain and manipulation of fellow inmates and the prison staff. The code generally varies among institutions, as does inmate commitment to the code.

institutional discrimination   The type of discrimination built into the structure of society.

internment camps   Places for refugees to be held until their release by the government is granted.

involuntary migration   The practice of bringing individuals to a new land against their will.

J

jail   Jails hold detainees awaiting trial and those sentenced to incarceration for less than a year. In most states jails are operated by county-level officials, typically sheriff's departments.

Jim Crow   An individual whose name is now associated with the label for the social, political, and legal separation of Whites and Blacks in all aspects of society.

Jocker   Also known as the Wolf, this type of inmate engages in homosexual activities and is viewed by his colleagues as a "man." To remain a "man" and still engage in homosexual acts, the Jocker has to present an image of exaggerated toughness. So the Jocker uses force: he rapes. The more violence that surrounds his sexual acts, the more he is seen as masculine. To maintain his status, he must also keep his sexual acts emotionless and impersonal.

judge's charge to the jury   a written document, prepared by a judge for a jury, that explains the parameters under which jurors may deliberate.

jury nullification   The practice of jurors acquitting particular defendants despite strong evidence suggesting guilt.

just deserts   A philosophy which argues that every person is equally responsible for their actions and should be punished according to what they have done.

K

kinesics   Body language, including gestures, facial expressions, eye behavior, and body movements.

L

Latino   A term that refers to people and cultures of Latin America.

London Metropolitan Police Act   Passed in 1829, this act led to the first formal police department, the London Metropolitan Police, led by Sir Robert Peel.

Los Braceros   A 1942 program that allowed the migration of contracted workers across the U.S.–Mexico border.

M

mandatory minimum sentencing   A sentencing structure in which offenders convicted of certain offenses are to be sentenced to prison for no less than a specified term of years, and non-prison sentences (e.g., probation) are not an option. Mandatory minimum sentences are typically imposed on violent offenders.

mandatory release   A policy in which inmates earn time off of their prison sentence through various incentives. Inmates are to be released when they've served the number of days they've been sentenced less good time.

manner   Tells the audience what sort of role the performer expects to play in the situation.

Marielitos   A term which refers to individuals who were herded on to boats by Cuban authorities in Mariel, the fishing port west of Havana.

marital rape   The raping of one's spouse.

material culture   Objects that are real to the senses (e.g., a baton, handcuffs, a judge's gavel) and contribute to cultural identity.

McJobs   Jobs in the lowest paying sectors of the market, including many minimum wage jobs.

melting pot   A society that blends together a variety of backgrounds and cultures into a cohesive whole.

minority group   a subordinate group whose members have significantly less control or power over their own lives than the members of the dominant group. While numerical size may be important and related, the issue is really one of power.

model minority myth   The belief that Asian Americans constitute an ideal minority because they have endured political, economic, and social obstacles.

multiculturalism   The embracing of cultural diversity.

N

National Advisory Commission on Civil Disorders   Also known as the Kerner Commission, this group was created to study the causes behind the 1960s rioting. The Commission identified a series of issues that contributed to the collective violence, including unequal justice, institutional racism, unemployment, and discrimination.

National Council of La Raza   The largest Hispanic civil rights organization in the U.S.

Nation of Islam   A religious, social, and political group that seeks to resurrect the mental, social, economic, and spiritual condition of Blacks.

neocolonialism   A type of dependence that arises when a country remains dependent on their dominators long after they separated from them politically.

Neoricans   Puerto Ricans who return to the island after spending time away, typically in New York.

Nineteenth Amendment   Ratified by Congress in 1920, it gave women the right to vote.

nolo contendere   Also known as "no contest", this plea has the legal effect of a guilty plea. Defendants may choose to enter a plea of *nolo contendere* instead of admitting guilt in attempt to cooperate with the court although they do not wish to directly admit guilt.

non-material culture   Shared beliefs and values which contribute to cultural identity; the social expectations individuals have for one another.

O

Office of Tribal Justice   An agency that serves as a liaison between the tribes and the federal government.

operationalization   The process of researchers defining terms and variables for the purpose of analysis.

overpolicing   The oppressive and extensive use of formal social control against minority groups.

overstayers   Individuals admitted to a country on temporary visas who either stay beyond the expiration of their visas or otherwise violate their terms of admission.

P

pardons   A type of clemency which involves the restoration of a former inmate's rights and privileges.

parole   Offender supervision in the community following a period of incarceration.

patronage   The practice of politicians rewarding friends and/or acquaintances.

perception   The act of becoming aware or apprehending something via the senses.

peremptory challenge   A motion through which attorneys can eliminate seemingly unfit or inappropriate members of the jury pool. Attorneys typically do not need to justify using a peremptory challenge, although they are limited in the number of peremptory challenges they can use.

personal front   Items of equipment that an audience identifies with performers and expects them to carry with them into the setting.

plea bargaining   An exchange between the prosecution and defense designed to encourage a guilty plea in exchange for a benefit for the defendant.

police discretion   Officer decision-making; it is evident in all aspects of police practices. It is necessary in policing as officers are consistently faced with difficult situations involving multiple variables.

police subculture   A distinct culture within policing; it promotes a particular working personality that encourages solidarity, authoritarianism, and sometimes the exclusion of females and minority officers.

political era of policing   The era (1840-1930) is characterized by police officers seeking an intimate relationship with the community and politics heavily influencing police departments and police practices.

poverty line   The income level at which people are entitled to public assistance such as welfare.

predictions   Evaluations of expected future developments based on instinctual feelings (or "gut feelings") that lack scientific validity.

prejudice   A negative attitude toward certain people based solely on their membership in a particular group.

preliminary hearing   A stage in criminal case processing in which a prosecutor demonstrates to a judge why charges have been filed and justifies continued processing.

President's Commission on Law Enforcement and Administration of Justice   Also known as the President's Crime Commission, this group focused on enhancing professionalization of policing and police officers. It suggested hiring more members of minority groups and encouraging departments to become more community-oriented.

Pressure Punk   An inmate who submits to homosexual behavior because he has been threatened or raped by other prisoners.

pretrial motions   Motions offered in court prior to the trial in which an attorney seeks an order of the court. These motions are presented to a judge and can be a determining factor in the outcome of a case.

pretrial release   Releasing defendants prior to trial. Release can be secured monetarily, as in the case of bail, or non-financially, such as release on recognizance.

prison   Correctional facilities that incarcerate inmates serving sentences of one year or more.

prisonization   Inmate adaptation to prison culture. A social and physical transformation of the individual in an effort to compensate for the pains of imprisonment.

prison play-families   An aspect of the social structure of prisons in which inmates assume the roles of different family members. Play-families are more common in female prisons than in male institutions.

probation   Offender supervision in the community in lieu of incarceration.

problem-oriented policing   A four-step approach to addressing specific crimes in the community. The steps include scanning communities to identify problems, analyzing the nature and extent of the problem, responding to the problem, and assessing whether or not the problem is properly addressed.

prohibition The period (1919-1933) in which the sale, transport, or manufacturing of alcohol was criminalized.

proxemics The space between the communicator and his or her audience.

public defenders Attorneys who work in offices that exist solely to provide indigent representation. They face many challenges, including responsibility for large caseloads and limited resources.

Punk A homosexual inmate with one of the lowest statuses in the institution. They are despised by inmates who see homosexual behavior as the result of either weakness in the face of pressure or a willingness to sacrifice his manhood to obtain goods and services.

qualitative approaches Consideration of non-numerical trends and patterns in attempt to anticipate future developments and changes.

quantitative analyses The use of statistics and trends to anticipate changes in society.

Queen A male inmate who prefers male sexual partners.

R

racial profiling Recognizing individuals as suspects based merely upon race.

racism The belief that people are divided into distinct hereditary groups that are innately different in their behavior and abilities. This also means that groups can be ranked as superior or inferior on the basis of those abilities and behavior.

recidivism rate The rate related to which individuals commit an undesirable act after one has been treated, or experienced a negative consequence for that behavior. It is also known as the re-offending rate.

reconstruction A new social, political, and economic portrait of the South created after slavery was abolished.

red-light districts Areas of a city frequented by prostitutes.

Red Power Movement A movement that was similar to the Black Power movement for African Americans in that it attempted to gain economic, social, and political equality for Native Americans.

reform era of policing Also known as the progressive era, it was a time (1930-1980) characterized by police-community relations suffering and police becoming increasingly reliant on technology and overly concerned with efficiency.

rehabilitation Attempts to "cure" or "fix" the ills leading to an offender's behavior.

reintegration Offenders reintegrating, or readjusting to life outside prison.

repatriation A government-sponsored deportation program to send Chicanos back to Mexico

reprieves A type of clemency which involves the postponement of a sentence. They are typically associated with delaying an execution.

restrictive covenants A private contract between neighborhood property owners which stipulated that property could not be sold or rented to certain minority groups, thus ensuring minorities could not live in the area.

retribution Punishment, or the "eye for an eye" approach.

reverse discrimination Claims that minorities are being hired for employment opportunities at the expense of those in the majority.

role The behavior that is expected of an individual who maintains a particular status.

S

sanctuary laws Laws that prohibit police officers from inquiring about a suspect's immigration status.

scenarios A method of forecasting the future in which narratives are used to describe anticipated future events and developments.

sentencing guidelines Guidelines used by some jurisdictions to provide consistency and parity in sentencing decisions. They involve a risk assessment of the offender based on current offense and past history.

setoffs Deductions from the money due equal to the cost of federal services provided to a tribe.

setting The physical scene that ordinarily must exist if the actors are to perform.

sex The biological characteristics that distinguish males and females.

sexual orientation A term used to describe a sexual attraction toward people either of the same gender, the opposite sex, or both.

showing only the end product Nondisclosure of all that precedes a particular performance.

situational homosexuality Instances in which homosexual behavior occurs between two otherwise heterosexuals.

slave codes Laws regulating slave behavior.

slave patrols Considered by some as the first American police departments, slave patrols were established as early as the 1740s. The patrols were tasked with preventing slave revolts and apprehending runaway slaves.

snakeheads Chinese human smugglers who lead illegal immigrants across borders.

social construction of race The concept in which every culture must determine which physical features are used to define membership in certain races.

social construction of reality   The process through which people mentally construct ideas about phenomena and thus create a reality.

social groups   Two or more individuals regularly interacting and feeling a sense of solidarity or common identity. Social groups typically share some norms and values while working to achieve common goals.

social interaction   The process through which individuals act and react in relation to other individuals.

status   The social position maintained by an individual.

subculture   The meanings, values, and behavior patterns unique to a particular group in a given society.

summons   A document informing individuals of their call to jury duty.

symbolic assailant   Particular individuals who are perceived by police officers to be potential sources of violence or as enemies to be reckoned with.

symbolic representation   Making our courts more representative of all racial/ethnic groups.

symbols   Items used to represent something else.

T

technical violation   Misbehavior by a probationer or parolee that is not by itself a criminal offense and generally does not result in arrest. Serious technical violations or continuous misbehavior, however, while on probation or parole can result in re-incarceration.

Termination Act   An act passed by Congress in 1953 which led to the termination of 13 tribes between 1945 and 1962. The Act also meant that certain tribes would lose tax exempt status for their lands.

"three strikes and you're out" sentencing   a sentencing structure targeted toward repeat offenders. "Three strikes" legislation demonstrates the public's disdain for crime and an attempt to target those who seem undeterred by criminal law and punishment. Three strikes laws vary among the states that use them, with offenders in certain jurisdictions facing life sentences following a third felony.

tokens   Individuals from underrepresented groups who are being hired, or received their position solely because of affirmative action policies, regardless of their ability to perform the job.

tribal courts   Allow tribes the authority to hear and decide cases relating to life on the reservation without interference of traditional U.S. Courts.

U

ultramasculinity   A primary concern for many prison inmates. The inmate subculture emphasizes being strong.

underpolicing   Actions not taken by the police to protect members of minority groups.

U.S. Probation and Pretrial Services System   The group responsible for, among other things, assisting the federal courts with pretrial practices and supervising federal probationers.

V

venire   A jury pool from which prospective jurors are selected and questioned.

vocalics   Also known as paralanguage, it refers to vocal characteristics such as inflection, tone, accent, rate, pitch, volume, and vocal interrupters.

voir dire   The process of questioning potential jurors regarding their suitability to serve on a jury.

voluntary migration   The process involving people who willingly immigrate to a new country looking for a better life.

W

Wolf   Also known as the Jocker, this type of inmate is viewed by his fellow inmates as a "man." To remain a "man" and still engage in homosexual acts, the individual has to present an image of exaggerated toughness.

Y

Yakuza   The Japanese version of organized crime.

yellow peril   A fear-based "threat" that actually resulted in strict immigration laws and the imprisonment of American citizens.

Credits

Index